'Of Kerns and Gallowglasses'

Irish Armies of the 16th Century, 1487–1587

Robert Gresh

Helion & Company Limited
Unit 8 Amherst Business Centre
Budbrooke Road
Warwick
CV34 5WE
England
Tel. 01926 499 619
Email: info@helion.co.uk
Website: www.helion.co.uk
Twitter: @helionbooks
Visit our blog http://blog.helion.co.uk/

Published by Helion & Company 2024
Designed and typeset by Mary Woolley, Battlefield Design (www.battlefield-design.co.uk)
Cover designed by Paul Hewitt, Battlefield Design (www.battlefield-design.co.uk)

Text © Robert Gresh 2024
Illustrations © as individually credited
Colour artwork drawn by Sean O' Brogain © Helion & Company 2024
Flag art work by Anderson Subertil © Helion & Company 2024

Every reasonable effort has been made to trace copyright holders and to obtain their permission for the use of copyright material. The author and publisher apologise for any errors or omissions in this work and would be grateful if notified of any corrections that should be incorporated in future reprints or editions of this book.

ISBN 978-1-804513-54-5

British Library Cataloguing-in-Publication Data.
A catalogue record for this book is available from the British Library.

All rights reserved. No part of this publication may be reproduced, stored in a retrieval system, or transmitted, in any form, or by any means, electronic, mechanical, photocopying, recording or otherwise, without the express written consent of Helion & Company Limited.

For details of other military history titles published by Helion & Company Limited contact the above address or visit our website: http://www.helion.co.uk.

We always welcome receiving book proposals from prospective authors.

Contents

Glossary		iv
Preface		vii
Introduction		ix
Part I: The Power of Irishmen		15
1	*A Description of The Power of Irishmen*	15
2	Tactics in Irish Warfare	44
3	Governor's Retinues, Garrison Troops, and the Rising Out of the Pale	56
Part II: 'The lord, the boy, the Galloglass, the kern' – Types of Irish Fighting Men		99
4	The Chieftain and his Military Role	99
5	The Horseman, or *Marcach*	113
6	The Galloglass	140
7	The Kern	156
8	The Horseboys: Dalonyes and Daltins	197
9	Scots Redshanks	203
Part III: Ships, Castles, Banners and Pipes		223
10	Irish Naval Power	223
11	The Tower House	229
12	Banners and Flags	241
13	The Pipers	249
Wilde Irishe Living History Group		257
Appendices:		
I: Muster of the Earl of Ormond's Kern, 1544		258
II: The Rate of the Wages of the Galloglas		261
III: Clergy Contributions to the Rising Out of the Pale, and the Militias of Corporate Towns.		264
Colour Plate Commentaries		267
Bibliography		272

Glossary

Battle – In Ireland, a company of galloglass. Also, in contemporary military parlance, one of the three divisions of an army in array.
Bawn – Outer wall surrounding the courtyard of a tower house. From the Irish *bó dún*, a cow enclosure.
Birred (Ir. *biorraeid*) – A pointed Irish cap, without a brim.
Blackrent – Protection money paid to neighbouring Irish clans by inhabitants of the Pale
Bonnaght (Ir. *bunnacht*) – Billeting of troops, particularly galloglass, upon householders. Sometimes used for the troops thus billeted.
Bonaght-Bonny (Ir. *buannacht bhuna*) – Basic bonnaght, or quartering of galloglass. As negotiated between a lord and his tenants.
Bonaghtbeg (Ir. *buannacht bheag*) – The substitution of a money rent intended for the hiring of galloglass, in place of providing actual bonnaght.
Bonney-Bur (Ir. *buannacht bhairr*) – An imposition above that of basic bonnaght, usually for additional galloglass hired during wartime.
Brogue (Ir. *bróg*) – The traditional Irish turn shoe, single soled, without a heel, and sewn with leather thong.
Cess – Billeting of troops upon a territory, particularly as practised by the English Administration within the Pale.
Coign and Livery (Ir. *coinnmheadh*) – Billeting and provision. Used particularly for the imposition of Irish mercenaries in the marches of the English Pale. 'Coign' was equated by some to 'man's meat', and livery to 'horse's meat', meat meaning food.
Consapal/Constábla – a Constable, or Captain, commanding a battle of galloglass.
Corughadh – a 'battle' or company of galloglass.
Cotún – see Jack.
Craiseach – A heavier variety of spear, for close combat.
Creach – A cattle raid. Also, the 'prey' of cattle and other livestock.
Creaght – A cattle herd and its attendants.
Crommeal (Ir. *croiméal*) – The large Irish moustache, repeatedly prohibited under English law.
Daloyne (Ir. *doílmhaineach*) – A horseboy. Literally, one free from liability, or a hired soldier.

GLOSSARY

Daltin (Ir. *dailtín*) – A kind of junior horseboy, ranking below the Daloyne. Meaning a brat, orphan or fosterling.

Daoine Uaisle – Nobles

Dart – The Irish throwing spear.

Fasagh (Ir. *fásach*) – Wasteland.

Foga – A dart.

Gae – A dart.

Galloglass (Ir. *gallóglaich*) – Irish heavy foot soldier, armed in mail and using a long axe.

Garrans (Ir. *gerráin*) – Small, study horses used for carriage and the plough. Represented today by the Kerry Bog Pony.

Gíománach – Camp servant to galloglass, derived from the English word 'yeoman'.

Glibbes (Ir. *glibeanna*) – long locks worn by the Irish hanging over the eyes.

Gorsoon (Ir. *garsún*) – Alternate term for horseboy, used in the south.

HEMA – Historical European Martial Arts. A modern revival of historical fighting styles, using period sword manuals and similar documentation.

Holding Kern – Professional kern retained by coign and livery.

Hosting Summons (Ir. *gairm shluaigh*) – The call to all freeholders to join the rising out, or muster, of their territory.

Jack (Ir. *seaca*) – A padded aketon, quilted longitudinally, in Ireland usually covering the kneecaps and sometimes called a 'side jack', meaning long jack.

Kern (Ir. *ceithern*) – Light armed Irish foot. Sometimes professional, sometimes part of the rising out. Technically plural, but generally used for the singular as well in English.

Kernagh (Ir. *ceithernach*) – An individual kern.

Kernety (Ir. *ceithern tigh*) – Household kern, permanently retained, serving as police and assisting in the collection of taxes. In Ulster, sometimes called *fircheithernn*, or 'true kern'.

Léine/Léine Croich – The large saffron shirt favoured by the Irish through this period.

Lord's Galloglass (Ir. *gallóglach tierna*) – Bodyguard and personal attendant to an Irish chief, chosen from among the galloglass.

Lucht tighe – A lord's military retinue, literally 'household people'. By the sixteenth century, the mensal lands surrounding the lord's residence.

Maghery (Ir. *macharie*) – A plain. Also, the inner core of the English Pale.

Marcach – An Irish horseman.

Marcsluagh – Irish cavalry, literally a 'horse-host'.

Marusgal – Marshal, responsible for organising, quartering and feeding the lord's troops.

Pale – The territory immediately surrounding Dublin, about twenty miles wide and running from Dublin to Dundalk, in which English custom and law prevailed.

Palesman – Inhabitant of the English Pale.

Pillion (Ir. *pillín*) – The Irish pad saddle, without stirrups.

Plashing – Near impenetrable barrier made of interwoven branches of fallen and standing timber, often used to channel enemy forces in conjunction with an ambush.

Quirren – Four pounds of butter.

Rising Out (Ir. *coimhéirghe*) – The muster of a territory's freeholders subject to the hosting summons.

Sciath – Irish for any shield, but originally referring to a wicker variety.

Scotici – Galloglass, as referred to in Latin documents.

Skean (Ir. *scian*) – A fighting knife, single-edged and acutely pointed. The *miodóg* was a shorter version, while the *scian fada* was almost a short sword with a blade up to twenty-two inches in length.

Sleag – A long, light casting spear.

Soren – An allowance beyond *Buannacht*, extracted from the people as spending money for the galloglass.

Sparr – A galloglass and his attendants, either one or two 'boys'. So named for the galloglass axe, or sparth.

Sparth – The galloglass axe. Called *tuagh* in Irish.

Sroan (Ir. *srubhán*) – An oatcake a foot and a half broad, reckoned equal to 1.5 gallons of oatmeal.

Stokaghe (Ir. *stocaire*) – A kern who served as a horn blower. Also, the larger boys among the servants of the kern.

Suaineamh – A throwing loop attached to a spear or dart.

Tánaiste – The designated successor to an Irish lord.

Targadha/Starga – Target, a round shield, usually of wood covered with leather.

Tierna – An Irish lord.

Trews/Trowses (Ir. *triúbhas*) – Irish trousers, closely fitted to the leg and either covering the feet or ending in instep straps.

Tuath – An Irish lordship.

Turbarii/Turbales – Kern, as referred to in Latin documents.

Uirrí – A sub-lord, subject to an overlord.

Ward (Ir. *bharda*) – the garrison of a tower house or castle.

Wood Kern (Ir. *ceithern coille*) – Outlaws or disbanded kern who lurked in woods.

Preface

> The merciless Macdonald...
> Of Kerns and Gallowglasses is supplied
> And Fortune on his damned quarrel smiling,
> Show'd like a rebel's whore.
> William Shakespeare, *Macbeth*, Act I, Scene II

Those lines, evoking the light and heavy Irish foot soldiers of the sixteenth century, were written within living memory of their service in the autonomous forces of the old Irish chieftains. The focus of this study is those native Irish armies of the Tudor era. It seeks to describe a traditional military system that functioned in the country up to 1587. That system began to undergo changes during the course of the century which accelerated during the two Desmond rebellions of 1569–1573 and 1579–1583, and were completed during the Nine Years' War, 1593–1603. In fact, Irish historians once spoke of the Fifteen Years' War, and dated this final conflict of Elizabeth's reign to 1588–1603. The armies of the Desmond rebellions and, most particularly, the Nine Years' War, require their own studies, and it is hoped the present effort will form a serviceable foundation for these. While this system had long been innately conservative, its structure and personnel would prove adaptable to rapid modernisation. Far from undergoing a purge, such as that of the janissaries in the Ottoman Empire, the members of the old Irish military system would take active roles in the modernised forces. The personnel and, to a large degree, the structures of the old system ultimately produced a military capable of standing up to and defeating the Crown's forces during the last decade of the century, until overwhelmed by superior resources. Because of the destruction accompanying these catastrophic wars, the society and culture that gave rise to this military system is under-documented, and its study requires consideration of all possible sources, including folklore. And it must be kept in mind that the surviving sources are heavily weighted towards the hostile viewpoint of English administrators and soldiers.

Sixteenth century Ireland was subject to misunderstanding abroad, even before the wars of conquest intensified in the second half of the century. The propagandist for the twelfth century Anglo-Norman invasion, Gerald de Barri, was widely read on the Continent, and Irish writers were still countering his misrepresentations four hundred years later. As a lineage based society, Gaelic Ireland placed emphasis on continuity with the past. This was seen in the conscious antiquarianism of settlement patterns, with ancient crannogs continuing to be occupied by some members of the Gaelic elite as a tangible link to remote antiquity. But the same lord whose primary residence might be an Iron Age lake dwelling could also sponsor the building of Roscommon Priory, his territory having the resources and skills to produce a massive and complex masonry structure for the new Dominican religious order, comparable to any priory in contemporary Europe. Likewise, in dress and personal appearance, the Gaelic Irish cultivated a deliberately anachronistic style. They sought to invoke the imagined past of the heroic sagas which had fuelled the Gaelic Resurgence of *c.* 1350–1500, during which large tracts of conquered territory had been recovered. If when braving the cold, barefooted and bareheaded they were viewed as archaic figures, it is arguable that this is exactly what they intended.

While the wars in Ireland constitute the major overseas financial expense of Elizabeth's reign, English historians have preferred to focus elsewhere. And service in the Irish wars was never popular with the contemporary Tudor elite, either. Sir William Skeffington, for example, insisted that if he was to serve as Governor in Ireland, the King would have to build him a bridge back to England. For a very long time, this was attributed to the nature of Gaelic Ireland itself, which historians depicted as squalid and unattractive. But that same society had largely assimilated the original settlers, and far from being repulsive, had the ability to seduce newcomers even during the final wars of conquest. The native military system will be seen to have been fit for purpose, and as such was adopted in its entirety by the English administration in Dublin, with one omission. The element of negotiation between freeholder and lord regarding the billeting of mercenaries was generally missing when the government 'cessed' troops upon the subjects.

Introduction

In 1485, at the onset of the Tudor era, Ireland was largely under native rule. The Lordship of Ireland, established after Henry II's invasion of 1171, had been weakened by the Black Death in the mid-fourteenth century. The plague devastated the English colony centred on Dublin and the loyal corporate towns, while having far less impact on the independent native Irish lordships, whose rural settlement pattern was more dispersed. Large tracts of conquered territory had thus been reclaimed by the Irish in the 'Gaelic Revival'. Ongoing intermarriage and gradual acculturation caused the descendants of the original Anglo-Norman settlers to become 'more Irish than the Irish themselves' (*Hiberniores ipsis Hibernis*), as the phrase went. The Hundred Years' War and the subsequent civil wars of England in the second half of the fifteenth century meant neglect for the Irish Lordship. Ireland thus enjoyed a kind of home rule in the early sixteenth century, with successive kings of England delegating what was left of the Crown's authority to the partly Gaelicised Anglo-Irish Fitzgerald Earls of Kildare.

Henry VIII's consolidation of centralised Royal authority in England, coupled with the impact of the Reformation, would soon change this situation. Furthermore, Ireland's strategic importance for England was widely recognised and noted in foreign courts, and hostile foreign intervention by Scotland or France was feared as early as the 1520s. Thus, starting fitfully after the 1534 Rebellion of 'Silken' Thomas Fitzgerald, 10th Earl of Kildare, a steadily intensifying Tudor conquest began, resulting in Ireland being reduced to colonial status by 1603. This centralising impulse was not the contemporary European norm, where in the Hapsburg realms, for example, local, de-centralised rule was practised, with allowance for diversity of language, dress, et cetera.[1] The burgeoning Tudor State would ultimately follow a very different course, moving, for instance, from separatist sumptuary laws forbidding the adoption of Gaelic Irish fashions by the English colonists to finally outlawing the native clothing altogether.[2]

---

1   Kenneth Nicholls, 'Celtic Contrasts: Ireland and Scotland', *History Ireland*, vol. 7, no. 3 (Autumn 1999), pp.22–26.
2   Sparky Booker, 'Moustaches, Mantles, and Saffron Shirts: What Motivated Sumptuary Law in Medieval English Ireland?' *Speculum*, 96/3 (July 2021), pp.726–770.

Consequently, after Henry VIII was declared King of Ireland and the former Lordship was incorporated into the Tudor State in 1541, there was an accompanying spate of sumptuary legislation outlawing Gaelic dress and other cultural markers. With the completion of the conquest after 1603, Sir William Parsons would state: 'We must change their course of government, apparel, manner of holding land, their language and habit of life.'[3] This was well under way by the last three decades of the century, as a class of 'New English' administrators doggedly pursued the centralising project, targeting the native aristocracy, both Gaelic and Anglo-Irish. The course of conquest proved increasingly costly, in part because the policy of demilitarising and disempowering loyal lords meant that they could offer little resistance to the great rebellion of O'Neill and O'Donnell in the last decade of the century.

In the early sixteenth century, Ireland was divided between three entities: first the Pale, a narrow strip of land 20 miles wide running west from Dublin to Dundalk, in which the King's writ ran and English custom prevailed; secondly, the great Anglo-Irish lordships (Kildare, Ormond and Desmond in the south, and the Burkes in the west); and finally the Gaelic Irish Lordships. The greatest part of the country was ruled by the more than 60 Gaelic Irish lords or 'Captains', formerly regional kings, each of whom was said to 'maketh war and peace for himself without any licence from the King, or of any other temporal person, save to him that is strongest, and of such that may subdue him by the sword.' It was in this sense that the Gaelic Irish poets, the *fili* whose ritualised praise poems gave legitimacy to a chieftain's rule, spoke of Ireland as 'sword land' (*fearann claíomh*). Within these independent Irish lordships, native brehon law prevailed, and land was held by the larger kinship group rather than being inherited by an elder son as in general European and English primogeniture. The organisation of the Irish chieftain's household is examined below.

Cattle were the basic measure of wealth in the Irish lordships, serving as a 'nominal currency'. The fully grown cow, called a *collop* or *sum*, was the basic unit of value, converted into equivalents of other livestock, e.g. five sheep equalled one cow. The chieftains maintained very large herds of cattle, which together with their attendants were known as *creaghts*. This term could refer to that portion of a community that departed in the spring for the upland pastures, moving between three or more summer pastures in a set pattern and returning in the autumn, a practice known as transhumance. A *creaght* could also designate the herds of a chief or military leader without land, wandering from place to place and master to master, often to be found in the *fásach*, or wasteland, on the frontier between the Gaelic and Anglo-Irish communities.

The Gaelic lordship or *tuath* was essentially an independent state, headed by the lord, or *tierna* (chieftain). The *tierna* and his designated successor, the *tánaiste*, were selected from among the *derbfine*, a patrilineal kinship

---

3   Daniel Corkery, *The Fortunes of the Irish Language* (Cork: Mercer Press Ltd, 1956), p.69.

group all sharing a common great-grandfather. Succession was often the outcome of dynastic feuding, which sometimes resulted in breakaway branches of a family being established. While this process brought a degree of instability, it also resulted in the emergence of strong leaders. Between serial wives and concubines, chieftains regularly produced more than 10 sons who typically constituted the core of the lordship's cavalry. So prolific were the chieftains that their descendants eventually came to squeeze out other families within the lordship. For instance, Turlough O'Donnell, the lord of Tyrconnell, had 18 sons by 10 different women and left 59 grandsons. In fact, as Kenneth Nicholls has shown, Gaelic society was clan-based, in spite of earlier Irish historians' reluctance to use the term 'clan' in describing it.[4] The clan might best be compared to a corporation which managed its land and resources. While lineage based, the clan's existence was in the political and legal spheres, and it lacked the solidarity of a family unit. By the sixteenth century, this system had largely been adopted outside the Pale by the Anglo-Irish community, or 'Middle Nation', as it was styled; neither fully English nor fully Irish.

The more powerful lords would seek to subjugate neighbouring *tuaths* to their overlordship, in order to impose rents and tribute. A subjugated lord became an *uirrí*, or tributary king. Stanihurst says: 'Those tyrants have chieftains of a lower rank in subjection and control, who are ready to go to war with a great number of levies whenever their prince raises the battle standard,' and should they avoid that duty, 'the prince is accustomed to compel them to arms; or if he find them very pugnacious or stubborn, he procures a band and forces, turns his battle standards on the defiant ones, expels them from their homes, turns them out from all their property.'[5] The *uirrí* was generally ready to break free at any sign of his overlord's weakening, and rival lords might wage war with one another to secure his tribute. Thus, the frequent hostilities between Tyrone and Tyrconnell had as their chief cause domination over the *uirrí* O'Dogherty of Inishowen.

There was a trend towards consolidation of regional power by the great lordships, such as O'Neill and O'Donnell in the north, and MacCarthy Mor in the south, and this was accompanied by an increasing reliance upon professional mercenary soldiery, both kern and galloglass. Available numbers of native mercenaries proved insufficient as the tempo of the English conquest picked up, resulting in the increasing employment of seasonal mercenaries from the Scottish Highlands, known as 'redshanks'. The decentralised nature of the native Irish political system is often assumed to have been its great weakness, but it can be argued that as long as the English commitment in Ireland was limited, the decentralised lordships could resist more effectively than a single monarch would have done. The

---

4   Kenneth Nicholls, *Gaelic and Gaelicised Ireland in the Middle Ages* (Dublin: Gill & MacMillan, 1972), p.11.
5   Katherine Simms, *From Kings to Warlords* (Woodbridge: Boydell & Brewer Ltd., 1987), p.128.

defeat of a theoretical Irish High King in battle would have decided the issue, whereas dealing piecemeal with a multitude of independent lordships was a much more drawn-out process.

While not politically centralised, the Irish had highly developed institutions by the ninth century, including a codified system of law and a standardised literary language and school of music. These institutions were of national scope, with little if any regional variation, something that modernist theories of nationhood would claim was impossible before the nineteenth century. There was a tradition of high kingship, which had become largely theoretical, centred on the national ritual centre at Tara. The national consciousness had been sharpened by the struggle with Viking invaders, recounted in the twelfth century history, *Cogad Gáedel re Gallaib* (the War of the Irish and the Foreigners). The Vikings were labelled *Gall* (foreigners) by the Irish, a name that was readily transferred to the incoming Anglo-Normans in the twelfth century. These invaders had been neutralised by the fifteenth century, with the loftiest Anglo-Irish lords, such as Butler and Desmond, comfortably using the Irish language, brehon law, and Gaelic military system, while pursuing dynastic marriages with Gaelic lineages.

The warlike nature of Gaelic society has been somewhat exaggerated. A recent appraisal of the military activity recorded in the Irish annals has revealed that during the period 1501 to 1550, only two years are without recorded raids or battles. This is largely due to the martial culture of the Irish lordships, whose chieftains achieved legitimacy through regularly raiding neighbouring lordships. Widespread though it was, this form of warfare resulted in few casualties. The situation in Ireland resembled that of the lineage based society of the Powhatan of Virginia, whose endless round of raids, ambushes and skirmishes also resulted in a limited amount of fatalities.[6] Thus, while the Irish lords held their position by the strength of their sword arm, the level of violence was relatively minor. At Towton, in 1461, it is thought that of the 76,000 soldiers engaged, as many as 28,000 may have been killed. By contrast, the battle of Knockdoe in 1504 probably involved no more than 10,000 total combatants on both sides, up to 4,000 of whom may have been killed. In fact, the trauma of that event may have discouraged similar actions among the survivors, who returned to the old pattern of raiding warfare.

Between 1501 and 1550, there are 95 raids reported in the annals.[7] David Edwards has shown that in the aftermath of Knockdoe, the 'battles'

---

6 David Edwards, 'The Escalation of Violence in Sixteenth Century Ireland' in David Edwards, Pádraig Leinihan and Clodagh Tait (eds), *Age of Atrocity: Violence and Political Conflict in Early Modern Ireland* (Dublin: Four Courts Press, 2007), p.41.

7 Colm Donnelly and Eileen M. Murphy, 'Violence in Later Medieval Ireland: the Osteoarchaeological Evidence and its Historical Context' in Eve Campbell, Elizabeth Fitzpatrick and Audrey Horning (eds), *Becoming and Belonging in Ireland AD c. 1200–1600* (Cork: Cork University Press, 2018), p.113.

noticed in the *Four Masters*[8] from 1505 to 1520 resulted in a maximum of 100 casualties and usually far less. For 10 of those 16 years, no battles are recorded at all. The low-level violence of raid and counter-raid was a form of economic warfare specifically meant to gain the services of earth tillers, and reduce a neighbouring lord to vassal status. In an underpopulated country, land itself was considered of little value without people to work it. Thus, the common people were intentionally spared, so that their productive labour could be exploited by the victorious lord. Added to this were the strong injunctions of the Church to avoid harming the unarmed – churchmen, women and children. Of course, the outcome of raids, while not immediately deadly, could nonetheless impose serious hardship on the population, with the burning of houses, destruction of crops and dislocation of populations leading to malnourishment. But the evidence from several collections of skeletal remains belonging to commoners in late medieval Gaelic graveyards reveals a remarkably low incidence of violent injury and death (1.0 to 1.8 percent). In fact, it appears to confirm a lower rate of violence than found in comparable data for earlier medieval Ireland, where higher rates of violent death are evident (3.4 percent), and is very comparable to rates of death indicated for contemporary England. Rates of violent death were also higher in fifteenth century England, due to the breakdown of law and order occasioned by the Wars of the Roses. The immediate burden of violence in early Tudor Ireland fell largely on the ruling lineages, which were subject to violence from members of rival neighbouring lineages or rivals within their own lineage.

Nor were the forces of the Irish chiefs particularly backward in comparison to their English foes in the century's first decades, as they eagerly made use of guns at about the same rate and time as England. The decisive change came with the acceleration in the use of firearms among the English garrison from *c.* 1550 onwards. The Irish military system was founded upon three categories of soldiers: horseman, galloglass and kern, and had remained essentially unchanged for the last 200 years. This system was also employed in the marcher regions of the English Pale, with the exception of the corporate towns, and was universally adopted among the Anglo-Irish magnates. The sheer numbers of armed men retained throughout the country raises the question of how they could have been paid for in an allegedly poor country. While a highly traditional society, Ireland was at no point isolated from Continental developments. For instance, Susan Flavin's work on sixteenth century Irish trade, largely focussed on the well documented south-east, has shown the active role played by Ireland in the development of the European Atlantic economy. Far from being limited to such raw materials as hide and fish, Ireland's exports included manufactured goods (cloth and clothing) which increased from about a tenth of total exports in the late fifteenth century to half of

---

8   John O'Donovan (ed.), *Annals of the Kingdom of Ireland, by the Four Masters*, 7 vols, (Dublin: Hodges, Smith & Co., 1856)

total exports by the 1540s, with a corresponding increase in the diversity of imports during the course of the sixteenth century.[9] A picture of economic stability throughout the country emerges for the first half of the sixteenth century, and imports would continue to grow periodically through the end of the century, in spite of the extensive ongoing wars of conquest. Similarly, Victoria McAlister's work on tower house settlement has offered a different interpretation of the astounding degree of encastellation in sixteenth century Ireland, which has often been interpreted as a sign of social instability. McAlister's research shows that the tower house's defensive function was limited and it in fact formed a kind of social and economic centre, often with firm commercial connections to port towns. The building of tower houses and church buildings was a significant economic activity in this era, reflecting the increased wealth made possible by political decentralisation, which allowed tolls and taxes to be retained and spent locally rather than going into the Royal coffers.[10] The key Irish economic event of the fifteenth century had been the arrival of shoals of herring migrating from Norwegian waters, driven by cooling temperatures to seek the warmer waters of Ireland's south and west coasts. This resulted in the increased wealth which helped fuel this building activity and paid for the large numbers of armed men retained by many of the Irish lords.

---

[9] Susan Flavin, *Consumption and Culture in Sixteenth century Ireland: Saffron, Stockings and Silk* (Woodbridge: Boydell & Brewer Ltd, 2014).

[10] Victoria McAlister, *The Irish Tower House: Society, Economy, Environment, c. 1300–1650* (Manchester: Manchester University Press, 2019)

Part I

The Power of Irishmen

1

A Description of The Power of Irishmen

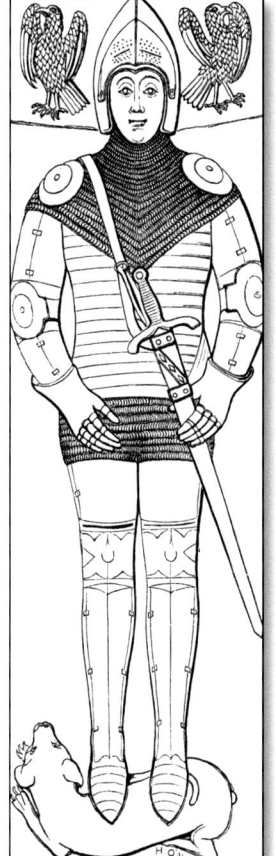

Piers Butler, 8th Earl of Ormond, *c.* 1539. From St Canice's, Kilkenny City. (Author's collection)

The most comprehensive contemporary source for Gaelic Irish military numbers and organisation is the document titled *A Description of the Power of Irishmen*. Published by Liam Price in 1932 from a manuscript in the British Museum, it was long considered to be of early sixteenth century date,[1] but it was subsequently dated to *c.* 1490. The figures in the tables below have been collated by Ellis and Maginn with an older version in the Hatfield House Papers, but the two are largely identical.[2]

The anonymous author was familiar with the eastern half of the country, for which the numbers seem reasonable. But some of the large forces attributed to certain lords of the north, west and south-west are likely exaggerated, and should be treated with some caution. Numbers of horsemen, galloglass and kern are given for each lord of the 'King's Irish enemies', otherwise known as 'wilde Irish', with two instances of the use of 'long galleys' noted (O'Driscoll and O'Malley), and in the case of Desmond, a battle of crossbows and gunners. The notes at the end of the document give the number of galloglass in a 'battle' as either 60 or 80. Taking 70 as a mean for the number in a battle, Ellis and Maginn have estimated the total

---

1 Liam Price, 'Armed Forces of the Irish Chiefs in the Early 16th Century', *Journal of the Royal Society of Antiquaries of Ireland,* vol. 62 (1932), pp.201–207.
2 Christopher Maginn and Stephen G. Ellis, *The Tudor Discovery of Ireland* (Dublin: Four Courts Press, 2015), pp.35–41.

of Gaelic Irish fighting men at around 23,000. With the addition of 'knaves' – one for each galloglass, one for every two kern, and three per horseman – the total rises to just over 40,000. Additionally, the numbers of Irish troops employed by the generally loyal Anglo-Irish lords of each province are appended to each table as an afterthought in the document. When these are added, the numbers rise to well over 50,000 Gaelic Irishmen in military service at the outset of the Tudor era, which would be over 20 percent of that demographic group.

The purpose for which this document was drawn up is not known, but as it is dated *c.* 1490, it was probably an intelligence brief prepared for Sir Edward Poynings prior to his Irish expedition in 1494. Henry VII also had the intention of leading an Irish expedition in 1506, and this document may have provided the King with an idea of what he would be up against. The version first published by Price had been copied out around 1560 by Lawrence Nowell during a visit to Ireland on behalf of Secretary William Cecil, at which point it was still considered a valuable source of information. The document was frequently quoted or paraphrased by officials during the reign of Elizabeth.

Table 1. Leinster

Lord	Horsemen	Battles of Galloglass	Kern
MacMurrough, Prince and Lord of Leinster	200 'well harneysed'	1	300
O'Byrne, Lord of Críoch Branagh	60	1	160
O'Toole, Lord of Fercullen and Imaal	24		80
Art MacDonogh MacMurrough, Lord of Hy Kinsellagh	16		60
Redmund MacShane O'Byrne, Lord of Gabhal Raghnaill	8		40
O'Murrough, Lord of iPhelimy	16		40
O'Nolan, Lord of Forth	12		20
O'Brennan, Lord of Odogh			40
O'More, Lord of Laois	60	1	200
O'Ryan, Lord of his country	12		24
MacGillipatrick, Lord of Ossory	40	1	60
MacMorish O'Connor, Lord of Irry	6		24
O'Dunne, Lord of Iregan	8		200
O'Dempsey, lord of Clanmaliere	24		100
O'Connor, Lord of Offaly	40	1	200
Total	**526**	**5**	**1,548**

Anglo-Irish of Leinster: Wexford, 60 horse and 200 kern; The Butlers in Kilkenny, 80 horse, 1 battle and 2,000 kern.

Table 2. Desmond

Lord	Horsemen	Battles of Galloglass	Kern
MacCarthy Mor, Prince and Lord of that portion	40	2	2,000
MacCarthy Reagh, Lord of Carbery	60	1	2,000
Donough Oge MacCarthy, Lord of Duhallow	24	1	200
MacTeige MacCormac MacCarthy, Lord of Muskerry	40	1	200
O'Keefe, Lord of his country	12		100
O'Crowley, Lord of his country	8		60
O'Donovan, Lord of his country	6		60
O'Driscoll, Lord of Baltimore – 'they use long galleys'	6		200
O'Mahony, Lord of Fonn Iartharach	16		120
O'Sullivan Beare, Lord of Kenmare and Bantry	16		200
O'Donoghue Mor, Lord of Loch Lene	12		200
O'Donoghue, Lord of Glenflesk	6		60
MacGillycuddy, Lord of his country			40
O'Connor Kerry, Lord of his country	24		60
O'Brien of Carrigogunnell	20		60
O'Brien of Aherlow	8		24
O'Brien of the Comeragh Mountains	6		24
Total	304	5	5,608

Anglo-Irish of Desmond: The Earl of Desmond and his kin, 400 horse, 8 battles, 1 battle of crossbowmen and gunners, 3,000 kern; Part of the Bourges called Bourg country, 24 horse, 1 battle, 200 kern; Part of the Butlers of Tipperary, 60 horse, 2 battles, 200 kern.

'OF KERNS AND GALLOWGLASSES'

Table 3. Thomond

Lord	Horsemen	Battles of Galloglass	Kern
O'Brien, Lord of Thomond	200	2	500
MacNamara, Lord of Clancullen	200	1	600
MacMahon, Lord of Corca Baiscinn	20		60
O'Connor, Lord of Corcomroe	24		100
O'Dea, Lord of Ifearmaic	8		24
O'Loghlen, Lord of Burren	20		100
Mac-I-Brien, Lord of Arra	40	1	100
MacBrien, Lord of Coonagh	16		60
O'Mulryan, Lord of Owney	24		100
MacTeig, Lord of Ormond	24		60
O'Kennedy, Lord of Lower Ormond	60	1	120
O'Carroll, Lord of Ely	80	1	140
O'Meagher, Lord of Ikerrin	16		100
O'Dwyer, Lord of Kilnamanagh	12		100
MacTeig MacPhillip, of Kinel Fogarty	6		40
Total	**750**	**6**	**2,204**

Table 4. Connacht

Lord	Horsemen	Battles of Galloglass	Kern
O'Connor Donn, Prince and Lord of that portion	120	2	300
O'Kelly, Lord of Hy Many	200	2	400
O'Flaherty, Lord of Iar-Connacht	14		300
O'Malley, Lord of Owles – 'using long galleys'	16		200
O'Gara, Lord of Coolavin	14		100
O'Hara Boy, Lord of Leyny	6		300
O'Dowd, Lord of Tireragh	20		60
O'Shaughnessy, Lord of Kinelea	12		40
O'Madden, Lord of Silanchia	14		120
MacDonagh, Lord of Tiraghrill	40	1	160
MacDermot, Lord of Moylurg	40	1	200
MacManus O'Connor [O'Connor Sligo] Lord of Carbury	40	1	100
O'Rourke, Lord of [West] Brefny	40	1	300
MacRannell, Lord of Munterolis	8		300
Magauran, Lord of Tullyhaw	6		200
MacKiernan, Lord of Tullyhunco	6		200
O'Farrell, Lord of Annaly	60	1	300
O'Reilly, Lord of [East] Brefny	60	1	400
Total	**716**	**10**	**3,980**

'OF KERNS AND GALLOWGLASSES'

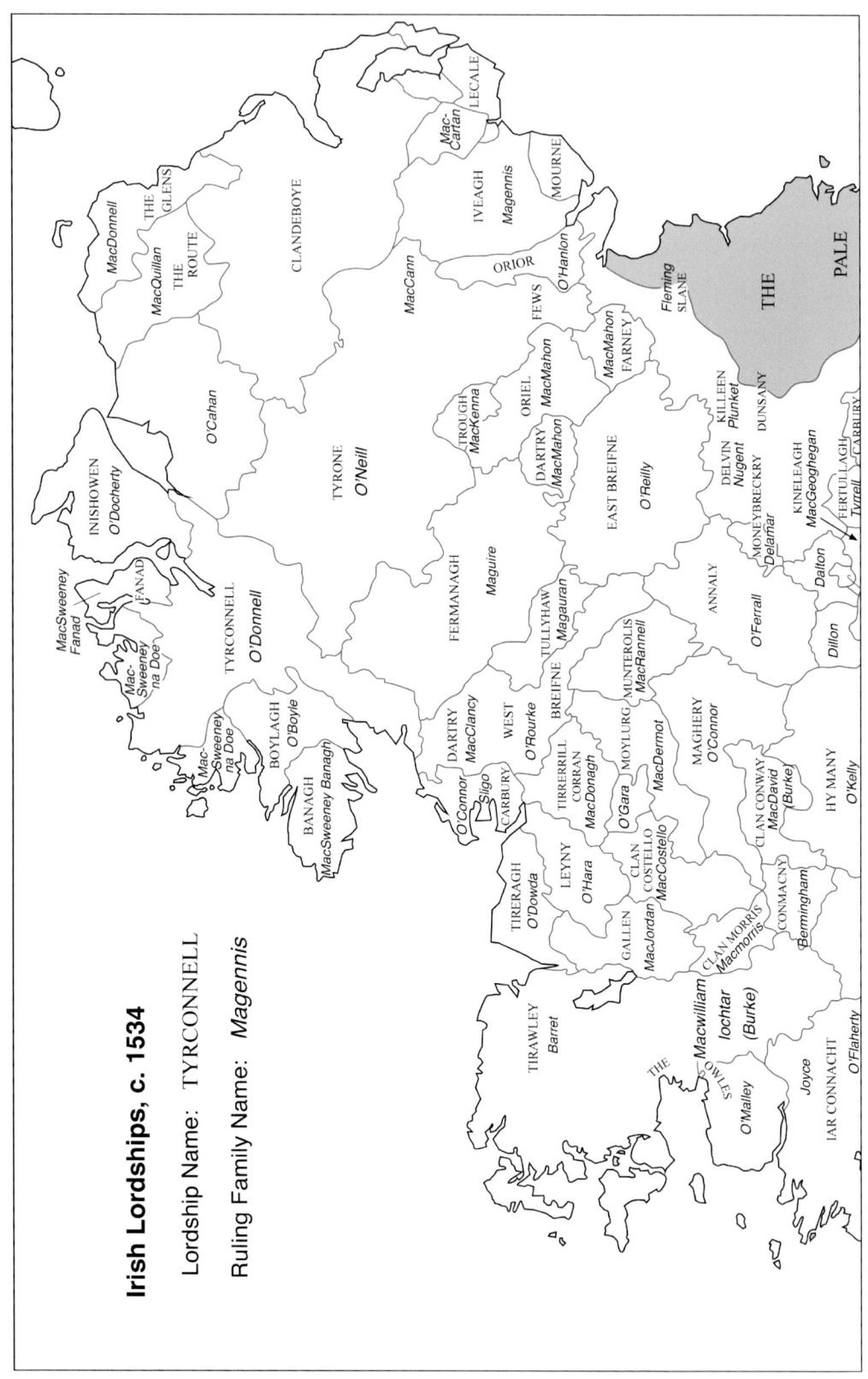

Irish Lordships, c. 1534

Lordship Name: **TYRCONNELL**

Ruling Family Name: *Magennis*

A DESCRIPTION OF THE POWER OF IRISHMEN

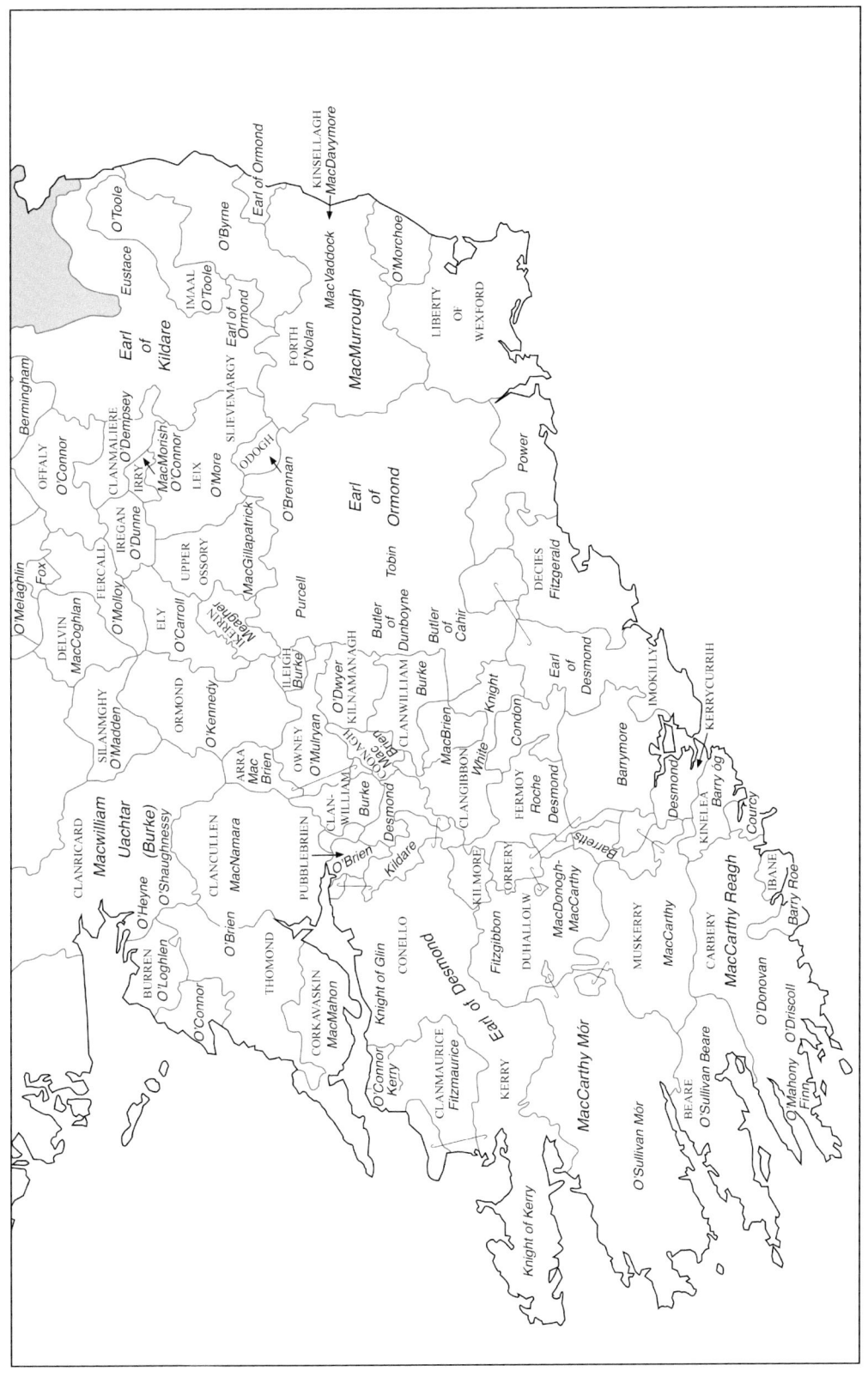

Ireland, showing the Irish and Anglo-Irish lordships. (Author's drawing, after K. W. Nicholls)

'OF KERNS AND GALLOWGLASSES'

Table 5. Anglo-Irish of Connacht

Lord	Horsemen	Battles of Galloglass	Kern
MacWilliam Upper [Uachtar] Burke, Lord of Clanrikard	120	2	300
MacWilliam Lower [Íochtar] Burke, Lord of Connyke Ghowle	200	3	300
Bermingham, Lord of Conmaicne of Dunmore	14		40
Nangle, Lord of Clan Costello	12		40
MacJordan, Lord of Gallen	12		60
MacAveely, Lord of Carra			120
MacDavy Burke, Lord of Clanconway	24		40
MacPhilbin Burke, Lord of Oyell			40
Total	**382**	**5**	**940**

Table 6. Ulster

Lord	Horsemen	Battles of Galloglass	Kern
O'Neill, Lord of that portion Tyrone	200	3	300
Con MacHugh Boy O'Neill, Lord of Clandeboy	200	3	200
O'Cahan, Lord of Irraght Ichan	60	1	100
MacEoin, Lord of the Glens	20		100
MacQuillan, Lord of the Route	20		100
Magennis, Lord of the Iveagh	60	1	200
MacCartan, Lord of Kinelarty	6		60
O'Hanlon, Lord of Oriel	24		60
MacMahon, Lord of Farney	40	1	300
Maguire, Lord of Fermanagh	40	1	300
MacKenna, Lord of Truagh	10		40
MacCawell, Lord of Kinel-Farry	8		40
O'Donnell, Lord of Tyrconnell	100	4	300
Savage, an Englishman, Lord of Ard	24	1	60
Total	**812**	**15**	**2,160**

Table 7. Meath

Lord	Horsemen	Battles of Galloglass	Kern
O'Melaghlin, Lord of Clonlonan	24		100
O'Molloy, Lord of Fircal	20		100
Mageoghegan, Lord of Kinelagh	24		80
Sionnach [Fox], Lord of Monthycagan	6		40
Magawly, Lord of Calrige	4		24
O'Breen, Lord of Brawney			60
MacCoughlin, Lord of Delvin	8		120
Total	**86**		**524**

The following examines in more detail the seven armies of the larger lordships, as they were numbered and organised in the decades following the Power of Irishmen document. Four of these are Anglo-Norman Magnates, Gaelicised to varying degrees but all using the Irish military system; Ormond, Desmond and the two Burkes in Connacht. The remaining three are the great Gaelic Lordships of MacCarthy Mor, O'Neill and O'Donnell.

Ormond Armies

Piers Rua Butler fought a campaign against the neighbouring MacGiollapadraigs in 1517 with a force of only 280 men. The Butler hosting steadily expanded afterwards to 750 men. By 1528, firearms had been added, with Piers Butler of Ossory loaning four gunners to the neighbouring O'Carrolls that year. But even at their peak in the 1530s, Butler armies never numbered more than 800–1,000 men. In 1535, Stephen Ap Harry with forces from the Pale was joined by Lord James Butler's hosting on the way to Cork, and reported it was only '202 horsemen, 312 galoglas, and 204 kernes, besides followers. I had 78 spearmen, 24 long bows and 5 handguns; every man well horsed.'[3] This corresponds fairly well to the 'Power of Irishmen' document.

---

[3] J. S. Brewrer and William Bullen (eds), *Calendar of the Carew Manuscripts*, vol. 1, 1515–1574, (London: Longman & Co., 1867), p.76, 6 October, Ap Harry to Cromwell.

The Butlers maintained a force of MacSweeney galloglass, noted in 1537 as 'being in nombre for the more parte 2 batelles conteyning xvii score,' i.e., two great companies totalling 340 men.[4] Complaint was made during the assizes at Clonmel in 1537 against 'the lord of Ossery's marshall, namyd Geffery Mawelorke & Jamys McDavy, for the galloghis .... useing blackbedds,' that is, making charges upon the tenants for dead or absent men.[5] The galloglass 'blackbedds' or 'blackmen' in Leinster were to number 16 out of a battle of 100, according to a 1524 indenture between Henry VIII and the Earl of Kildare.[6] If this was applied to Ormond's galloglass, then assuming 84 galloglass 'on their feet', there would be four battles of 84, totalling 336, equivalent to the 17 score mentioned above. Another 100 galloglass appeared later in South Kilkenny under David FitzGerald of Brownesford, imposing upon Kilkenny's tenants the greatest burden of galloglass billeting (*bunnacht*) in Ireland.[7] An indenture of 1572 exists between Thomas, 10th Earl, and the MacSweeney galloglass, and they remained in Ormond's service until as late as 1575, when five MacSweeney galloglass captains of Ormond appeared before Lord Deputy Sidney at Cork, during his progress. He noted that they held no lands but were as feared as any landowner, and that they generally served on the side of the government.[8]

The Walshes (Brenaghs) of the Walsh Mountains and the McCody Archdekins of Ballybawnmore were Gaelicised Anglo-Irish clans who served the Butlers as sergeants. Ormond's 120 man kernety, or household kern, organised in two companies of 60, were drawn from these McCody Archdekins and also the Purcell family of Foulkesrath.[9] The Butler kern were maintained by coign and livery. In 1537, complaint was made of Butler's '2 severall companyes of kernes' going quarterly from town to town, taking their victuals, or money in their stead: 'And Edmundo Purser and William Purser, brethren, ar captaynes of the one kerne, and Robert Astyken and Jamys Astyken ar captaynes of thother kernes.'[10] Edmund Purcell died in 1549 and his tombstone at St Canice's Cathedral in Kilkenny bears the inscription, *Capitanus Turbariorum Comitis Ormoniae* (Captain of Kern to the Earl of Ormond). Individual landholders were liable for smaller numbers, such as the 10 swordsmen due from the Graces of Courtstown. These, along with the wards maintained in castles across the lordship, some as large as 7–8 men, would have added another 100 kern.

---

4   Herbert Hore and James Graves (eds), *The Social State of the Southern and Eastern Counties of Ireland in the Sixteenth Century* (Dublin: University Press, 1870), p.109.
5   Hore, *Social State*, p.245.
6   *Cal. Carew Mss*, p.28, 4 August, Henry VIII to Kildare.
7   David Edwards, *The Ormond Lordship in County Kilkenny, 1515–1642* (Dublin: Four Courts Press, 2003), p.156.
8   Cyril Falls, *Elizabeth's Irish Wars* (London, Methuen & Co., Ltd., 1950), p.77.
9   Seán Duffy (ed.) *Medieval Ireland: An Encyclopaedia* (New York: Routledge, 2005), p.332.
10 Hore, *Social State*, p.98.

The two companies of 80 kern that Ormond sent to France in 1544 each included 18 gunners, initially the only firearms in the Irish contingent. The Butler's rising out of 80–100 horse was the most expensive part of their array. They were raised upon the gentry by similar means to those used for the kern, with small detachments fitted out by landowners, some only one or two horsemen. Armour was supplied by the Butlers. Walshes, Comerfords, Dens, Shortals, Blanchvilles, Fitzgeralds, and Galls formed the sub-commanders of these forces, both horse and kern.

In the 1550s, the 10th Earl's brothers emerged as marcher lords, fragmenting the Butler army. The Earl himself maintained only two castle garrisons of eight men each in the 1560s, while his brother Edward, for instance, maintained 20 armed men at Cloghgrenan Castle, including three gunners, 20 men at Tully Castle, 40 men on his Carlow estates (including five gunners, six horsemen and one galloglass) and six men at Ballinahinch Castle, three of them galloglass.[11] This made it increasingly difficult for the Earl to control his lordship's forces.

At the last private magnate battle, a rent dispute fought between Ormond and Desmond in May of 1565, the Earl 'put up a thing of red silk upon a staff' to avoid being accused of displaying banners while not on Crown Service, and marshalled a mere 100 horsemen and 300 or 400 kern and galloglass.[12] Shortly afterwards, Sussex praised the Earl of Ormond for willingly serving the Crown with horsemen, galloglass, gunners, and kern, unlike the Earl of Desmond, who performed no service. In 1568, the Earl's brother, Edward Butler, then in a rebellious mood, appeared on foray at the head of 'six hundred gunners and kern, one hundred galloglass, sixty horsemen, and three hundred slaves, knaves and boys.'[13] Edward feared the loss of his 'Captainship' and military autonomy, as the Butler lordship was targeted for Anglicisation and de-militarisation. In open revolt by September of that year, he and his brother Edmund hired extra troops, totalling 100 horsemen, 200 galloglass, 100 gunners and 500 kern. By November, this had increased to 200 horsemen, 400 galloglass, 200 gunners and 600 kern, the largest force the Butlers would ever field.[14] They were allied with Turlough Luineach O'Neill in the north and James FitzMaurice in the south, the latter joining them to besiege Kilkenny in July 1569. Intervention by the government's army raised the siege, and by September the brothers had obtained pardons. However, the rank-and-file soldiers who followed them now found the local gentry unwilling to 'book',

---

11   David Edwards, 'The Butler Revolt of 1569' in *Irish Historical Studies*, vol. 28, no. 11 (May 1993), pp.228–255.
12   Richard Bagwell, *Ireland Under the Tudors*, vol. 2, (London: Longmans, Green, and Co., 1885), p.87.
13   *Calendar of State Papers Ireland: Henry VIII, Edward VI, Mary and Elizabeth*, vol. 1, 1509–73, ed. Hans Claude Hamilton, (London: Longman, Green, Longman & Roberts, 1860), p.388., 18 September, FitzWilliams to Cecil.
14   David Edwards, *The Ormond Lordship in County Kilkenny, 1515–1642* (Dublin: Four Courts Press, 2003), p.193.

'OF KERNS AND GALLOWGLASSES'

James Butler, 9th Earl of Ormond, c. 1546. From St Canice's Cathedral, Kilkenny City. (Author's collection)

or hire, them. They thus became 'masterless men' subject to execution, and were purged under martial law. Coign and livery was eliminated, and the remaining horsemen and kern consolidated directly under the Earl of Ormond. The Earl appointed John Sweetman as Marshal, and his new kernety were distributed as 6 horsemen and 12 footmen per barony.[15] The Purcells remained prominent in the organisation, Ferdorrough McEdmund Purcell being a captain of the kernety in 1577.[16]

Desmond Armies

The *c.* 1490 'Power of Irishmen' document credits the Earl of Desmond with 400 horse, eight battles of galloglass, one battle of crossbowmen and gunners, and 3,000 kern. Similarly, the State Papers record the Earl of Desmond's defeat by his Munster rivals at the battle of Mourne on 25 September 1520, claiming that he lost '18 banners of galoglas, which bee comonly in every banner 80 men, and the substance of 24 banners of horsemen, which be 20 under every baner, at the leest; and under some, 30,

---

15   Edwards, *Ormond Lordship*, p.211.
16   Edwards, *Ormond Lordship*, p.221.

40, and 50.'[17] While this last account is clearly exaggerated, the 'Power of Irishmen' document's claim of eight battles of galloglass (640 men) aligns well with later figures. In April of 1529, James, 11th Earl of Desmond, met with the ambassador of the Emperor Charles V, who said he was accompanied by '500 horse and as many halberdiers', the latter being galloglass. James boasted to the ambassador that he could raise 16,500 foot and 1,500 horse, but the documented full musters of Desmond were about an eighth of that.[18]

In the second Desmond Rebellion, the Earl's forces were estimated at 600 galloglass and 2,000 kern, besides horse and his battle of gunners. The company of gunners was still being tracked down and eliminated in 1583, as the rebellion wound down. They are not included in lists of figures dated 1569, which otherwise confirm the later estimate of Desmond's strength. Carew added comments to these lists, but they were possibly drawn up by Sir Humphrey Gilbert during his term as President of Munster.[19] Carew lists 300 *Bonogh beges* belonging to Desmond, which means the substitution of a money payment to support galloglass, in place of actually quartering them. Assuming a strength of 80, these figures come very close to the '8 battles of galloglass' assigned to Desmond in the 'Power of Irishmen' document. Carew also adds 'A note how galliglasses have been cessed' in Cork, and as the number cessed totals 380, it may account for the actual quartering locations of most of the 300 *Buannacht Bheag* listed in the last column. As such, these figures have been added in parenthesis in the 'Galloglass' column. Of course, not all of these claims for rising out would be honoured, and some of these lords, such as the Viscount of Decies, actively opposed Desmond's claims over them. Carew's figures are summarised in the table below.

---

17 *State Papers published Under the Authority of His Majesty's Commission: King Henry VIII*, vol. 2, part 3. Correspondence of the Governments of England and Ireland, 1515–1538 (London: HMSO, 1834), p.46, 25 September, Lord Lieutenant to Henry VIII.

18 Constancia Maxwell, *Irish History From Contemporary Sources* (London: George Allen & Unwin, 1923), p.92.

19 *Calendar of the Carew Manuscripts*, vol. 1, 1515–1574, J.S. Brewrer and William Bullen eds (London: Longman & Co., 1867), pp.393–395, n.d., Notes touching the Presidentship of Mounster, by G. Carew.

'OF KERNS AND GALLOWGLASSES'

Table 8. Earl of Desmond's Forces, *c.* 1569

Lord/Territory	Horse	Kern	Galloglass	Galloglass 'Bonogh beges'
The Earl of Desmond's Country in Kerry	20	240	200	
The Earl of Desmond in Conologh	30	300	160	96 sparres
John of Desmond in Limerick	12	100		
Sir Thomas of Desmond in Coshbryde	12	100		
Sir Morrice Fitzgerald, Viscount Decies	20	200		30 axes
MacMaurice, Baron of Lixnaw	24	200		48 sparres
O'Connor Kerry	6	100		96 axes
Imokilly, Cork	12	80		30 axes
Condon's country in Cork	8	60	(60 sparres)	
Lord Roche's country in Cork	36	100	(80 galliglasses)	
Lord Barrey's country in Cork	30	200	(160 galliglasses)	
The White Knight's country, called Clan Gibon, in Cork	10	100	(80 sparres)	
The Knight of the Valley in Limerick	10	140		
Total	230	1,920	360 (380)	300

Some of the Desmond galloglass were descendants of the Fánad line of MacSweeneys, but like MacCarthy Mor, the Earls also maintained MacSheehy galloglass. In 1593, holdings of 3,260 acres which had belonged to Owen and Turlough MacSweeney, of the Ballynoa and Newtown sept, were awarded to an English undertaker. The chief septs of MacSweeneys under Desmond, holding even larger estates, were at Lisnaculla Castle and Ballyalinan Castle. This is in contrast to the galloglass captains of Ormond, who were not landowners.[20] In early 1565, Manus Oge MacSheehy, a captain of galloglass to Desmond, had taken 400 galloglass and 200 shot and horsemen across the Shannon into Thomond, where they interfered in an O'Brien succession dispute.[21] Shortly afterwards, Desmond seems to have brought a similarly sized force on a rent-seeking expedition into

---

[20] G. A. Hayes-McCoy, *Scots Mercenary Forces in Ireland (1565–1603)*, (London: Burns, Oates & Washbourne, 1937), p.67.

[21] *Calendar of State Papers Ireland: Elizabeth*, vol. 2, 1574–1585, Hans Claude Hamilton ed., (London: Longmans, Green, Reader and Dyer, 1867) p.245, 2 September, Sir. T. Cusake.

the Decies. This resulted in the Battle of Affane in February 1565 where he led 80 to 100 horsemen, 300 to 400 foot, and several hundred camp followers and plunderers against the forces of Ormond.[22] In 1566, while Sidney invaded Ulster, the Earl of Desmond loyally joined in the defence of the Pale with 100 horsemen, 300 galloglass, and 92 gunners.[23] Desmond seems to have brought no kern for this service. The 'battle' of 92 gunners is still present, as in 1490, and this probably gives a good idea of the power which the Earl could routinely project.

During the first Desmond Rebellion, at the height of his strength in July of 1569, James FitzMaurice of Desmond was reportedly encamped near Waterford with 1,400 galloglass, 400 mailed pikemen, 400 shot, and 1,500 kern. These numbers included the forces of the other Desmond chiefs, such as MacCarthy Mor, the White Knight, et cetera.[24] This seems to be the first appearance of pikemen and such large numbers of shot in an Irish force. The fact that the pikemen were in mail suggests they may have been rearmed galloglass, though this is far from certain. In 1596, Captain John Dowdall would claim that the Irish had converted their galloglass into pikemen, but he is the only commentator to claim this explicitly. FitzMaurice's situation deteriorated and later that month, Rory MacSheehy, Captain General of the Earl of Desmond's galloglass, submitted to Sidney at Limerick.[25] In October of 1572, Fitzmaurice obtained substantial aid from the rebellious sons of the Earl of Clanricard, Ulick and Shane, who are reported crossing the Shannon into Limerick with 1,200 Scots, though the Recorder of Limerick claimed they had 1,400 Scots and 2,000 Clandonnell galloglass, and many horsemen.[26] Edward and Edmund Butler, brothers of the Earl of Ormond, had recently been in rebellion, and to redeem themselves, they were sent upon Fitzmaurice and his Scots, killing 100 of them. Old Clanricard then persuaded his wild sons to submit, and the mercenaries melted away, leaving Fitzmaurice with 600 men. These were surprised near Kilkenny by Edmund Butler with 300 Ormond galloglass and 60 horse. FitzMaurice's men were scattered and the rebellion ended shortly thereafter.

A decade later, in the early stages of the second Desmond Rebellion, Sir Humphrey Gilbert gave the Earl's own total strength as 100 horsemen, 500 galloglass, and 800 kern.[27] This was a reconstituted force, risings out

---

22 Bagwell, *Ireland Under*, p.85.
23 Herbert Hore, 'The Hosting Against the Northern Irish in 1566,' *Ulster Journal of Archaeology*, vol. 1 (1853), p.161.
24 Claude Ronald Sasso, 'The Desmond Rebellions, 1569–1573 and 1579–1583'. Unpublished Loyola University of Chicago PhD thesis, 1978, p.126.
25 Bagwell, *Ireland Under*, p.166.
26 *Calendar of State Papers Ireland: Henry VIII, Edward VI, Mary, and Elizabeth*, vol. 1, 1509–1573, ed. Hans Claude Hamilton (London: Longman, Green, Longman and Roberts, 1860), p.487, 26 October, Lord Deputy to Burghley.
27 *Calendar of the Carew Manuscripts*, vol. 2, 1575–1588, J. S. Brewrer and William Bullen, eds (London: Longman & Co., 1867), p.175, 26 November, Probably by Sir Humphrey Gilbert.

and coign and livery having been taken from him in 1574 after the first Rebellion.[28] At Monasternenagh in 1579, with the Earl himself still wavering in the wings, his brother John, the Captain of Desmond, reportedly fielded 2,000 horse and foot. In his report on the battle, Captain Malby claimed there were 1,200 galloglass among the foot, for 'Desmond joined his force of 600 galloglass with the 600 of his brethern.'[29] Pelham reported in February of 1580 that if Desmond was joined by MacCarthy Mor and Fitzmaurice, he would command 80 horse, 600 galloglass, 1,600 kern and 200 shot.[30] In October of 1582, the Council in Dublin declared that Desmond was as strong as ever, commanding 2,000 men distributed thus: the Earl and the Baron of Lixnaw, 1,000 men in Kerry; Patrick Condon, 300 in Roche's country; Gerald MacThomas of Connuelo and Donough MacCormac, 300 in Aherlow; the Seneschal of Imokilly, '200 footmen, picked kern, and expert fellows, sixty shot, and twenty-four horsemen' in the Decies, all of them reportedly reaping the peasant's corn and burying it in grain pits in the woods – an activity that frequently accompanied rebellion.[31]

After the crushing of the first Desmond Rebellion, many MacSheehy galloglass were among the hundreds of Irish military men executed by Sir William Drury, Lord President of Munster. The second Desmond Rebellion resulted in the utter destruction of the Desmond lordship and the devastation of the province of Munster, with about 9,000 adult males killed in the fighting, and an estimated 36,600 people starving in the subsequent famine.[32] The galloglass Goran MacSweeney was one of the 15th Earl of Desmond's last faithful followers in 1583. In September of that year, Ormond sent Burghley a long list of 'principal leaders of companies as were executed,' including 'A Capten of Galloglass of the MacShihies in his company' and 'Rory Moyle MacConegan, Capten of Galloglas.'[33] Some MacSheehy and MacSweeney survivors became roving mercenaries in the north. In 1589, Bingham, Governor of Connacht, reported 'There be 200 of the M'Shees, of Munster, in Tirconnel,' who had just come from Turlough Luineach O'Neill's service. Bingham wanted to hire them, lest they join the 'traitor' Brian O'Rourke.[34] They were led by the famous mercenary Captain, Murrough na Mart ('of the beeves') MacSweeney, himself a refugee of the Desmond war.

---

28 *Calendar of State Papers Ireland: Elizabeth*, vol. 2, 1574–1585, Hans Claude Hamilton ed. (London: Longmans, Green, Reader and Dyer, 1867), p.25, 31 May, Mr Garret to Kildare.
29 *CSP Ireland*, p.190, 12 October, Malby to Walsingham.
30 *Cal. Carew Mss*, p.214, 9 February, Pelham to Wallop.
31 *CSP Ireland*, p.ciii, 10 October, Lord Justices to Privy Council.
32 Colm Lennon, *Elizabethan Ireland: The Incomplete Conquest* (Dublin: Gill & Macmillan, 2005), pp.216–218.
33 *CSP Ireland*, p.cxi, 10 September, Ormond to Burghley.
34 *Calendar of State Papers Ireland: Elizabeth*, vol. 4, 1588, August to 1592, September, Hans Claude Hamilton ed. (London: Longman, 1885), p.157, 26 April, Bingham to Lord Deputy.

MacCarthy Mor Armies

'The Power of Irishmen' document aligns well with other sources for the MacCarthy Mor lordship. The first element of MacCarthy Mor's army was the 'rising out' of the several septs of the MacCarthys and dependent lord's territories: 'Garemsloage (*gairm shluaig*) is a rising upon a warninge given of all the able men of the countrye with sufficient weapon and three day's victuals; and for every default, to be fined at a choice cow or xx livres of old money.'[35] For instance, the rising out of Florence MacCarthy's personal territory of Carberry was 300 kern, which is the force he would lead in English service in the later stages of the second Desmond Rebellion. The rising out of MacGillicuddy of the Reeks was 700 kern, while the Earl's own freehold was charged with a 'rising' of 40 horsemen, 'each with two horses and three boys as often as the Earl might need to employ them' et cetera.

The second element of MacCarthy Mor's army were the kernety, or household kern. These were permanently maintained kern, quartered like the galloglass in groups of 20 per quarter of land upon his sub-chieftains. O'Sullivan Beare, the Marshal of MacCarthy Mor's forces, was also to provide his personal guard, '5 gallowglasses or 5 kerne out of every arable quarter.' There were 39 quarters in O'Sullivan Beare's territory, each supporting 5 galloglass or kern, for a total of 195 men. As we will see below, O'Sullivan Beare only provided for 50 galloglass, so the remaining 145 men were likely kernety. And upon a hosting, if any of these men were missing the sub-chieftain was to pay 6s 8d or one beef at the Earl's choice.

When Donal MacCarthy Mor submitted in 1565 and was made Earl of Clancare, his military strength was enumerated by Sir William Herbert. Herbert's summary records 257 galloglass maintained on eight subject 'countries' within the lordship, or 774 men and boys.[36] Herbert closely parallels the 'Power of Irishmen' document's total number of galloglass for MacCarthy Reagh and MacCarthy Mor (240), adding that the latter had one battle of 80 MacSweeney galloglass, and one battle of 80 MacSheehy galloglass. The distribution of their quartering rights was as follows:

---

35 John Dorney, 'Florence MacCarthy and the conquest of Gaelic Munster, 1560-1640.' Dissertation submitted to National University of Ireland in partial fulfilment of requirements for the degree of MA at University College Dublin, September 2003, p.10.

36 William Butler, *Gleanings From Irish History* (London: Longmans, Green and Co., 1925), p.45.

Table 9. MacCarthy Mor Galloglass Quartering Rights

Muskerry (MacCarthy Mor)	30
Duhallow (MacCarthy Mor)	27
O'Sullivan Beare and Bantry	50
Dunkerron (O'Sullivan Mor)	50
MacGillicuddy of the Reeks	30
Kerslawny (MacCarthy)	40
MacFineen Dubh (MacCarthy)	15
Clan Dermond (MacCarthys)	15
Total	**257**

The galloglass listed above 'were a company that never stirred from one place all the year long.' Other lands were charged with the 'bonnyburr' of 'galloglass coming forth of any foreign country which were in one place but one quarter of the year.' This provided meat for the hiring of additional galloglass and boys, 'and drink for the time at the country charge.'[37] The *Carew Calendar* records the 'ordinary forces' of the Munster lords during the presidency of Sir John Perrot, 1570–1573. Butler felt the numbers given for the MacCarthy Mor lordship (see table 10) were too low to represent the full strength of the 'rising out'. He therefore suggested that this might represent a standing force of 2,726 mercenaries, horse and kernety, maintained upon the freeholders. In wartime, with the addition of the 'rising out', Muskerry could raise 1,000 men and Carbery could raise 2,000 to 3,000. A list of 'The Forces of Irish Borderers' c. 1537, gives the MacCarthy Mor lordship 3,728 men, horse, galloglass and kern. But this does not include O'Sullivan Mor, and the Carbery forces are only listed as 40 horse, 80 galloglass, and 200 kern. With the addition of the 2,492 estimated for Carbery, this gives a total of 6,220. This aligns with the Power of Irishmen estimates above, and is close to Nicholas Browne's claim that the combined forces of the followers of MacCarthy Mor could raise 7,000 to 8,000 men.[38] The galloglass figures in quotes in the table below are drawn from Carew's 'A note how galliglasses have been cessed,' as referenced above in the table for Desmond forces. Thus, these galloglass figures may include, in part or in their entirety, the 'bonnyburr' of additional hired galloglass, 'which were in one place but one quarter of the year.'

---

37 Thomas Westropp, 'Notes on Askeaton, County Limerick', *Journal of the Royal Society of Antiquaries of Ireland*, ser. 5, vol. 34 (1904), p.127.
38 Butler, *Gleanings*, pp.103–104.

A DESCRIPTION OF THE POWER OF IRISHMEN

Table 10. 'Ordinary Forces' of the MacCarthy Mor Lordship

Lord/Territory	Horse	Kern	Galloglass
MacCarthy Mor, with O'Donoghue Mor, O'Donoghue of the Glens, and McGillycuddy McFinnin	8	400	'240 axes'
O'Sullivan Mor in Cork	2	240	
O'Sullivan Beare in Cork	2	200	
Muskerry, Sir Dermot McTege's country in Cork	20	300	'160 galliglasses'
Carbery, Sir Donough MacCarthy Reagh's country in Cork	30	1,000	'240 axes'
MacDonough in Duhallow	8	100	'180 axes'
MacAuliffe, follower of MacDonough	6	200	
O'Keefe	3	100	
O'Callaghan	7	100	
Total	86	2,640	820

A table of MacCarthy Mor forces provided by George Carew, given below, may help clarify the above.[39] It was based largely on the 'Power of Irishmen' document, although with minor changes. The grand total is 6,202, and this is close to the estimate of 6,220 quoted above. It does not include possible additional galloglass, hired using 'bonnyburr.'

Table 11. Carew's List of Forces of the MacCarthy Mor Lordship.

Lord/Territory	Horse	Kern	Galloglass
MacCarthy Mor, Prince of that portion	40	2,000	160
MacCarthy Reagh, Lord of Carbery	60	2,000	80
Donough MacCarthy of Duhallow	24	200	80
Teig MacCormac of Muskerry	40	200	80
O'Keefe	12	100	
MacAuliffe	80	60	
O'Donovan	6	60	
O'Driscoll of Collinmore and Baltimore	6	200	
O'Mahon of Ivaghe	26	120	
O'Sullivan Beare and Bantry	10	200	
O'Donogh More of Lough Lene	12	200	
O'Mahoney of Brin	46	100	
Totals	362	5,440	400

---

39 Daniel MacCarthy, *The Life and Letters of Florence MacCarthy Reagh* (London: Harrison and Sons, 1867), p.9.

MacCarthy Mor gathered his host in support of the rebel James Fitzmaurice in 1569, obtaining arms from Spanish merchantmen.[40] This was the likely source of the arms for Fitzmaurice's 400 mailed pikemen and 400 shot seen near Waterford in July 1569, as noted above under Desmond Armies. On 26 September 1571, the lords of MacCathy Mor's territories were constrained to sign an agreement with Sir John Perrot, President of Munster, to raise specified forces for Crown Service for the space of six months. These are given in the table below. The Earl of Clancare (MacCarthy Mor) was to command them, and in his absence, Lord Barry. They would divide any booty taken in proportion to the number of men each commanded.[41] In 1580, when Ormond was operating against the rebel Desmond, he brought with him to Castlemaine 'Clancare, O'Sullivan Bere, and O'Sullivan More, Mac Fynyn of the kerne, MacDonogh, O'Keefe, O'Callaghan, MacAuliffe, O'Donoghue More, and all the other chiefs of Desmond, except O'Donoghue of Glenfesk, who remained with the traitor earl.'[42] The 'Mac Fynyn of the kern' seems to have had charge of the kern of MacCarthy Mor, but it is not clear if this refers to the Mac Finin Dubh branch of O'Sullivans.

Table 12. MacCarthy Mor Lordship forces raised for Crown Service in 1571

Lord/Territory	Horse	Shot	Galloglass	Kern
MacCarthy Mor	6	24	126	100
MacCarthy Reagh	8	10	40	50
Sir Donough MacTeige MacCarthy of Muskerry	6	10	20	40
MacDonough of Kanturk	4	8	20	30
the Lord Courcy	2	4	6	8
the Lord Barry	6	10	30	20
Totals:	32	66	242	248

O'Neill Armies

The 'Power of Irishmen' reflects the strength of the O'Neill's of Tyrone at the time of Con Mor O'Neill, *c.* 1490. A sixteenth century document, *Rights of O'Neill* (*Ceart Uí Néill*), lists *bunnacht*, or billeting rights, for the considerably larger number of 1,615 hired soldiers. Like a similar Irish document pertaining to the O'Donnells, some of these claims were

---

40 Sasso, 'Desmond Rebellions', p.103.
41 Charles Smith, *Ancient and Present State of the County and City of Cork* (Dublin: 1749), p.46.
42 Bagwell, *Ireland Under*, p.49.

aspirational, and reflect the political situation *c*. 1395. Certainly, 1395 was the approximate date at which the Clan Alasdair MacDonnells became galloglass to O'Neill, headquartered at Cnoc-na-Cluithe, in the 'galloglass country.'[43] They provided 300 galloglass, possibly three 'battles' of 100 each. However, some of the billeting rights listed in the document are of sixteenth century date, such as the claim upon O'Reilly, while other families named were already extinct. The O'Donnellys are named as 'the marshals of O'Neill; one fortieth goes to them as levying share. A penny out of each man's provision on account of a raid or of encampment. One of them should be present at a parade. They have the heads and hides the first night on changing ground from one tribal land to another.' O'Devlin, MacCowell and MacMurrough were O'Neill's 'true kern' (*fírcheithearna*), 'to keep watch for the first three nights of an encampment, and at a hosting.'[44] Other members of the *Lucht Tighe*, or household people, were O'Quinn, the quartermaster, and O'Hagan, the seneschal. Together with the O'Donnellys, these household families provided O'Neill's horsemen. Pettiplace, an English pirate familiar with Ulster, remarked in 1567 that the O'Donnellys 'are three hundred gentlemen to whom he hath given livings and countries.' MacCaffrey was hereditary Standard Bearer to O'Neill.

There were four septs of MacDonnell galloglass serving O'Neill in Tyrone and Armagh. Gillespic, of the Colla Balbh sept, was made 'MacDonnell Galloglach' in 1537. When an existing rift with O'Neill worsened, Gillespic submitted to the Crown in 1542, agreeing to serve in Ulster with '120 spears well harnessed.' Lord Deputy Bellingham called on him do so in 1548, saying he 'appointed McDonnell to bring with him forty sparres besides their boys, who has brought six score.'[45] When Gillespic died in 1549, Conn O'Neill, bitterly opposed to the Anglicising policy of the Dublin government, switched to the Clann Somhairle Mor sept for his new MacDonnell Galloglach. This was Eoin mac Somhairle MacDonnell, who took over the seat of Cnoc-na-Cluithe in Annagh Townland. The sept of Colla Balbh were then resettled south-east of Armagh in the district of Clancarney. Eoin MacDonnell Galloglach, Constable of O'Neill, was killed by the MacSweeneys at Farsetmore in 1567, while serving Conn's successor, Shane O'Neill. He was succeeded by his son Feardorcha, as 'McDonell, chief of Galloghglasses and Art McDonnell, their captain,' who remained in the post until at least 1590. In 1570, Feardorcha and Art took revenge for Eoin's death at Farsetmore, killing Torloch Og MacSweeney Fánad and Murchad

---

43 Katherine Simms, *From Kings to Warlords* (Woodbridge: Boydell & Brewer, Ltd, 1987), p.139.
44 Éamon Ó Doibhlin, 'Ceart Uí Néill: A Discussion and Translation of the Document', *Seanchas Ardmhacha: Journal of the Armagh Diocesan Historical Society*, vol. 5, no. 2 (1970), pp.324–358.
45 Donald M. Schlegel, 'The MacDonnells of Tyrone and Armagh: A Genealogical Study', *Seanchas Ardmhacha: Journal of the Armagh Diocesan Historical Society*, vol. 10, no. 1 (1980–81), pp.193–219.

Mall MacSweeney na dTuath at Dun-na-long, in the presence of Turlough Lunieach O'Neill.

Starting in 1559, Shane O'Neill had militarised the lordship: 'he furnished all the peasants and husbandmen of his countrie with armour and weapons, and trained them up in the knowledge of the wars.'[46] This included forming a company of gunners, captained initially by Niall M'Shane Boy, who was killed in 1563 during one of Sidney's incursions into Ulster.[47] Pettiplace, the English pirate, reported: 'For ammunition and powder he hath that made in his country as good as need be, and for harquebusses, skulls, and shirts of mail, he was and is furnished by Spaniards and Frenchmen, yea, and by Englishmen.'[48] The training was likely in weapons handling, and does not seem to have affected tactics.

In June 1564, Shane is reported in the State Papers at the head of a 'great host of men, 300 horsemen, 400 galloglass, 200 long bows, Scots born in Ireland, 120 gunners, and 500 kerne.'[49] Prior to Sidney's invasion of Ulster in 1566, Shane reportedly now had 200 harquebusiers, 400 horsemen, 1,500 galloglasses, 800 redshanks under MacLean, 2,000 kern 'and other raskals of his country.'[50] This roughly confirms Sidney's own estimate in November of that year, that Shane commanded 700 horse and 4,000 foot.[51] For pitched battles with native enemies, such as Glentasie in 1565, and Farsetmore in 1567, Shane fielded about half this number. But at the Battle of the Red Sagums in 1561, engaging in a more cautious kind of warfare against government forces, Shane overthrew Stanley's rearward with a selected force of only 12 horsemen, 300 Scots, and 200 galloglass, and with no kern.[52] Pettiplace did not see many Englishmen in Shane's service, and those that were present were charged with his cannon, which had been purchased from foreign merchants. But he noted that Shane had broken down many of his castles, and trusted rather to the woods and crannogs, which proved impenetrable to Sidney during his incursions into Ulster. Shane had prior knowledge of the Lord Deputy's intentions a full day in advance, 'as if he were in Dublin,' and knew beforehand his numbers and route of approach, as well as the duration of the expedition.

Shane's less belligerent successor, Turlough Luineach O'Neill, actually increased the size of the army of Tyrone through the increased use of Scots mercenaries. In June of 1581, Turlough commanded 700 horse, 1,500

---

46 G. A. Hayes-McCoy, *Irish Battles: A Military History of Ireland* (Dublin: Gill and Macmillan, 1980), p.74.
47 *Calendar of State Papers Ireland: Henry VIII, Edward VI, Mary and Elizabeth*, vol. 1, 1509-73, Hans Claude Hamilton ed. (London: Longman, Green, Longman & Roberts, 1860), p.217, 11 May, Lord Lieutenant to Privy Council.
48 Herbert Hore, 'The Hosting Against the Northern Irish in 1566' in *Ulster Journal of Archaeology*, vol. 1 (1853), p.161.
49 *CSP Ireland*, p.xxvi, 13 June, Sir Thomas Cusack to Lord Justice Arnold.
50 Hore, 'The Hosting Against', p.160.
51 *CSP Ireland*, p.318, 12 November, Lord Deputy to Privy Council.
52 Bagwell, *Ireland Under*, p.24.

galloglass, 2,500 Scots, and 'an infinity of kern.'[53] The table below, from a government intelligence report of April, 1575, gives much smaller numbers. Turlough's forces varied is size, depending on need. The report was titled, 'A brief note of the number of horsemen, galloglasses, and Scots and kernaghes entertained at this present by the Lords and chief men inhabiting within the Province of Ulster.'[54]

Table 13. Forces of the Chiefs of Ulster, 1575.

Lord	Horse	Galloglass	Scots	Kern	Gunners
MacMahon of Farney	50			200	
O'Neill of the Fews	30			100	
MacMahon of Dartrey	100			600	
Baron of Dungannon	60			300	
O'Hanlon	12			120	
Art McDonnell Galloglass	20	300			
Henry McShane's sons	30			100	
Turlough Breslaghe and the McKanes	40			200	
McGuinness	50			300	40
Maguire	80			600	
Turlough Luineach	200	400	400	1,000	
O'Neill of Clandeboy	600			800	
MacQuillan of the Route	24			100	
Alexander Oge MacDonnell	12			100	
Sorley Boy MacDonnell	40		200		
O'Donnell of Tyrconnell	20	600		1,000	
Total	**1,368**	**1,300**	**600**	**5,520**	**40**

The total muster of Ulster was therefore 8,828, though the report gives it as 8,356. Note that, as a landholder, 'Art MacDonnell Galloglass' of the Clann Colla Balbh sept, could raise cavalry like any Irish lordship. As noted above, Feardorcha, of the Clann Somhairle Mor sept, was actually MacDonnell Galloglach at this time, serving with 'Art McDonnell, their captain.' The number of gunners is low, since in March 1581 Trollope had written, with some exaggeration, that Turlough Luineach could 'make' 6,000 men, and whereas in times past they were armed but with darts and axes, they were

---

53   Falls, *Irish Wars*, p.147.
54   *Calendar of the Carew Manuscripts*, vol. 2, 1575–1588, J. S. Brewrer and William Bullen, eds (London: Longman & Co., 1867), p.9, April, A Note of Ulster, Malby.

now 'furnished with all kinds of munition, and were as practised therein as Englishmen.'[55] The report adds a note on the wages of each class of soldier:

> The bonnaught or wages of galloglass for a quarter of a year, when it is best cheap, is one beef for his wages, and two beefs for his feeding and diet. The wages of a Scot is like. The captain of galloglass hath for a quarter, one chief horse and a hackney, or for the hackney an habergeon, and in a band of 100 he hath to advance his wages, 13 dead pays out of the 100; so the band of 100 is but 87 men. The captain is also allowed for his own victuals six men's allowances. The captain of 100 Scots and the captain of 100 gunners have the like. The horsemen hath for his wages as the galloglasse hath, besides horsemeat allowed him. The captain of the horsemen hath as the captain of the galloglasse. The captain of 100 kernaghes hath for his pay 8 men's pay and the allowance of their meat, and at his first entrance hath as in a way of reward over and above his quarter's wages commonly 10 kine to bestow as a benevolence among his gentlemen, which they look for as a common duty. The kernagh hath quarterly one heifer, valued at 8s. sterling, and his victuals.

O'Donnell Armies

The O'Donnell lordship benefited from a succession of strong rulers from 1461 to 1555, after which internal issues brought about a decline. In 1555, Maghnus became ill and was deposed by his son Calvagh, who was supported by a force of Mac Ailin (Campbell) mercenaries with 'brass ordnance', led by Archibald Campbell, heir to the Earldom of Argyll, as well as James MacDonnell of Dunnyveg, who was tied to Argyll by feudal bonds. In 1560, Calvagh signed a 'bond of manrent' with Argyll, giving him nominal control over the lordship. At the same time Calvagh married Catherine MacLean, who brought a dowry of 1,000 to 2,000 redshank mercenaries. Although he defeated his rival, Shane O'Neill, in 1557, Calvagh was subsequently captured by Shane. Hugh MacMaghnus, Calvagh's successor, also defeated Shane in battle, in 1567 at Farsetmore. But the lordship thereafter was in decline and would not see a resurgence until 1592, when the famous 'Red Hugh' was inaugurated as chief.[56]

The 'Power of Irishmen' estimate for the O'Donnell lordship – 100 horse, four battles of galloglass, and 200 kern – is relatively accurate. The household

---

55 *Calendar of State Papers Ireland: Elizabeth*, vol. 2, 1574–1585, Hans Claude Hamilton ed. (London: Longmans, Green, Reader and Dyer, 1867), p.xvii, Trollope to Walsingham.
56 Muríosa Prendergast, 'Scots Mercenary Forces in Sixteenth Century Ireland' in John France (ed.), *Mercenaries and Paid Men: The Mercenary Identity in the Middle Ages* (Boston: Leiden, 2008), pp.363–381.

families (*lucht tighe*) of Tyrconnell provided 200 kern and 60 horsemen, commanded by O'Gallagher, the Marshal of O'Donnell's host. McGroarty was hereditary Standard Bearer to O'Donnell, riding into battle bearing the *Cathach*, a book shrine of St Columba. The MacSweeney Banagh Galloglass sept also provided a bearer for the talismanic red stone and mail shirt of St Columba.[57] The three septs of the MacSweeneys provided O'Donnell with 300 sparrs of galloglass. First appearing in Tyrconnell in the mid-fourteenth century, the MacSweeneys had settled there later in the century. They became part of the political structure and were second in importance only to their O'Donnell lords. Their organisation was based on a *corughadh* (battle) of 60 men, with MacSweeney Doe and MacSweeney Fánad each providing two *corughaidh*, and MacSweeney Banagh, one *corughadh*. These details are from a manuscript preserving the recollections of O'Donnell's steward, and are discussed in greater detail in the chapter on the Galloglass.

The same manuscript source of O'Donnell's steward also records O'Dogherty of Inishowen providing 60 horse and 120 kern for the rising out. From the fourteenth century, the O'Doghertys had been noted for maintaining large numbers of horsemen. In 1600 Dowcra wrote that they were able to make 300 foot and 60 horse. Dowcra goes on to describe a skirmish in which O'Dogherty had 'about 400 foot & 60 horse', as well as a subsequent fight in which O'Donnell had '600 foote & 60 horse,' probably the same horsemen.[58] The *Annals of the Four Masters* describes O'Donnell returning from a raid in Connacht in 1600 and dismissing his allies and mercenaries, retaining only 'five hundred heroes of his choice soldiers, and sixty horsemen, of his own faithful people.'[59]

As with the O'Neills, the O'Donnells held an old Irish Charter recording their billeting rights on the Province of Ulster. These are recorded in the *Book of Ó Scingin*, which is dated 1542, but has its origins in the 1340s. In it, a claim is made for billeting rights for a total of 605½ men. The list includes:

> The equivalent of forty men on Tír Conaill; Sixty on Clannaboy; Fifty-five and a half on Ó Catháin; Sixty on Cineal Maoin; Forty per quarter year on O Flynn; Forty on Mac Gilla Muire; Sixty on Uí Eachach; Forty on the Oirtheara; the same on the Oirghialla; Forty on Fir Manach; Forty on Tír Fiach of Ardstraw; Forty on MacCaul (Campbell); Twelve on MacCann; Thirty-two on Muintir Bir; Six on O Caragain Birn.[60]

---

57 Darren McGettigan, *Red Hugh O'Donnell and the Nine Years' War* (Dublin: Four Courts Press, 2005), p.26.
58 Katherine Simms, 'Late Medieval Donegal' in William Nolan, Liam Ronayne and Mariead Dunleavy (eds), *Donegal History and Society: Interdisciplinary Essays on the History of an Irish County* (Dublin: Geography Publications, 1995), p.188.
59 John O'Donovan (ed.), *Annals of the Kingdom of Ireland, by the Four Masters*, 7 vols, (Dublin: Hodges, Smith & Co., 1856), p.2201.
60 Ó Doibhlin, 'Ceart Uí Néill', p.332.

The *Annals of the Four Masters*, in their obituary for Hugh Roe O'Donnell in 1505, record a similar list, asserting that he was lord of Tír Conaill, Cineal Maoin, Inis Eoghain, and North Connacht, and that he had submissions from Fir Manach, Clannaboy, the Route, Ó Catháin, et cetera. The very pro-O'Donnell *Annals of the Four Masters* also record a meeting on the bridge at Ardstraw in 1514 between Hugh Dubh O'Donnell and Art O'Neill, where they seem to have ratified this O'Donnell charter and the O'Neill's own equivalent, *Ceart Uí Néill*. The only conflict between the O'Neill and O'Donnell charters is that both claimed lordship over Ó Catháin and Fir Manach. The annals say: 'New Charters as well as the ratification of old Charters were given by O'Neill to O'Donnell for Cineal Moain, Inis Eoghain and Fir Manach.'[61]

The O'Donnell fleet is described in the chapter below on Irish naval power. The O'Donnells were very forward in the adoption of firearms, and in 1487, Godfrey O'Donnell made the first recorded use of a gun in Ireland when he killed an O'Rourke during an incursion into Breifne. In 1513, Hugh Dubh O'Donnell conducted negotiations with James IV of Scotland for the delivery of an impressive supply of munitions. These were to include one cannon drawn by twenty-six horses, one large culverin drawn by eight horses, two carts with eight barrels of powder, two carts with gun stands, one cart with pikes, sculls, mattocks and a trellis for the cannon, as well as two Scottish 'wrights,' or gunners, with a French overseer, and eight sappers for undermining castles.[62] In the end however, this supply could not be sent. The O'Donnells made temporary use of the guns of a French ship to reduce a castle in 1516, and in 1536, a Scottish cannon was finally delivered. This last may have been the 'great gun' which Hugh Dubh used to intimidate his enemies during an invasion of North Connacht in 1537.

Clanwilliam Armies

'The Power of Irishmen' gives Mac William Lower (*Íochtar*) 200 horsemen, 240 galloglass and 300 kern. This is a reasonable assessment, and the next full account is the *Compossicion Book of Connaught*,[63] which gives the following in 1585:

---

61 Ó Doibhlin, 'Ceart Uí Néill', p.333.
62 Darren Mac Eiteagáin, 'The Renaissance and the Late Medieval Lordship of Tír Chonaill, 1461–1555' in William Nolan, Liam Ronayne and Mariead Dunleavy (eds), *Donegal History and Society: Interdisciplinary Essays on the History of an Irish County* (Dublin: Geography Publications, 1995), p.215.
63 A. Martin Freeman (ed.), *The Compossicion Booke of Conought* (Dublin: The Stationery Office, 1936), p.52.

A DESCRIPTION OF THE POWER OF IRISHMEN

Table 14. Rising Out of Richard Burke, the Mac William Lower (Íochtar), 1585

Territory	Horsemen	Horseboys/ Horses	Galloglass	Kern	Mercenaries (Scots?)
Ballyoviachan				100	8
Ballyboha				100	8
Cashelaffa				100	8
Ballinlocha				100	8
Barony of Tirawley	60	180		120	
O'Malley's Country			120		
O'Kelly's Country	120		120	120	
O'Conor-Rua/ MacDermott	120		120	120	
Carra					160
Clan Costello	Costello's horse?		60		60
Barony of Gallen	60		60	60	
Total	**360**	**180**	**480**	**820**	**252**

Tirawley was the seat of the lordship. The first four townlands were within Mac William Burke's own lordship, and each owed 'a rising-out, rations and hill-billeting,' and eight mercenaries 'in addition to his galloglass.' The mercenaries were probably Scots or possibly hired kern. Galloglass numbers are enumerated as 'six-score mail' et cetera. The galloglass of O'Malley's country were 'bringing their own provision, excepting the first nights meat.' The rest of the rising out were 'on their own provision.' Horseboys/horses were only specified for Tirawley, and 'MacCostello's standard of horse' was not enumerated. Horsemen were specified as being 'armed and accoutered.' Mac William Burke's fines for men missing were, 'in lieu of every man in armour he should have a beef; in lieu of a horseman, two beeves; in lieu of a kern, one beef.'

The Mac William Burkes of Mayo hired large numbers of Scots in the 1570s and 1580s. After Richard an Iarainn's rebellion in 1580, Captain Malby wrote: 'Mac William raised 1,200 galloglasses, and had complete 800. Agreed to pay for 700 Scots, and had complete 600, Loose Kerne 300, Horsemen 20.'[64] When he submitted, Richard owed the Scots £16,800, but was able to banish them without payment.

---

64 Hubert Knox, *The History of the County of Mayo* (Dublin: Hodges, Figgis & Co., 1908), p.194.

The MacDonnells of Mayo were galloglass to Mac William. According to Captain Malby: 'The Clandonnells were accounted always invincible people, and the most strongest sept of Galloglas in Ireland, and the only men of force in Connaught.'[65] Justin MacDonnell, Constable of galloglass, had accompanied Mac William's brief venture into Munster in 1572, to assist Fitzmaurice's rebellion. When Lord Deputy Sidney visited Galway in 1576, he received submissions from 'seven principal men of the Clandonnells, for every of their several lineages one, of that surname …. all by profession mercenary Soldiers, by the name of Galloglas; they are very strong, and …. they are able to go where they will, and with the Countenance of any mean Lord of Force, to make war with the Greatest.'[66] They were MacWilliam's chief strength, and Sidney sought to neutralise them by indenturing them to the Queen instead.

With the second Desmond Rebellion, in 1579, Fitzmaurice again entreated Justin MacDonnell and Randall MacColla MacDonnell of Mayo to join the rebellion in Munster, this time unsuccessfully. But in 1580, they joined Richard an Iarainn Burke's rebellion, and Captain Malby seized Cloneen Castle, Ferragh MacDonnell's seat, and Moelle Castle and town, belonging to Marcus MacYnabbe, Chief of the Clandonnells.[67]

Clanricarde Armies

The 'Power of Irishmen' numbers also seem reasonable for MacWilliam Upper (*Uachtar*), Lord of Clanricarde. The 2nd Earl of Clanricarde, Richard Sassenach ('the Englishman') Burke, was the most zealous Queen's man of the Irish of Connacht in the 1550s and 1560s. At the Battle of Shrule, in 1570, 420 'axes' of Clanricarde's MacSweeney galloglass stood alongside the Government's MacDonnells of Leinster.[68] In 1578, the Earl wrote a memorandum recalling the forces he had commanded on various occasions in Crown service during the middle of the century.[69] It is summarised in the table below, with the 'Power of Irishmen' numbers on the first line:

---

65 Knox, *History Mayo*, p.188.
66 Knox, *History Mayo*, p.183.
67 Knox, *History Mayo*, p.206.
68 Kenneth Nicholls, 'Scots Mercenary Kindreds in Ireland, 1230–1600' in Seán Duffy (ed.), *The World of the Galloglass* (Dublin: Four Courts Press, 2007), p.104.
69 *CSP Ireland*, pp.xlvii–li., 8 March, Clanricarde to Burghley.

Table 15. Hosting of Clanricarde Burke, 1550s

Year	Horsemen	Galloglass	Shot	Kern
c. 1490	120	160		300
1555	100	200	100	200
1556	120	320	120	'a number of kerns well appointed'
1557	132	300	120	250

However, the Earl's sons, Ulick and John, were 'wild children' who caused their loyal father much grief, and they were repeatedly in rebellion from 1570 onwards. Returning from their submission in Dublin, they stripped off their English clothes and put on Irish attire in sight of the garrison of Athlone, having safely crossed the Shannon first. The brothers frequently hired Scots redshanks when going into rebellion. They led 1,200 to 1,400 Scots into Limerick in 1572, in support of the second Desmond Rebellion. When the 2nd Earl died in 1582, Ulick murdered his brother John to secure the title for himself, and remained steadfastly loyal until his death in 1603.

2

Tactics in Irish Warfare

Warfare in Ireland was characterised by mobility and shaped by the landscape. The heavily wooded and boggy terrain allowed the Irish to avoid contact until a time of their own choosing. The essence of Irish warfare was summarised by the Irish Kings who explained it to Edward Bruce in these terms: 'Our custom is to pursue and fight, and fight when retreating, and not to stand in open hand-to-hand conflict until the other side is defeated.'[1] This chapter will examine the institution of the cattle raid, and the pattern of warfare among rival lordships, sometimes leading to a set-piece battle, and will conclude with reviewing the increasing adoption of firearms and ordnance into Ireland.

The Cattle Raid

The cattle raid, or *creach*, was an ancient aspect of Gaelic Irish culture. A ritual proof of manhood with deep Indo-European roots, it forms a dominant element in the earliest Greek heroic tradition. As Hermes had lifted Apollo's cattle, so Herakles lifted those of Geryon, and alongside the abduction of women, the cattle raid was the most obvious *causus belli* in a heroic society.[2] Both of these practices remained in Gaelic Irish culture, with 'marriage by capture' being dubbed 'foudagh' (*fhuadach*).[3] The *Táin Bó Cúailnge,* or Cattle Raid of Cooley, is the national epic of Ireland, and it is just one of 11 Irish tales bearing the title *Táin Bó*.[4]

---

1   Katherine Simms, 'Warfare in the Medieval Gaelic Lordships' in *The Irish Sword*, vol.12 (1975), p.98.
2   Peter Walcot, 'Cattle Raiding, Heroic Tradition, and Ritual: The Greek Evidence', *History of Religions*, vol. 18, no. 4, (May 1979), pp.326–51.
3   James Berry, *Tales of Mayo and Connemara* (Salem: Salem House, 1984), p.120.
4   Bruce Lincoln, 'The Indo-European Cattle-raiding Myth', *History of Religions,* vol. 16 (August 1976), pp.42–65.

Besides the acquisition of easily portable wealth, the cattle raid was a means of enforcing domination over a neighbour, with no intention of taking their land or lives. Raiding warfare was thus a particularly appropriate method of establishing power relationships in a relatively underpopulated country, and its suitability to Irish environmental and demographic conditions meant that it was adopted by the Anglo-Irish as well. Thus, in the sixteenth century, it was still the first duty of a newly elected chief to conduct a 'king's raid' (*creach riógh*). The inauguration of Rory MacTeige MacRory Oge MacDermott in 1549 was concluded by a raid in which the annals enumerate the prey that he took from the traditional sub-chieftains of the MacDermotts, including 1,200 cows from Clann-Pilib. These cattle were promptly handed over to the poets, whose praise was key to establishing the new chief's legitimacy.[5] In other circumstances, the cattle taken might be returned to the owners if the latter submitted to the new lord – the goal was to obtain ongoing annual rents or tribute. By 1576, there was some modification of this practice in the MacCarthy lordship, where every freeholder was levied one cow upon the new MacCarthy Mor 'taking the rod.' 'This levy was called "Rod money" and its object was to provide the new chieftain with a stock of cattle, instead of following the old custom of *Sluaigheadh ceadnais raidhne*, or the excursion on receiving the headship …. which, besides giving proof of the capacity of the new chief in plundering, supplied him with cattle.'[6]

In 1561 the Dublin apothecary and occasional government poisoner, Thomas 'Bottle' Smyth, painted a vivid picture of the traditional cattle raid, although coloured by his anti-Gaelic bias. He says the poets, or *fili*, will make a poem to any young scion of the 'septs of Oes or Macs' who has half a dozen followers. They make him run mad with flattery, reciting the deeds of his ancestors, whom they compare to Scipio or Hercules. 'Then will he gather a sort of rake-hells to him, and other he must get him a Proficeer, who shall tell him how he shall spede (as he thinks). Then will he get him lurking to a side of a wood, and there keepeth him close till morning.'[7]

The contemporary poem book of the O'Byrnes says the raiders constructed rough sleeping huts of wattles close to their objective, preferably in a wood with a stream nearby. There, tested warriors would 'lie on a layer of fresh foliage.' In the pre-dawn hours: 'His steed is beside every man; horse-shoes are being put on by candle-light; Conlá's descendant [Aodh O'Byrne] has to make hasty forays because of his terror of men of poetry.'[8]

---

[5] Bernadette Cunningham and Raymond Gillespie, *Stories From Gaelic Ireland* (Dublin: Four Courts Press, 2003), pp.30–31.
[6] Herbert Hore and James Graves (eds), *The Social State of the Southern and Eastern Counties of Ireland in the Sixteenth Century* (Dublin: University Press, 1870), p.272.
[7] Herbert Hore, 'Irish Bardism in 1561', *Ulster Journal of Archaeology*, 1st. ver., vol. 6 (1858), p.166.
[8] Seán Mac Airt, *The Book of the O'Byrnes* (Dublin: Dublin Institute for Advanced Studies, 1944), pp.343–344.

'OF KERNS AND GALLOWGLASSES'

Smyth concludes by saying that at first light the raiding party descends on the villages, giving their enemies a chilly rousing out:

> Then will they drive all the kine and plow horses, with all other cattle, and drive them away. Then must they have a bagpipe blowing afore them; and if any of these cattle fortune to wax weary or faint, they will kill them, rather than it should do the owners good. If they go by any house of friars or religious house, they will give them 2 or 3 beeves, and they will take them, and pray for them, yea and praise their doings, and say his father was accustomed so to do; wherein he will rejoice; and when he is in a safe place, they will fall to the division of the spoils according to the discretion of the captain.[9]

Derricke's depiction of a cattle raid. A body of men armed with axes appears at left, led by a piper. These *may* be galloglass, possibly unarmoured for speed during a cattle raid. The mounted man of rank is similarly unarmoured. Some of the kern are barefoot. The three at the centre carry their darts on their shoulders, with what appear to be a shield, a pot and a bag slung from them. (Creative Commons)

The number of men conducting a cattle raid could be quite small. Two fifteenth century examples comprised of only 140 kern and 12 horsemen, and 60 kern and six horsemen, respectively.[10] In the Pale, the raiders of the O'Connors and other bordering clans often seem to have been largely mounted. A Statute of 1460 says the Irish 'ryde upon the King's subjects …. by night.' And in 1537, two tower houses are to be built in the marches to put 'a stopp to keep hym and all the Yrishemen from invading your Pale with any horsemen.'[11] During larger raids, harrying an entire territory, the

---

9 Hore, 'Irish Bardism', p.166.
10 Simms, 'Warfare in', p.104.
11 Steven G. Ellis, *England's Irish Pale, 1470–1550: The Making of a Tudor Region* (Woodbridge: The Boydell Press, 2021), pp.53 & 106.

TACTICS IN IRISH WARFARE

invading force often split into several separate raiding parties. Thus the *Annals of the Four Masters* describe O'Donnell's scouring of Connaught in late January 1597: 'Having reached the very centre of Hy-Many, he sent forth swift-moving marauding parties through the district of Caladh, and the upper part of the territory; and they carried off many herds of cows and other preys to O'Donnell, to the town of Athenry.'[12] The numbers of cattle taken could be considerable. An estimate of 2,400 cows were taken in a raid in Connacht in 1462.[13] On such large-scale raids, there might be little fear of pursuit. After O'Donnell's great raid of the Burren in Co. Clare in 1599, he marched out of the territory with ostentation:

> He placed the attendants, the raw levies, and the unarmed in front of the line of march with their preys and spoils and booty. He himself marched with the nobles and chosen men of the great host accompanying him in the middle of the same line of march behind the party he had put in charge of the prey. He ordered his soldiers, his youths, and his shooters to remain in the rear to fight for them if they should be pursued. They went then in the early part of the day by the roadways of ancient Burren eastwards with much noise and great shouting.[14]

Raiding involved a great deal of planning and logistics, not least because much of it was carried on in darkness. The annals frequently mention 'night incursions' and the State Papers preserve a letter from the Mayor of Cork from November, 1548, saying: 'Certain wild Irish, coming one night to make a prey near Cork, were met by Lord Barrymore, who was going to do the like on certain other wild Irish; the Lord Barrymore killed eighty of them.'[15] Folklore sometimes preserves details of the activities engaged in during cattle raids. We learn that the crossing of a stream provided an opportunity to count the *creach*, and that mounted friars sometimes accompanied the raiders. M'Sparran adds an interesting tradition of this sort:

> It was customary, or rather one of the feudal laws prevailing in those days, that the enemy who could forcibly take the property of another past three crosses situated at a mentioned distance from each other, then became the lawful possessors of it; and therefore O'Donnell had placed one cross at the Bann side, another somewhere in a central

---

12 O'Donovan (ed.), *Annals Ireland*, p.2009.
13 Simms, 'Warfare in', p.101.
14 Lughaid O'Clery (Paul Walsh ed.), *Beatha Aodh Ruadh Uí Domhnaill (The Life of Hugh Roe O'Donnell)*, (Dublin: Irish Texts Society, 1948), p.207.
15 *Calendar of State Papers Ireland: Henry VIII, Edward VI, Mary and Elizabeth*, vol. 1, 1509–73, Hans Claude Hamilton ed. (London: Longman, Green, Longman & Roberts, 1860), p.92, 18 November, Mayor of Cork to Bellingham.

direction, and the last beyond the old church at Drumachose. .... In this place was erected a large cross with a bough of holly bound to the top.[16]

The chief and horsemen would have led the incursion into enemy territory, while the kern burnt houses and rounded up livestock. When exiting with the prey, the chief's place was in the rear, while the galloglass, if present, would form a moveable 'castle of bones', stationed at some pass or ford along the line of retreat, which the raiders would aim for as a refuge. Horsemen are described as using the galloglass as a bastion from which to issue forth to make counter attacks against their pursuers. Curiously, Derricke's woodcut of a cattle raid includes a body of axemen with a piper playing before them. Are these unarmoured galloglass accompanying the raid? The poets spoke of 'the reaver's track in the grass,' and skilled trackers were paid to follow the raiders. If the pursuit, or *toraigheacht*, caught up with the raiders, they were far more likely to be victorious than the raiders.[17] Remarkably, one of the folklore collections made by school children in Co. Cork in the early twentieth century recounts such a pursuit. When the men of Carbery drove a big *creach* away from Dunboy, Donal Cam O'Sullivan Beare's mother urged him to pursue:

> Donal got up and took his father's sword and called the men of Dunboy and they followed the robbers and killed some of them at Doire Cann Diarmuda and took some of the cattle off them. They overtook them again near Cooranial and killed five of them and the graves are to be seen still. The blood ran down to Derrynafulla and the froth of the blood of a man named Randal ran down to Cooranial. They followed them on and overtook them again at Doire Creithe and they were shivering there. They killed the last of them at Carraig na Caointe and it was there the women of the men that were killed wept for the death of their husbands.[18]

This outcome is a reminder of the frequent fate of the more humble raiders. In 1583, Mably, Lord President of Connacht, wrote that Clanrickard had 'embraced civility' by applying the customary punishment of hanging a cattle thief with a quarter of a beeve around his neck. A song on this class of raiders was translated by Rev. Hanmer of Dublin in the later sixteenth century, and a very close version, given below Hanmer's translation, was still being sung in Irish in Ballyvourney, Co. Cork, in 1943.

---

16 Archibald M'Sparran, *The Irish Legend, or M'Donnell and the Norman de Burgos* (Coleriane: J. M'Combie, 1854), pp.82, 101.
17 A. T. Lucas, *Cattle in Ancient Ireland* (Kilkenny: Boethius Press, 1989), p.175.
18 NFCS 279: 162–3. Glengariff School, County Cork, 1937/1938. Teacher: Caoimhín Ó Séaghdha.

You and I will go to Finegall.
You and I will eat such meats as we find there.
You and I will steal such beef as we find fat.
I shall be hanged and you shall be hanged. What shall our children do?
When teeth do grow unto themselves, as their fathers did before.

Racha mise, racha tusa, síos fén ngleann.
Goidfe mise, goidfe tusa, bó 'gus gamhain.
Crochfar mise, crochfar tusa, 's cad a dhéanfaidh ár gclann?
Cuma mise, cuma tusa, nuair ná beimíd ann![19]

Campaign and Battle

While tower houses and crannogs were suitable for defence against cattle raiders, a determined invasion by a superior enemy was countered by melting into the landscape. There simply wasn't enough room in either type of fortification to defend all the lord's cattle and followers. Therefore, if the attackers were not stopped at one of the fords or passes leading into the chief's territory, he sent his people and herds into the forests and hills. He would protect them there with his own forces, either avoiding contact altogether, or looking for an opportunity to engage the invaders to advantage. He might try to draw them onto difficult terrain of his own choosing, or attack them on the march by blockading a pass with plashed trees. A frequently noted tactic of the Irish in these kinds of running battles was the feigned retreat. Fynes Moryson, for instance, wrote: 'In fighting they will runne away, and turne agayne to fight, because they thincke it no shame to runne away, and to make vse of the advantage they haue in swift running, yet haue they great Corage in fighting, and I haue seene many of them suffer death with as constant resolution as euer Romans did.'[20] The measures adopted to man outposts and defend the borders of an Irish lordship against the incursion of the English army are described in the Chapter on the Irish Horseman, where the close relationship between the horsemen and kern and their role in guarding the *creaght*, or cattle herd, is also discussed. Camden describes an Irish army setting out on foray, saying: 'To give an acclamation and shout unto every footman or horseman as he goeth out of the gate, is counted lucky and fortunate: he who hath no such applause is thought to have some mischeife portended unto him.'[21] In 1835,

---

19   G. M., 'Review of Irish Poetry from the English Invasion to 1798 by Russell K. Alspach', *Studies: An Irish Quarterly Review*, vol. 33, no. 132 (1944), p.563.
20   Graham Kew, 'The Irish Sections of Fynes Moryson's Unpublished Itinerary', *Analecta Hibernia*, no. 37 (1998), p.102.
21   William Camden, *Britain, or a Chorographical Description of the most Flourishing Kingdomes, England, Scotland, and Ireland* (London: F. Kingston, R. Young and I.

John O'Donovan, the great Irish scholar, recorded a sample of the sort of march that would be sung on such occasions from the O'Mullans of Derry.[22] It is remarkably similar to a *piobaireachd* march shared by the MacIntyres and Stewarts, the Gaelic lyrics of which are given here below O'Donovan's translation of the O'Mullan's march:[23]

> I will walk the great road,
> I will walk the great road,
> I will walk the great road,
> No thanks to my enemies.

> *Gabhaidh sinn an rathad mór,*
> *Gabhaidh sinn an rathad mór,*
> *Gabhaidh sinn an rathad mór,*
> *Olc air math le càch e.*

In 1548, Paolo Giovio described Conn O'Neill as a warlike man 'who leads his life in settled encampments among the Irish; the rain he avoids in the military manner, protected by the shelter of foliage or in tents, covered with hides and canvas [*linteis*].'[24] Contemporary poem books, such as that of the MacSweeneys, refer to two spears being used as tent-poles, forming a *teach caoilshleagh*, or hut of slender spears.[25] The camp of Conn's son and ultimate successor, Shane, was vividly described in the *Annals of the Four Masters*. Having invaded O'Donnell's country in 1557, Shane's army constructed booths and tents, spending their time 'very happily in the camp …. for they carried on the buying and selling of mead, wine, rich clothing and other necessaries.'[26] Two O'Donnell spies, a Campbell and a Maguire of Fermanagh, were able to infiltrate the O'Neill camp because of 'the mix of people' there, including English renegades from the Pale:

> The two persons aforesaid proceeded from one fire to another, until they came to the great central-fire, which was at the entrance of the son of O'Neill's tent; and a huge torch, thicker than a man's body, was constantly flaming at a short distance from the fire, and sixty

---

Legatt, for George Latham, 1637), p.147.

22 T. H. Mullin and J. E. Mullan, *The Ulster Clans* (Belfast: The University Press, 1966), p.183.
23 Henry Whyte, *The Martial Music of the Clans* (Glasgow: The Celtic Monthly Office, 1904), p.32.
24 Jason Harris, 'Ireland in Europe: Paolo Giovio's Description (1548)', *Irish Historical Studies*, vol. 35, no. 139 (2007), pp.286.
25 Katherine Simms, 'Images of Galloglass in Poems to the MacSweeneys' in Seán Duffy (ed.), *The World of the Galloglass* (Dublin: Four Courts Press, 2007), pp.118–119.
26 O'Donovan, (ed.), *Annals Ireland*, p.1551.

grim and redoubtable gallowglasses, with sharp, keen axes, terrible and ready for action, and sixty stern and terrific Scots, with massive, broad, and heavy-striking swords in their hands, ready to strike and parry, were watching and guarding the son of O'Neill. When the time came for the troops to dine, and food was divided and distributed among them, the two spies whom we have mentioned stretched out their hands to the distributor, like the rest; and that which fell to their share was a *ceinn-bheart* [helmet] filled with meal, and a suitable complement of butter.[27]

Regarding the 'huge torch,' Joyce says, 'It was usual to keep a *ríchainnell* or king-candle (*rí,* 'a king'), or Royal candle, of enormous size, with a great bushy wick, burning at night in the presence of a king …. during war it blazed outside his tent-door; and on night-marches it was borne before him.'[28]

In the relatively rare set-piece battle, the Irish were said to fight with many 'loose wings' of kern on their flanks, while the battles of galloglass would have formed the centre, arrayed in linear formation.[29] The cavalry, if they didn't dismount and take their place among the galloglass, were drawn up on one flank or the other, and their formations and tactics are discussed in the Chapter on the Irish Horseman. The roles played by galloglass and horse are suggested by an entry for 1495 in the *Annals of the Four Masters* relating that Con O'Donnell had in his 'great little army' no more than 'twelve score axemen, for making a standing fight, and sixty horsemen, for following up the rout.'[30] With the battle lines thus drawn up, in 1548 Giovio says, 'They spark battle not by the sounding of a trumpet, but with the bellowing of a great twisted wooden horn.'[31] At the Battle of Knockdoe in 1504, when Clanricarde's forces drew up in formal array, 'they sett forward their galeglass and fott men in one mayne battayll, and all ther horsemen on ther lyfte syde, and so came one.' After giving three great shouts, 'the Irishe galeglas came on, to whome the English archers send them such a showre of arrows that ther wepons and ther hands were put faste together.'[32] The galloglass were true to form that day, biding the brunt to the death: 'And the place wherein were nine battalions of galloglass in compact array of battle, there escaped not alive of them but one thin battalion alone.'[33]

---

27 O'Donovan (ed.), *Annals Ireland*, p.1552.
28 P. W. Joyce, *A Social History of Ancient Ireland*, vol. 1, (New York: Longmans, Greene & Co., 1904), p.371.
29 James Logan, *The Scottish Gael* (London: Smith, Elder, and Co., 1831), p.111.
30 O'Donovan, (ed.), *Annals Ireland*, p.1220.
31 Harris, 'Paolo Giovio', p.287.
32 G. A. Hayes-McCoy, 'The Gallóglach Axe' in *Journal of the Galway Archaeological and Historical Society*, vol. 17 (1937), p.111.
33 Hayes-McCoy, 'The Gallóglach Axe', p.103.

Hayes-McCoy and others have speculated on the reasons for the galloglass's exclusive reliance upon the two-handed axe. This was also largely the case with the huscarls of Anglo-Saxon England and the Varangian Guard of Byzantium, bodies of elite axemen who shared a Norse origin with the galloglass. The axe was purely a cutting weapon and precluded deploying shoulder to shoulder like billmen, since it would have required something like four feet on either side to wield it without endangering one's comrades. This would be particularly true if figure-of-eight flourishes were used, as suggested by some Historical European Martial Arts (HEMA) practitioners. But they would have been deployed close enough to prevent the enemy passing through, while leaving enough room to use their weapons to defend themselves.

While organised in companies for administrative purposes, the galloglass retained the status of elite individual warriors whose chosen weapon required strength and skill to wield. They would likely have arrived on the battlefield in compact formation, capable of marching and manoeuvring, but would have shaken out into a looser order before engaging the enemy, necessary because of the nature of their weaponry. Their principal tactic would be a headlong assault on the enemy, 'mouthing their aboos like bulls bellowing' with pipes skirling, which would devolve into a series of individual duels.[34] At Monasternenagh in 1579, Stanley described the MacSweeney galloglass making their assault against the English pike and shot 'as resolutely minded …. as the best soldiers in Europe could.'[35] A woodcut in Derricke's *Image of Ireland* depicts the final outcome, with a disordered battle of galloglass put to flight by harquebusiers, their piper shot down at their head.

Derricke's text describes the onset of the Irish, 'With three and three in rankes beset.'[36] This is very reminiscent of the 'ancient and simple manoeuvre' of the Highlanders during the 1745 Rebellion, a column of three files which allowed them to negotiate narrow passes. With a quarter turn to the left or right, the column became a line of battle, three ranks deep. The first rank consisted of the fully armed Highland gentlemen, backed by their retainers and ghillies in the second and third ranks.[37] Might Derricke be referring to something similar, with the galloglass forming the first rank, backed by 'his harness bearer and boy' in the second and third ranks? These two servants, 'wherof sume have speares sume have bowes,' could have provided fire support from the two rear ranks. Indeed, the organisation of Scots redshanks during the sixteenth century – one-third mailed *daoine uaisle* with two-handed swords, and two-thirds unarmoured

---

34 G. B. O'Connor, *Elizabethan Ireland, Native and English* (Dublin: Sealy, Bryers and Walker, 1907), p.218.
35 *CSP Ireland*, p.190, 12 October, Stanley to Walsingham.
36 John Derricke, *The Image of Irelande, With a Discouerie of Woodkarne* (London: John Daie, 1581), p.62.
37 Christopher Duffy, *The '45: Bonnie Prince Charlie and the Untold Story of the Jacobite Rising* (London: Cassell, 2003), p.117.

bowmen – would have lent itself perfectly to this formation for set-piece battles. It was in much this way that Sir Mungo Campbell's men at the Battle of Auldearn were 'shot onto their objective' by bowmen at their rear.[38] The galloglass themselves would have thrown their darts first. St Leger, in 1543, said the servants of the galloglass carried for them three darts, which they threw before coming to the 'hand strife.'[39] Paolo Giovio in 1548 said much the same of the galloglass: 'He uses a German axe after he has thrown his javelin at the beginning of the battle. Out from among these while the battle stands disposed in the middle of the field and the bagpiper plays, the light infantry rushes from the wings and fights with darts and arrows which they fire from short wooden bows.'[40] Giovio thus places the battle of galloglass in the centre, with wings of kern. Derricke describes the attack of the kern, 'who leauyng the order of battaile raye, beyng neare the combat, fall into a cluster; therein they suppose their saftie to consiste, makyng a moste terrible noyse of criyng to terrifie (if it were possible) the whole hoste of Englishe men.'[41] Spencer remarks on the shout of Ferragh! Ferragh! (Watch! Watch!), 'which their kern use at their first encounter.'[42]

The author of the 'Power of Irishmen' earlier says the Irish are 'Good watchers in the night, as good souldiours by night as others by daye.' Night operations were practised in the cattle raid, and were frequently resorted to in campaigns against opposing armies as well. In 1435, a nighttime 'camp assault' was made by Henry O'Neill upon Nechtain O'Donnell; O'Neill's men marched forward 'quietly, silently' until they reached the camp and surprised the sentries. The rival galloglass of the MacDonnells and MacSweeneys then fell in with one another, but friends and enemies could not be distinguished 'through darkness of the night.'[43] Manus and Hugh Dubh O'Donnell defeated Conn Bacagh O'Neill at Knockavoe in 1522 again by staging a night assault upon his camp. And Calvagh O'Donnell repeated the tactic successfully in 1557, assaulting Shane O'Neill's camp by night and chasing him out the back side of his tent.

Stanihurst describes the aftermath of battle: 'Those who come off the battle line unscathed carry their wounded comrades home on an eight-man litter. There, standing by, they have 'empirics' who attempt to cleanse the infection by applying crushed herbs.'[44] These doctors belonged to hereditary families of physicians. Stanihurst dismisses them for their rote memorisation of Hippocrates, and for thinking themselves qualified if they

---

38 Stuart Reid, *Highland Clansman, 1689–1746* (London: Osprey, 1997), p.20.
39 Maxwell, *Irish History*, p.221.
40 Harris, 'Paolo Giovio', p.287.
41 Derricke, *Image of Irelande*, p.62.
42 Henry Morley, *Ireland under Elizabeth and James the First*, (London: G. Routledge & Sons, Ltd, 1890), pp.92, 96.
43 B. MacCarthy (ed.), *Annala Uladh, Annals of Ulster* (Dublin: Her Majesty's Stationery Office, 1895), p.137.
44 Richard Stanihurst (John Barry and Hiram Morgan, eds), *Great Deeds in Ireland*, (Cork: University Press, 2014), p.127.

can use a surgeon's probe to explore a wound and bind it with a bandage, and use a rod to beat eggs together with chopped and pounded herbs in a bowl. There was a very large body of medical treatises of a practical nature in the Irish language, but as an alchemist, Stanihurst faulted the Irish doctors for a supposed lack of esoteric 'theoretical' knowledge. Surgeons accompanied the levies of kern for overseas service in 1544 and again in 1550.

Later Changes

The first recorded use of a gun in Irish warfare is the killing of an O'Rourke by Godfrey O'Donnell with a hand-gun in 1487.[45] The Earls of Desmond had maintained a battle of crossbowmen and gunners since *c.* 1490, and they still existed as a company of harquebusiers and were being tracked down and slaughtered as the second Desmond Rebellion drew to its close in 1583. Dedicated bodies of shot became more common among the Irish as the century progressed. For instance, in 1562 Maguire impeded Shane O'Neill's advance into his territory by blocking a pass with 'certain hagbuteers that I have.'[46] As mentioned above, by 1575 'The wages of the Irish men of war' recorded for the Province of Ulster gave the captain of 100 gunners and his men the same pay as a company of galloglass or Scots.

Garret Mór, 8th Earl of Kildare, had reduced many castles with the Royal artillery during his Governorship from 1500 to 1513. The English use of ordnance in Ireland is covered in the chapter on the Pale. Among the Irish, the O'Donnells made great efforts to obtain and use artillery, as noted in the chapter on the 'Power of Irishmen.' Ordnance much heavier than anything seen later in Elizabeth's reign was used in the earlier decades of the century, both by the Crown Forces and the Irish. In 1537, O'Brien's fortified bridge over the Shannon was defended by 'a great piece of iron' which shot balls a big as a man's head. The ward was made up of galloglass, horsemen, and gunners, and they also had 'a ship piece, a Portingall piece, and certain hagbusshes and hand guns.'[47]

The pike makes its first appearance in Irish hands during the first Desmond Rebellion in 1569. In July of that year, the rebels near Waterford had 400 mailed pikemen and 400 shot, along with their galloglass and kern.[48] During the second Desmond Rebellion, the Baltinglass rebels were reported charging with the pike.[49] These are isolated instances, however, and the use of the pike would remain rare for the Irish until the years immediately preceding the Nine Years' War later in the century. The second

---

45   G. A. Hayes-McCoy, 'The Early History of Guns in Ireland' in *Journal of the Galway Archaeological and Historical Society*, vol. 18 (1938), p.47.
46   Bagwell, *Ireland Under*, vol. 2, pp.55–6.
47   Maxwell, *Irish History*, p.99.
48   Falls, *Irish Wars*, p.105.
49   Falls, *Irish Wars*, p.146.

TACTICS IN IRISH WARFARE

Desmond Rebellion also saw the appearance of bodies of Irish targeteers, as in April of 1580, when the ward of Desmond's Castle of Ballygleaghan were described issuing out, 'some in brown apparel with swords and targets.'[50] In the State Papers in November 1582, Sir Warham St Leger wrote that the Desmond rebels were still in great strength, and had gained in hardiness by continually lying in the woods and travelling in foul weather. In December, he complained that they were buying horses, armour and weapons, 'So that every horseman of them is as well appointed for light horsemen as any be in Christendom.'[51] Does this mean that some of Desmond's horsemen had adopted a standard saddle and stirrups? He went on to say that their footmen were appointed in like sort, and allowed only 'pick'd fellows' in their company, banishing the infirm and making 'baser sorts of people' into their drudges. We get an idea of the arms being purchased from Pelham's plot for Munster in 1580, which had advocated fortifying the coast to stop 'Portingalls and Spaniards, that yearly come to fish in those harbours, bringing with them powder, calivers, sculls, targets, swords, and other munition, whereby the idle men of this realm are most plentifully replenished.'[52]

Detail from Derricke's depiction of a battle, 1581. Galloglass overcome by English shot. Their piper lies on the ground, the drones clearly issuing from separate stocks. The galloglass wear long habergeons of mail, with three quarter length sleeves. They are without pisane collars and wear simple skulls rather than bascinets. (Creative Commons)

---

50   David Edwards, (ed.), *Campaign Journals of the Elizabethan Irish Wars* (Dublin: Irish Manuscripts Commission, 2014), p.79.
51   *CSP Ireland*, p.413, 26 November, St Leger to Queen.
52   *Cal. Carew Mss*, p.285, 28 July, Plot by Pelham.

3

Governor's Retinues, Garrison Troops, and the Rising Out of the Pale

Retinue to Garrison

Since the 1350s the incoming governors had received a subsidy of £500 per annum which paid for a small personal retinue of 20 men-at-arms, providing a professional core for the 'rising out' of the English Pale. During the fifteenth century, these retinues usually numbered 200–300 men, but some were small armies. They were almost always Englishmen. However, as soon as a Governor was recalled, his retinue would be disbanded.[1] See Table 16 below for examples of Governor's retinues:

Table 16, Governor's Retinues

Sir John Tiptoft, Earl of Worcester (1467–70)	700 archers
1479, Earl of Kildare (1479–1494)	80 yeomen 'abled' archers and 40 other horsemen called spears
Sir Edward Poynings (1494–95)	653 archers and gunners
Thomas Howard, Earl of Surrey (1520–22)	50 mounted archers and demi-lances, 50 foot (all Englishmen), 50 Irish horse and 150 kern
Sir William Skeffington (1534–35)	100 mounted archers, 50 foot

---

1   Steven G. Ellis, 'The Tudors and the Origins of the Modern Irish States: A Standing Army' in Thomas Bartlett and Keith Jeffery (eds), *A Military History of Ireland* (Cambridge: Cambridge University Press, 1997), pp.119–120.

GOVERNOR'S RETINUES, GARRISON TROOPS, AND THE RISING OUT OF THE PALE

The Ordinances prepared in the lead up to Surrey's expedition specified that the Deputy was to have in continual wages and retinue '100 goode tall yemen and 20 gonners, everye yeman havyng his bowe, shief, iacke, sallet either stoul [scull] and an horse, some of them havyng two horses and weapon, and to have among theme ten pavyces, everie gonner to have his horse, breastplate other brygundyse, his stoule or sallet.'[2] He was also to maintain 60 galloglass, 200 kern, and 40 Irish horsemen, though it was admitted there were not enough revenues for this. In the event, Surrey's expedition of 1520 consisted of 'the King's guard 400, of the King's gunners 24, of Irish horsemen 100,' which together with his personal retinue of 300 listed above, constituted the entire Royal army during his uneventful campaign of 1520–21.[3] In fact, the number of yeomen of the guard actually sent over was reduced to 220, rather than 400, and they were found unsuitable to the conditions of Irish warfare.[4] Starting in 1496, the Earls of Kildare would be criticised for habitually employing an entirely native retinue at Crown expense instead, being followed by a 'multitude' of Irish galloglass and kern.

In 1474 a military guild called the Brotherhood of Arms of Saint George had been founded at the instigation of the 7th Earl of Kildare, who served as its chief captain. It consisted of 13 Pale magnates, including the Mayors of Dublin and Drogheda, who mustered 120 mounted archers, 40 horsemen ('spears'), and 40 pages. The Brotherhood was abolished in 1475, but restored in 1480 by Gearóid Mór, 8th Earl of Kildare. Finally suppressed by Henry VII in 1494, The Brotherhood had constituted the entirety of the Crown's standing forces in Ireland.[5] Besides the mayors mentioned, the original membership of it included the Seneschal of Meath, High Sheriff of Kildare, the Irish Chief Justice and other administrators. Even after the disbandment of this guild in 1494, it was commonly the case that whenever a major hosting was underway, the business of government in the Pale ground to a halt. Being a relatively small community, many prominent citizens were usually among those undertaking a 'journey' against the Irish. In 1521, inquiries from London regarding the state of the colony's revenues had to wait as 'the officers and clerks be so occupied in the hosting gone forth that almost no man is left at home.'[6]

At the outset of the 'Silken' Thomas Rebellion (1534–1537), efforts were made to recruit from foreign sources '300 good harquebusmen who would pursue the Irish into their woods and bogs.' While the value of firearms

---

[2] Christopher Maginn and Christopher, Stephen G. Ellis, *The Tudor Discovery of Ireland* (Dublin: Four Courts Press, 2015), p.99.
[3] Raymond James, *Henry VIII's Military Revolution: The Armies of Sixteenth Century Britain and Europe* (London-New York: Tauris Academic Series, 2007), p.97.
[4] Anita Rosamund Hewerdine, 'The Yeomen of the King's Guard 1485-1547'. Unpublished PhD thesis, University of London, 1998, p.94.
[5] Thomas Moore, *History of Ireland,* vol. 2 (London: Longman, Orme, Brown, Green and Longmans, 1837), p.285
[6] Ellis, 'The Tudors', p.119.

was thus well appreciated, no such troops could be employed.[7] In the end, Skeffington recruited a total of about 2,500 men, mainly Welsh. The largest contingent of 1,600 men sailed from Chester, but of whom less than 400 were reported to have weapons upon landing. The total number had fallen below 1,000 by 1536, when Lord Deputy Grey had to discharge a further 500–600 for lack of funds.[8] This continued into 1538–1539, with the garrison reduced to 340, enforcing an essentially defensive posture. Skeffington's army had also included about 300 northern horse from the West Marches, under 'four Cumberland gentlemen', two of whom were veterans of Irish service. This type of horseman would be preferred in Ireland throughout the Tudor era. There were many complaints about the quality of bows supplied, 'for many would not hold the bending,' and on campaign in wet conditions the archers could not defend themselves 'for their strings were so wet, and most of the feathers of their arrows fallen off.'[9] A further 400–500 'hackbutiers' do seem to have been sent in 1535. In spite of these problems, the ample siege train detailed below under Artillery brought success in a number of sieges, starting with that of Maynooth Castle in 1535. Maynooth was defended by Kildare's extensive ordnance and 60 gunners, the entire garrison receiving 'the Pardon of Maynooth' from Skeffington, i.e., being summarily executed after having surrendered on terms.

After the collapse of the Kildare Ascendancy, the 'Kingdom of Ireland' was created in 1542, imposing direct rule by the Crown of England. Henceforward, Governors would be appointed exclusively from England. By 1542 the number of gunners in the 'King's Irish retinue' had risen to 100.[10]

Table 17. The King's Irish Retinue, 1542

Lord Deputy St Leger's Retinue	100 horsemen, 9d; grand captain, 4s; petty captain, 2s
Mr. Robert St Leger's Retinue	100 horsemen, 9d; grand captain, 4s; petty captain, 2s
Master of Ordnance's Retinue	100 hakebuttiers, 50 @ 9d, 50 @ 8d; grand captain, 4s; petty captain, 2s
Mr. Brereton's Retinue	150 archers, 6d; grand captain, 4s; captain, 3s; petty captain, 2s
Knight Marshal's Retinue	32 horsemen, 9d; grand captain, 4s
Clerk of Check's Retinue	10 horsemen, 9d
Treasurer's Retinue	40 horsemen, 9d

---

7   James, *Henry VIII's*, pp.104–106.
8   Mark Charles Fissell, *English Warfare, 1511–1647*, (New York: Routledge, 2001), p.42.
9   Ellis, 'The Tudors', p.126.
10 *Calendar of the Carew Manuscripts*, vol. 1, 1515–1574, J. S. Brewrer and William Bullen, eds, (London: Longman & Co., 1867), p.200, n.d., Revenues of Ireland.

GOVERNOR'S RETINUES, GARRISON TROOPS, AND THE RISING OUT OF THE PALE

After 1550, the rising out of the Pale was increasingly relegated to 'home guard' duties, while garrison troops sent from England replaced the old retinues, and were used to spearhead offensive actions. The garrison's numbers rose steadily between 1546 and 1567, during which years Crown forces were on campaign in the eastern half of the country at least once a year. The sharp increase seen in 1566–67 was in anticipation of a planned invasion of Ulster:

Table 18. English Garrison Troops, 1546–1567

1546–1551	900
1551–1556	2,010
1556–1565	2,200
1566–1567	4,000

During the first Desmond Rebellion of 1569–73, the garrison never exceed 2,000, and in 1573 totalled 1,928, comprising 221 horse, 559 foot, and 225 Irish kern to secure Leinster, leaving 194 horse and 729 foot 'for the service of Munster.' The garrison increased sharply to 8,892 during the second Desmond Rebellion of 1579–83, but had fallen to 2,000 again by 1584.[11] It is difficult to be precise about these numbers, as there were always great fluctuations. The numbers include both English companies and Irish kern, for kern remained indispensable on campaign. In 1561, for instance, the totals given above include 640 kern. When the numbers of kern were reduced in 1580, Pelham advised the Privy Council that 'these bands of kerne must be revived upon the entry into any long journey, because without them we cannot drive the woods.'[12] While the Royal Army may seem small, it was quite sufficient to deal with any opposing native force. And unlike the Crown, the Irish lords were not able to keep their forces in the field except for relatively brief excursions, which limited their geographical reach. Critically, the English companies were increasingly equipped with firearms. Of the 4,000 men on the books in 1566–67, 1,140 were 'gunners'. This increase in firepower could not be matched by the Irish lords, and was a major factor in the gradual success of the Crown's policy down to the 1590s.[13] The tables below, drawn from the Fitzwilliam Accounts, offer

---

11 Falls, *Irish Wars*, p.47.
12 *Calendar of the Carew Manuscripts*, vol. 2, 1575–1588, J. S. Brewrer and William Bullen eds (London: Longman & Co., 1867), p.266, 9 July, Pelham to Council.
13 Edwards, David, 'The escalation of Violence in sixteenth century Ireland' in David Edwards, Pádraig Leinihan, Clodagh Tait (eds), *Age of Atrocity: Violence and Political Conflict in Early Modern Ireland* (Dublin: Four Courts Press, 2007), pp.65–6.

a snapshot of the Crown Forces during the war against Shane O'Neill.[14] In May 1561 new troops had arrived, consisting of archers and harquebusiers, with no additional equipment or armour, except a sword and dagger. The tables include the troops which were likely present under Sir George Stanley at the 'Battle of the Red Sagums' in July 1561. The Battle was given this name by the Irish because of the red cassocks worn by the English who fell there. No more than 600–700 of Stanley's 1,200 men were English on this occasion, including 200 horse and seven and a half companies of English foot. The remainder of his force were 200 galloglass, 100 hired Scots, and 'all the kerne in camp.'[15]

Table 19. English Garrison Companies 1561–1562, Bands of Footmen

Captain, 4s per diem	Petty Captain/ Lieutenant, 2s	Officers, 12d	Harquebusiers, 8d	Archers, 6d
Captain Manners	1	3	50	50
Captain Delves	1	3	100	100
Captain Cuff	1	3	50	50
Captain Audley	1	3	50	50
Sir Nicholas Bagenal	1	4	45	50
Sir William FitzWilliams	1	4	50	50
Sir Henry Radclief	1	3	50	50
Sir Henry Radclief (ex Captain Lippiat)	1	3	25	25
Sir George Stanley	1	3	50	50
Jacques Wingefeld	1	4	44	50
Captain Warren	1	4	100	
Captain Collie	1	4	50	50
Captain Portas	1	3	25	25
Total	**13**	**44**	**689**	**600**

---

14 Longfield, Ada K., (ed.), *Fitzwilliam Accounts 1560-65* (Dublin: Irish Manuscripts Commission, Dublin 1960), pp.48–53.
15 Bagwell, *Ireland Under*, vol. 2, p.24.

GOVERNOR'S RETINUES, GARRISON TROOPS, AND THE RISING OUT OF THE PALE

Table 20. English Garrison Companies 1561–1562, Bands of Horsemen

Captain, 4s per diem	Petty Captain, 2s	Standard Bearer, 12d	Trumpeter, 12d	Horseman 9d
Sir Henry Radclief	1	1	1	40
Sir George Stanley	1	1		30
Jacques Wingefeld	1	1		24
Francis Agard	1	1	1	40
Captain Girton	1	1	1	40
Captain Heron	1	1	1	20
Mounted Harquebusiers				
Captain Warren	1	1	1	40
Total	**7**	**7**	**5**	**234**

These appear to be bands actually under arms, and do not include four wards of 10–20 men each and similar numbers of soldiers detached to the personal retinues of state officials. To this total of 1,523 men should be added the 640 kern enumerated below under 'Government Kern', making a total of 2,163. The absence of pikes, or even bills or halberds, is notable in the tables above, and while a large independent band of foot mentioned later in the same accounts includes 60 'armed men' and an ensign, along with 140 harquebusiers, this was subsequently converted to 200 arquebusiers. By May 1563, the English bands were 275 horsemen, and 600 arquebusiers, archers and pikemen, besides 96 wards of forts.[16] This force of 'bowmen, hargabusses, billmen, and pikemen, and a few horsemen, driving 2,000 kine,' is described in the *Book of Howth* as marching in the usual three 'wards' during Sussex's incursion into Ulster in April 1563.[17] With the advent of the Trained Bands, the composition of foot companies sent to Ireland would soon change to equal numbers of pike and shot, with a portion of halberdiers, as illustrated in John Derricke's famous woodcuts depicting scenes from Sir Henry Sidney's second Lord Deputyship of 1575–1578.

In respect of the cavalry supplied out of England, Lord Deputy Surrey had complained in 1520 that of 100 horsemen sent to him, only 30 were 'spears', the rest being 'ill-horsed' mounted archers, of which there were already too many in the rising out of the Pale. Throughout the century, deputies such as Surrey would express a preference for 'northomberland speris,' that is Northern 'border horse.' These were considered the elite of

---
16 Falls, *Irish Wars*, p.92.
17 *Calendar of the Carew Manuscripts, Miscellaneous: The Book of Howth*, J. S. Brewer and William Bullen eds, (London: Longman & Co., 1871), p.201.

the army, 'without whom no notable exploit can be doon.'[18] In the State Papers in 1563, Lord Deputy Sussex wrote to the Privy Council saying '200 jacks, 200 northern saddles and furniture desired.'[19] And border horse wearing mail and carrying targets appear prominently in Derricke's illustrations of the English army in Ireland, 1575–1578. Apart from border horse, the English horse sent to Ireland were classified as light horsemen. In 1575, five light horsemen from Yorkshire were to be sent to Ireland, armed with a plate coat (brigandine?), and a scull or sallet, with sword, dagger and spear. They were to have a blue cap over the headpiece, and a blue coat, with doublet, hose and a pair of boots. The Bishop of Chester also provided light horsemen for this levy, who were to have 'redd clokes, lined, without sleeves and of length to the knees, dubletts, hose, hatts, boots.'[20] Captain Warren's 40 mounted harquebusiers in the table above, who did good service in the otherwise unfortunate battle of July 1561, were a rarity. So too were the demi-lances in plate armour illustrated by Derricke.

Robert Damport, an English military servitor. Damport was commissioned to execute martial law in Connacht and held property at Athlone in 1579. He was Provost Marshal of Connacht in 1586. Carved panel from Athlone Bridge, 1567. (Journal of the Royal Society of Antiquaries of Ireland, 6th series, vol. V, no. 2 (1915), facing p.122)

Although the levies of 1561–62 listed above wore red coats, this would only become ubiquitous in the 1590s. During the Silken Thomas Rebellion, as the rebels raised their siege of Dublin in autumn 1534, Holinshed recalled a 'company of white cotes, with reddde crosses' being landed as reinforcements from England.[21] This white coat had been the mark of the English soldier in the first half of the century. Beginning in the 1560s foot soldiers levied for Ireland most typically wore coats of watchett (light blue), red coats only becoming more common after 1580. For

---

18   James, *Henry VIII's*, pp.98, 107.
19   *Calendar of State Papers Ireland: Henry VIII, Edward VI, Mary and Elizabeth*, vol. 1, 1509–73, (London: Longman, Green, Longman & Roberts, 1860), p.213, 9 February, Sussex to Privy Council.
20   W. Y. Carman, *British Military Uniforms from Contemporary Pictures* (London: Leonard Hill, 1957), p.11.
21   Raphael Holinshed (Liam Miller and Eileen Power, eds), *Holinshed's Irish Chronicle, 1577*, (Dublin: Dolmen Press, 1979), p.276.

instance, Lancashire archers for service in Ireland in 1566 had a cassock of blue cloth with two small guards of white cloth, a scull covered by a red cap, and buckskin jerkins.[22] Captain Malby, visiting from his post in Connacht, witnessed the overthrow of the Royal army at Glenmalure, Co. Wicklow, in 1580. He said that the 'new-come men' in their coats of red or blue were obvious to the rebels, who concentrated on them. He advised that the coat money be used to 'clothe themselves here with jerkins and hose of frieze, and with the same money bring them every man a mantle which shall serve him for his bedding and thereby shall not be otherwise known to the rebels than the old soldiers be.'[23] Only occasionally do English troops appear to have been clothed locally, usually in outlying garrisons like Coleraine. Schemes for clothing the English garrison entirely with Irish goods would be proposed by Captain Thomas Lee and other experienced captains right up to the end of Elizabeth's reign. While authorities remained reluctant to officially source clothing in Ireland, they did occasionally alter specifications for levies being sent there. In 1584, these were to have 'convenient dublletts and hose, and also a cassocke of the same motley, or other sadd greene colour or russet.' Berkshire troops for this same levy for Ireland were to have coats 'of some dark or sadd colour, as russett or suchlike and not so light colour as blew and redd which heretofore hath commonly been used.'[24]

Artillery, Ordnance and Armourers

Garret Mór, 8th Earl of Kildare, had used the King's ordnance to reduce numerous castles during the period of his Deputyships (1477–1513). These were probably the 'two or three falcons' his grandson, Thomas, would turn against Dublin Castle in his rebellion of 1534. Surrey had also used this artillery to reduce O'Connor Faly's chief castle of Monasteroris, 'the strongest hold within the Irishry,' in 1520–21. O'Connor Faly subsequently built a new castle further west at Daingean, 'of such strength as we have not hitherto seen the like in this land,' but this was in turn reduced by artillery in 1537.[25] This was during the Silken Thomas Rebellion of 1534–37, which saw the most extensive use of artillery in this period, including demi-cannon three times the size of anything used in Elizabeth's reign. The ordnance sent with Skeffington in 1534 is listed below and it included six iron-shod English carts. The resultant mobility difficulties meant that such

---

22 Carman, *British Uniforms*, p.10.
23 Bagwell, *Ireland Under*, vol. 3, p.62.
24 Carman, *British Uniforms*, p.11.
25 Rolf Loeber, 'An Architectural History of Gaelic Castles and Settlements, 1370–1600, in Patrick J. Duffy, David Edwards and Elizabeth Fitzpatrick (eds), *Gaelic Ireland: Land, Lordship & Settlement c. 1250–1600* (Dublin: Four Courts Press, 2001), p.308.

a train would not be seen again in Ireland during the sixteenth century. Lighter brass 'campaign pieces' were also used in the field by both Surrey and Skeffington. While they could never match the Crown's resources, the Irish themselves had been eagerly taking up the use of artillery and firearms, and this drove the increasing deployment of gunpowder weapons in Ireland during Henry's reign.

Administrative offices within the English garrison after *c.* 1550 tended to be lifetime sinecures. The master of ordnance, for example, was Jacques Wingfield from 1558–1587. Wingfield's tenure was marked by corruption and inefficiency, and he will appear below also drawing income from a band of kern. The offices of master gunner and chief engineer were likewise held for life by incumbents who appear not to have performed the relevant duties.[26] It has been claimed that the Ordnance Office in Dublin 'at the black fryares' was nothing but a warehouse from which weaponry sent from the Tower of London would be distributed.[27] However, during the period covered, there are frequent references in urban centres to 'smiths and armourers', as well as locksmiths, lorimers, sword makers and arrowsmiths. There were certainly enough smiths capable of making mail, plate and helmets to fulfil at least a portion of Ireland's needs. In the thirteenth and fourteenth centuries, a full-time smith had been retained at Dublin Castle, and a 'Richard Gonner, smith' was already making guns there in 1394. In 1515, smiths and craftsmen were dispatched from the Castle to the towns of the Pale, to forge 'gonnes and saletes'. A master of the ordnance account existed by 1537–39, disbursing wages for smiths and rent money for forges. The work was outsourced to independent smiths within Dublin. Better quality Spanish iron (*ferri hispanici*) was purchased in 1558–59 for 'chambers for gonnes' for the city ordnance. In 1550 John Morgan had been appointed smith of the Irish ordnance, 'To repair and mend the King's ordnance in Ireland' and received a house 'built for that purpose' in Dublin Castle. In 1584 Morgan remained 'chief smith of the great ordnance and artillery [of Ireland] - with the right to buy iron, coal, forges and tools.' He held the office until 1597.[28]

---

26   Cairan Brady, 'The Captains' Games: Army and Society in Elizabethan Ireland' in Thomas Bartlett and Keith Jeffery (eds), *A Military History of Ireland* (Cambridge: Cambridge University Press, 1997), pp.148–9.
27   Fissell, *English Warfare*, p.42.
28   Rondelez, Paul, 'Ironwork in late Medieval Ireland: AD 1200 to 1600'. Unpublished University College Cork PhD thesis, 2001, p.146.

Table 21. Ordnance for Ireland, 1534[29]

	A Proportion thought necessary to be sent to Ireland
(i)	A demi-cannon of brass mounted with shod wheels, with ladle and sponge, and 60 iron shot to the same
	2 brass falcons mounted with shod wheels
	2 falconets and 240 iron shot for the falcons and falconets
	40 iron 'hagbushes'
	3½ last of serpentine powder
	4 half barrels of corn powder
	½ last of saltpetre
	4cwt. brimstone
	500 yew bows
	2 barrels bow strings
	1,000 sheaves of livery arrows
	300 northern spears
	1,000 horseshoes and 8,000 nails for them
	6 carts shod with iron
	8 pr iron-shod wheels for sakers and falcons
	3 dozen scythes
	a gin
(ii)	Parcels that require to be provided:
	60 great horses to draw the ordnance, to be bought in Northamptonshire
	6 cart horse harness, at 20s. each
	200 spades and shovels
	3 dozen rammers and forms for charging ladles, at 2s per dozen
	6 forms for cartouches, at 3d each
	30 chests for bows and arrows
	2 barrels soap
	10 horse hides 'whyt tawyd' [tanned]
	4 iron crows, weighing in all 5½cwt, at 1½d per pound
	100 pickaxes weighing 1,007lbs at 2½d per pound
	100 felling axes, 12d each
	2,000 iron spikes weight 5cwt at 14s per cwt
	Total £95 1s 0½d
(iii)	Artificers and carters
	1 wheelwright
	6 carters
	20 tons elm timber

---

29   Constancia Maxwell, *Irish History From Contemporary Sources* (London: George Allen & Unwin, 1923), p.95.

The Pale

Throughout the fifteenth century, England had been distracted by civil wars at home and overseas wars in France, leading to neglect of the Irish colony. The combined threat of France and Scotland was the chief priority in the first half of the sixteenth century. Consequently, the Crown was unable to perform the basic medieval duty of protecting its subjects in Ireland. Left to its own devices, the Irish Parliament of 1460 declared Ireland 'corporate of itself'. The colony in Ireland had become self-sufficient in matters of defence by *c.* 1470, saving the Crown an estimated £3,000 annually, which was the cost of an English Governor and his retinue. The years 1470–1534 mark the Kildare Ascendancy, during which the Crown delegated governance to the Earls of Kildare, despite their Yorkist leanings. Two Yorkist pretenders to the English throne would be launched from Ireland in this period. But in the brief interludes during which Englishmen were appointed Governor in place of Kildare, they proved less effective as they lacked the broad affinity the Kildares had built up across the country.

The Pale was that area surrounding Dublin in which English law and custom prevailed. The coastal plain here was especially fertile and was coming under increasing cultivation in the early sixteenth century, leaving it largely treeless. Just prior to Sir Edward Poynings's arrival as Lord Deputy in 1494, the defences and militia of the Pale's 'four loyal shires' (Dublin, Louth, Meath and Kildare) had been reorganised. The old medieval frontier had relied upon defence in depth, with a wide stretch of wasteland (*fásach*) dividing the Gaelic lordships from the English colony. With the contraction of Royal authority to a region 30 miles long by 20 miles wide, it has been argued that this frontier was now consolidated into a sharply delineated defensive perimeter.[30] However, archaeology indicates it was never entirely fortified. By 1494, the four shires were collectively being called the 'Pale', from the Latin term *palus*, meaning a stake forming part of a palisade.

The Great Earl of Kildare's Parliament in 1488 had produced an Act of Marches and Maghery, which on paper at least, divided the colony into a clearly defined inner heartland, or maghery (*machaire*, or 'plain' in Irish), surrounded by outlying marches. Parts of the maghery borders were protected by a broad dike with ditches on either side and topped by a palisade (hence the term 'Pale'), which was supplemented with tower houses and fortified bridges. Traces of the maghery ditches remain to this day, although it never formed a continuous barrier. Poynings's Parliament of Drogheda in November, 1494, attempted to extend these defences outwards:

---

30 Steven G. Ellis, 'The Tudors and the Origins of the Modern Irish States: A Standing Army' in Thomas Bartlett and Keith Jeffery (eds), *A Military History of Ireland* (Cambridge: Cambridge University Press, 1997), pp.116–135.

GOVERNOR'S RETINUES, GARRISON TROOPS, AND THE RISING OUT OF THE PALE

As the marches of four shires lie open and not feasible in fastness of ditches and castles, by which Irishmen do great hurt in preying the same; it is enacted that every inhabitant, earth-tiller, and occupier in said marches …. do make and build a double ditch six feet high above the ground at one side or part which meareth next unto Irishmen

to be maintained by the tenants, with the bishops and sheriffs of the four loyal counties appointed Commissioners

with full power to call the inhabitants of said four shires to make ditches in the waste or Fasagh land without the said marches.[31]

The degree to which this was complied with remains unclear, as the boundary of the marches was always very fluid.

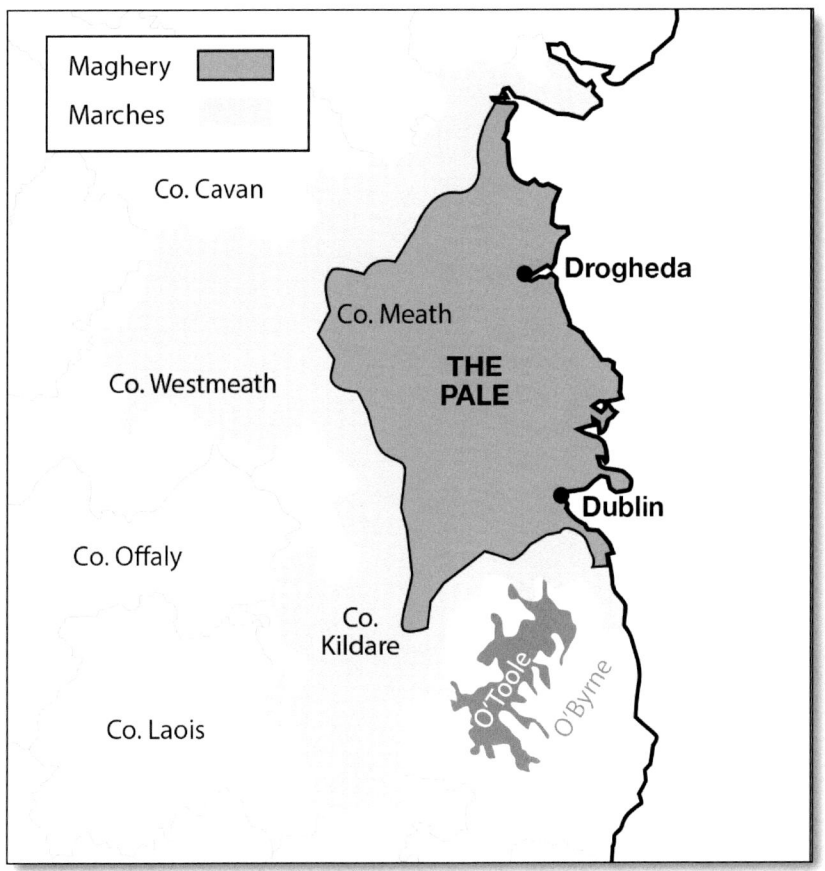

The English Pale, showing the maghery and marches.

---

31   Rev. Denis S. J. Murphy, 'The Pale' in *The Journal of the County Kildare Archaeological Society*, vol. 2, no. 1 (1896), p.51.

'OF KERNS AND GALLOWGLASSES'

The northern boundaries of the maghery ran south of a natural drumlin belt in Central Meath and Louth. At the southern end of the maghery, castles were particularly thick round the bend of the Liffey. Most had been built before the legislation of 1488; these were the famous '£10 castles', encouraged by a statute of 1429 that offered a £10 subsidy to inhabitants of the four shires who would build a 'sufficiently embattled' tower house of a specified minimum size. The most typical form of Pale tower house is distinguished by the projecting turret, one to four in number and containing stairs, garderobes, and small chambers.[32] The narrow southern end of the Pale in Co. Dublin was the most heavily defended, as it fronted upon the abrupt uplands of the Wicklow Mountains which were held by the hostile clans of the O'Byrnes and O'Tooles. Unlike the other marches, it was administered directly by the Dublin government, which launched more expeditions there than at any other part of the Pale's borders.

A local tax called 'smoakesilver' had been levied in the marches since 1461 'to defray the charge of the watchmen or ward' maintained 'for the better preservation & custody of the country & to resist the King's Irish enemies & rebels thereof'.[33] These watchmen maintained a system comparable to the Armada beacons along England's southern coast, with a raised iron basket (much like that depicted on the modern Wicklow town arms), and materials to make both smoke and fire signals.

These defences were intended to discourage cattle raiding, the ditches in particular impeding the exit of the Irish when they would be burdened with their 'prey'. Nonetheless, the Palesmen continued to pay 'black rent' (protection money) to neighbouring Irish lordships. In 1515, the *State of Ireland* report found that the county of Uryell (Louth) paid O'Neill £40 annually, while Meath paid O'Connor £300, Kildare paid O'Connor £20, the King's Exchequer paid MacMurrough Kavanaugh 80 marks, et cetera.[34] This payment continued even after it was legislated against in 1534. Deputy Surrey's campaigns of 1520–21 would begin the process of damping the neighbouring Irish of the Midlands, starting with the O'Connors and O'Mores. These clans, who had been such a scourge to the English colony in the fifteenth century, would see their lands shired and planted with military colonies in 1556. Thus the Pale served as a bridgehead from which the area under English control could be gradually extended outward. While the maghery heartland of the English Pale provided men armed after the English manner, the marches on the periphery were to maintain Irish-style troops, both horsemen and kern, with the later addition of galloglass. Thus,

---

32   Tadhg O'Keefe, 'Medieval Frontiers and Fortification: The Pale and its Evolution' in F. H. A. Aalen and Kevin Whelan (eds), *Dublin City and County: From Prehistory to Present* (Dublin: Geography Publications, 1992), pp.1–34.
33   Ellis, 'The Tudors', p.117.
34   *State Papers Published Under the Authority of His Majesty's Commission: King Henry VIII*, vol. 2, part 3. 'Correspondence of the Governments of England and Ireland, 1515–1538,' (London: HMSO, 1834), p.9, 1515, n.d., State of Ireland and Plan for its Reformation, anon.

this extension of English control would be accomplished to a degree by the government's quartering of Gaelic soldiery, first upon the English marchers, and subsequently upon neighbouring Irish lordships, as discussed below.

The Rising Out of the Maghery

In the fourteenth century, Anglo-Irish forces had included men-at-arms, hobelars, mounted archers, foot archers and armed infantry. By the fifteenth century, the portion of the 'rising out' of the English Pale that was armed 'after thEnglyshe maner' had resolved into just two troop types, 'Speres and bowes', that is to say, light horsemen and mounted archers. The mounted archers fought on foot and used horses only on the march. The whole rising out was generally mounted because of the need for mobility in keeping pace with fast moving Irish raiders. These forces were distinct from the muster of the Pale marches, on the peripheries of Westmeath, Louth and Kildare, which provided Irish-style horsemen and kern, and which will be dealt with separately.

Military service was universal for men aged 16 to 60. The 1534 'Ordinances for Government of Ireland' required that a justice of the peace be made in each shire, a warden of the peace in each barony, and constables in each parish. They were to keep musters every quarter of the year.[35] Normally the quarter days were reckoned to be Lady Day 25 March, Midsummer Day 24 June, Michaelmas 29 September, Christmas Day 25 December. But according to Richard Stanihurst, the Palesmen's four annual musters took place between early April and late June, on Blackmonday ('which is the morrow of Easter Day'), on Mayday, St John the Baptist's Eve, and St Peter's Eve.[36]

Upon proclamation of a hosting against the Irish, each landowner in the maghery was to send a longbowman for every £20 of his annual income, and no Englishman dwelling within the maghery could bring a spear unless he also brought a longbow. The Act of 1465, still in place, required that 'Every Englishman and Irishman that dwells with Englishmen …. shall have an English bow of his own length and one fist mele – between the necks with 12 hafts of the length of ¾ of the standard.'[37] The 1534 'Ordinances for Ireland' ordered 'that shooting be used in every parish within the English pale.' Each parish was thus to be provided with a pair of butts, and the constables ordered to call the parishioners before them to 'shoot up and down 3 times every feast day between 1st March and last day of July,' if the weather was fair. The prohibition against maghery men answering the muster with a spear, 'excepte he have a bowe or pavyce,' is based on

---

35   *State Papers: Henry VIII*, p.214, 1534, n.d., Ordinances for Ireland, anon.
36   Holinshed, *Irish Chronicle*, p.42.
37   Thomas J. DeBurgh, 'Ancient Naas (Parts I. and II.)', *Journal of the Kildare Archaeological Society*, vol. 1, no. 3 (1891–95), p.188.

the general preference for the longbow. The pavise could be an infantry shield, but may also indicate the crossbow, which continues to appear in Anglo-Irish wills into the 1570s. However, there is an ethnic element to the prohibition, as the 'spere' being discouraged here is not the horseman's lance, but rather an Irish dart. The adoption by English colonists of the Irish language, hairstyles, dress, weapons and manner of riding had been legislated against since 1366, and was a continuing source of anxiety for the Dublin administration.

The Pale elite were proud of their English military traditions, and this included an emphasis on good archers. However, from the latter fifteenth century it was increasingly recognised that the bow was not as effective in the close country of bogs and scrubby woodlands that lay between the Pale and the Irish lordships. As early as 1515, the 'State of Ireland' report on the Pale's defences had called for those unable to shoot a longbow to be instructed in the use a crossbow or a gun, since these required minimal training. A growing administrative appreciation of firearms is seen during the crisis of the Kildare revolt of 'Silken' Thomas in 1535, when the Imperial Ambassador Chapuys reported that four or five hundred English 'hackbutiers' had been sent into Ireland, amid numerous complaints about the quality of bows available there.[38] Nonetheless, it is remarkable that the armament of the rising out of the maghery of the Pale itself seems to have remained virtually unchanged as late as 1601.

A typical 'hosting' of the English Pale was carried out in July of 1560, to guard the borders during Lord Deputy Sussex's 'journey' upon Shane O'Neill. A Royal Commission for the Musters, still proclaimed by writ in medieval Latin, provided instructions to the chief landowners. The Commissioners identified the quotas assigned to the various baronies and named the captains. Captains and petty captains were elected by the shire gentry from amongst the wardens and constables. The 1515 'State of Ireland' report specifies that wardens of Meath (and other shires) were to be accompanied by a standard of St George, while the constables were to have a guidon of St David of Wales (a red dragon on a white over green field). The standard of St George was superseded by an ensign with the same device in 1557.[39] For the 1560 muster, the constables of each barony were instructed to appear on 22 July, at the customary place of muster, bringing a book with the names of all residents between 16 and 60 in their parishes. The constable's books were to be 'certified and delivered on their oaths,' and the persons named in the lists were to appear in person on the day of the muster. Each of them was to bring 'all such horses, harness, armour, bows, arrows, guns, weapons, and all manner of warlike apparel as they by any means can put in readiness against that time for the service of the Queen's Majesty and the defence of the realm.' The penalty for absence was an amercement of

---

38 James, *Henry VIII's*, pp.109.
39 G. A. Hayes-McCoy, *A History of Irish Flags from the Earliest Times* (Boston: G. K. Hall & Co., 1979), p.25.

GOVERNOR'S RETINUES, GARRISON TROOPS, AND THE RISING OUT OF THE PALE

20 shillings or 10 days imprisonment.[40] The traditional place of muster for a general hosting was the Hill of Tara in Co. Meath, a convenient location with political resonance as the ancient centre of Ireland's sovereignty.

At the muster, the Commissioners were to examine each man present for the 'hableness' of his body and 'furniture'. In the margin of the muster book, they were to make notes in coded letters next to each man's name:

> that is to say, upon every hable man, archer h.a., upon every hable harquebus h.ha., upon every hable billman h.b., upon every hable horseman h.h., upon every hable kernagh h.k., and upon him that you fynde not so hable to leave out the first h. But also note in like sorte by writing what horse, armour, and weapon each of them shall then have by these letters. For a horse h.o., for a jacke j., for a spear s.p., for a bow b.o., for a sheaf of arrows s.h., for a bill b., for a gun g., for a sword s., for a habergen of mail h.m.[41]

These muster books, signed by the constables, were to be delivered to the Lord Lieutenant by 1 August. The muster was liable to be called to a 'hosting' with six days notice, to last no more than 40 days. Each hundred men was commanded by one grand and one petty captain. In 1535, when serving beyond their own locality, the daily wages of each grand captain were 4s, and of each petty captain 2s.[42]

It is clear that the mounted archer was central to the Pale's militia. As Oman noted of the original twelfth century invaders: 'None of the barons who won Ireland ever marched forth without a large provision of bowmen, and after a time they habitually mounted them.'[43] Mounted archers probably maintained horseboys, as they had done earlier. In an indenture of 1420, written in French, a retainer of James, Earl of Ormond, agrees to maintain six mounted archers, and 'shall have them well armed, harnessed, and mounted after the fashion of England. Every two of said archers to provide for themselves three horses, and one horseboy (*garsoun*) to guard them.'[44] Garsoun was the name frequently applied to horseboys in the south of Ireland during the sixteenth century, and survives in the modern term gossoon (*garsún* – boy) in Munster Irish. A decay in archery skills was bemoaned in 1460, such that the Irish enemies 'dare ride upon the kings subjects …. by night.' It was emphasised, therefore, that subjects with £20 of income per annum must provide 'one archer mounted and

---

40 John Gilbert (ed.), *Facsimiles of National Manuscripts of Ireland*, pt. 4.1 (Dublin: Public Records Office, 1884), Appendix V.
41 Gilbert, *Facsimiles*, part 4.1, Appendix V.
42 *State Papers: Henry VIII*, p.243, n.d., Skeffington to Henry VIII.
43 Sir Charles Oman, *A History of the Art of War in the Middle Ages*, vol. 1 (London: Methuen & Co. Ltd, 1924), p.404.
44 *Calendar of Ormond Deeds*, vol. 3, 1413–1509, Edmund Curtis, ed. (Dublin: The Stationery Office, 1935), p.27, 1 March, Earl of Ormond to Thomas Petyt.

arrayed defensively with a bow and arrows fit for the war according to the English fashion.'[45] Yet, the 1519 Ordinances indicate an attempt was made at that time to save costs by limiting the number of horses. They specify that no yeoman was to ride to battle, 'but every vi yemen to take an hackeney and ladde to beare their iackes, stoulles (skulls) bowes and arrows, and all bowmen to go on foote except the greate capytayne.'[46] At about the same time, the Earl of Kildare's Rental Books for 1518 list 'the cessing of the cartes' in each barony of Kildare for a general hosting, giving a total of 39 carts. Not surprisingly, both of these measures were found wanting, and the use of mounted archers was quickly resumed, while the carts would be converted to the handier pack horses or 'garrans'. Thus, the *State Papers* in August 1548 record a partial hosting that was to meet at Trim under Patrick Barnewall, consisting of 120 mounted archers, 53 horsemen, and 60 kern.[47] Later that month, 30 horsemen under the Marshal Nicholas Bagenal met with a party of O'Connors driving a prey out of the Pale, 'and as many as were archers, not past ten, lighted afoot, and rescued the prey.'[48] The accompanying table lists four general hostings of the Pale later in the century, indicating the muster was limited to horsemen and mounted archers, and in which it can be seen that 5 'garrans' were substituted for each cart. See the discussion of transport under Carriages below.

---

45 Steven G. Ellis, *England's Irish Pale, 1470–1550: The Making of a Tudor Region* (Woodbridge: The Boydell Press, 2021), p.52.
46 Ellis, *Irish Pale*, p.56.
47 *Calendar of State Papers Ireland: Henry VIII, Edward VI, Mary and Elizabeth*, vol. 1, 1509–73, Hans Claude Hamilton ed. (London: Longman, Green, Longman & Roberts, 1860), p.84, 18 August, James Everard to Bellingham.
48 *CSP Ireland*, pp.86–7, ? August, Lord Deputy to Privy Council.

GOVERNOR'S RETINUES, GARRISON TROOPS, AND THE RISING OUT OF THE PALE

Table 22. General Hostings of the English Pale, 1556[49], 1566[50], 1593[51], 1601[52]

Barony	Horsemen 1556/1566	Archers on Horseback 1556/1566	Carts 1556	Carts converted into garrans 1556	Horsemen 1593/1601	Archers on Horseback 1593/1601
Dublin						
Balrothery		32 / 20	10	50		25 / 26
Cowlocke		28 / 30	6	30		31 / 30
Newcastle		11 / 15	10	50		18 / 18
Castleknocke		11 / 8	7	35		10 / 11
Rathdowne		6 / 6	[blank]	[blank]	- / 12	10 / 10
Total		**88 / 79**	**33**	**165**	**- / 12**	**94 / 95**
Kildare						
Sawlte		'Remayned at home for the deffense of the bordres'			8 / 8	14 / 14
Upper Naas		"	"	"		13 / 13
Nether Naas		"	"	"		5 / 5
Kilcullen		"	"	"	8 / 8	2 / 2
Narragh		"	"	"		2 / 2
Reban & Athy		"	"	"		3 / 3
Kilkea		"	"	"	1 / 1	2 / 2
Offaly		"	"	"	1 / 1	4 / 2
Connall		"	"	"		3 / 3
Clane		"	"	"		2 / 2
Okethy		"	"	"		5 / 5
Carbery		"	"	"		4 / 4
Total:					**18 / 18**	**59 / 57**

---

49   *Facsimiles,* Gilbert, pt. 4.1, Appendix V.
50   *Manuscripts of Charles Haliday, esq., of Dublin, Acts of the Privy Council in Ireland, 1556–1572,* J. T. Gilbert (ed.), (London: Eyre and Spottiswoode, 1897), pp.161–66
51   Brendan Scott and Nicholls, Kenneth (eds), 'The Landowners of the late Elizabethan Pale', *Analecta Hibernica,* no. 43 (2012), pp.1–15.
52   Fynes Moryson, *Itinerary,* vol. 3, (Glasgow: James MacLehose and Sons, 1907–8), p.382–385.

Meath						
Duleek		26 / 27	10	50		30 / 30
Scryne	24 / 24	21 / 24	9	45	24 / 24	31 / 30
Ratouthe		5 / 6	5	25		13 / 13
Dunboyne		1 / 2	3	15		3 / 3
Deece		7 / -	12	60		17 / 17
Moyfenraghe		- / 18	[blank]	[blank]		12 / 4
Lane		12 / 8	6	30		- / 8
Navan		38 / 37	10	50	3 / -	44 / 48
Kells	13 / 16	2 / 2	9	45	16 / 16	6 / 6
Slane	8 / 6	9 / 7	5	25	6 / 6	9 / 11
Fower	4 / 28		2	10	28 / 28	
Morgallen	4 / 7		5	25	8 / 7	- / 1
Total:	**53 / 81**	**121 / 131**	**76**	**380**	**85 / 81**	**165 / 171**
West Meath						
	- / 60				60 / 60	2 / 2
Total:	**- / 60**				**60 / 60**	**2 / 2**
Louth						
Gerrard		6 / 14			- / 4	29 / 26
Athirdee	33 / 27		4	20	15 / 16	12 / 13
Total:	**33 / 27**	**6 / 14**	**4**	**20**	**15 / 20**	**41 / 39**
Grand Total:	**86 / 168**	**215 / 224**	**113**	**565**	**178 / 191**	**361 / 364**

Arms of the Palesmen

The 'State of Ireland' report of 1515, discussed above, provides our most complete record of the expected equipment for the rising out of the Pale. It is found in the *State Papers* and was carefully analysed by John Hunt.[53] The document complains that Palesmen had abandoned 'bowes and arrows …. swords and bucklers, jacks and sallets' in favour of short Irish bows, et cetera. It then sets out that each man with from £10 to £20 worth of property should have: a doublet or coat of fence called a jack, 'no langre to the knee,' a sallet (or sculle), a sword, an English bow, or with an Irish bow and his arrows, or a spear charged with a bill or glaive.

---

53 John Hunt, *Irish Medieval Figure Sculpture: 1200–1600*, vol. 1 (Dublin: Irish University Press, 1974), pp.63–65.

GOVERNOR'S RETINUES, GARRISON TROOPS, AND THE RISING OUT OF THE PALE

Those who could not make or purchase a jack would be provided with a back and breast from the armoury. However, it was acknowledged that it was easier for a man to bear a 'cote of fence, callyd a jakke, then a brest, and better shall defend a mannes body from Iryshe arrowes and darttes. The breste leavyth the leggs nakeyd, and the back is more uneasye and paynfull to bere, for footemen, then a jakke.'[54]

These were the requirements for the best armed men. Others would have been unarmoured. During the revolt of 'Silken' Thomas Fitzgerald in 1534, three degrees of armament were specified based on income. Every man worth £4 to £10 in goods was to have a bow, half a sheaf of arrows, a bill and a sallet or a 'scull'. Every man worth £10 to £20 was to have a jack or coat of defence, a bow, a sheaf of arrows, and a bill, a sallet or a scull. And paid servants receiving yearly wages above 13s 4d were to have a bill and scull, or a bow and arrows.[55]

The horsemen, or 'lords, knights, squires, gentlemen and all others so horsed and harnessed,' were to have their horse, harness and spears 'after the maner of Walshe speres.' He could ride in 'whyt harnoyse', or 'in his jakke, with his halbryk and his gorgete, so that he shall bare his spere in the rest, at his pleasure, when nede shall require.' Later in the document, this is reiterated, with each man 'of noble folk' being required to have 'his jakke, his halbryk, his gorget, his basenet, his swerde and his spere, reddy allwaye after the maner of this lande; soo that every horsseman of landes, or of substaunce, have a payre of grayves and a gauntlet for his lyfte hand.' He is to ride a 'barbeyd horse,' which Hunt points out would be limited to a shaffron and crinet with a steel saddle.

The jack referred to in this document is the Irish 'side jack,' reaching to the knees. This eliminated any need for leg armour, apart from greaves. The 'halbryk' cannot be a mail hauberk, as it has a lance rest fastened to it. Hunt equates it to the 'halkrig' used in contemporary Scotland, which was a plate back and breast with tasses. In Scotland the halkrig was usually paired with splints for the arms, but the use of a 'lyft gauntlet' indicates that splints were not used by the horsemen of the Pale. The gorget is likewise not an item of plate armour, but the deep pisane collar of mail, characteristic of Ireland where it was paired with the peculiarly Irish style of bascinet. The specification of the archaic bascinet here is linked by Hunt to depictions of the more complete magnate harness found on tomb sculpture. The full harness as used by Pale magnates would have been relatively rare, as is discussed below.

The 'archer on horseback' was seen as increasingly obsolescent, while horsemen, or 'speres' were never available in adequate numbers. During times of crisis, as in 1520, the *State Papers* record Governors pleading that

---

54 Hunt, *Irish Sculpture*, pp.63–64.
55 *State Papers: Henry VIII*, p.208–9, 1534, n.d., Ordinances for Ireland.

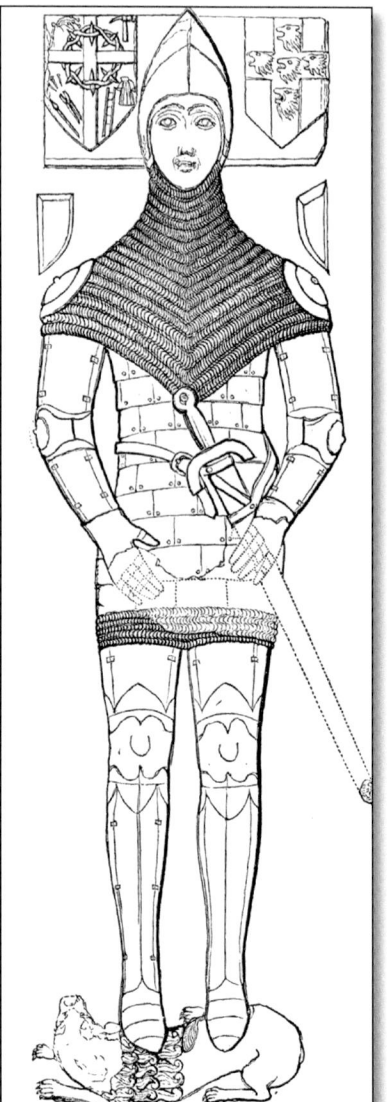

James Schorthals, 1507. In St Canice's Cathedral, Kilkenny City. (Author's collection)

they be reinforced by the Crown with 'Northomberland speris, and with somme Walshe speris, and not with bowes on horsbak.'[56]

Anglo-Irish Armour: 'Harnoyse After the Manner of this Land.'

By the Tudor era, a 'national' style of armour had evolved among the elite of the Anglo-Irish men-at-arms. This was styled 'the harnoyse after the maner of this lande,' and was distinguished from 'whyt harnoyse, after the Maner of England.'[57] As there are no surviving examples, study of this harness is based on funerary effigies in the Dublin and Ossory Pales. According to John Hunt's authoritative art-historical study this 'native' Irish style was frozen around the year 1370, and would remain unchanged for the next 200 years. It was a practical and effective type of armour, harking back to earlier times, but with its own distinct features. The retention of this armour was driven by the demands of Ireland's raiding style of warfare and the geographical conditions of the country. A magnate like Piers Butler, 8th Earl of Ormond, was familiar with the English Court and could afford any luxury he desired, yet his effigy of 1539 shows this style of armour. In his will, Piers leaves to his son *meam loricum*, i.e., not his best habergeon but his only habergeon. Similarly, the will of another Anglo-Irish magnate, Gerald Fitzgerald, 9th Earl of Kildare, leaves a friend 'the haberion and pisayn that Donyll Oge had' and bequeaths to the Piers Butler just mentioned above, 'an habergeon.'[58] Far from being an artistic anachronism, Hunt was confident that Piers Butler's effigy shows him 'as he appeared to his enemies when on foray with his gallowglasses and kerns.'

This style of armour is characterised by a typically Irish high crowned bascinet, rising to a central apex, with a pronounced keel. This helmet was common to both the Gaelic and Anglo-Irish communities, with the latter adding a visor pierced by slits for 'sights' surrounded by breathing holes, or 'breaths'. These bascinets are close fitting, gracefully tapered, and drawn in towards the bottom. There are no vervelles for attaching an aventail. Instead, an ample pisane collar protected the neck and shoulders, and is interpreted by Hunt as being attached to an arming cap fitted with a padded burlet, as seen in the effigy of Edmund Purcell. This pisane fully covers the shoulders and often falls to a point in front. Thus, the bascinet was independent of the pisane and could be

---

56 *State Papers: Henry VIII*, p.47–8, 25 September, Surrey to Wolsey.
57 Hunt, *Irish Sculpture*, p.80.
58 Hunt, *Irish Sculpture*, p.63.

GOVERNOR'S RETINUES, GARRISON TROOPS, AND THE RISING OUT OF THE PALE

removed at will. The foundation was a relatively short mail habergeon or possibly an arming doublet with mail voiders for the arms coupled with a mail skirt. A hip length coat of plates with a moderately inflected waist was worn over the mail, constructed of overlapping horizontal lames riveted to a canvas or leather foundation and overlaid with fustian, velvet or silk. The plate breast of the coat of plates is obscured by the deep pisane collar. The mail habergeon or skirt extends several inches below the coat of plates, just covering the groin.

A distinctive characteristic of this harness is the use of large, plain besagews laced onto the pisane collar and usually covering the wearer's armpits. The arms are generally in full plate, the upper arms defended by a rerebrace, with a cowter for the elbow joint and vambrace on the forearm. The cowter usually has a rondel riveted to it, of identical size and appearance to the besagews used on the pisane collar. The hands are protected by gauntlets with bell-mouthed cuffs and articulated fingers with prominent gads on the knuckles. The legs are protected by all-round plate cuisses, with slotted turning joints. Poleyns defend the knee, with full greaves below them with hinges sometimes evident on the outside and inside. Sabatons of overlapping lames defend the feet.

The elite figures depicted on the Anglo-Irish effigies would have been horsemen, armed with the spear. Their secondary weapon was a sword with a characteristic wheel pommel and straight quillons with tips angled sharply downward. This Anglo-Irish type of hilt is consistent with that in use across the Irish Sea, where it distinguishes lowland Scottish swords from their Gaelic Highland counterparts. These swords were carried in a frog of relatively uniform pattern, the sword belt being worn either on the waist or 'baudrewise' over the shoulder, which is how the King girded Piers Butler when creating him Earl of Ossory in 1528.[59] Holinshed, in his *Irish Chronicle* under the year 1532, refers to the Earl of Kildare's 'painted scabbard'.[60]

Edmund Purcell, c. 1549. Captain of kern to the Earl of Ormond. In St Canice's Cathedral, Kilkenny City (Author's drawing)

---

59 Edwards, *Ormond Lordship*, p.87.
60 Holinshed, *Irish Chronicle*, p.262.

'OF KERNS AND GALLOWGLASSES'

The use of full round cuisses in English armours of *c.* 1370 reflects the habit of English knights and men-at-arms of dismounting for combat. The presence of full round cuisses on these Anglo-Irish effigies may also reflect this practice. While most warfare in Ireland took the form of flight and pursuit, for which the wearers of these armours would have remained in the saddle, cavalry played little role in the relatively rare linear battles. Instead, Irish horsemen, both Gaelic Irish and Anglo-Irish, are often described as dismounting for a standing fight, in the manner of the medieval English, as discussed in the chapter on Irish horsemen.

Because of the supposedly outdated appearance of this armour, some have suggested that the funerary figure sculptures depicting this Anglo-Irish style are examples of unconscious antiquarianism. Hunt argues convincingly that this is not the case. It is quite possible that many of the pieces depicted were very old, as a well cared for armour can easily last 100 or 200 years. And Hunt points out that the woodcuts of Dürer depict harness of almost identical form, while the works of Holbein, Bosch and Breughel also display many corresponding details. He concluded:

> Ireland was one of the toughest and most merciless schools of fighting in Europe, and the Irish early discovered that light defences capable of being worn night and day under very rough conditions were preferable to elaborate panoplies of plate, which were too heavy to be worn for more than brief periods and which required for their proper donning a company of squires, pages and the constant attention of armourers.[61]

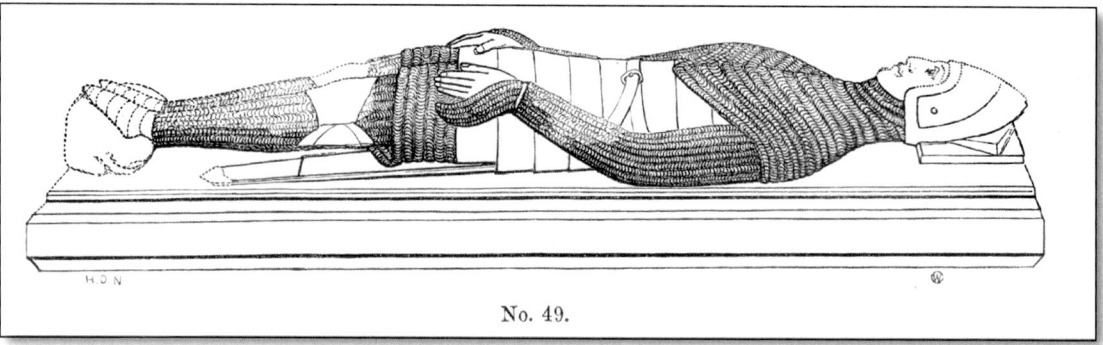

John Grace, c. 1552. A particularly archaic version of Pale harness. In St Canice's, Kilkenny City. (Author's collection)

The Carriages

While carts and wagons were common enough in the English Pale, and indeed in the Kildare and Ormond lordships, they were found to be unsuitable for carrying supplies on a 'hosting journey' against the Irish. The Pale had good roads, some of which were metalled, but the *fasagh*,

---

61 Hunt, *Irish Sculpture*, p.62.

GOVERNOR'S RETINUES, GARRISON TROOPS, AND THE RISING OUT OF THE PALE

or wasteland which had to be crossed in the disputed region was wooded, boggy and without many bridges. Thus, carriages, or pack horses, were levied upon the farmers of the Pale instead. The horses employed were small, sure-footed native geldings, called garrons or garrans (*gearráin*) in Ireland. This breed of horse, replaced wholesale in the eighteenth century by donkeys from Iberia, survives today as the Kerry Bog Pony. They were about the size of a donkey, an anonymous description of an elderly English settler who was captured by rebels in 1597 says 'they mounted him upon a poor garrounde …. his bare feet almost towchinge the grownede.'[62]

The number of carts required from each barony in Meath is listed by Sheriff Cusack in 1510, the assessed total of 71½ being very close to the 76 carts called for in 1556, but by then garrans were being substituted for the carts.[63] As noted, the use of carts for the general hosting in 1519 seems to have been part of the cost saving measures. Thomas Alen had complained of one levy of Irish carts in 1549: 'They bear the name carts, but good cars would bring as much.'[64] The carts in question were probably the block-wheeled low-backed car, which survived even in the Dublin area well into the nineteenth century. These were drawn by one horse, and in 1560 we read of a cess of '50 garrons with 50 cars.' These carts were levied for building fortifications in newly shired Laois and Offaly, and were not being taken on a 'journey'.[65] In 1567, a hosting for 'Her Majesties service in the North' required a 'cesse of 200 garrons and 100 men to drive them furnished with their victuals for one month for the carriage …. 6d ster. per diem the leader, and 4d per diem the garron.'[66] The load of one cart and its driver was reckoned equal to that of five garrons, which also required multiple drivers, so that had carts proven practical the savings would have been substantial. But we know the return to garrans was permanent, and the general hosting of 1575 for service with the Lord Deputy in Ulster included the 'hire of 300 garrons and 150 drivers at 14d sterling per diem for every two garrons,' the same rates as in 1567.[67]

We have a more complete record of a similar levy from 1 May 1581. The Sheriff of Kildare was commissioned by the Lord Deputy and Council to cess '108 able garrons with straddles and for every 5 garrons 2 sufficient drivers, furnished with three weeks' provisions, for three weeks' service for

---

62 Hiram Morgan and Kenneth Nicholls (eds), 'Dialogue of Sylvynne and Peregrynne', Author H. C., CELT, the Corpus of Electronic Texts., p.37.
    <http://research.ucc.ie/celt/document/E590001-001>
63 Ellis, *Irish Pale*, p.119.
64 *CSP Ireland*, p.104, 21 June, Thomas Alen to Lord Deputy.
65 *Calendar of the Carew Manuscripts*, vol. 2, 1575–1588, J.S. Brewrer and William Bullen eds (London: Longman & Co., 1867), p.93, June 1577, Extracts from the Council Books relating to Cesse, by John Chaloner.
66 *Cal. Carew Mss,* p.98, June 1577, Extracts from the Council Books relating to Cesse, by John Chaloner.
67 *Cal. Carew Mss,* p.99, June 1577, Extracts from the Council Books relating to Cesse, by John Chaloner.

the hosting journey intended by the Lord Deputy.' Similar commissions were sent to the Counties of Dublin, Meath, Westmeath and Louth, with a double proportion upon Meath. At the same time, a Commission was sent to the Sheriff of Dublin 'to levy forthwith 50 pioneers or labourers with spade and picks to attend the Lord Deputy in this hosting journey fixed for the 14th instant with three weeks' provisions'.[68] The straddles mentioned were simple wooden pack saddles with horns for suspending a pair of wicker panniers, or creels. This was an ancient form of transport that survived well into the twentieth century. The State Papers record in 1596 that 'O'Donnell did cut on the country .... 500 garrans for carriages, and two baskets to every Garran.'[69] We get some idea of the loads carried this way in the State Papers for January 1567, where 'furniture wanting for the service at Derry' includes 'furnishing of small tents meet for the camp to be carried on garrons' backs.'[70] Garrans were in fact the usual overland transport for goods in sixteenth century Ireland, for instance, 'The manner of carrying wine in Ireland is in little barrels on horses' backs.'[71]

The proportions of garrans called up in 1581 mirrored the requirements placed upon the same counties for fighting men, as seen also in the accompanying table for the general hosting of 1556. In 1600, as Lord Deputy Mountjoy prepared to campaign in Ulster, he had: 'written to the five shires of the Pale to attend his Lordship with their rising out,' as Deputy Burgh had done three years previously, but at the general hosting at the Hill of Tara, he dismissed the Pale levies to home guard duties, only taking a portion of their carriage horses.[72] Driving garrans for the army was not without its risks, as during Sussex's 1563 incursion into Ulster, the State Papers record 'the murder of about ten churls who stole away with their garrans on the night of 11 April, and were surprised by certain of Shane's men, returning from the borders.'[73] Captain Nicholas Dawtrey, an Irish veteran with 30 years of service, had warned of the ruinous consequences of these requisitions for 'journeys' against the Irish: 'And let this be noted by the way, that of the Cariage horses or garinus (as they tearme them) in Ireland, the third horse, nor the third leader of such cariage horses, wilbe able to return home into the English Pale, which would be mighty destruction to the husbandry.'[74]

---

68 David B. Quinn, 'Calendar of Council Book of Dublin, 1581–1586', *Analecta Hibernia*, no. 24 (1967), p.117.

69 Darren McGettigan, *Red Hugh O'Donnell and the Nine Years' War* (Dublin: Four Courts Press, 2005), p.77.

70 *CSP Ireland*, p.326, ? January, Lord Deputy to Cecil.

71 Timothy O'Neill, *Merchants and Mariners in Medieval Ireland* (Dublin: Irish Academic Press, 1987), p.91.

72 Falls, *Irish Wars*, p.423.

73 *CSP Ireland*, p.218, 26 May, Sussex to Cecil.

74 Hiram Morgan (ed.), 'A Boke of Questions and Answars', *Analecta Hibernia*, no. 36 (1995), p.99.

GOVERNOR'S RETINUES, GARRISON TROOPS, AND THE RISING OUT OF THE PALE

The Rising Out of the Marches

An Irish farmer from the marches of the Pale, driving a 'garran', or packhorse. Each driver would mind at least two garrans. He is dressed in the Killery costume, a surviving suit of clothing woven from white and black sheep's wool, which originally included a sheepskin cap. This is as set out in the Ordinances of the Black Earl of Ormond, which forbade labourers from using coloured cloth. The clothing is of fifteenth or sixteenth century date, judging from the medieval tailoring, which matches a known sixteenth century coat from Tipperary.

The muster of the 'maghery', or inner core of Dublin and Meath, was entirely mounted archers and light horsemen called 'spears', and as we have seen, they were armed in the English manner. By contrast, the muster of the Pale marches of Meath and Dublin, and the counties of Kildare and Carlow, provided Irish-style horsemen and kern. Further kern and Irish horsemen were provided by indentured Gaelic chieftains outside the Pale. Upon proclamation of a hosting, all gentlemen dwelling within the Pale marches were to send an Irish-style horseman for every 10 marks of annual income, and all marcher gentry were to quarter Irish kern upon the tenants of their march land, under the quasi-Gaelic quartering system known to the Palesmen as 'coign and livery'. The 1488 Act proscribed the use of coign and livery by landowners within the maghery, while permitting it to these landowners in the marches, provided that their quartering of kern and horsemen was limited to their own tenants. In 1533, administrator Robert Cowley said the Pale's strength 'consisteth in the marches of the said four shires,' that is, among these kern and Irish-style horsemen, with the eventual addition of Crown galloglass.[75]

It has been suggested that this use of Irish troop types in the marches was because they were cheaper than their Anglo-Irish counterparts. This is belied by a memorandum of 1520, which clearly states that 'the Deputy can neyther well defend the Englishery from invasion ne doo conveniently displeas[u]re the enymys without galoglas and kerne.'[76] Therefore, the memorandum further explained, coign and livery could not be dispensed with. 'The marchouris of Englishmen next adioynyng vnto the Irishmen bee enforced to reteyn .... galoglas and kerne for the defence of their lands which been not hable to defend without the said galoglas and kerne,' and these could not be supported without coign and livery. The charge was said to rest upon the lords and not the tenants, who received a recompense in their rents for quartering troops. Without these Irish troops, the Deputy

---

75　Ellis, *Irish Pale*, p.55.
76　James, *Henry VIII's*, pp.97–8.

would have no answer to the King's Irish enemies, for 'Irishmen bee light and delyver soo that when the Englishmen shuld follow theym they shuld labo[ur] all in vayne and not prevail in pursuyng theym.' If the English followed them into the woods, 'theym neyther having experience nor knowledge .... they shuld not oonly retourn w[ith]out doing any good but also be in great danger and p[er]ill.' Things were still much the same in September, 1582, during the height of the second Desmond Rebellion, when the State Papers record Edward Barkley's recommendation to convert English foot to 'horsemen and kern of the country, for that our English footmen are able by no means to annoy them for want of footmanship.'[77] For as Sir John Perrot had declared in 1571, while serving as President of Munster, 'I must have kerne against kerne, and gallowglass against gallowglass.'[78]

While these Irish-style troops secured the borders of the Pale, the effect of maintaining them created a paradox, as it drove out 'The pore Englishe erth tillers of the English pale,' who couldn't bear the imposition of coign and livery. Thus the lords 'bring into the hart of the Englishe pale Irishe tenantes, whiche neither can speke thEnglishe tonge, ne were capp or bonnet, and expulseth ofte the aunciert good Englishe tenantes.'[79] Such were conditions along the frontier, and Robert Cowley noted that even the captains of the 'Englyshe marche borderers .... use Iryshe apparell, and the Iryshe tounge,' fostering their children among neighbouring Irish clans.[80]

Marcher 'Holding Kern'

The loyal contingents of indentured Irish lords from outside the Pale actually constituted the bulk of the general hosting of 1556, and the numbers recorded (see below) did not include further contingents expected from nine other lords, including O'Hanlon, Maguire, the Earl of Tyrone, the Baron of Upper Ossory, and the Earl of Ormond, each of whom was to appear 'in parson, with his rysing oute of horsemen and kerne.' These might easily have doubled the number of Irish horsemen and kern present.

---

77 *Calendar of State Papers Ireland: Elizabeth*, vol. 2, 1574–1585, ed. Hans Claude Hamilton, ed. (London: Longmans, Green, Reader and Dyer, 1867), p.400., 25 September, Barkley's advice.
78 Hayes-McCoy, *Scots Mercenary*, p.44.
79 *State Papers: Henry VIII*, p.449, n.d., Cowley to Cromwell.
80 *State Papers: Henry VIII*, p.479, n.d., Lord Deputy Gray to St Leger.

GOVERNOR'S RETINUES, GARRISON TROOPS, AND THE RISING OUT OF THE PALE

Table 23. The Rising Out of Irish Lords and Captains, 1556[81]

Lord	Horsemen	Kern
O'Bynre	12	24
Kavanagh	12	30
O'Carroll	12	24
MacGeohegan	4	24
O'Molloy	6	40
O'Melaghlin	4	24
O'Madden	4	12
Hugh O'Madden	4	12
MacGuinness	12	24
MacMahon	8	15
Captain of Farney	10	30
O'Reilly	40	100
Total:	128	359

The rising out of indentured Irish lords and captains as specified for the general hosting of 1601 remained almost identical to that of 1556, including, for example; 'O'Byrne, horsemen 12, Kern 24; and Kavanagh, horsemen 12, Kerne 30; etc.' The totals on this occasion were 128 horsemen and 361 kern. These figures do not appear to include the kern and horsemen 'that lay placed and divided at cess' in the marches of the Pale.

The term 'holding kerne' was used for the kern quartered in the marches, indicating that they were maintained by coign and livery. The 1519 Hosting Ordinances required the 'gentles' of the marches of Meath to cess upon their lands 60 of their own kern for every hosting, with a captain elected for them with a 'lytle bann[er] and all the kerne to followe' him, and to be 'always redye togetthres'. The marches of Louth and Dublin were each to cess 40 kern with a captain, while Counties Kildare and Carlow were each to cess 60 'kerne and their capitaynes to be elected and everie capytayne their lytle gytton [guidon]'. The total of 'holding kern' was thus 260 in 1519.[82] Subsequently, the contribution of Co. Dublin was reduced from 40 to 24 kern, but this was more than offset by the additional kern supported by the expansion of marcher lands which ultimately resulted in the creation of Co. Westmeath in 1543.

The 1534 'Ordinances for Ireland' record that 'the gentyls of the marches of Myth [Meath] shall cesse on their marche landes 120 kerne .... and the shyre of Uriell [Louth] to cesse 80 kerne; the marche of the countie

---

81 *Facsimiles,* Gilbert, pt. 4.1, Appendix V.
82 Ellis, *Irish Pale,* p.56.

'OF KERNS AND GALLOWGLASSES'

Kern, c. 1544. Note the left gauntlet hung from a lanyard round the neck. (Biblioteka Cyfrowa, Creative Commons)

of Dublin 24 kerne; the kerne of the countyes of Kyldare and Cartlagh [Carlow], as the Erle of Kyldare used to cesse there.'[83] Counties Kildare and Carlow each cessed 60 of the Earl of Kildare's 120 'Keating kern' and their 90 boys. These two companies of Kildare's kern were always commanded by and largely recruited from members of the Keating family. Thus, the total in 1534 of 344 'holding kern' is very close to the total of 361 kern in the 'rising out' of loyal Gaelic chieftains given for 1556 and 1601. Yet, the indentured loyal chieftains were to appear 'in parson' with their rising out, so we know they were not merely being assessed for the payment of a nearly equivalent number of 'holding kern' cessed in the marches.

The total of kern paid for service in a general hosting therefore included both the indentured kern of loyal chieftains and 'holding kern' cessed in the marches. This can be seen in the general hosting of July 1544, were 660 kern were provided for. The counties of Tipperary, Waterford, Kilkenny, and Wexford were each to provide money to hire 60 kern in place of their usual rising out. This totalled 240 kern, serving for a quarter of a year at the cost of £204 13s 4d sterling. These were probably the kern of indentured loyal chieftains. Likewise, Counties Kildare and Carlow were to provide money for 120 kern (the Keating kern), Oriel (Louth) for 60 kern, and Westmeath, Eastmeath, and Dublin for 240 kern, for a total of 420 kern serving for a quarter of a year at the cost of £647 10s. These last were the 'holding kern' cessed in the marches.[84]

The Keating Kern and the Kern of the Pooles

The two companies of Kildare's Keating kern had joined in the Kildare Rebellion until their commander, William Keating, was taken prisoner in August 1535. He was released 'upon hostages' and attracted most of the Keatings away from 'Silken' Thomas Fitzgerald. William was now

---

83 *State Papers: Henry VIII*, p.213, n.d., Ordinances for Ireland.
84 *Carew Mss*, p.87, June 1577, Extracts from the Council Books relating to Cesse, by John Chaloner.

GOVERNOR'S RETINUES, GARRISON TROOPS, AND THE RISING OUT OF THE PALE

to drive Thomas and his ally O'Connor from their fastness in Kildare, 'For no doubt, this war against O'Chonnor and Thomas must be most excellent by kern.'[85] In 1552 the same William Keating was to command 30 kern in Catherloghe (Carlow) and Leighlin, and the duties of his kern are spelled out: 'apprehension of thieves and other like malefactors, and therein and all other services to use themselves uprightly and faithfully, upon loss of such entertainment as they either have or shall have at the King's Majesty's hands.'[86] William Keating and another commander of kern, Robert Hartpole, held adjacent lands in Slievemargy in 1563.[87] Hartpole is named in a pardon with several Keatings in September of 1578, almost certainly for their involvement in the notorious massacre of the O'Mores at Mullaghmast. Redmond Keating appears in records as early as 1585, and in 1588 the Crown paid him 16d a day for his services as captain of 16 kern. The Keatings would remain in government service to the end of Elizabeth's reign, still commanded by Redmond Keating. Keating, in 1599, is castigated by Captain Thomas Lee as 'that huge unweldy Rebell whom a horse cannot carrye,' and a rebel, even though he had 'entertaynment from her Majestie as a Captayne of her Kerne' to the value of £120 per annum.[88]

After the collapse of the Kildare lordship in 1539, the Keating kern had been taken directly into the pay of the government. Confusingly, when the Earldom of Kildare was restored to the 11th Earl in 1555, he was initially allowed to resume command of a force of 100 horsemen and 100 kern, though a portion of the Keatings continued in direct government service to the end of Elizabeth's reign. In 1562, Richard Keating and his kern are noted as preying upon English settlers in Wexford with impunity, shielded by their patron, the 11th Earl of Kildare.[89] By 1566 William Keating had been transferred from government service to the command of the 11th Earl's kern, and it was now alleged 'there be 8 score ketynge kerne, which by his mayntenaunce have coyn and livery 2 dayes and 2 nyghtes quarterly in every barony in the countie of Kildare …. doyng no service for the same, but pilfre and steal, conductyng the enemies lykewyse to suche places where they se is best oportunitie to spoyle the subjects.'[90]

---

85   *Cal. of the Carew Manuscripts*, vol. 1, 1515–1574, J. S. Brewrer and William Bullen eds (London: Longman & Co., 1867), p.72, 21 August, Gerald Alymer to John Alen.
86   *Cal. Carew Mss,* p.233, 30 April, Order of Lord Deputy and Council.
87   John Kelly, 'The Collection of Cess and Pardons and Fines in Carlow in the 1570s' in *Carloviana: the Journal of the Carlow Historical and Archaeological Society* (2017), pp.110–120.
88   John McGurk (ed.), 'The Discovery and Recovery of Ireland with the Author's Apology', Author Thomas Lee, ff.44–45, CELT, the Corpus of Electronic Texts. <https://celt.ucc.ie/published/E590001-005.html>.
89   Richard Bagwell, *Ireland Under the Tudors*, vol. 2, (London: Longmans, Green, and Co., 1885), p.44.
90   Hore, *Social State*, p.170.

In 1571, the 11th Earl persuaded his gentry to assist with the regular maintenance of his two 80 man companies of kern, now commanded by Shane and Meyler Keating, in a composition meant to replace the hated 'cess' with fixed rents.[91] Three years later, Kildare had these two Keating captains killed to eliminate witnesses, as they had been involved in subversive activities, plundering his enemies on his behalf.[92] Kildare never attained the hegemony of his predecessors, but assumed the position of General of the Leinster forces, commanding the 'home guard' of the Pale when the Lord Deputy was on campaign. Although permitted to expand his command with up to 200 additional 'choice kern' in times of crisis, his attempt to obtain funding for an additional 600 kern in 1574 was limited to three months service from January of that year, to deal with a Midlands revolt. The furore aroused by the imposition of these kern upon the Pale was instrumental to the final abolition of coign and livery.[93]

Like the Keating kern, the 'kernes of the Pooles' in Westmeath were another band of kern traditionally recruited from and commanded by an Anglo-Irish family. The Pooles are found consistently providing 100 kern from 1558 to 1601. For instance, on 23 September 1558, '100 kerne of the Polles with 31 days' victuals' were cessed to serve in the North with the Lord Deputy. They were to be captained by Thomas Flemyng, who would receive the pay of 20 of them 'for his pains for leading of the rest.' The kern were to receive 6d per day on this occasion rather than the usual 4d, 'the journey being painful', but this was not to be considered a precedent for the future.[94] In 1573, during the Earl of Essex's unsuccessful attempt to colonise Ulster, he complains in the State Papers about the Pooles: 'Thomas Flemyng's kerne, who being hired to serve, and coming to the place where their service should have been seen, turned their weapons against us, and are now with the rebels.'[95]

Government Kern Later in the Century

Kern remained in great demand even after the decisive change to reliance upon garrison troops sent from England. The companies in pay during the campaign against Shane O'Neill in 1561 are given below. The companies

---

91 Vincent P. Carey, *Surviving the Tudors: The Wizard Earl of Kildare and English Rule in Ireland*, 1537–1586 (Dublin: Four Courts Press, 2002), p.152.
92 Carey, *Surviving Tudors*, p.173.
93 Carey, *Surviving Tudors*, p.163.
94 *Calendar of the Carew Manuscripts*, vol. 2, 1575–1588, J.S. Brewrer and William Bullen eds (London: Longman & Co., 1867), p.92, June 1577, Extracts from the Council Books relating to Cesse, by John Chaloner.
95 *Calendar of the Carew Manuscripts*, vol. 1, 1515–1574, J.S. Brewrer and William Bullen eds (London: Longman & Co., 1867), p.445, 2 November, Earl of Essex to Edward Waterhouse.

GOVERNOR'S RETINUES, GARRISON TROOPS, AND THE RISING OUT OF THE PALE

of those captains marked by an asterisk were temporarily retained for the duration of the war.

Table 24. Government Kern, 1561–62[96]

Francis Cosbie, 'General over the said Kerne'	100
Sir Henry Radclief	40
Jaques Wingfeld	50
Owen Mc Hewgh	40
Richard Ketinge	40
Henry Collie	20
Sir George Stanley *	100
Captain Heron *	100
Thomas Fleminge, 'kernes of the Pooles' *	100
John Plounket *	50
Total:	**640**

The fierce campaign against the Midlands clans resulted in their dispossession and the shiring of Laois and Offaly in 1556, with 100 strong garrisons of English soldier-settlers planted at 'Fort Governor' (Phillipstown/An Daingean) and 'Fort Protector' (Maryborogh/Portlaoise) by 1564. Nevertheless, in April of that year, during a campaign against the surviving O'Mores and O'Connors, and O'Reilly, the numbers of kern employed actually increased. The borders of Meath were to be defended with 200 kern cessed upon the whole county of Meath. Also to be cessed for six weeks upon Co. Kildare, 120 'Keating kerne', and on Co. Carlow, 120 kern. And 300 kern were cessed upon Co. Westmeath, giving a total of 740 kern in 1564.[97] In September that year, the cess of 600 of those kern was renewed in Westmeath, with the cess of '100 kern and 50 boys' renewed in Kildare, and the cess of '80 holding kerne and their 40 boys' renewed in Meath and Kildare. In addition to these 780 kern, the 11th Earl of Kildare himself was to have entertainment for 200 kern of his own choosing, 'to pursue the rebels of the O'Connours,' divided: in Offaly 30 kern; in McVadoke's, McEdmond Duffe's and the county of Wexford and Fassaghbentry, 60 kern; in Westmeath, 30 kern; Louth 40 kern; Dublin, 40 kern, for a total of 200 kern, and their 100 boys.[98]

---

96   Ada K. Longfield (ed.), *Fitzwilliam Accounts 1560-65* (Dublin: Irish Manuscripts Commission, Dublin 1960), pp.43, 52–3.

97   *Calendar of the Carew Manuscripts*, vol. 2, 1575–1588, J.S. Brewrer and William Bullen eds (London: Longman & Co., 1867), p.94, June 1577, Extracts from the Council Books relating to Cesse, by John Chaloner.

98   *Cal. Carew Mss*, p.95, June 1577, Extracts from the Council Books relating to

'OF KERNS AND GALLOWGLASSES'

A recurring figure in the period after 1550 is the professional English soldier-adventurer serving in the border regions in command of native Irish kern. Increasingly in the 1560s and 1570s, these captains operated under commissions of martial law, which granted them a third of the goods of any rebel they killed. Captain Robert Hartpole, mentioned earlier, was typical of such ambitious, ruthless servitors. He had been in Ireland for 18 years when appointed Constable of Carlow in 1567, holding a command of 100 kern and their 50 boys till his death in 1594. He was married to Grainne O'Byrne, who could serve as interpreter for him, while her brother, Owen Dowlagh O'Byrne, was his bailiff and 'common extortioner'. Hartpole's troop of kern were captained by Donal MacGerald of Moyle, and staffed by many O'Byrnes of the Coulteman sept, often surnamed Mac Fir. They are found frequently serving alongside Captain Henry Davell's company of kern, commanded by Art Duff, and together involved themselves in shady dealings with disloyal borderers and oppressions within the Ormond lordship.[99] A pardon was issued to Hartpole in 1571 for 'cessing the inhabitants with strange kern, taking every meal for every kern, 2 white groats, and for every boy, a white groat.' Francis Cosby, the Queen's 'Captain General of the Kern', stood accused of similar oppression and commerce with rebels. In Connacht during the 1570s and 1580s, the provincial Lord President, Captain Nicholas Malby, likewise employed in each barony 'strange kern which they call sheriff's kernety' as bailiffs, and these were also accused by the local lords and people of extortion and oppression.[100]

The post of Captain General of the Kern seems to have been largely a sinecure, always held by an Englishman, and without apparent administrative or tactical significance. A patent roll of Philip and Mary records Sir Francis Cosby being made the first 'General of all the Kerne in Ireland' in 1558, and he held the post until his death in 1580. For service in 1559–1562, against Shane O'Neill, Cosby as 'generall over the said Kerne' received 3s 7d, with 100 kern paid '3d le pece per diem.'[101] Cosby is again recorded in 1576 being generously paid as 'General, for term of life, at 3s 8d a day; 32 kernes at 3d ster. a day.' The same document records other captains, however, being allowed similar commands of kern, such as Francis Agard, 40 kern, and Owen MacHugh O'Byrne, 20 kern.[102] Cosby appears once more in 1579 as 'General over Her Majesty's kerne: - himself, 4s 8d; and 32 kerne at 4d a day,' and was ordered to Munster with 100 kern to serve against the Desmond rebels.[103] Although Cosby's kern were recruited in

---

Cesse, by John Chaloner.

99   John Kelly, 'Robert Hartpole, Constable of Carlow' in *Carloviana, the Journal of the Carlow Historical and Archaeological Society* (2016), pp.72–84.
100 Rory Rapple, *Martial Power and Elizabethan Political Culture: Military Men in England and Ireland, 1558–1594* (Cambridge: Cambridge University Press, 2009), p.219–20.
101 Longfield, *Fitzwilliam Accounts*, p.52.
102 *Cal. Carew Mss*, p.45, 31 March 1576, Charges of Ireland, anon.
103 Edwards, *Campaign Journals*, p.65.

GOVERNOR'S RETINUES, GARRISON TROOPS, AND THE RISING OUT OF THE PALE

Connacht, at the Battle of Glenmalure they were persuaded to defect to the O'Byrnes of Wicklow, after killing Cosby himself as he reluctantly led them into the glen at the head of the English column. That day he commanded the vanguard of '300 Irish kerne, amongst whom was also mingled certain of your Majesty's galloglass …. these kerne and galloglass turned their backs to the enemy and their weapons to our bosom,' cutting up the supporting English 'loose shot' along with their own commander.[104] Sir Henry Duke succeeded Cosby, and appears in the State Papers in a 1585–86 listing of troops, under the heading 'Bands of Kern – Henry Duke, General of Her Majesty's Kerne.' Duke appears again in 1588, receiving wages for 'himself at 2s 8d, and 30 kerne at 4d le piece per diem.'[105]

Captain Thomas Lee was appointed by Lord Deputy Russell as General of the Kern in February of 1596. The following year, Lee's company tracked down and killed the rebel Fiach MacHugh O'Byrne, Lee describing himself afterwards as 'your bog Irishman' in a letter to the Queen. Like Captain Hartpol, Lee married a local woman, Anglo-Irish in Lee's case, who served as interpreter and occasionally sided with her kinsmen against her husband. Lee's life-sized portrait of 1594 by Marcus Gheeraerts, hangs in the Tate Gallery, London. The painting is saturated with political messages and 'civility v. savagery' symbolism, all of which has been extensively analysed. Lee is depicted barefoot and bare legged, in a glorified version of Irish kern dress, and it is often assumed that the shirt embroidered with black work and the gold laced jerkin were too extravagant for service in Ireland.[106] But it is known that captains wore their wealth in their clothing, and the arms depicted, including a 'graven morion', are reasonable for a man of his rank. Compare this with Sir George Bourchier, another captain who had fought through the Desmond Wars and who is frequently found serving alongside Lee in command of kern during the 1590s. Hooker says of him, 'If he served upon foot he was apparelled

Captain Thomas Lee, General of the Kern. His fish tail pistol is likely of Scottish manufacture, while the engraved morion and target are likely Milanese. He holds a remarkably slender Irish throwing spear or dart, the pointed butt spike is visible although the head is out of view. His forefinger rests in the throwing loop. Painted by Marcus Gheeraerts in 1594. (photo: Tate)

---

104 Edwards, *Campaign Journals*, p.142.
105 *Calendar of State Papers Ireland: Elizabeth*, vol. 3, 1586–88, July, Hans Claude Hamilton ed. (London: Longman & Co., 1877), p.40, 31 March, Book of the Garrisons.
106 Brian de Breffny, 'An Elizabethan Political Painting' in *Irish Arts Review*, vol. 1, no. 1 (1984), pp.39–41.

in the manner of a kerne, and a foot soldier, and was so light of foot as no kerne swifter, for he would pursue them in bogs, in thickets, in woods, in passes and streights.'[107]

Marcher Horsemen

The 1519 Hosting Ordinances commanded the marcher gentry to send 'an horseman well appoynted' for every 10 marks of yearly income. They were to elect a 'capytayne for the speres of their shyre,' which captain was to have a banner, provided that he had at least 40 men on horseback.[108] The marcher horsemen were armed and mounted in the native Irish fashion, and they are specifically exempted from long-standing legislation forbidding inhabitants of the English Pale to wear the Irish mantle and ride on an Irish pillion. Thus the Ordinances of 1534 required gentlemen to 'ryde in a saddle and weare inglyshe apparel …. except in warre.'[109] The mantle was admitted to be very useful when on campaign and the marcher horsemen were noted for being very skilful with their 'Irish weapons', which they simply could not use from an English saddle. Details of arms, mounts and tactics are covered in the chapter on the *marcagh*, or Irish horseman.

The horsemen cessed in the marches were supported by ploughlands, otherwise called 'horsemens beds'.[110] The 'Earl of Kildare's Rental Book', begun in 1518, listed 44½ horsemen thus provided for across Co. Kildare by 28 gentlemen. The Earl himself accounted for 5 of these horsemen, 3½ coming from Bermingham's Country of Carbrery, and 3 horsemen from Co. Carlow, with lesser numbers from the rest. By 1537, the Earl was sending 60 horsemen from Kildare and Carlow to every hosting. These horsemen were to remain resident on their holdings, and were frequently of Gaelic Irish extraction. For example, in 1540, the Earl of Kildare maintained two horsemen at Rathangan on 205 acres – Magnus O'Coyne at Carrick Everly Castle, and Miler O'Fay at Ballinure Castle. These two trusted servitors were to guard a key pass against the incursions of O'Connor Faly.[111]

The marcher horsemen would have had a 'chief horse' and two hackneys, each with its own horse boy. In a document of 1524 advocating reform, Kildare was to set limits on coign and livery, with 'every horseman and captayne of kerne and galloglasse' on campaign to have bread, ale and flesh on flesh days, with fish or butter on fish days. The 'kyrnne and boyes' were to accept as 'coygn' whatever fare the host farmer was eating, or else 2d a meal for a horseman, 1½d for a footman, and 1d for a horsekeeper. Every

---

107 Holinshed, *Irish Chronicle*, p.370.
108 Ellis, *Irish Pale*, p.56.
109 Sparky Booker, 'Moustaches, Mantles, and Saffron Shirts: What Motivated Sumptuary Law in Medieval English Ireland?' in *Speculum*, 96/3 (July 2021), p.755.
110 Hore, *Social State*, p.190.
111 Ellis, *Irish Pale*, pp.89, 96.

chief horse would have 'livery' of 12 sheaves of oats for a night and a day, every 'bereing horsse' 8 sheaves, and only one boy was allowed per horse. Fodder was valued at 1d for 6 sheaves, and 8d for a bushel of oats.[112]

Leinster Clandonnells: the Government Galloglass

The ancestors of the Leinster MacDonnells emigrated from the Scottish Highlands to Ulster in the second quarter of the fourteenth century. They subsequently moved to Connacht, where they served the O'Kellys and were constables to O'Connor Roe. By 1430, Turlough MacDonnell had moved from the O'Kellys' service to Wicklow, settling in the 'Debatable Lands' around the north-west base of the Wicklow Mountains and founding the original Wicklow sept of Leinster Clandonnells. This initial settlement was in the townlands of Ballydonnell and Baltyboys, known for the next two centuries as 'Clann Donnell's Countrie'. By 1435, Turlough had acquired lands at Tinnakill, Co. Laois, where a second sept of Leinster MacDonnells was established. With the temporary weakness of the Kildare Lordship due to succession issues, this was an ideal time to become established as defenders of the Dublin Marches, separating the Pale from the O'Byrnes and O'Tooles. Turlough's son, John Carragh who died in 1466, was referred to as 'Constable of the Pale' and 'best captain of the English.'[113] The MacDonnells had been taken into the service of the Earls of Kildare during the time of Gearóid Mór, the 'Great Earl', who was generally Lord Deputy from 1479–1513. An Alexander MacTurlough, of the Wicklow sept, is recorded in 1541 as acquiring lands at 'Great Grange' (Monksgrange), Co. Laois, where a third sept had been established at Rahin.[114]

The Great Earl was responsible for the introduction of his own kern and MacDonnell galloglass into the service of the Dublin administration. As Lord Deputy he was able to cess his galloglass upon the landholders of the Pale. The Great Earl's son Gerald (Gearóid Óg) became Lord Deputy in 1513 and continued the practice, contemporaries complaining that rather than a retinue of bills and bows, the King's Deputy was now followed by a multitude of Irish galloglass. The Ordinance of 1519 states that 'if the deputie be drywen that he must have a battayll or battaylles of galloglasse goyng to any hostyng or iourney, that they be lyveried by the kyng's herbynger by bylles after the forume as is afore in the lyvery of Irishmen that shall come to hostynges or iourneyes'.[115] When the Earl of Kildare's Irish troops were thus billeted within the four loyal shires of the English Pale, the king's harbinger

---

112 Hore, *Social State*, pp.150–1.
113 John Marsden, *Galloglass, Hebridean and West Highland Mercenary Warrior Kindreds in Medieval Ireland* (East Lothian: Tuckwell Press, 2003), p.53.
114 Lord Walter Fitzgerald, 'Macdonnells of Tinnakill Castle', *Journal of the Kilkenny Archaeological Society*, vol. 4, no. 3 (1904), pp.205–215.
115 Maginn and Ellis, *Tudor Discovery*, pp.102, 104.

preceded them, and was to pay for every galloglass, horseman and kern's meal 2d., and for every boy's meal 1d. There was to be no harbinger in the four shires but the king's harbinger, and he was to send no bill that was not sealed with the sign of the horse's head. He was to register the bills in his book, along with the day and year. This king's harbinger was likely identified by wearing a tabard bearing the royal arms of England quartered with those of France, and he may in fact have been the royal herald who was part of the deputy's household in the Tudor era, who is later found keeping accounts for the provisioning of the lord deputy's household. While this office is not heard of later, the rates quoted for the soldier's two daily meals – 2d per man and 1d per boy – were current throughout this period, with kern normally receiving 4d per diem.

After the downfall of the House of Kildare following the rebellion and attainder of Gearóid Óg's son, 'Silken' Thomas Fitzgerald, the Kildare galloglass were permanently transferred into Crown service. 'Silken' Thomas had been served by 240 galloglass in his rebellion of 1534–5, doubtless three battles of 80 sparrs each, and these were the galloglass transferred to the Crown's service after his defeat. By 1549 they are styled the 'King's galloglasses of the Clandonnells', and a few years later as the 'King's Scotici, otherwise galloglass', later becoming the 'Queen Majestie's Galloglass.'[116]

In 1547, Gerald Fitzgerald, the half-brother and sole heir of the executed 'Silken' Thomas Fitzgerald, returned from exile and worked to regain a portion of his family's lands. After strenuous efforts, he succeeded in getting the Earldom of Kildare restored, and in 1554 Gerald was made 11th Earl. While he was able to regain command of a portion of the 'Keating kern', his attempts to recover control of the MacDonnell galloglass of Leinster were thwarted. In 1557 four old captains of MacDonnell galloglass were examined by Crown authorities in regard to Gerald's claims. It was found that the Great Earl of Kildare had indeed received bonnaght from loyal Gaelic chieftains for the quartering of galloglass upon their lands, but only when acting as Lord Deputy, and never in his capacity as Earl of Kildare. The galloglass captains included Alexander mac Turlough mac Donnell and Domhnaill mac Uithne, whose testimony was hearsay, as he had been employed in the north by O'Neill in those days.[117] Nonetheless, by 1564 the 11th Earl had a standing force of 200 horse, 160 'Keating kern' and 160 galloglass. The latter were separate from the government galloglass, and it is not clear whether they were also MacDonnells.[118]

The captains of the three septs were established as land owners in the wake of the plantations of Laois and Offaly in 1556. In 1562, they received the following grants: Tinnakill Castle and townland to Calvagh Mac Turlough MacDonnell, formerly an O'Connor Faly holding; Rahin-Derry townland to Maelmurry mac Edmund MacDonnell, formerly an O'More

---

116 Nicholls, 'Scots Mercenary', p.86.
117 Hore, *Social State*, pp.152–3.
118 Carey, *Surviving Tudors*, p.94.

GOVERNOR'S RETINUES, GARRISON TROOPS, AND THE RISING OUT OF THE PALE

holding; Newcastle townland to Turlough Mac Alexander MacDonnell, formerly an O'More holding. In return, they paid rent and were each to personally maintain 9 or 12 'able galloglass on sayde Castel and land', as specified (Colla was to have 12, Maelmurry Mac Edmund and Turlough Mac Alexander, 9). They were also required to adopt the English language, dress and law as far as they reasonably could, and to maintain fords, bridges and 'pavements' or metalled roads on their properties. They also had to appear for muster before the Constable or Sheriff on 1 September annually with all their followers, aged 16 to 60, and deliver a book of their names and answer for their deeds in the year past. The upkeep of the captains' full battles, or companies, was laid upon Gaelic clans bordering the Pale.[119]

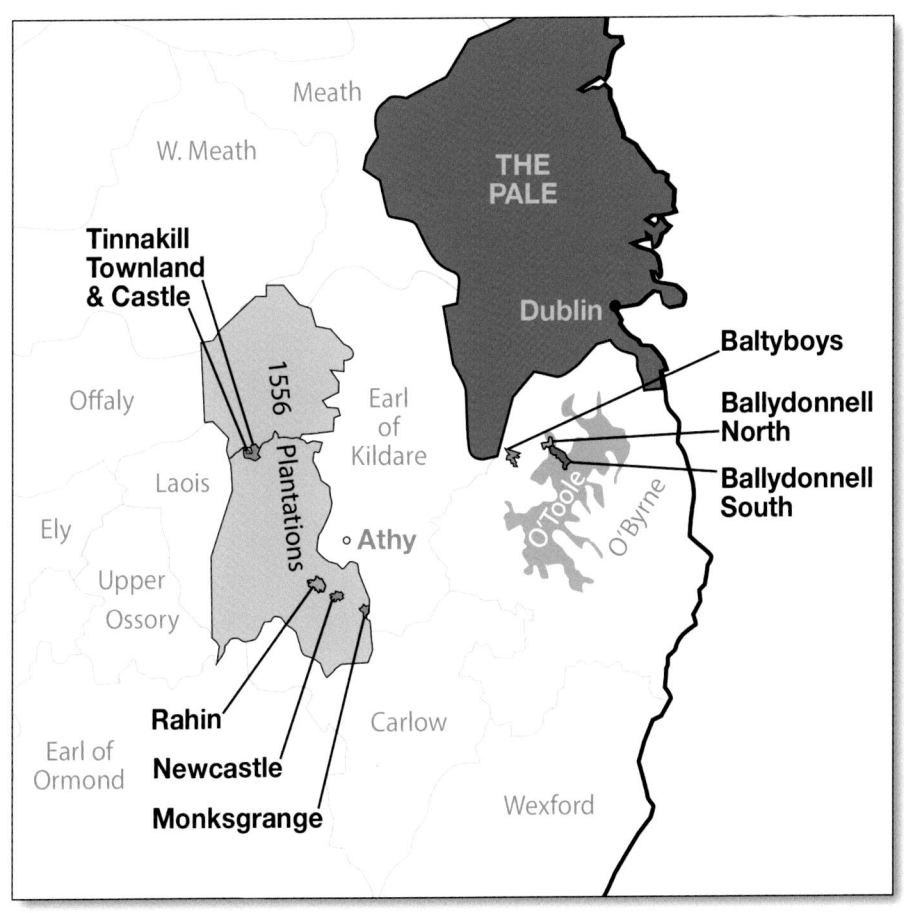

Land Holdings of the Clandonnell Galloglass

---

119 Fitzgerald, 'Macdonnells of Tinnakill', pp.205–207.

With the death of chief captain Donough MacOwen in 1561, a succession dispute arose between the captains of the three septs. This was resolved on 17 June, when Lord Lieutenant Sussex promulgated an Act of the Privy Council in Ireland abolishing 'the chiefe captenry of the three seiptes of galloglasses, but that they should all bee alike.'[120] Additionally, to avoid debate in the levying of bonnaght, the three captains would cast dice for each 'countrey', to decide which of them would get first, second or third choice. The districts in which the galloglass were to take their bonnaght are listed by Sussex in 1560 as:

Table 25. Bonnaght of Government Galloglass, 1560[121]

Irishmen that border on the Pale	Sparrs
O'Byrnes	120
Kavanaughs	120
Baron of Upper Ossory	80
O'Carroll	80
O'Meagher	40
O'Molloy	60
MacCoughlan	40
O'Melaghlin	60
Kellys	120
O'Madden	60
The Annaly	120
MacMahon	80
Magennis	80
Total:	**1,060**

As the marches of the English Pale were pushed out further, the MacDonnells were quartered upon these adjacent Irish clans to weaken them and maintain their submission. Each of the Irishmen bordering on the Pale listed above bore his quota of galloglass sparrs for only one-quarter of the year. Thus, the total reflects 265 sparrs circulating among these districts quarterly, indicating roughly 88 galloglass in each of the three battles. It is likely that there were 12 'dead pays' out of 100 men. This is close to the 87 men 'on their feet' in a battle of galloglass quoted in the 1575 report

---

120 J. T. Gilbert (ed.), *Manuscripts of Charles Haliday Esq. of Dublin, Acts of the Privy Council in Ireland, 1556–1572*, (London: Eyre and Spottiswoode,1897), pp.123 & 264.

121 *Calendar of the Carew Manuscripts*, vol. 1, 1515–1574, J .S. Brewrer and William Bullen eds (London: Longman & Co., 1867), p.303, 11 September, Earl of Sussex.

GOVERNOR'S RETINUES, GARRISON TROOPS, AND THE RISING OUT OF THE PALE

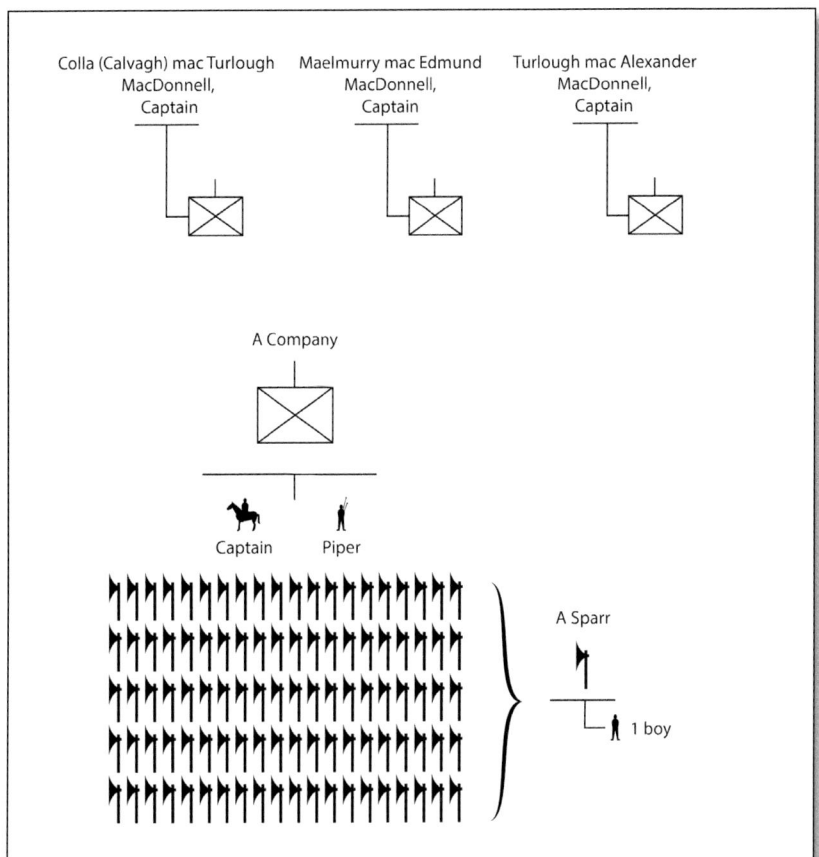

MacDonnell of Leinster organisation, *c.* 1560–80

on Ulster, discussed under the O'Neill Armies above. Nonetheless, officials usually spoke of 'three hundreth' sparrs of Clandonnell galloglass. In 1553, Thomas Cusack (governing as Lord Chancellor during the Lord Deputy's absence), wrote of his expedition to Ulster in support of Conn O'Neill's son, the Baron of Dungannon, during which he 'cessed in the country 300 galloglass', probably the three septs of the Leinster Clandonnells.[122] The *Acts of the Privy Council in Ireland* preserve the form used by the Lord Lieutenant the Earl of Sussex on 22 July 1560 to call up the Queen's Galloglass for service in Ulster against Shane O'Neill:

> Trustie and wellbeloved we grete you well : And wheare for the service of the Quenes Highness we have thought good at this present to entertayne three hundreth sparres of Her Majesties gallowglasses under your conducte for one quarter of a yere : we lett you witt that we have directed our severall mandates unto Obyrne and unto Omoloy and unto captaynes of the Analy to furnyshe you of your bonaght for the same accoordingly, the which mandates you shall receyve

---

122 *Cal. Carew Mss*, p.245, 8 May, Cusack to Northumberland.

'OF KERNS AND GALLOWGLASSES'

herewith to be delyvered unto them and therefore will and chardge you and every of you to assemble and prepare your saide numbre of sparres of gallowglasses and with all expedicion receyve your said bonaght appointed and furthewith be with them in readynes to Her Majesties service as you shall from us have comandement. Herof se you faill not in any wise.[123]

Queen Majesty's galloglass, from the Dublin City Charter, 1583 (Special Collections, The Catholic University of America, Washington, DC)

For the hosting of 1566, the agreement between the Lord Deputy and the galloglass captains required them to 'bring to the hill of Tarragh the 15th of August next three hundreth armyd men furnished for six weekes.'[124] For this hosting, each sept received an imprest of 300 marks, to be repaid by their bonnaght, and an imprest of 40 marks to hire 40 garrans. The Leinster Clandonnells were only allowed one boy per sparr as they utilised carriage horses like the rest of the hosting of the Pale.

A conference with the captains of the three septs of the Queen Majesty's Galloglass was held in Dublin in 1568, setting the wages to be paid in money and victuals. Galloglass taking bonnaght in Ulster, Munster and Leinster received wages of 5s 8d Irish per quarter year 'for every sparre (which maketh two men)'. They also received daily sustenance, half as 'diets in victuals' of bread corn and butter, and half in 'diets in money' amounting to 1d sterling per meal, which totalled 40s 6d Irish per quarter. The 'diets in victuals' due to each sparr per quarter were 122 bread-cakes and 366 quarts of butter, at a rate of three quarts of butter to each cake, and reckoning five quarts to a gallon.[125] If cessed for less than a full quarter, they drew only their wages and 'diets in money', with no 'diets in victuals'. Galloglass taking bonnaght in Connacht received wages of 7s Irish per quarter year (see Appendix II).[126]

---

123 J. T. Gilbert (ed.), *Manuscripts of Charles Haliday Esq. of Dublin, Acts of the Privy Council in Ireland, 1556–1572*, (London: Eyre and Spottiswoode, 1897), p.88.
124 *Manuscripts Haliday*, p.177.
125 Although this seems unusual it is as cited in 'Rate and Wages of the Galloglass'. See Appendix II
126 Richard Butler, (ed.), 'The Rate of the Wages of the Galloglas' in Richard Butler, Acquilla Smith and James Hardiman (eds), *Tracts Relating to Ireland*, vol. 2 (Dublin: M. H. Gill, 1843), pp.87–90

GOVERNOR'S RETINUES, GARRISON TROOPS, AND THE RISING OUT OF THE PALE

However, it proved difficult for the galloglass to collect their bonnaght from the Irishmen bordering the Pale, so that the Government often had to provide payment in lieu. Therefore, an Indenture of Composition was executed on 7 May 1578, commuting the bonnaght to a money payment made into the hands of the 'three cheefe Captaynes of the three septs of Clandonills, Her Majesty's galloglass': Hugh Boy Mac Callagh (Calvagh) MacDonnell of Tinnakill; Maelmurry Mac Edmund MacDonnell of Rahin; and Turlough Óg Mac Alexander MacDonnell of Wicklow. This took the form of a pension of £300, one-third for themselves, and the rest for their septs. They were to forgo all bonnaghts, sorens, and dead pays, and were to furnish 90 sparrs of galloglass as required, serving no one but the Queen, unless licensed by the Lord Deputy. They were to continue to perform the same duties as before, including 'approches and assaultes, and prepuracones of approaches and assaultes of castelles and ffortresses, all such officers and sapires, as by her Majestie's galloglass ought to be supplyed, executed and done.'[127]

The emphasis here on galloglass serving as sappers and assaulting castles is interesting. Sappers in eighteenth century European armies always carried a heavy axe, since these can be useful in breaking down doors and other defences. There are indications that galloglass served this purpose in sixteenth century Ireland. As late as January 1595, in the last days of the galloglass, Hugh Maguire laid close siege to Enniskillen Castle, employing 40 picked men dressed in mail and armed with axes to assault the castle. These were apparently galloglass, and they broke into the bawn (the outer wall) and forced the ward to retreat into the tower.[128] Not surprisingly, there is also evidence that the Queen Majesty's Galloglass may have been accompanied by pipers. The Fiants of Elizabeth record a pardon in 1573 for Hugh Boy Mac Calvagh MacDonnell's brothers, Alexander, Walter, Donough and Brian, as well as 66 others, among whom are two bagpipers – Alexander, piper, and Turlough, piper.[129]

With the outbreak of the second Desmond Rebellion in November 1579 the three chief captains mentioned above received a commission reading: 'By your indenture dated 7 May 1578, you have covenanted to serve with 90 spears of gallowglass.' They were now to assemble at Carrick-on-Suir to serve under the Earl of Ormond against the proclaimed traitors, the Earl of Desmond and his brothers.[130]

---

127 Erasmus Borrowes, 'Tennekille Castle, Portarlington and Glimpses of the MacDonnells' in *Ulster Journal of Archaeology*, vol. 2, (1854), p.38.
128 James O'Neill, 'Three Sieges, Two Massacres: Enniskillen at the Outbreak of the Nine Years' War, 1593–92' in *The Irish Sword: The Journal of the Military History Society of Ireland*, vol. 30, no. 121 (2016), pp.241–250.
129 Fitzgerald, 'Macdonnells of Tinnakill', p.210.
130 *Calendar of the Carew Manuscripts*, vol. 2, 1575–1588, J. S. Brewrer and William Bullen, eds (London: Longman & Co., 1867), p.168, 19 November, Deputy and Council.

'OF KERNS AND GALLOWGLASSES'

The Leinster Clandonnells remained faithful servants to the Crown until the end of Elizabeth's reign. From the start, galloglass in general had been noted for their long-term loyalty to their employers, which influenced their rivalries with other galloglass lineages as they spread across the country. The MacSweenys, for instance, having taken service initially with the Butler-aligned O'Donnells of Tyrconnell, continued to serve only with other families loyal to the Butler faction. The MacDonnells, on the other hand, first took service with the Kildare-aligned O'Neills of Tyrone, and continued to serve families that were loyal to the Kildare faction. And it was this Kildare connection which had brought the MacDonnells of Leinster into government service. However, despite the injunction to renounce their allegiance to the Papacy and to adopt the English language, dress and law, which came with their land grants in 1562, the Leinster Clandonnells retained a Gaelic cultural identity. Like other Gaelic chieftains, they sponsored Irish poets and produced a family *dunaire*, or book of bardic poems dedicated to the family (and paid for handsomely it must be said). Intermarriage with the O'Mores helps explain the Clandonnell's actions during the crisis of the 1590s, when most became rebels subject to Acts of Attainder. Only the Tinnakill sept retained its lands by 1603.

Part II

'The lord, the boy, the Galloglass, the kern' – Types of Irish Fighting Men

4

The Chieftain and his Military Role

In setting out the Irish military hierarchy, Stanihurst placed the horseman highest, 'next to the lord and captain', who occupied the loftiest position. By the sixteenth century, the former Irish regional kings were being referred to in government documents as 'captain of his nation' or 'captain of his surname.' But the Gaelic poets in their encomiums continued to espouse their patron's right to kingship and to refer to the inauguration ceremony as a 'King making' (*rígad*). The ceremony continued to be carried on outdoors, usually on a traditional mound (*tulach tinóil*) where the candidate stood on an inauguration stone, frequently receiving the white rod of lordship and having a single shoe thrown over his head or fastened on his foot. The gathered clan then repeatedly shouted the surname aloud, for example proclaiming the candidate 'O'Neill'.[1] In previous centuries, the assembly would have proclaimed the candidate 'king', but this evolution of kingship into lordship had actually been accompanied by increasing regional power over greater territorial units and the employment of larger and more professional military forces. And a primary kingly attribute that

---

1 Katherine Simms, *Gaelic Ulster in the Middle Ages* (Dublin: Four Courts Press, 2020), pp.233–235.

continued to be praised by the court poets throughout the sixteenth century was the chief's personal military prowess. Katherine Simms has shown that this imagery was functional, and was not merely a rehearsal of meaningless clichés.[2] She cites many instances of near suicidal personal bravery on the part of chieftains forcing 'the Gap of Danger' (*An Bearna Bhaoil*) upon their enemies.

It has been argued recently that the leaders of galloglass always led from the front, 'in sharp contrast to the cautious Irish lords …. getting their kerns and "hirelings" to do their fighting for them.'[3] In 1461, the *Annals of Connacht* describe the Irish chieftain Cairbre O'Connor leading the pursuit of his enemies, 'harassing their rear on horseback and performing deeds of prowess upon them with an axe belonging to one of his own foot soldiers.' Apparently, having lost his spear, he seized the axe out of the hands of one of his hired galloglass.[4] Similarly, in 1572, Sir Edward Fitton said his column narrowly escaped being attacked from ambush by Ulick Burke, who eagerly 'took a gallaglass axe in his hand, and said he would join with the gallaglass himself; but Hugh McSwine, their captain, answered he would take a better time, and so we saw them not.'[5] In fact, a chieftain's rise to lordship was traditionally dependent on his own fighting abilities, since he lived in a martial culture that required that he demonstrate his personal fighting prowess and skill at cattle raiding. An English official commented in 1515: 'Also, the sonne of eny of the said capytaines shalle not succede to his fader, withoute he be the strongeist of all his nation …. he that hathe the strongyst armye and hardeyst swerde among them, hath best right and tytill.'[6] As noted in the Introduction, it was in this sense that the Gaelic Irish poets, the *fili* whose ritualised panegyric verses granted legitimacy to a chieftain's rule, spoke of Ireland as 'sword land' (*fearann claíomh*). The ethos of personal combat among the chiefs lasted down to the end of Elizabeth's reign. In 1589, the State Papers recalled that Clanricarde, 'seeing Morogh ny Morth keeping the rereward of O'Rourke's men called to him, and desperately ran upon him, and a shot made upon him missed him, but he most valiantly ran the shot through.'[7] This heroic combat between champions remained a part of Irish warfare, as it had been at Knockdoe in 1504 when MacSweeney cried out for 'great Darcy' amidst the melee. Well known examples of later

---

2 Katherine Simms, 'Images of Warfare in Bardic Poetry' in *Celtica*, vol. 21 (1990), p.608.
3 Fergus Cannan, *Galloglass, 1250-1600: Gaelic Mercenary Warrior* (London: Opsrey, 2010), p.12.
4 Katherine Simms, 'Images of Galloglass in Poems to the MacSweeneys' in Seán Duffy (ed.), *The World of the Galloglass* (Dublin: Four Courts Press, 2007), p.117.
5 *Calendar of the Carew Manuscripts*, vol. 1, 1515–1574, J. S. Brewrer and William Bullen, eds (London: Longman & Co., 1867), p.420, 19 May, Fitton to Fitzwilliam.
6 *State Papers: Henry VIII*, p.5, n.d., State of Ireland, anon.
7 *Calendar of State Papers Ireland: Elizabeth*, vol. 4, 1588, August–1592, September, Hans Claude Hamilton ed. (London: Longman, 1885), p.185, 21 May, Mordant to Lord Deputy.

date are the mounted duel between Hugh O'Neill, the Earl of Tyrone, and Seagrave, the giant Palesman, at Clontibret in 1595, which ended with them grappling on the ground, and Hugh Maguire's impromptu fight with St Leger at Cork in 1600, which resulted in both their deaths.

The English official commenting in 1515 went on to note that the process for selecting a successor to the chieftainship often bypassed the chief's own son, settling instead on the senior heir, who was frequently the previous leader's brother. While seniority was honoured, the key to leadership was having the greatest number of clients and supporters within the kin group, as well as a strong arm. Along with the greater use of professional soldiery, it could be argued that this preference for age and experience in selecting a chief reflected a less active role, and in some cases this was indeed true. But the poets continued to idealise the active chieftain, guarding his borders through the night, sitting in the saddle at the ford while freezing rainwater ran down the spearshaft in his hand.

The Adoption of English Dress

In temporising with the increasingly intrusive Dublin government, the Irish chiefs came under strong pressure to adopt English dress. When submitting to the Crown's authority, they were not only presented with 'the robe and collar of essys' for appearances in Parliament, they were expected to change their everyday garments and 'go like an Englishman.' When overawed by the Government's power, they might 'come even to the Castle of Dublin, stripped of their Irishe weades, and appareled with English atteyre, craving the winge of Her Majesty's government to overshadow them.'[8] The process could be gradual, and as late as 1598, Magennis of Iveagh was commended because of his 'civility' and 'every festival day weareth English garments amongst his own followers.'[9] When Shane O'Neill presented himself before Elizabeth in London in January of 1562, his guard of galloglass made a vivid impression with their axes, saffron shirts and hairy mantles. But Shane himself was clad in English clothes, having delayed the trip for months because his clothing wasn't yet ready.

It became a sign of rebellion to reassume Irish dress. In 1573, The State Papers reported of Gerald, 15th Earl of Desmond, that: 'He and his wiefe put on Irish rayment and made proclamation that no deputie nor constable nor sheriff should practice their office in his country.'[10] When

---

8 *Calendar of State Papers Ireland: Elizabeth*, vol. 2, 1574–1585, Hans Claude Hamilton ed. (London: Longmans, Green, Reader and Dyer, 1867), p.cxxxv, 4 June, Archbishop Long to Walsingham.
9 Edmund Hogan, *The Description of Ireland in Anno 1598* (Dublin: H. M. Gill & Son, 1878), p.7.
10 Susan Flavin, *Consumption and Culture in Sixteenth century Ireland: Saffron, Stockings and Silk* (Woodbridge: Boydell & Brewer Ltd, 2014), p.117.

James FitzMaurice Fitzgerald was killed at Barrington Bridge in 1579, he was wearing an Irish saffron shirt. He had met with the Pope, and the Kings of France and Spain while in exile, but notwithstanding that he had been 'brought up in all civilitie, he was no sooner come home, but away with his English attires, and on with his brogs, his shirt, and other Irish rags.'[11] Similarly, in 1576, Lord Deputy Sydney said the sons of Clanricarde, the 'two beggarly bastard boys', John and Ulick, rebelled and cast off their English clothes, cutting them to pieces in sight of the garrison of Athlone, 'and put on their wonted Irish weede.'[12] Their father was the 2nd Earl of Clanricarde, Richard Sassenach ('the Anglicised') Burke. Not surprisingly, Richard's surviving tailor's bill, in the State Papers under 1578, features doublet and hose of satin 'cut, raised and laced', with doublets of 'yellow canvas pinkt' and green Venetian breeches with leather pockets and ash coloured hose for his sons.[13] The 1580 genealogy of the MacWilliam Burkes of Mayo depicts at least one family member in civil cap, doublet and trunk hose. But most of the figures are depicted attired in thoroughly Gaelic habergeons, pisane collars, and helmets of Lough Henny type. Likewise, the more Anglicised Clanricarde Burkes nonetheless rode in the native Irish style as late as 1589, when Ulick Burke, having become the 3rd Earl, was described as taking a fall on horseback and catching his spur in the fabric of his Irish 'pillion' saddle.

One exception to the pressurised adoption of 'civil' dress may be the O'Donnell lords of Tyrconnell. In the first half of the century, the remote O'Donnell lordship maintained close relations with the Scottish Crown, which was their foremost influence. But Hugh Dubh (d. 1537) travelled widely and spent time in Italy. His successor, Manus, sent diplomatic communications in 'a kingly style' to the Kings of France. Deputy St Leger was surprised in 1541 to see Manus O'Donnell clad like a renaissance prince in a coat of crimson velvet with aiguillettes of gold, a cloak of crimson satin guarded with black velvet, and a feathered bonnet, also 'set full of aggletts of gold.' He was accompanied by his advisers, 'five or six persons right honestly apparelled.'[14] His father, Hugh Dubh, had visited the King of Scotland in 1513, receiving on that occasion a satin gown lined with taffeta, a coat of furred russet, a doublet of cream satin, and scarlet hose lined with velvet.[15]

---

11 John Dymmock, 'A Treatice of Ireland' in *Tracts Relating to Ireland*, vol. 2 (Dublin: M. H. Gill, 1842), p.69.

12 Arthur Collins, *Letters and Memorials of State*, vol. 1 (London: T. Osborne, 1746), pp.119–20.

13 Daniel MacCarthy, 'My Lord Clanricarde's Tailor's Bill', *Journal of the Kilkenny and South-East of Ireland Archaeological Society*, vol. 1, new series (1858), pp.247–250.

14 Mac Eiteagáin, 'Renaissance Tír Chonaill', p.220.

15 Paul, James Balfour (ed.), *Accounts of the Lord High Treasurer of Scotland*, iv 1507-13 (Edinburgh: Her Majesty's General Register House, 1902), pp.434–434.

Armour of an Irish Chieftain

Early in the sixteenth century, some chieftains in closer proximity to the Pale wore a variant of the harness of the Anglo-Irish men-at-arms, described above. More typically, the Irish chieftain wore the same 'horseman's apparel' as any other Irish cavalryman (covered in the Chapter on the Irish Horseman). It would have consisted of a *cotún*, or padded aketon, worn under a habergeon of mail, with a pisane collar and a scull or bascinet. As late as 1593, Bishop Edmund MacGuaran was described by Richard Bingham in the State Papers as riding thus: 'One M'Gwaran who terms himself Primate, doth much mischief riding on his chief horse, with his staff and shirt of mail.'[16] This is a reminder that bishops, such as the infamous Miler Magrath, were often to be found occupying tower houses like secular lords. And they might ride in armour and take part in cattle raids, as in the example of John Purcell, the Bishop of Fernes, who was accused of joining in a cattle raid involving the robbery of 20 houses in 1537: 'the bp, who was on horseback, frequently called for fire, to burn the said houses.'[17] The discussion of the Irish horseman's armour mentions the gift of a scull made to Turlough Lynagh O'Neill in 1589 by the Lord Deputy. Like clothing, armour could be given to Irish chiefs to symbolically bind them in loyalty, much as the chiefs themselves did with their own followers. When Brian O'Neill, briefly Earl of Tyrone, was killed by Turlough Lynagh in 1562, the Government sought the return of a jack and shirt of mail they had given to him, the *Fitzwilliam Accounts* detailing 'Sondry extraordinary payments: George Garven and Thomas Bathe of Dundalk, merchants, for redeeming of a jacke and hebergine belonginge to therle of Tyrone which was given him by way of reward per warrantum datum primo Septembris, 1562, xvli.'[18]

The Irish chieftain pictured in John Derricke's *Image of Ireland*[19] wears an unusual helmet and armour that have never been satisfactorily explained.

Burke effigy, Glinsk, County Galway. A thoroughly Gaelicised Anglo-Irish clan, wearing the full panoply of the Gaelic elite, here with what appear to be splint protection on the forearms. (Journal of the Royal Society of Antiquaries of Ireland, Vol. 37 (1908) p.306)

---

16   *Calendar of State Papers Ireland: Elizabeth*, vol. 5, 1592, October–1596, June, Hans Claude Hamilton, ed. (London: Eyre and Spottiswoode, 1890), p.103, 6 June, Bingham to Burghley.
17   *Letters and Papers, Henry VIII*, vol. 12, pt. 2 (London: Eyre and Spottiswoode, 1891), p.313, 12 October, Presentments of jury at Wexford.
18   Longfield, *Fitzwilliam Accounts*, p.64
19   John Derricke, *The Image of Irelande, With a Discouerie of Woodkarne* (London:

They have been interpreted as a doublet and hat of English fashion, and are sometimes cited as evidence of the chiefs adopting elements of English clothing, even as their followers clung to traditional Irish dress. Derricke pictures this chieftain prominently in plates I, III and IV, without any accompanying written description. His helmet is of spangenhelm type, with a brow band and cross bands of iron, showing clear signs of rivets. These bands frame four panels that feature interwoven, cross-barred straps intersecting at right angles. At the apex of the skull, the cross bands are joined by a ring to which a crest is affixed. The crest in plate I resembles a fur pom-pom, while in plates III and IV, it has an upright, spreading appearance suggesting horsehair or possibly cock feathers.

The chieftain's body armour is a jacket tailored like a doublet, buttoning down the front with a high collar, shoulder wings, and a slightly flared skirt covering the hips. It is patterned like the helmet, with intersecting, cross-barred straps, each square of the fret possibly containing a rivet. By contrast, the Irish horsemen in plate IX wear shirts of mail, the same as the galloglass in the background. The helmet of Derricke's chieftain may well be the *cathbarr*, which appears to have been a peculiarly Irish helmet. It means 'top of battle', and was also a Gaelic personal name, as in Cathbarr O'Donnel, brother of the famous Red Hugh. It is described in an Irish text of 1419 (*Sid na mBan*) as a 'crested (*cír*), plated, four-edged helmet (*cathbarr*) of beautiful refined gold.'[20] The reference to four edges sounds like a cross-barred spangenhelm type helmet, and since such helmets appear in Derricke's *Image of Ireland* (1581), they have been equated with the *cathbarr*. Other evidence, including the references to gold and a crest, can be seen to support this identification.

While the chieftain's helmet is not specifically mentioned in Derricke's text, his 'Description of the Irishman, as well the Lordes, as of the galliglasse,' has them 'with sculles upon their poules, in stead of civill Cappes.'[21] And 'skull' is the term used to describe such an Irish helmet in *Beware the Cat* (1553) by William Baldwin[22]. Baldwin had knowledge of Ireland, and in the previous year had written plays for court such as 'An Irish Play of the State of Ireland.' In *Beware the Cat*, he describes Patrick Apore, 'a kern of John Butler' (though he is in fact an armoured horseman), returning home after a raid on Cahir MacArt Kavanaugh (d. 1554). 'When he was come home and had put of his harnes (which was a Corslet of maile made like a Shirt, and his Scul covered over with gilt lether and crested with Otterskin), all weary and hungry.'[23] The practice of covering a helmet with leather is not

---

John Daie, 1581).
20 Peter Harbison, 'Native Irish Arms and Armour in Medieval Gaelic Literature, 1170–1600' in *The Irish Sword*, vol. 12, no. 48 (1976), p.178.
21 Derricke, *The Image of Irelande*, p.49.
22 William Baldwin (William A. Ringler Jr. and Michael Flachman, eds) *Beware the Cat*, (San Marino: Huntington Library Press, 1988).
23 Baldwin, *Beware the Cat*, p.14.

widespread, but there is a reference to a bascinet belonging to King Philippe de Valois of France (reigned 1328–50) being covered with white leather (*Bacinet couvert de blanc cuir*).[24]

The fact that the crest was of otter skin has significance in Gaelic culture. In Roderic O'Flaherty's *West or H-Iar Connaught*,[25] his list of Ireland's native wildlife includes '... the amphibious otter, of which kind the white-faced otter is very rare. It is never killed, they say, but with loss of man or dog, and its skin is mighty precious.' A footnote adds: 'White-faced otter. – Called by the Irish *Dobhar-chu*.' Martin in his interesting description of the Western Islands of Scotland,[26] says that in the Isle of Skye, 'the hunters say there is a big otter above the ordinary size, with a white spot on its breast, and this they call the King of otters; it is rarely seen, and very hard to be killed. Seamen ascribe great virtue to the skin, for they say that it is fortunate in battle, and that victory is always on its side.' The helmet crest as depicted in Derricke's plate could be interpreted as a fur pom-pom, like that on the skull of the galloglass in the contemporary Charter of the city of Dublin, which is quite possibly by Derricke's own hand. In Derricke's other depictions of Irish horsemen's crests they seem to spread and flow, and are thus interpreted as horsehair, though Wilde thought they might in fact be cock feathers.

Derricke's chieftain prepares for a raid. (Creative Commons)

Nineteenth century writers thought Derricke's chieftain wore 'a leathern helmet, chequered with bars of iron,' rather like a seventh century Vendel helmet (e.g. Sir Walter Scott's reprint of *Image of Ireland*, in which in his commentary on Derricke's plate IV, on p. 127, he says 'having laid aside his leathern helmet, checkered with bars of iron, and his large broad sword'). However, by the sixteenth century, a skull would have had plates between the spangens. In light of William Baldwin's reference to gilt leather covering the skull of his Irishman, we may consider whether this cross-barring in fact represents a decoration of some sort, made in gilt leather, rather than interwoven iron bars. A contemporary Irish bardic poem, written for Cú Connacht Mág Uidhir (Lord of Fermanagh, 1566–1589) says:

The Maguires in the thick of battle are not people who should be tackled;
From your massed warriors there are many gold-lined helmets left without a wearer in the fight.

---

24 Joseph Strutt, *A Complete View of the Dress and Habits of the People of England* (London: Henry G. Bon, 1842), p.60.
25 Roderic O'Flaherty (James Hardiman ed.), *The Territory of West or H-Iar Connaught*, (Dublin: M. H. Gill, 1876).
26 Martin Martin, *Description of the Western Islands of Scotland* (London: Andrew Bell, 1703), p.159.

The words are: *feilm líneadh n-óir* – gold lined helmets. *Felim* is a loanword from the English 'helm'. The word *líne* is line, or linear ornamentation, and *líneach* means lined, ornamented, as in engraved. This could very well describe the skull of a *cathbarr* if it was covered over with tooled gilt leather.[27] As it happens, there was precisely such a cross-barred pattern used in gilt leather, and called *fretatus de auro*, meaning 'fretted with gold,' the term fret deriving from heraldry, where it designates an ornament of small slats intersecting each other at right angles, interlaced like a lattice. This pattern of decoration was noted by John Sobeiski Stuart in *Costume of the Clans*: 'Sandals of purple, fretted with gold 'fretatus de auro,' are mentioned among the parts of dress worn by King John; and the buskins of his son, Henry III, were checked with gold, and sprinkled with the lions of England.' Stuart continues, 'even those of the parish schoolmaster were carved 'like Paules windows,' (Chaucer's *Miller's Tale*) that is, "fretatus" or chequered, as far as he could in imitation of his superiors.'[28]

As with many luxury products imported by Gaelic Ireland in the sixteenth century – saffron, wine, sword blades – gilded leather was a product of Spain, traded by the vast fleets of Basque fishermen that paid annual visits to the southern and western coasts. In Spain painted or gilded embossed leather was called *guadamecil*. Cordovan was the centre of the art, and 'cordovan' or Spanish leather was famous throughout Europe, most prized being the scarlet leather dyed with kermes. This was particularly used by shoemakers, so much so that they became known in English as 'cordwainers'. Edmund Spencer refers to the Irish horseman as wearing 'riding shoes of costlie cordwaine.'[29] Shoes of such red leather are still to be seen worn by Sir Neil O'Neill as a part of traditional Irish dress in his portrait painted by Michael Wright in 1680, now in the Tate Gallery, London.

When preparing gilded leather, the smooth side of the cordovan leather was sized with glue, and a sheet of silver foil, beaten tissue-thin, was applied. Although referred to as gilded leather, no gold was used in the process. The golden colour was imparted by a 'changing' lacquer applied to the foil, the colouring agent of which was saffron. Polychrome decoration could then be applied in oils. Although manufactured in panels for wall hangings, it was put to other uses, notably in Japan, where armour and scabbards were covered with it. The Irish also seem to have used it for covering helmets and leather jacks. The 'pelles aurei' (i.e., golden or prepared skins) imported into early sixteenth century Ireland could possibly be a reflection of this trade.[30]

---

27 David Greene, *Duanaire Mheig Uidhir: The Poembook of Cú Connacht Mág Uidhir* (Dublin: Dublin Institute for Advanced Studies, 1972), p.11.

28 John Sobieski Stuart, *The Costume of the Clans* (Edinburgh: John Grant, 1892), p.51.

29 H. F. McClintock, *Old Irish and Highland Dress* (Dundalk: Dundalgan Press, 1943), p.59.

30 Ada K. Longfield, *Anglo-Irish Trade in the Sixteenth Century* (London: George Routledge & Sons, Ltd., 1929), p.71.

THE CHIEFTAIN AND HIS MILITARY ROLE

Spencer's character Irenaeus in *A View of the Present State of Ireland*[31] describes those parts of Irish dress that he would permit, as being suited to the conditions of the country:

> the leather quilted jack in journeying and in camping, for that it is fittest to be under his shirt of mail for any occasion of sudden service, as there happen many, and to cover his thin breech on horseback …. for the Quilted leather jacke is Old English; for it was the proper weed of the horsemen, as ye may read in Chaucer, where he describeth Sir Thopas his apparell and armoure, when he went to fight agaynst the Gyant in his robe of shecklaton, which shecklaton is that kind of gilden leather with which they use to embroider theyr Irish jackes.

Spencer's Irenaeus then recommends limits to the use of the jack:

> I would not have it laid away, but the abuse thereof to be put away, for being used to the end that it was framed, that is, to be worn under a shirt of mail, it is allowable, as also the shirt of mail and all his [the Irish horseman's] other furniture. But to be worn daily at home and in towns and civil places, it is a rude habit and most uncomely, seeming like a player's painted coat.

Derricke's chieftain sits down for a feast (Creative Commons)

Eudoxus notes the Irish footmen also wear a quilted jack, but Irenaeus finds it not unseemly:

> not as used in war, for it is then worn likewise of a footman under a shirt of mail, the which footman they call a galloglass.

When Sir Walter Scott republished Derricke's lost book in 1809, he equated the chieftain's jack to Spencer's 'shecklaton'. Scott's notes on plate IX say the chieftain's armour is the chequered quilted jacke, which the same poet [Spencer] likens to a player's painted coat.[32]

---

31 Edmund Spencer, *A View of the Present State of Ireland*, (1596), unpaginated, CELT, the Corpus of Electronic Texts. <https://celt.ucc.ie/published/E500000-001/>
32 Derricke, *The Image of Irelande*, p.138.

Spencer would return to this article of dress in the *Faerie Queen*,[33] describing the character Disdayne: 'But in a Jacket quilted richly rare, Vpon checklaton he was straungely dight.' This term 'checklaton' is reminiscent of the checked appearance of the *fretatus de auro* design for gilt leather described above, as well as the Irish term *feilm lineadh n-oir* for gold lined, or engraved, helmets. And we know from Baldwin's 1553 description that Partrick Apore's skull was covered with gilded leather and crested with otter skin. All of these seem likely contemporary descriptions of the kind of checked leather helmet and jack seen on Derricke's Irish chieftain. And they are seconded by the account of an anonymous Spaniard who probably accompanied James Fitzmaurice Fitzgerald's expedition to Ireland in 1579 and reported in Latin to the Vatican: 'The [Irish] nobility are clothed in garments made of skin and adorned with various colours.'[34] This puts one in mind of Spencer's description of the Irish quilted leather jack being 'like a player's [actor's] painted coat.' A 'Gilt lether cot' is listed in *Henslowe's Diary* among horsemen's coats and cloaks in an inventory of the Lord Admiral's Men, *c.* 1600.[35] Extensive searching in Elizabethan theatre sources has not revealed any image of the gilt leather coat in the Lord Admiral's Men inventory, but as it was listed among horsemen's coats, it would have been longer than a doublet, perhaps like the 'coats' of Sir Henry Sidney's trumpeters in Derricke's prints.

O'Cleary's *Life of Hugh Roe O'Donnell*[36] describes Hugh's brother Manus as wearing an armour of skins, when during a fight at Lifford in 1600, the traitor Nial Garve O'Donnell gave him a thrust of a long lance under the shoulder blade, piercing the armour and wounding him mortally. O'Cleary distinguishes this from Nial Garve's coat of mail, on which he was struck three times on this occasion.[37] So a leather jack could be worn alone, without mail covering it, as we see in Derricke. In fact one would think a quilted leather jack embroidered with gilt leather would be rubbed and damaged by having mail worn over it. We do have other references to leather jackets worn by Irishmen without any suggestion of armour. In September 1581, MacCarthy Mor and Lord Morrys were described at Dublin: '. . . the best robe or garment that they wore, was a russet Irish mantle, worth about a Crown apiece, and they had ech of them a hatt, a lether jerken, a payre of hosen, which they call trowes, and a pair of brogues, but all not worth a noble that eyther of them had.'[38] And from the first half of the seventeenth century, *Parliament Chloinne Tomáis* describing Gaelic peasants says 'your

---

33   Edmund Spencer, The Faerie Queene (London: William Ponsonbie 1590), book vi, canto vii.
34   Maxwell, *Irish History*, p.320.
35   Robert I. Lublin, 'Costuming the Shakespearean Stage', Unpublished PhD Thesis, Ohio State University, 2003
36   Lughaid O'Clery (Paul Walsh ed.), *Beatha Aodh Ruadh Uí Domhnaill (The Life of Hugh Roe O'Donnell)*, (Dublin: Irish Texts Society, 1948)
37   O'Clery, *Beatha Aodh Ruadh*, pp.271 & 273.
38   McClintock, *Old Irish and Highland Dress*, p.65.

leather coats, your thick bottomed birredhs with crooked ear-pieces, . . . and your stinking trews with flap flies' (*bhur gcótuidhe croicinn, agus bhur mbiorraéid bhunramhra chluaschama, . . . agas bhur dtrúisa lobtha lapa.*)³⁹

It seems Derricke's jack and chieftain helmet are defences being worn in both civil (the feast) and martial (the raid) activities, as Spencer complained of. The chieftain's skull is covered with gilt leather as described by Baldwin in 1553, and this same gilt leather decorates his jack, as Spencer described in 1596, after 15 years' experience in the country. The Gaelic Irish chieftain class seem to have adopted a leather upper garment in the mid- to-late sixteenth century, tailored in an interpretation of English fashion. It is variously described as a 'lether jerkin', 'garments of skin adorned with various colours', or 'a quilted leather jack .... like a player's painted coat.' The garment described by these writers, and depicted by Derricke, was worn in peace and war. It had defensive properties, but would not have been unduly heavy. We nowadays think of a jerkin as being without sleeves, but this was not necessarily the case in the sixteenth century. Also, jack began to be applied occasionally to non-defensive garments, as in 'jackett' – i.e., initially meaning an abbreviated jack. What we are still missing is any English or Continental analogy. Once again, the Irish seem to have been unique in this regard.

Household of an Irish Chieftain

The Gaelic chieftain lived in a close and informal relationship with his immediate followers, and there seems to have been a genuine affection among the common folk for the ancient ruling families. In stark contrast to the fate of the Anglo-Irish Earl of Desmond, when Hugh O'Neill was reduced to skulking in Glenconkeyne woods after Kinsale, it never occurred to his Gaelic followers to claim the price on his head. Even after the defeat, when Con O' Neill of Clannaboy returned home after obtaining a pardon, his people turned out in large numbers to welcome him, mostly on foot but with the better-off riding horses with 'pannels', or straw saddles. They greeted him with a homage of 'beeves, colpaghs [two-year-old heifers or bullocks], sheep, hens, bonnyclabber, graddan-meal-strowans [oat cakes]; with snush [marrow] and bolean [soft cheese] as much as they could get to regale him.'⁴⁰

These cultural attitudes were long-standing. In 1394, Froissart records how four Gaelic Irish Kings were brought to conformity by the steward when making their submissions at Dublin:

---

39 N.J.A. Williams, (ed.), *Parlement Chloinne Tomáis* (Dublin: Dublin Institute for Advanced Studies, 1981), p.74.
40 A. T. Lucas, 'A Hay-rope Pack-saddle from County Louth', *Journal of the County Louth Archaeological Society*, vol. 15, no. 1 (1961), pp.13–16.

> When these kings were seated at table, and the first dish was served, they would make their minstrels and principal servants sit beside them, and eat from their plates and drink from their cups. They told me, this was a praiseworthy custom of their country, where everything was in common but the bed. I permitted this to be done for three days; but on the fourth I ordered the tables to be laid out and covered properly, placing the four kings at an upper table, the minstrels at another below, and the servants lower still. They looked at each other, and refused to eat, saying I had deprived them of their old custom in which they had been brought up.[41]

Nonetheless, the remaining Gaelic gentry continued to mix freely with their servants three hundred years later, when in 1681 Thomas Dineley wrote: 'They are at this day much addicted (on holidayes after the bagpipe, Irish harpe, or Jews harpe) to dance after their countrey fashion the long dance one after another of all conditions master, mrs, servants.'[42] A Gaelic 'Big House' culture clung on precariously through the eighteenth century in very remote places like the O'Connell's house at Derrynane. In *Hidden Ireland*, Daniel Corkery credited the exposure to poetry and music afforded the large staff of hangers-on in these rustic halls with having elevated the state of poetry among the Munster peasantry. Until his death in 1726, Munster poet Aodhagán Ó Rathaille composed bardic poems praising the Big Houses of Munster's fading Gaelic aristocracy, poems whose tropes – swords being whetted, chess played, poets paid, harps, mead – were highly traditional and aristocratic. Whatever one thinks of Corkery's thesis, it is an undisputed fact that Ó Rathaille's poems remained on the lips of 'illiterate' Kerry farmers into the twentieth century.[43]

In 1594, at the very outset of the Nine Years' War, an interesting collection of customs of the Gaelic Irish was gathered by Meredith Hanmer, Chaplain to the Earl of Ormond, and Treasurer of Christ's Church, Dublin. He gives an interesting and unique list of the members of an Irish chief's household, stating what portion each of them received when a cow or sheep was slaughtered.[44] The idea that sixteenth century Irish Gaelic society provides a 'window on the Iron Age', like a bee preserved in amber, is discredited, but it must be admitted that Hanmer's list preserves an archaic practice and is reminiscent of the 'champion's portion' in the tales of the heroic cycles, and the semi-fabulous seating arrangements recorded for the great hall of ancient Tara. In eighteenth century Big Houses, a sheep was killed every

---

41 Simms, Katherine, 'The Barefoot Kings: Literary Image and Realty in Later Medieval Ireland', *Proceedings of the Harvard Celtic Colloquium*, vol. 30 (2010), p.6.
42 Evelyn Philips Shirley, 'Extracts from the Journal of Thomas Dinely', *Journal of the Royal Society of Antiquaries of Ireland*, ser. 2, vol. I (1856), p.182.
43 Corkery, *Fortunes Irish Language*, pp.42–67.
44 Herbert Hore, 'Gaelic Domestics', *Ulster Journal of Archaeology*, 1st. ver., vol. 3 (1855), pp.117–126.

THE CHIEFTAIN AND HIS MILITARY ROLE

week, and a bullock once a month. A cow was reckoned to feed 40 people. Hanmer says it was divided as follows:

> Cow – The head, tong, and feet to the smith. Neck, to the butcher. 2 small ribbs, that goe with the hind quarters, to the Taylor. Kidneys, to the physitian. Marybones to the dony-lader. Udder, to the harper. Liver, to the carpenter. A peece to the garran-keper. [*gearrán*, packhorse] Next bone, from the knee to the shoulder, to the horse-boy. Choise pece of the beef to the Shott. The hart, to the cow-heard. Next choise pece to the housewif of the house. The third choic to the nurse. Tallow, for candles. Hide, for wyne and aquavitae. Black poodings for the plowman. Bigge poodings for the wever. Kylantony [Kyl-Anthony?], the a–e pooding, to the porter. Dowleagh, a brode long pece, lying upon the gutts, to the calf-keper. Sweete-bred, to hor that is with child. Rump, to him that cutts the beef. [i.e., the Chief]. Tripes to the kater. The drawer of water hath the great bigg poding.
> Mutton – Head, the horse boy. Neck, the garran-keeper. Lyver, the carpenter. Sholder, to the astronomer. Bag pooding, for the man that brings water. The hart and the feet for the shepherd. Skyne, for the cook.

Not surprisingly, this all mirrors Highland practice, recorded by Dr Johnson at the end of the eighteenth century during his tour of the Hebrides, where he noted that when a cow was killed for the house, individual parts were earmarked for particular workmen, such as the smith, who received the head, and the piper, who received the udder. The smith was a non-producer of food with semi-magical powers, and he was entitled to a tribute of first fruits – the heads of slain beasts were his perquisite. The 'nurse' was not a wet nurse, but a woman who tended the sick and wounded. 'Astronomer' indicates the 'physitian', who used astrology in his practice. The horseboy is discussed in a separate chapter. 'Him that cutts the beef,' and receives the choice rump, is no doubt the lord himself.

The dony-lader (*duine laidir*) literally 'strong man', was probably the lord's galloglass, or *gallóglach tighearna*. He is discussed in the chapter on Galloglass. The porter had a significant role, with quarters just inside the castle door where he kept watch. The shot constituted the ward of the castle, having replaced the galloglass in this role during the course of the century. The cator, or caterer, was a professional thief on foot, retained to plunder the Queen's true subjects, and there are many references to the chiefs' caterers in the official records. Most beef eaten in the houses of Irishmen bordering on the Pale was supposedly obtained this way.

Finally, although he is missing from Hanmer's list, note should be made of the chief's 'knowne messenger.' In the famous woodcut, Derricke's messenger Donole O'Brean delivers his chief's message of defiance, folded and closed with a wax seal, to Lord Deputy Sidney with the word 'shogh' (*seo* or 'here' in Irish, informal bordering on rude in this context). His spear with a knarled staff resembles some seen in fourteenth century French illuminations of hunting scenes. The Irish chief's messenger is noted in the account of the Dublin apothecary Thomas Smyth in 1561. Smyth, noting the division of spoil after a cattle raid, says: 'And the messingers that goithe of their errants cleamith the gottes [guts] for their parcell; – bycause it is an aunscient custome they will not break it.' Herbert Hore, who published Smyth's writings in 1855, commented: 'The Messenger' mentioned by the writer, performed so active and useful a part in old Gaelic social life, that his services seem but meagrely rewarded by the offal which all records agree was his share of a feast. Captain Rich, who was quartered at Coleraine, and printed his quaint *Description of Ireland* in 1610, observed that 'every great man of the country hath his rymer, his harper, an his knowne messenger, to run about the country with his letters.' The Gaelic names for one of these couriers were *eaclach*, and *gilli-cosh*. The latter word signifies 'lad of the foot.'[45] The proverbial footmanship of the Irish is examined in the chapter below on the horseboy.

---

45 Herbert Hore, 'Irish Bardism in 1561', *Ulster Journal of Archaeology*, 1st. ver., vol. 6 (1858), pp.165–167.

5

The Horseman, or *Marcach*

Fynes Moryson noted of the Irish cavalry, 'Their horsemen are all gentlemen (I mean of great septs or names, how base soever otherwise).'[1] Cavalry were thus the least numerous portion of an Irish army, making up between 10 and 15 percent of the total. This was also due to the unsuitableness of much of the country for mounted warfare. Those districts with fewer woods and bogs are often found providing larger numbers of horsemen. Thus, the O'Dogherty's of the barren Inishowen peninsula furnished the bulk of O'Donnell's horsemen, and the O'Reillys of sparsely wooded Cavan were famous for maintaining large numbers of horsemen.

The Irish horseman, being commonly 'a gentleman born' (*duine uasal*), is listed highest in Stanihurst's enumeration of Irish troop types, being 'the chiefest next the lord and captain.' Interestingly, he adds: 'These horsemen when they haue no stay of their own, gad and range from house to house like arrant knights of the round table, and they neuer dismount vntill they ride into the hall, and as far as the table,' indicating that some horsemen at least on occasion might be landless, and available to serve any lord.[2] However, in a smaller sized Irish lordship, the horse host (*marcsluagh*) was generally made up entirely of the chief's sons and other close kinsmen. Thus, we read of the chief of Clandeboye, who has 'eight tall gentlemen to his sons and all they cannot make past 24 horsemen.'[3] In the High Medieval period, larger Irish lordships had often included 'household families' (*lucht tige*), whose lands were exempt from ordinary taxation, but whose occupants owed service as the lord's horsemen. By the Tudor era, the *lucht tige* had become more of a land designation, and had often lost its connection to particular duties. But in the O'Neill lordship of Tyrone, certain old *lucht tige* families,

---

1   C. Litton Falkiner, *Illustrations of Irish History* (London: Longmans, Green, and Co., 1904), p.284.
2   Raphael Holinshed, *Holinshed's Irish Chronicle, 1577*, eds Liam Miller and Eileen Power (Dublin: Dolmen Press, 1979), p.114.
3   Katherine Simms, 'Warfare in the Medieval Gaelic Lordships', *The Irish Sword*, vol.12 (1975), p.105.

notably the O'Donnellys, continued to be known as 'O'Neill's horsemen', and served as such to the end of Elizabeth's reign.

Origins: The Hobelar?

In recent years, the distinctive Gaelic Irish light horse of the sixteenth century have often been referred to loosely as hobelars. This is not entirely correct, as the hobelar was a type of Anglo-Irish cavalryman that enjoyed a relatively brief existence in the earlier fourteenth century. References to them largely cease after 1350, though the 1366 Statutes of Kilkenny limit the demands made by 'Soldier Hobler, or Kernagh.'

At the turn of the fourteenth century, the Anglo-Irish lords had provided support for the Scottish wars of Edward I, including the light horsemen known as hobelars. These excelled in skirmishing and reconnaissance, and we read of Robert le Brut, 'an Irish hobelur . . . retained to spy the passings and haunts of the enemy by night and day.'[4] It is assumed that the hobelar had developed to meet Irish conditions and may have been influenced by Gaelic Irish practice.

The origin of the term hobelar is disputed, some claiming it derives from the Irish *obann*, meaning swift, while others cite the French term *hobeler*, to skirmish. The name hobby certainly was applied to the distinctive Irish horse ridden by these cavalrymen, a breed examined in more detail below.

Hobelars, even in small numbers, were in great demand for campaigns against the elusive and mobile Scots, and came to be imitated by horsemen raised in England. These, however, lacked the small, fast ponies that gave the Anglo-Irish hobelar his advantage. The English hobelar's equipment is specified as a haqueton, hauberk, and bascinet, with a sword, long knife and lance for offensive arms. They were particularly distinguished by riding *discoopertus* (unarmoured) ponies. All of this presumably reflects the Anglo-Irish original, and certainly matches the equipment of the Tudor era Gaelic Irish horsemen. After his brief heyday, by the mid-fourteenth century the hobelar had been superseded at home and abroad by the mounted archer who would characterise English forces for the next two hundred years.

This entire narrative of the hobelar's history was disputed recently by Robert Jones, who assigns to him a Welsh origin.[5] However, Jones' suggestion that the hobby ridden by his Welsh-derived Irish hobelar was not much different from any other mount is simply not true, as will be seen below when examining the significance of that breed. Likewise, his assertion that there is little evidence of cavalry being used by the Irish

---

4   James F. Lydon, 'The Hobelar: An Irish Contribution to Medieval Warfare', *Irish Sword*, vol. 2 no. 5 (1954), pp.12–16.
5   Robert Jones, 'Re-Thinking the origins of the 'Irish' hobelar', *Cardiff Historical Papers*, vol. 1 (2008), pp.1–20

until after the Anglo-Norman invasion needs qualification. Irish cavalry (*marcsluagh*) is mentioned as early as the ninth century, and appears with increasing frequency from the eleventh century onwards.[6] It is true that, as in Tudor times, the earlier medieval Irish cavalry did not play a notable part in pitched battles, and was not very numerous. It is thought they may have been largely unarmoured, and thus, the suggestion that the armoured native Irish horseman of the later Middle Ages and Tudor era reflects the influence of Anglo-Norman military culture is not unreasonable. As mentioned the equipment of the Tudor Irish horseman matches perfectly that of the English-raised hobelars of the fourteenth century, but it would probably be more correct to refer to him as a horseman (*marcach*), as his contemporaries did.

In fact, the closest foreign parallel to the Gaelic Irish horseman is the Spanish *jinete*. Like his Irish counterpart, the *jinete* operated in underpopulated and difficult terrain, conducting a low-intensity warfare of fast moving raids. Fighting *à la jineta* involved the use of 'Morrish tactics'; the feigned charge, followed by a false retreat to induce pursuit, doubling back upon the pursuer if he became disordered by the terrain. Ramón de Perilhos had noticed the similarity as early as 1397, saying of the Irish horsemen, 'their manner of warring is like that of the Saracens, and they shout in the same way.'[7] Like the Irishman, after casting his initial dart, the *jinete* turned his horse tightly, falling back to take up a second dart, with the shield habitually worn on his back providing protection in this manoeuvre. This demanded a particular style of horsemanship and the use of light, nimble horses. Interestingly, the Spanish *jinete* breed of horse was an ambler, like the Irish hobby. Unlike the hobelar, the Irish horseman and *jinete* were skilled in the use of what Froissart called the *darde enpenné*, or feathered dart. Along with a lance, a handful of darts were carried, and more could be provided by attendants on foot. According to the military Ordinances of Juan I, by 1385 a *jinete* was armed with a lance, two or three darts, a shield, habergeon, aketon, bascinet, sword and knife, mirroring the armament of the contemporary Irish horseman. Half of the Spanish mounted forces would remain '*jinetes*' until *c.* 1550.[8]

The Horseman's 'Feat of War'

Perhaps no part of the Tudor Irish armies has been subject to as much criticism as the cavalry. In particular, their lack of stirrups and a conventional saddle are faulted for leaving them unable to engage more heavily armoured

---

6   Andrew Halpin, *Weapons and Warfare in Viking and Medieval Dublin*, Medieval Dublin Excavations 1962–81, ser. B, vol. 9 (Dublin: National Museum of Ireland, 2008), p.12.
7   Simms, 'Warfare', p.105.
8   Arnold Blumberg, 'The Jinete' in *Medieval Warfare*, vol. 3, no. 1 (2013), pp.18–21.

horsemen using deep war saddles and couched lances. The Irish cavalry shoulder much of the blame for the defeat at Kinsale in 1601, where they avoided the charge of the English horse by fleeing headlong through the ranks of their own foot. The insinuation is that their persistence in using a pad saddle without stirrups was simply a perverse backwardness. Typical of such comments is Barnaby Rich, who wrote:

> The Horse-men of *Ireland*; againe, are not fit to serue in the time of fight, neither against Horse nor foote, vntill it doth come to a flat running retraite, and then in a chace they are good for execution . . . The reason is, by defect of their appointment, for they are armed with a Skull, a Shirt of Maile, and a Staffe, which as they vse to cary, is of no seruice, but for execution in a chace: and their Horse likewise, being as slightly furnished with a Padde, wherein the Rider hauing neither Stirrops nor stay, no otherwise then if he shoud sit on the bare Horse backe, is therefore quickly vnhorsed and easely ouerthrowne.[9]

However, Gerald of Wales, the chronicler of the Anglo-Norman invasion of Ireland in 1171, was quite specific about the fighting conditions there, and how they differed from those in France. It is clear that little of what Gerald describes had changed between his own time and the Tudor era. In Ireland's rough, wooded country, Gerald says heavy armour was an embarrassment, and fights were won through mobility, not by making a firm stand. Thus, he says, 'when the fighting takes place only within a restricted space, or over wooded or boggy ground, where there is scope for foot soldiers rather than horsemen, light armour is far superior.' Gerald noted that much of the fighting in Ireland was against light armed foot, and was lost or won at the first encounter:

> In that situation it is inevitable that an enemy who is mobile and in retreat over confined or difficult terrain can only be routed by an equally mobile force pressing hard on them, and only lightly armed. For owing to the weight of that armour with its many layers, and saddles which are high and curved back, men have difficulty in dismounting, even more difficulty in mounting, and find advancing on foot, when the need arises, most difficult of all.[10]

Ease of mounting and dismounting, and occasionally opting to fight on foot were all features of the Gaelic Irish horseman's 'feat of war'. In a

---

9   Barnaby Rich, *A New Description of Ireland*, 1610, (Early English Books Online Text Creation Partnership, 2011) <http://name.umdl.umich.edu/A10713.0001.001>

10   Gerald of Wales (A.B. Scott and F.X. Martin, trans.), *Expugnatio Hibernica*, (Dublin: Royal Irish Academy, 1978), pp.246–7.

THE HORSEMAN, OR *MARCACH*

formal battle, the aristocratic Irish horse appear to have drawn up on one or the other flank of the army. Hayes-McCoy points out that, apart from any tactical considerations, this allowed them to engage with their social equals, the opposing horsemen. Clanrickard's cavalry at Knockdoe in 1504 were drawn up on the left, which is also where Derricke's woodcut of a battle places them. In the picture map of the Battle of the Erne Fords in 1593, the cavalry are on the right flank of Maguire's force, and this is where Sussex placed them when he approached Limerick in battle array in 1558 with 'all the Irish horsemen on the right wing.'[11] In these illustrations they are drawn up in what appear to be columns of five, and in the illustration of the Erne Fords there is a rectangular banner in their midst, apparently bearing a cross pattée. 'Banner' is used as a synonym for a troop of horse in the Irish annals, and likewise appears, for instance, as 'MacCostello's standard of horse' in government documents such as the *Composition Book of Connaught* of 1585. In 1520, the Earl of Desmond's horsemen were described as '24 banners of horsmen, which be 20 under every baner, at the leest; and under some, 30, 40, and 50.'[12] Nonetheless, at the end of the century, Fynes Moryson said dismissively that the Irish horsemen 'are more fit to make a bravado and offer light skirmishes than for a sound encounter …. They assail not in a joint body but scattered, and are cruel executioners upon flying enemies.'[13] In the far more typical raiding warfare, the noble Irish horsemen scouted ahead when entering the enemy's territory. While the kern burnt houses and rounded up cattle, the horsemen were expected to do most of the actual fighting. And when returning from the raid guarding a 'prey', or *creach*, of cattle, or when defending their own people and herds fleeing from an enemy attack, the horsemen would form the rearguard. This was the post of

Irish horseman, sixteenth century. Note the prominent upturned nasal, and *cotún* worn without mail. From Glenarm Abbey, County Antrim. (Author's drawing)

---

11 G. A. Hayes-McCoy, *Irish Battles: A Military History of Ireland* (Dublin: Gill and Macmillan, 1980), p.82 ;Cal. Carew Mss, p.275, 25 July , Sussex's Journey, anon.
12 *State Papers: Henry VIII*, p.46, 25 September, State of Ireland., Lord Lieutenant to Henry VIII.
13 Falkiner, *Illustrations Irish History*, p.287.

honour, occupied by the chief and his close kinsmen, in which they fulfilled their role of protecting the common folk and foot soldiers.[14]

Thus, most warfare in Ireland took the form of flight and pursuit, with the horsemen being heavily involved and generally remaining mounted. However, cavalry played little role in the relatively rare linear battle. Quite apart from tactical considerations, horses were valuable and the riders might not be inclined to risk them to a shock encounter. At the great set-piece battle of the earlier Tudor era, Knockdoe in 1504, Ulick Burke's cavalry completely avoided the melee of axemen and billmen, sweeping instead around the enemy's right flank to raid the baggage train. And there is no reference to horsemen at all in the several accounts of night battles. Indeed, Irish horsemen, both Gaelic Irish and Anglo-Irish, are often described as dismounting for a standing fight, in the manner of the medieval English men-at-arms. For instance, the fourteenth century *Triumphs of Turlough* says of the Irish horsemen before battle, 'they required their crimson-broidered actons, bright mail, flashing blades and far-reaching spears; as they handed over to their horseboys their horses to lead them to the rear, pursuant to their resolve that never would they desert their chief.'[15] Similarly, in 1522, in a bitter war with O'Neill, 'O'Donnell, having arrayed and marshalled, excited and earnestly exhorted his small army, commanded them to abandon their horses, for they had no desire to escape from the field of battle unless they should be victors,' meaning that if they were beaten, they had no desire for horses on which to flee, a measure of resolve, perhaps. However, it may have been as much a tactical choice.[16] At the Battle of Shrule in 1570, the *Annals of the Four Masters* says of MacWilliam Burke and his allies: 'They resolved first to convert their cavalry into infantry, and having done so, they formed into order and array.'[17] In 1581, the State Papers add a further instance among the Baltinglass rebels in Leinster: 'The gentlemen among the traitors [i.e. the horsemen] left their horses, encountered our men on foot, and charged them even unto the pikes.'[18] Likewise, at the Battle of the Curlew Mountains in 1599, Hugh O'Donnell deployed his horsemen as infantry: 'The place was not one suitable for deploying or fast riding, so he made foot soldiers of his cavalry in the midst of his warriors.'[19] As late as 1600, when the Earl of Tyrone's shot were skirmishing with the English in close country, an English officer reported: 'We saw many of them killed, and

---

14 Katherine Simms, *Gaelic Ulster in the Middle Ages* (Dublin: Four Courts Press, 2020), p.426.
15 Standish Hayes O'Grady (ed.), *Caithréim Thoirdhealbhaigh, The Triumphs of Turlough*, 2 vols (London: Irish Texts Society, 26, 27, 1929), p.40.
16 John O'Donovan (ed.), *Annals of the Kingdom of Ireland, by the Four Masters*, vol. 5, (Dublin: Hodges, Smith & Co., 1856), p.1357.
17 O'Donovan, *Annals of Ireland*, p.1645.
18 *Calendar of State Papers Ireland: Elizabeth*, vol. 2, 1574–1585, Hans Claude Hamilton ed., (London: Longmans, Green, Reader and Dyer, 1867), p.299, 21 April, Briskett to Walsingham.
19 O'Clery, *Beatha Aodh Ruadh*, p.227.

after understood they lost a great number, whereof many were horsemen, of the best sort, that had lighted to incourage their men to fight.'[20]

An veteran of 30 years' service in Ireland, Captain Nicholas Dawtrey, described the defensive strategies of an Irish lordship, including the horsemen's role. He said that while the Irish kern were footmen, 'yett they serue chiefly with the horsemen.' This was because, while hired soldiers were paid by the chiefs, this was not true of 'the horsemen and kernes, who are the riseings out of the Country as they term them. The reason is, that all the horsemen are gentlemen of the best ability in the Country, and all the kernes are ther servants, and do waite upon ther Maisters a foote, being men so well breathed, as wheresoeuer ther Maisters ride they followe at hand with them.'[21] John Hooker had claimed the second degree of Irish soldier after the horseman, who was a 'gentleman born', was the 'kernaugh, & he also is a gentleman or a freeholder borne, but not of ability to mainteine a horse.'[22] Dawtrey says the cavalry and kern, together, 'do always lie where their *creaghts* [cattle herds and drovers] feed …. because the horsemen may be ready to entertain the enemies, if any sudden force should break in amongst them.'[23] This close relationship between the noble horsemen, their kern and the wealthier cattle owners of the *creaghts* is made clearer by understanding that 'the herdsmen amongst the Irish which keepe their cowes, their stod meares their swine and sheepe, are altogether most commonly of the best bloud and discent amongst them.'[24] When so great a lord as Hugh O'Neill seized a sudden opportunity to flee the country in 1607, he had to leave his son Conn behind as the child was in the mountains with the *creaghts* and could not be located.

Regarding the outposts maintained on a lordship's borders, Captain Dawtrey says that while hired foot soldiers man the watch in woods and bogs, the watches at 'dashes or fords' are always horse-patrols, or *marcsluag cuartagti*. Probably these operated in pairs, like the 'ii horsemen of Tyrone's' seen patrolling along the Blackwater River in 1601.[25] Furthermore, Dawtrey says these watches maintain scouts at least 8 or 10 miles distant from the *creaghts*, with a standing every quarter of a mile along each passage leading inwards towards the camp. He says that upon any discovery of an

---

20   Fynes Moryson, (Litton Falkiner ed.), *Itinerary*, vol. 2, *The Rebellion in Ireland, AD 1600*, (London: J. Beale, 1907), p.338.
21   Hiram Morgan (ed.), 'A Boke of Questions and Answars', *Analecta Hibernia*, no. 36 (1995), pp.90–1.
22   Raphael Holinshed, *Holinshed's Chronicle, 1587*, vol. 6 (Abingdon: Routledge, 1965), p.132.
23   Morgan, *A Boke*, p.95.
24   Hiram Morgan and Kennith Nicholls (eds), 'Discourse of the Mere Irish of Ireland', anon., CELT, the Corpus of Electronic Texts, p.29.
      <https://celt.ucc.ie/published/E600001-004.html>
25   Hiram Morgan (ed.) Hatfield House, Cecil Papers 88/121-2, 'Thomas Walker's Narrative, written to Sir Robert Cecil, 1601', CELT, the Corpus of Electronic Texts, p.3. <https://celt.ucc.ie/published/E600001-003/>

'OF KERNS AND GALLOWGLASSES'

approaching English force, the sentinels ride 'as fast as a bird can fly' into the camp 'and cry Hugat on slo, or Hugat on Sassany,' that is, 'the army is coming, or the English are coming.' Thus, before an English force can come within four or five miles of them, the *creaghts* are driven into the woods and the straights and passages are manned by the hired foot soldiers.

Perhaps the best testimony to the usefulness of Irish-style cavalry was their employment by their English adversaries. As discussed in the chapter on the forces of the English Pale, during the first half of the sixteenth century the Anglo-Irish lords of the Pale were required to maintain large numbers of horsemen in their marcher lands to cope with fast moving Irish raids. The horsemen thus maintained were often of Gaelic extraction and were specifically ordered to be armed and mounted on a pad saddle in the native Irish style. They were thus exempted from the 1499 enactment requiring Palesmen in general to ride in a saddle 'after the Englishe guise.' These marchers, 'being skylfull in their Irishe wepens, whiche they cannot use in a saddle,' it was deemed 'right perillouse' to force them to do otherwise.[26] It was these very Irish horsemen of the Pale marches that Sir Anthony St Leger had offered to King Henry for possible service in France in 1543, 'And assuredly I think for their feat of war, which is for light scourers, there are no properer horsemen in Christian ground, nor more hardy, nor yet that can better endure hardness. I think our Majesty may well have of them five hundred, and leave your English pale well furnished.'[27]

An Italian pilgrim to Lough Dearg, Paolo Giovio, visited Conn Bacach O'Neill, and wrote this description of Conn's horsemen in 1548 (translated here from the original Latin):

A horseman is protected by a mail shirt and a helmet; he carries a Spanish lance and the reins together in his left hand, and with his right

Irish horseman. After the Book of the De Burgos, 1571–80. Note the long spear, and helmet of Lough Henny type, with upturned nasal guard. (Author's drawing)

---

26 *State Papers: Henry VIII*, p.449–50, 25 September, State of Ireland, Lord Lieutenant to Henry VIII.
27 *State Papers: Henry VIII*, p.444, 6 April, St Leger to Henry VIII.

he hurls with great strength a javelin fitted with a throwing loop [literally, an *amentum*], and he is accustomed to carry more either contained in his sword-belt or compressed in place under his thigh; others are supplied by attendants on foot. Thus, at long distance he battles with javelins, while at close quarters he quickly switches his lance from his left hand to his right and uses it to fight at mid-distance with repeated blows from on high. Each knight [*eques*] has two horses, one to ride outside the battle, the other an outstanding warhorse that has no rider and which he can easily mount when the battle-signal calls to arms. Indeed, the knight has such agility for controlling and spurring on a horse that, dodging with marvelous twists of his body while swaying from side to side, he may evade enemy weapons and seize scattered ones by reaching out with his left hand while hanging from the saddle held on by only one bent knee.[28]

Writing 40 years later, the Dubliner Richard Stanihurst sounds very similar, particularly regarding the dramatic swaying of the body to avoid being struck by an enemy:

> The first rank is the cavalry. But Irish horsemen differ much from the practice of other nations. They grip their spears – and these are quite heavy – about the middle with their hands; they do not hold them underarm into their side, but brandish them above their heads by strength of muscle. They have excellent docile horses, on which they launch themselves at the packed ranks of the enemy; or if the odds are against them they can avoid the attack by a swerve of the body. All this is done with no great effort on the part of the horseman, even though he holds the reins very slack, for nothing is more manageable than an Irish horse.[29]

Interestingly, Moryson also remarked on the Irish horsemen's 'weighty spears'.[30] O'Sullivan Beare described the contrasting fighting styles of the Irish and English cavalry in 1598. He says the English horse carried lances six cubits (nine feet) long while, 'The light armed [Irish horse], having longer lances which they grasped in the middle and held above their right shoulder, rarely struck except at advantage, at other times hurling wooden darts tipped with iron and about four cubits long,' and he adds that, 'excelling in dexterity and speed and wheeling their horses again and again returned to the fight, inflicting many wounds but giving ground, however, all the

---

28   Harris, 'Paolo Giovio', p.287.
29   Stanihurst, *Great Deeds*, p.123.
30   Falkiner, *Illustrations Irish History*, p.285.

'OF KERNS AND GALLOWGLASSES'

Swaying to avoid enemy weapons in *juego de cañas*. Author's drawing, after António Galvão de Andrade, *Arte da Cavalaria de Gineta, e Estardiota* (Lisbon: Joam da Costa, 1678)

time.'[31] Fynes Moryson echoes this, saying: 'darts they also use to carry and cast them after their enemies when they wheel about.'[32] This casting of darts from horseback was a feat of considerable skill. Anyone who has thrown a dart fitted with a finger loop will appreciate the difficulty of setting up a shot while on horseback.

In 1595, Felim Riabhach Mac Davitt of Inishowen, a district that provided the bulk of O'Donnell's cavalry, made a particularly deft cast of a dart. Bingham, the governor of Connacht, reported O'Donnell's cavalry had been showing themselves on the hills above Sligo, and came pricking (skirmishing) close to the town. Mac Davitt was one of this party of O'Donnell's horsemen which had been assigned to lure the English horse under Bingham's nephew, Captain Martin, into an ambush by fleeing before them. However, Mac Davitt's horse let him down and he was in danger of being overrun by Martin, who was foremost in the pursuit. Turning in the saddle to defend himself: 'He put his finger in the string and he drew the javelin boldly, and the shot of the dart struck Captain Martin with such force that it passed through the border of the foreign armour at the hollow of the armpit straight and it pierced his heart in his breast.'[33]

Edmund Spencer, writing of the Irish horseman's 'feat' in 1596 was as complimentary as St Leger had been 50 years earlier:

---

31 Don Philip O'Sullivan Bere (Matthew J. Byrne ed.), *Ireland Under Elizabeth* (Dublin: Sealy, Bryers & Walker, 1903), p.110.
32 Falkiner, *Illustrations Irish History*, p.285.
33 O'Clery, *Beatha Aodh Ruadh*, p.376.

nether is the same yet counted an uncomlie manner of rydinge; for I have hearde some greate warryors say, that, in all the services which they had seen abroad in forraygne countreyes, they never saw a more comelie horseman than the Irish man, nor that cometh on more bravely in the charge; nether is his manner of mountinge unsemly; though he lacke stiropps; but more readie than with styrroppes; for in his gettinge up, his horse is still goinge, whereby he gayneth way. And therefore the styrrop was called soe in scorne, as yt were a stayre to gett up.[34]

This manner of vaulting into the saddle was called *ech-léim* or 'steed-leap'. In 1584, Stanihurst wrote:

> Also, they do not mount their horses by means of iron steps – stirrups as some call them – nor do they permit such nugatory aids (such is their opinion of them) to be attached to the harness. Instead with the left hand they grasp the stiff hair of the mane, which sticks out at the forehead, or the ears of the horses. The horses, moulded to such willingness by their trainers, such is their docility, lean quietly with bowed heads as the horsemen, even when wearing mail shirt or mantle (*loricis aut sagis*), leap up with amazing agility and in one movement are seated on a horseblanket which is not unlike a saddle. Such mounting is so widely practised among them that it is not so much praiseworthy to be able to do it as it is shameful not to be able to.[35]

A late sixteenth century bardic poem condemning an Irishman who has adopted English ways said the people 'laugh as you set foot on the mounting-block'.[36] There is a rather suspect engraving from Abraham de Bruyn, dated 1577 and titled 'Wild Irish Rider', which seems to reflect a confused reading of such accounts. The de Bruyn artist may have read something akin to this description by an anonymous Spanish traveller in 1579: 'They mount their horses, seizing them by the left ear, and using nothing to support their feet,' since he has his horseman riding along with a firm grip on his horse's left ear.[37] The de Bruyn figure is otherwise derived from a more plausible engraving of an Irish kern, a version of which, by Caspar Rutz, is titled *Hybernis Miles*. While vaulting was not widely practised outside Ireland, it continued to be taught as a kind of circus trick, and in 1641 William Stokes published a book on the subject, *The Vaulting Master*. Interestingly, the only

---

34 Spencer, *A View*, unpaginated.
35 Stanihurst, *Great Deeds*, p.123.
36 Osborn Bergin (ed.), *Irish Bardic Poetry* (Dublin: Dublin Institute for Advanced Studies, 1970), pp.49–50.
37 Maxwell, *Irish History*, p.320.

'OF KERNS AND GALLOWGLASSES'

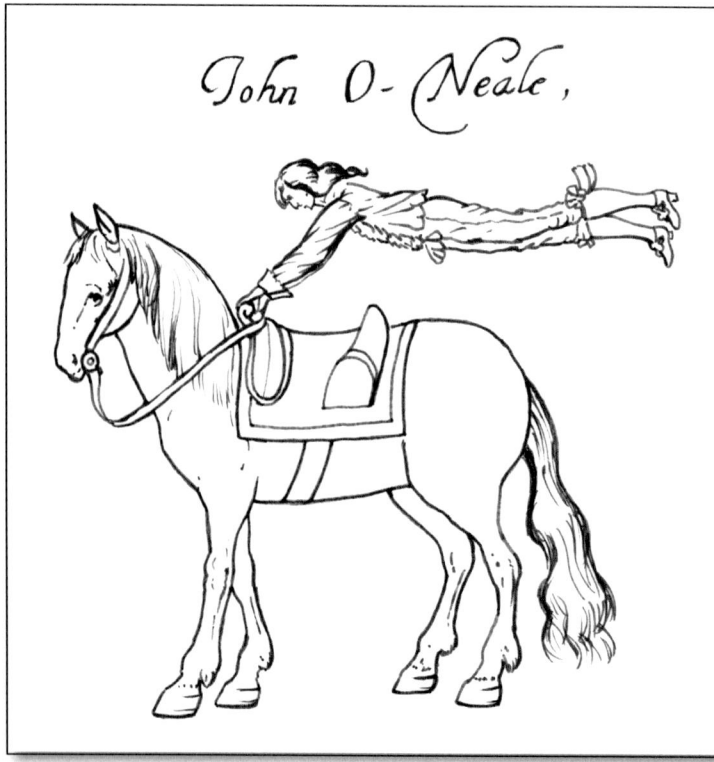

Mounting without stirrups. The horse should be underway, presumably. John O'Neale performing. (Author's drawing, after William Stokes, *The Vaulting Master: or the art of vaulting: Reduced to a method, comprized under certaine rules, and now primarily set forth, by Will. Stokes* (London: I. Okes, 1641)

practitioner of this art identified by name in Stoke's book is John O'Neale, an Irishman who is depicted in mid-vault. The vaulting practised by the old Irish horseman, getting up 'while his horse is still going, whereby he gaineth way,' can be seen in today's Mounted Games, a fast-paced team competition centred in Britain.

The Horseman's Training: 'The Ancient Irish Pickering'

Speaking of the Irish 'captaynes', or chiefs of their name, the author of the *Power of Irishmen* says: 'Their sonnes learne to be men of warre from the age of 16 yeares & be continually practysed in toyles thereof.'[38] This is in keeping with old Irish law, under which a warrior received his first shield and spear when his fosterage ended at age 17, or 14 at the earliest. But the legendary Ulster hero Cú Chulainn had demanded arms at the age of seven! For a time at least, at the cusp of the fifteenth century, this unlikely precociousness seems to have been imitated literally among the Gaelic Irish elite.

A fascinating feature of the 'Gaelic Revival', which was at its height in the years *c.* 1350–1450, was a resurgence of enthusiasm among the Gaelic elite for the cycle of stories centring on Cú Chulainn and the Warriors of the Red Branch. Besides fostering the production of new manuscript editions of the tales which today form our main source for them, this revival extended to a kind of re-enactment of the imagined historical past. This included the construction of a temporary feasting hall on the site of the Iron Age hill fort of Emain Macha, the seat of the Red Branch Warriors, and extended to going bare foot and bare legged among the elite, even in winter. Besides being a public display of hardiness, these practices were an interpretation of the fashion of the heroic era. The bare footedness among the elite is attested to by French and Catalan visitors to the court of Niall Og O'Neill, *c.* 1400, both of whom remarked on the cultural self confidence of the Irish chiefs, who were interested in the habits of foreign courts, but felt their

---

38   Price, 'Armed Forces', p.207.

THE HORSEMAN, OR MARCACH

own customs to be best. With the emergence of relative peace after *c.* 1450, the practice may have been modified, and as discussed in the section 'The Chief and his Military role,' some chiefs begin to appear in the height of renaissance fashion in the early sixteenth century.[39] Yet there are indications that instances of this kind of thinking continued into the sixteenth century, such as the account of Laurent Vital's visit to Kinsale in 1518. Thus, in 1395, the interpreter for a group of Irish Kings being prepared for a knighting ceremony before Richard II was told:

> they were knights already …. I asked when they were made; they answered at seven years old; that in Ireland a king makes his son a knight, and should the child have lost his father, then the nearest relation; and the young knight begins to learn to tilt with a light lance against a shield fixed to a post in a field, and the more lances he breaks the more honour he acquires. 'By this method', they added, 'are our young knights trained, more especially king's sons.'[40]

This early initiation age seems to have been part of the 'Gaelic Revival' practices mentioned above, here imitating the legendary Cú Chulainn, and we have seen elsewhere that a more believable age of 16 is given in *c.* 1490. But the method of training is of interest. Sir James Ware recalled something of the training of the old Irish horsemen: 'I know not whether it may be worth the while to remember here the Martial exercises of the *Irish* horsemen, which they perform'd only for shew, and therefore with Darts not headed with iron; and their hunting of the Stagg, a Recreation much resembling the affairs of War, and (if we believe Xenophon in *Cyropaedia*) productive of Valour.'[41] In 1597, James McDonnell of Dunluce put on an equestrian display of this type when he:

> came to Scotland to wait upon King James VI and the King received him very kindly; he rode a white horse and all his train together, the King was highly pleased to see James McSourl with their brave horses and armour. James has shown his Majesty and the nobility the ancient Irish pickering or riding in their high pillions made all of pure velvet and scarlet to the imaginable satisfaction of King and Court.[42]

---

39 Simms, 'Barefoot Kings', pp.1–21.
40 Simms, *Gaelic Ulster*, p.424.
41 James Ware, *The Antiquities and History of Ireland* (Dublin: A. Crook, 1705), p.32.
42 Archibald MacDonald (ed.), 'A Fragment of an Irish MS. History of the MacDonalds of Antrim', *Transactions of the Gaelic Society of Inverness*, vol. 37 (1934–1936), p.269.

'OF KERNS AND GALLOWGLASSES'

It is significant that these equestrian exercises appear to have a Spanish origin. The breaking of lances on a shield fixed to a post, recorded in an Irish context in 1395, was known in the Spanish realms as the 'saracen joust', and was the origin of the quintain. Likewise, Ware's description of the Irish horsemen's exercise with 'darts not headed with iron' is the 'game of reeds' or *juego de cañas*, another Spanish equestrian exercise. In the game of reeds, two teams of six horsemen alternated between chasing and fleeing from one another. Those in pursuit attempted to strike their fleeing opponents with headless cane darts, while those in flight attempted to block the dart with their leather *adarga* shield. Thus, it was a game of flight and pursuit, a neat microcosm of Irish raiding warfare. Like their Spanish counterparts, Irish horsemen carried 'round leather targets in the Spanish fashion,' as noted by Edmund Spencer in *View of the State of Ireland*. And as mentioned above, Paolo Giovio in 1548 said the Irish horseman 'carries a Spanish lance' and described him swaying his body dramatically to avoid the blows of his opponent and snatching spent darts off the ground, all perfectly mirrored by illustrations in Iberian equestrian manuals describing *juego de cañas*.[43] While this is thought to have been introduced to Iberia by the Moors, the game may ultimately descend from the ancient Roman *hippica gymnasia*. These exercises are another indicator of the cultural connection between Spain and Gaelic Ireland. Other examples of a military nature include the use of fletched darts by lightly armed foot soldiers carrying shields, and the preference for barbute helmets with nasal guards projecting from the forehead.

Snatching darts off the ground in *juego de cañas*. After Galvao Anrade's *Arte de Cavalaria de Gineta e Estardiota*, 1678. (Author's drawing)

Along with the 'game of reeds', Ware also implies the hunting of the stag from horseback using darts, which he suggests much resembles 'the affairs of war.' This is interesting in light of the connection we have seen Nicholas Dawtrey draw between the Irish horsemen and their kern, suggesting that the two habitually served closely together in time of war. The hereditary service kindreds of an Irish

---

43 Gregorio Tapia y Salcedo, *Exercicios de la gineta al principe nuestro señor d. Baltasar Carlos* (Madrid: D. Diaz, 1643)

chief included numbers of kern, some of whom specialised as horn blowers (*stocaire*) and keepers of hounds, each with his own holding among the lands of the clan's *lucht tighe* (household people). For instance the O'Connor Roe lordship in Macharie Connacht included several kern of the MacBranan family, holding land in return for service as *stocaire* or *ceatharnach*, for by tradition, 'MacBranan has the rearguard of O'Connor, and the stewardship of his hounds and the leadership of his kerns.'[44] The MacBranans occupied Dumha Selga ('the mound of the hunt'), and would all have taken part in their chief's 'great huntings', which could be on a grand scale. Moryson said the Irishman 'catched his stags by driving them into nets, shouting with a great noise upon the contrary side from the nets.'[45]

The anonymous English author of a *Discourse on the Mere Irish* tells us more about the 'hunting of buck and stag …. a commendable exercise for Noble and gentlemen,' which he would nonetheless prohibit. This is because of the great numbers of 'Idle creatures [who] assemble from all corners thereabouts and their office must be to be hewers [beaters] and these commonly are so many in number at those meetings as they compass in a forest wood or mountain of four or five mile or more.'[46] The hunt being concluded, it is 'a custom among the Irishry to cess the horse and foot, their dog hounds and their dog keepers upon the gentlemen and husbandmen …. and it falls out very often that every dog has three or four attendants of these fellows.' Instead, he says the nobles that love to hunt should 'be driven to keep their hounds and huntsmen …. and not permit them to forage and range abroad.' These exactions for the keep of the lord's huntsmen and dogs were known as *gille con* and *dow-gollogh*, respectively. It should be noted that the red deer stag is as large as a North American elk, and quite dangerous.[47]

'Horseman's apparel after the Irish order'

The armour of a sixteenth century Irish horseman consisted of the knee length padded aketon (called *cotún* in Irish, or 'long jack' in Anglo-Irish documents), a coat of mail and a bascinet, the later occasionally being called a 'scul' in contemporary language. Ramón de Perilhos in 1397 described it:

44　Elizabeth Fitzpatrick, 'Gaelic service kindreds and the landscape identity of lucht tighe' in Eve Campbell, Elizabeth Fitzpatrick and Audrey Horning (eds), *Becoming and Belonging in Ireland AD c. 1200–1600* (Cork: Cork University Press, 2018), pp.167–188.
45　Falkiner, *Illustrations Irish History*, p.323.
46　Morgan, 'Discourse Mere Irish', p.31.
47　Richard Swinney and Scott Crawford, 'Medieval Hunting as Training for War Insights for the Modern Swordsman', *Acta Periodica Duellatorum*, vol. 2, no. 1 (Bern: Universität Bern, 2014), pp.179–193.

'OF KERNS AND GALLOWGLASSES'

He has indeed forty horsemen, riding without saddle on a cushion …. they are armed with coats of mail, and wear them girded, and they have throat pieces of mail and round helmets of iron [*capelines*], with swords and knives [*cotelhs*] and lances very long, but very thin in the manner of the ancient lances, and they are two fathoms [12 feet] long; the swords are like those of the Saracens, which we call Genoese; the pommel and the cross are of another form. The pommel has the shape of an extended hand. The knives are long and narrow like the little finger, and twisted, and they cut very well …. and they put their spurs upon their bare heels.[48]

Irish horsemen, John Derricke, 1581. Sculls of iron or spangenhelm type, as discussed above in the chapter on the chief. Both types have upturned nasals in Derricke's woodcuts of Irish horsemen. Note the targets on their backs. (Creative Commons)

This is the horseman's panoply described as early as the fourteenth century in the *Triumphs of Turlough*: *lúirech, cotún, clogad, cloidhem agus cráisech* – mail shirt, aketon, bascinet, sword and spear.[49] This remained unchanged until very late, a party of O'Reilly horsemen being described in 1579 as 'armed in mail, with pesantes and skulls, and riding upon pillions,' the 'pesantes' being the ample pisane collar of mail, called *sgabal* in Irish.[50] This in no way differs from the harness of the galloglass, and we may surmise that the Irish horsemen, when fighting on foot, took their place in the front ranks of the galloglass. Derricke's woodcuts of 1581 show Irish horsemen with a slightly simplified version this harness, with a plain round skull fitted with an upturned nasal in place of the bascinet, and no pisane collar. Derricke's horsemen all have circular shields slung about their necks, and depending on whether they are advancing or retreating, these cover the chest or back. In size and shape, they resemble the two known surviving Irish shields, and differ little from the Highland targe. These are discussed in the chapter on the kern. Shields are not seen in other depictions of Irish horsemen, but are frequently referred to in Irish poetry, one horseman being described as bearing a red *starga* on his back which bounced foreign spears from his shoulder. While *starga* is cognate with target, the older word *sgiath* is also used for shield without great distinction between the two. Under either name, shields are described as being slung by shield-straps (*sciathrach*).[51] References to shields in outsider's accounts are rare. A German traveller in 1591 says the Irish horsemen were: 'dressed in a mail-coat, with a shield over their arm.'[52] And in 1597, Captain Dawtrey also noted: 'They are light horsemen, furnished with jackes, and Habergines

---

48   J. P. Mahaffy, 'Two Early Tours of Ireland' in Members of Trinity College, Dublin, eds, *Hermathena*, vol. 40 (London: Longmans, Green & Co., 1914), p.7.
49   Standish Hayes O'Grady (ed.), *Caithréim Thoirdhealbhaigh*, The Triumphs of Turlough, 2 vols (London: Irish Texts Society, 26, 27, 1929), p.68.
50   Longfield, *Irish History*, p.222–3.
51   Peter Harbison, 'Native Irish Arms and Armour in Medieval Gaelic Literature, 1170–1600', *The Irish Sword*, vol. 12, no. 48 (1976), pp.197–8.
52   Donall O Fionnain (ed.), 'A German Visitor to Monaincha in 1591' in *Tipperary Historical Journal*, County Tipperary Historical Society (1998), p.230.

THE HORSEMAN, OR *MARCACH*

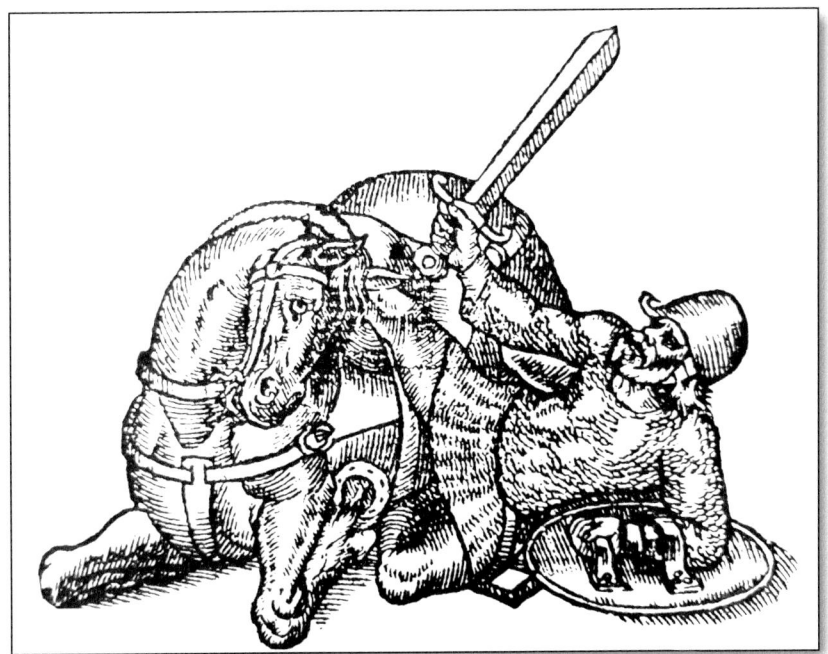

Irish horseman, John Derricke, 1581. Simple mail shirt without pisane collar, scull with upturned nasal, and target. (Creative Commons)

of maile, and each man hath a small scull upon his head, a targett, and a chasing stafe.'[53]

This panoply of an Irish horseman was known in Irish as *culaidh mharcaigh*, translated accurately in contemporary English documents as 'horseman's apparel'. It was a symbolic medium of exchange in several circumstances in Gaelic Ireland. For instance, *taurastal* was an ancient custom whereby a Gaelic chief could bestow gifts of horses and/or 'horseman's apparel,' and thus bind the recipient to serve him.[54] In 1549, Conn Bacach O'Neill sought the return of eight horses and, 'an armed tunic, otherwise called a "jacke," and an "habergyne," which he gave Magwyre as a stipend for his service.'[55] The 'jack' here is the quilted armour which was usually called *cotún* in Irish, though sometimes *seaca*. On occasion, however, the gift of horseman's apparel might be made to an equal or superior lord, as a 'buying' or 'kenaght' (*ceannuigheacht*) to secure protection or assistance. This occurs in the State Papers, where on 29 September, 1562, we read that Sorley Boy MacDonnell shall foster with Shane O'Neill, and shall give him 500 kine, and eight horseman's furnitures for a buying, and shall serve him with four or five hundred men in every journey.[56] The same source records a similar exchange when in 1568 Turlough Lynagh O'Neill received a gift

---

53 Morgan, '*A Booke*', p.90.
54 Kenneth Nicholls, *Gaelic and Gaelicised Ireland in the Middle Ages* (Dublin: Gill and Macmillan, 1972), p.43.
55 *Cal. Carew Mss*, p.245, 20 June, Earl of Tyrone to Magwyre.
56 *Calendar of State Papers Ireland: Henry VIII, Edward VI, Mary and Elizabeth*, vol. 1, 1509–73, Hans Claude Hamilton ed. (London: Longman, Green, Longman & Roberts, 1860), p.205., 29 September, Lord Lieutenant to Queen.

of a 'horseman's apparel' from Con O'Donnell.[57] As late as 1594, the State Papers record James Oge MacSorley Boy MacDonnell placing Neal M'Brian Fartuogh under extortion with the threat of taking preys from him 'except he promise to give him two horsemen's apparel after the Irish order which be worth 100 L. sterling.'[58]

Chiefly inaugurations were another occasion upon which horsemen's apparels were exchanged. The early seventeenth century manuscript *Cíos Mhic Mathghamhna*, or the Rights of MacMahon, recalls the inauguration practices of *c.* 1442.[59] MacMahon then had three hereditary sub-chieftains (Ó Buidhellan, Mac Ceanaith and Duthach), and at his inauguration MacMahon gave to each chieftain a horseman's apparel, or 40 marks of old silver in its stead (*culaidh mharcaigh úadha do gach taoiseach*). During the inauguration, MacMahon's Chief Marshal, Ó Connalaigh, supplied him with a horse, jack, sword, helmet, and great spear for the ceremony (*an seaca, an claidhiomh, an ceinnbeart, agus an ga mor*).[60]

The *ga mor*, or great spear presented to MacMahon above is apparently the 'horseman's staff' so often referred to in English documents. Like the full horseman's apparel, it could be given as a diplomatic gift. This is seen in an entry in the State Papers for 1588 recording O'Rourke's letter to MacMahon, saying: 'He has not a good harp in his country but sends two great spears, and two skeans.'[61] And a little later, in September, 1589, the Lord Deputy is recorded giving a 'scull' to Turlough Lynagh O'Neill: 'After delivery of your Honour's "scoule" [skull], to O'Neill, he took it in his hand and kissed it at least half-a-score times, and then presently sent for two hogsheads of wine and christened your scull, and he put on his shirt of mail and his jack .... and said I am now 10 years younger by reason of this scull.'[62]

Regarding the size of the *ga mor*, or great spear, Perilhos in 1397 says the Irish horsemen carry 'lances very long, but very thin in the manner of the ancient lances, and they are two fathoms [12 feet] long.' Accordingly, O'Sullivan Beare says that in 1598, while the English horse had lances six cubits [nine feet] in length, those of the Irish horse were longer. He also says the Irish horse carried darts 4 cubits [six feet] in length.[63] Paolo Giovio called the Irish horseman's spear 'a Spanish lance', almost certainly meaning

---

57   *CSP Ireland*, p.369, 23 March, Lord Justices to Queen.
58   *Calendar of State Papers Ireland: Elizabeth*, vol. 5, 1592, October–1596, June, Hans Claude Hamilton ed. (London: Eyre and Spottiswoode, 1890), p.103, 8 March, John Dallway to Lord Deputy.
59   Katherine Simms, *From Kings to Warlords* (Woodbridge: Boydell & Brewer Ltd, 1987), p.67.
60   Elizabeth Fitzpatrick, *Royal Inauguration in Gaelic Ireland, c. 1100–1600: A Cultural Landscape Study* (Woodbridge: The Boydell Press, 2004), p.7.
61   *Calendar of State Papers Ireland: Elizabeth*, vol. 4, 1588, August–1592, September, Hans Claude Hamilton ed. (London: Longman, 1885), p.54, 12 October, O'Rourke to MacMahon.
62   *CSP Ireland*, p.234–5, 12 September, John Garland to Sir John Perrot.
63   O'Sullivan Bere, *Ireland Under*, p.110.

the *lanza jineta* carried by the contemporary Spanish *jinete*, whose fighting style was similar to that of the Irish horseman. Suárez de Peralta, in the sixteenth century, says the *lanza jineta* should 'be up to 18 or 19 spans [11.9 to 12.5 feet] long, not very thick or thin.'[64] This is the Spanish lance seen in Titian's equestrian portrait of Charles V, depicting him riding *a la jineta* at the Battle of Mühlberg in 1547.

The same Turlough Lynagh O'Neill spoken of so wryly in the State Papers is described arming in a more dignified manner in a bardic poem. The poem lists his padded jack, his *feilm* or helm, and his spurs.[65] Two hundred years earlier, Art MacMurrough Kavanagh was described as wearing spurs on his, then-fashionable, bare heels. Large star-shaped rowel spurs seem to have been preferred, and are seen in Derricke and on the DeBurgo horseman. In 1589, the State Papers record that the Earl of Clanricarde, in action against O'Rourke, was thrown when his horse shied from an arquebus shot. The horse's plunge threw the 'Earl to the ground, the spur sticking in the pillion, and by force teared the spur off his foot,' – indicating that this loyalist Irish lord, whose tailor's bills show that he dressed in the height of Elizabethan fashion, was still riding in the Irish manner at this late date.[66] For his spur to have been caught this way, he probably had a pillion of 'chequered blanketting', as described below. Some writers later in the century, such as Fynes Moryson, say the Irish horsemen wore no spurs. But this was during the Nine Years' War in the 1590s, at which point many changes occurred. Moryson also says they were then wearing no armour but for a morion, and Don Juan Del Águila, writing from Kinsale in 1601, seconds this: 'all that can be levied in Ireland or that they have are small horses, and the soldiers are unarmed, who only fight with half-pikes and saddle without stirrups.'[67]

The Pillion Saddle: 'Strange-Fashioned Pads'

At the time of the Anglo-Norman invasion in 1171, the medieval Irish are described as riding without a saddle upon a simple horsecloth called *diallait*, which is the modern Irish word for a conventional saddle. The old *diallait* often covered the entire animal. It is indicated thus in illustrations in the *Book of Kells*, and appears remarkably unchanged in wall paintings at Clare Island Abbey (rebuilt around 1460), as well as in the 1582 De Burgo genealogy. References to the Irish riding without a saddle were also made during the Irish expeditions of King John (1210) and Richard II (1394–1395). For example, this is a description of Art MacMurrough Kavanagh in

---

64 Juan Suárez de Peralta, *Tratado de Caballería de la Gineta y de la Brida* (Seville: 1580)
65 Simms, 'Images of Warfare', p.612.
66 *CSP Ireland*, p.186, 21 May, Mordant to Lord Deputy.
67 Thomas Stafford (Standish O'Grady, ed.), *Pacata Hibernia*, vol. 1, (London: Downey & Co., 1896), p.284.

'OF KERNS AND GALLOWGLASSES'

1395: 'He had a horse without saddle or saddle tree' *(Un cheval ot sanz sale ne arçon).*[68] However, other sources indicate that by this date, the Irish were in fact using a pillion saddle. Henry Chrestide, esquire to King Richard II on his Irish expedition, recounts in *Froissart's Chronicles* that the Irish: 'rode on a kind of saddle used for pack horses, without stirrups. It was only with great difficulty that I got them to ride on the kind of saddles we have.'[69] A similar description appears in Monstrelet's *Chronicle* of the Siege of Rouen, in 1418, where he says of the Irish cavalry: 'Those who were on horseback had no saddles, but rode excellently well on small mountain horses, and were mounted on such panniers as are used by the carriers of corn in parts of France.'[70] In 1397, Ramón de Perilhos visited Niall Óg O'Neill and wrote 'He has indeed forty horsemen, riding without saddle on a cushion,' clearly indicating a pillion saddle.[71] The modern English word 'pillion' is derived from the Irish word for this saddle, *pillín*, which in turn comes from the Latin *pellis*, meaning a skin.

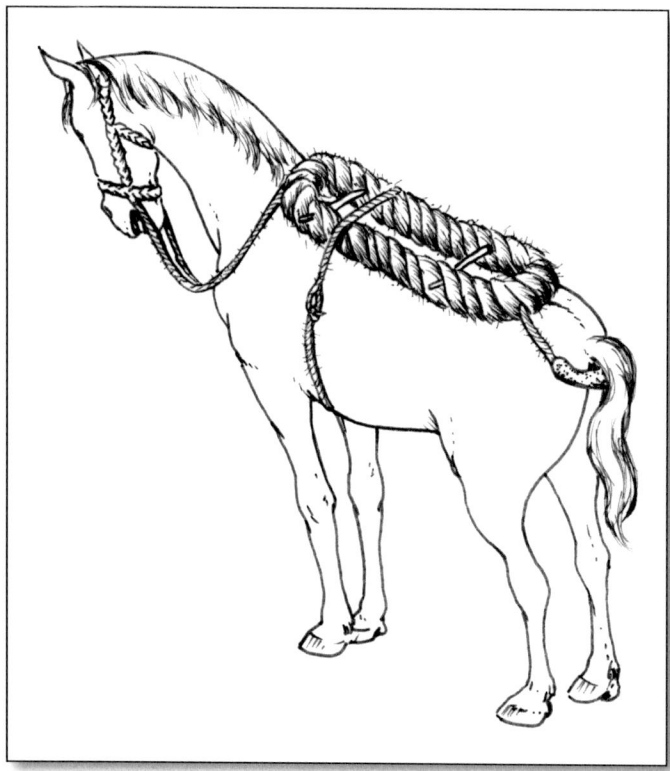

Horse with straw harness and *súgán saic* saddle. (Author's drawing)

These comparisons of the Irish pillion saddle to a pack saddle are of great interest. This is usually assumed to be a reference to the conventional 'crossbuck' or 'sawbuck' pack saddle with two pairs of crossed wooden bars for attaching sling ropes. The four 'horns' of the conventional pack saddle have led to speculations of the Irish using something like the old Roman saddle, whose four 'horns' helped keep the rider in place. However, there is a traditional piece of Irish horse tack made of *súgán* (straw rope) that survived into the twentieth century, used both for carrying burdens and as a riding saddle. It was called a *súgán saic*, in reference to its being used to carry sacks of grain. This is likely the type of pack saddle Monstrelet referred to above, used to carry corn. The *súgán saic* doubled as a riding saddle among Irish farmers, and the

---

68 Daphne Machin Goodall and A. A. Dent, *The Foals of Epona* (London: Galley Press, 1962), p.126.
69 Jean Froissart, *Chronicles of England, France, Spain and adjoining countries*, vol. 2, trans. Thomas Johnes (London: H. G. Bohn, 1857), p.580.
70 Enguerrand de Monstrelet (Thomas Johnes tr.), *The Chronicles*, vol. 5, (London: Longman, Hurst, Rees, Orm and Brown, 1810), p.42.
71 Mahaffy, 'Two Tours', p.7.

shape of its long, narrow pad as well as the overall arrangement of the tack, greatly resembled the pillion saddle and harness of the Irish *marcach*.

This straw rope saddle is referred to as early as 1605, when the 'Montgomery Papers' record Con O'Neill's followers meeting him upon his return from Dublin while riding on 'pannels' or 'bughams', words of English and Scots derivation, respectively. Panel was the term used for the *súgán saic* when speaking English. In the early eighteenth century Jonathan Swift spoke of an Irishman 'riding on a sougawn', and the Halls in their early nineteenth century travelogue wrote of Kerrymen being mocked as they rode to Cork on little horses with straw bridles and coarsely plaited straw saddles.[72] Doubtless, this straw rope saddle was in use during the Tudor era, and may have served the horseman's servants, the horse boys, as their riding tack. It is from Luke Gernon, an Englishman writing in 1620, that we get our most complete description of the old Irish saddle and tack:

> The Irish saddle is called a pillyon, and it is made on this forme. The tree is as of an ordinary saddle, but the seate is a playne table of two foote longe, and a foote broad or larger, high mounted, and covered with a piece of chequered blanketting. It is not tyed with girths, but it is fastned with a brest plate before, and a crupper behind, and a sursingle in the middle. The men ryde upon it astryde, with theyr leggs very farr extended, and towards the horse neck. If the horse be dull, they spurregall him in the shoulder. It seemeth very uneasy to us, but they affirme it to be an easy kind of ryding. If it be, it is very usefull, for a man may ryde astryde, a woman may ryde a syde, and a man may ryde with a woman behind him, all upon the like saddle. It is an excellent fashion to steale a wench, and to carry her away.[73]

Writing about the same time, Fynes Moryson says, 'they use no saddles, but either long narrow pillions bumbasted or bare boards of that fashion.'[74] Spencer briefly summed up this Irish horse tack: 'his strong brass bit, his sliding reins, his shank pillion without stirrup.'[75] The shank pillion is the 'long narrow pillion, bumbasted,' the 'shank' being the 'playne table' of wood, mounted on an ordinary saddle tree. The brass bit is the snaffle, unchanged since antiquity. Unlike the curb bit in use by English horsemen, it did not interfere much with grazing. With regard to 'sliding reins' it has been suggested that they were double reins, slipped through the snaffle-rings without being sewn to them, giving great play, but that if the rider released the top rein, and drew in the lower, it would slide up the neck and

---

72 Anne O'Dowd, *Straw, Hay & Rushes* (Dublin: Irish Academic Press, 2015), pp.381, 384, 387-388 & 395.
73 Falkiner, *Illustrations Irish History*, p.360.
74 Falkiner, *Illustrations Irish History*, p.284.
75 Goodall, *Foals of Epona*, p.154.

'OF KERNS AND GALLOWGLASSES'

Irish saddle and tack. Horseboy holding a chieftain's mount. John Derricke, 1581. (Creative Commons)

cause a gag reaction behind the ears. This does not seem to be confirmed by surviving iconography.

These descriptions agree in all details with Derricke's detailed illustrations of Irish saddles and horse tack, published in 1581. Gernon says the 'table' was 'covered with a piece of chequered blanketing,' which must mean the pillion itself. Such check blanketing was used for horse and donkey tack in Ireland and elsewhere, well into the twentieth century, and seems to be indicated by the pillions in Derricke's illustrations. Alternatively, Derricke's illustrations of the pillion have been interpreted as a diamond-quilted leather cushion. As noted, the very name pillion (*pillín*) indicates the saddle was made of skin. The mid-seventeenth century Irish literary source, *Pairlement Chloinne Tomáis*, satirises the antiquated Gaelic peasantry for their horsehair halters and 'wide, colourful pack saddles (*lóiste*) of pigskin or calfskin under our rumps.'[76] Elsewhere in the same source, the pillions are described as 'wide-patched' and 'soft-edged'. A red cordovan leather,

---

76   N. J. A. Williams (ed.), *Parlement Chloinne Tomáis* (Dublin: Dublin Institute for Advanced Studies, 1981), p.109. '*Lóiste*' appears in the glossary as 'straw-stuffed saddle, cushion', and is equivalent to '*pillín*'.

called 'rede leshe', was imported into Ireland in the first half of the sixteenth century and sold in strips for use in making up the Irish pillion or pad saddle (*pillín* or *lóiste*). Completed 'cushions' of the same leather were also imported. Longfield, in her study of Anglo-Irish trade, presumed that these pillions were for riding, and that the appearance of many dozens of pillions implied their use among the early Tudor 'Inglishrie' as well as the native Irish.

After 1550, standard saddles, saddle trees, bits, bridles, horse bells, girth web and curry combs began to appear in imports, all catering for the English style of saddlery.[77] The Irish saddle and tack could occasionally be of finer materials. In 1597 as referred to above James McSourl is recorded riding in 'high pillions made all of pure velvet and scarlet,' and in 1602 Mountjoy presented Don Juan Del Águila with 'a choice Irish horse, with a rich pad and furniture.'[78] However, a half a century earlier Polydore Virgil says the Irish horsemen rode 'with no decorative bosses' (phalerae).[79] Similarly, an Act of the Irish Parliament in 1447 against 'gilt Bridles, and Peytrels and other gilt harness' appears to be specifically directed against Gaelic poets wandering into the English Pale, rather than ordinary Irish horsemen.[80] Finally, Gernon noted that the Irish saddle could accommodate a female passenger 'riding pillion' behind the rider, and the Irish saddle was used this way for military purposes as well. In 1589, O'Rourke raided Westmeath with 'a hundreth horsemen, and as many shot mounted behynde them.'[81]

The Hobby: 'a gallant stouryng Steede'

The Irish hobby, called a 'gallant stouryng Steede' by John Derricke in 1581, is key to understanding the tactics and effectiveness of the Irish cavalry. Sixteenth and seventeenth century commentators were universally of the opinion that the old Irish hobby horse was derived from the Asturcón, a breed of small black 'Celtic' ponies anciently prized by the Romans and surviving today in the mountains of Asturias in northern Spain. They retain their ambling gait, although they are seldom ridden now and are considered degenerate from their classical ancestors.

Primarily renowned for its speed, the Irish hobby was also notable in that, rather than trotting, it usually ambled or paced. This was an inherited trait. The 'easy-going' pace is a lateral two-beat gait in which both feet on

---

77 Ada K. Longfield, *Anglo-Irish Trade in the Sixteenth Century* (London: George Routledge & Sons, Ltd., 1929), p.189.
78 Stafford, *Pacata Hibernia*, p.249–250.
79 Polydore Virgil (Dana Sutton ed.),,, *Anglica Historia*, Book XIII, 1555, (The Philological Museum, University of Birmingham) unpaginated. <https://philological.cal.bham.ac.uk/polverg/>
80 Sparky Booker, 'Moustaches, Mantles, and Saffron Shirts: What Motivated Sumptuary Law in Medieval English Ireland?' in *Speculum*, 96/3 (July 2021), p.755.
81 Morgan, 'Dialogue of Sylvynne and Peregrynne', p.85.

one side of the body move in unison. The result is a point of equilibrium in the saddle area, thus giving a smooth ride ideal for long journeys. While modern pacers can sway uncomfortably, the hobby evidently had a fast, comfortable pace, like the modern Icelandic pony. It is clear that the hobby also performed the amble, a slower, even, four-beat gait which is even smoother than the pace. The ambling gait is not cultivated now in Europe, though it survives in the Icelandic pony. A living tradition of riding ambling horses in Spanish America includes, for instance, the Andadura riding of Puerto Rico, and the Asturcón del Camino horse of Columbia.

The old canard that the hobby and its modern descendant, the Connemara pony, have their infusion of Spanish blood due to the horses washed ashore from the wrecks of the Armada in 1588 can be dismissed. Both English and Spanish sources state that the Duke of Medina Sidonia had ordered all horses and mules thrown overboard while still off England's east coast, as the men were already on short water rations. This is confirmed by a neutral captain who reported seeing hundreds of the animals swimming, or floating dead, in those waters.[82] Rather, the seaway from 'The Groyne' (La Coruña) in North-West Spain to Britain and South-West Ireland had been frequented since ancient times, and was heavily trafficked by both merchant ships and pilgrims going to Santiago. And La Coruña was adjacent to the homeland of the Asturcón.

Andadura pacing achieves speeds of 30–40 mph, is done bareback, and occasions a seat very like that described by Luke Gernon for the old Irish horsemen, 'with the legs very far extended towards the neck,' exactly as depicted in old Irish manuscript illustrations. The rider extends his feet far forward on the horse's shoulders, and rocks back in the saddle, 'sitting on his back pockets,' as Irish equestrian specialist Lynn Williams put it. This type of fast riding on ambling ponies is also practised in Turkic-speaking parts of the Russian Federation, where it is called Yorga Atlar. The riders adopt exactly the same feet-forward seat as seen with Andadura riders, and as described for the Irish horsemen. The Columbian Asturcón del Camino riding utilises the ambling gait for a more collected and elegant form of equitation, with very rapid movement of the hooves. This breed of horse is small and black, but more finely featured than its wild namesake in Spain. The size and conformation resemble that seen in depictions of the old Irish hobby.

Both the gait and the seat of the rider were advantageous in a wooded Irish environment. A breeder has noted that the amble of the Puerto Rican Paso Fino horse 'gives them the ability to climb and descend rough, steep terrain almost as well as a mountain goat, even meander between trees in trail-less deep forests in a blink of an eye.'[83] This cutting in and out among trees was facilitated by the old Irish saddle, as equestrian reenactor, Dave

---

82   Goodall, *Foals of Epona*, p.148.
83   Stella Manberg-Wise, *The American Paso Fino Horse*, <https://spanishhorsetack.com/spanish-horse-breeds/the-american-paso-fino-horse/>

O'Reilly's, experiments have demonstrated. With the riders legs raised and nearly crossing around the horse's neck, the horse can shimmy between the narrowest gaps without fear of the rider bashing a knee or catching a stirrup. And if a fall occurs, saving oneself is easier without stirrups. Likewise, an account of the Tartar ambling pony during the Crimean war also makes it clear why this gait would be valuable in boggy country. Panaev, a Russian officer, described the Crimean ponies he rode as being able to move at speed across muddy tracts, while his Cossack escort had to continually slip off their horses to scrape the accumulating mud off their legs. He attributed this to the ambling gait and noted that 'the placing and raising of the pony's leg appeared to be one movement: as soon as firm ground was touched, it immediately withdrew its leg from the mud in a short quick motion'. When pursued by hostile Tartar picquets, Panaev's 'pony went like an arrow over the swampy field,' the Tartars calling after him, 'It's a good thing you have one of our horses, or you wouldn't get away.'[84] This recalls Stanihurst's comments regarding travel on an ambling hobby; 'When equipped for a journey they never cling to their horses: no matter how muddy the track, so high do they raise their calves and so smoothly do they ride, without any shaking, that they do not in the least splash their boots with dirt and filth.'[85]

The old Connemara pony of unmixed stock stood from 12 to 14 hands high, probably reflecting the height range of the earlier hobby. In 1619, Thomas Gainsford noted that 'their horses are for the most part unshod behind,' whereas we might expect the reverse as is depicted in Derricke's woodcut of an Irish chief's horse, where it is the front hooves that are unshod, while the rear are shod.[86] The DeBurgo horseman of 1583 has four horseshoes with caulkins and protruding nails for better purchase on soft ground, rather like Chaucer's knight in the Ellesmere Ms. The hobbies depicted in the DeBurgo genealogy and Derricke's woodcuts are carefully groomed and appear to have hogged manes, while the DeBurgo horseman's mount sports a braided forelock. A late fifteenth century Irish medical treatise on horses speaks of the common colours:

> Brown horses with white heads are the best colour. The black is soft and given to sweating. Light is a good colour. The swarthy is strong. Red horses are bad and the yellow is worse. The best horses are those with a black streak along their back. Dun-coloured horses are good. The grey is seldom praiseworthy. The dark-swarthy black is good; and dappled horses are often good. And the white-headed brindled horse is good.[87]

---

84 A. A. Panaev (Mark Conrad, trans.), 'The Eupatoria Affair', *Russkaya Starina*, vol. XIX (1877), p.304.
85 Stanihurst, *Great Deeds*, p.123.
86 David Beers Quinn, *The Elizabethans and the Irish* (Ithica: Cornell University Press, 1966), p.169.
87 Brian Ó Cuív, 'Fragments of Irish Medieval Treatises on Horses', *Celtica*, vol.17

These colourings are pretty consistent with those of the modern Connemara pony. The 'old dun-type' Connemara pony with dorsal stripe is clearly indicated. A fourteenth century poem in the Book of Fermoy suggests the dun was considered a noble mount in the Gaelic world, and refers to 'many the vehement rider of a dun steed (*eich duinn*).'[88] Further evidence of the common horse colourings comes from the Rental and Memorandum Book of the 9th Earl of Kildare. While Kildare's racing stud was the best documented, numbering from two to three hundred stud mares, the Earls of Desmond and the Barons of Upper Ossory were not far behind as breeders of racing hobbies in Ireland. Kildare's gifts of hobbies to subordinate Kavanagh clansmen bound them to his service, and the colours were recorded. Thus, in 1514, 'To McMorowe, a bay horse, and to his wife a gray hackney; To Morairtagh Kavanagh, a black; To Morice Kevanagh, a bay,' and in 1520, 'to O'Morowe, a bay; to Gerald Kevanagh, a grey,' and in 1524, 'To M'Morowe, a sorell; To Art M'Gerald Kavanagh, a dun.'[89]

While breeds in the modern sense did not exist in the Tudor era, the Irish hobby type was internationally recognised as distinct. Recent DNA studies have shown that the hobby features prominently in the ancestry of the modern thoroughbred, contributing the 'speed gene'. Hobbies were thus highly valued and given colourful names, such as *Mac De, mac diabhail* (Son of God, son of the devil), and *Mac an Iolair* (Son of the Eagle), this last being a horse taken as booty at Farsetmore in 1567.[90] In addition to their use in the hunt and war, the hobby was raced, and the poet Tadgh Dall O Huiginn's poem on Enniskillen recalled that no herb grew around that castle, as the green was upturned by the hooves of coursing steeds.[91] In 1548, Paolo Giovio observed: 'Pacing-horses, however, throughout Ireland are produced in a pure stock; they are called "hobbies" by the English on account of their extremely gentle gait for which they are much sought after by fops.'[92]

Richard Stanihurst (1577) left the fullest description of the Irish hobby: 'The Horsses are of pase easie, in running woonderfull swift', though he faulted their galloping. He distinguished three types of hobby; 'The Nagge', the 'chief horse', and the 'moongrel hobby.' First, the 'nag or Hackeneie is very good for traueiling, albeit others report the contrary, and if he be broken accordinglie, you shall have a little Tit, that will traueyle a whole daie without anie bait.' Next, 'Their Horses of Seruice are called Chiefe Horses; being well broken, they are of an excellent courage. They reine passinglie, and champe vppon their bridles brauely; commonly they amble

---

(1985), pp.119.
88 Goodall, *Foals of Epona*, p.104.
89 Herbert Hore, 'Clan Kavanagh Temp. Henry VIII', *Journal of the Royal Society of Antiquaries of Ireland*, Seventh Series, vol. 2, no. 1 (1858), p.73.
90 Quinn, *Elizabethans and Irish*, p.169.
91 Eleanor Knott, *The Bardic Poems of Tadhg Dall Ó Huiginn* (London: Irish Texts Society, 1922), p.50.
92 Harris, 'Paolo Giovio', p.287.

not, but galloppe and run. And these Horses are but for skirmishes, not for traueilyng, for their stomackes are such as they disdaine to be hacknied, thereof the report grew that the Irish Hobby wyll not hold out in traueilyng.' Finally, 'You shall have of the third sort, a bastarde or mongrel hobbie, neere as tall as the horse of seruice, strong in traueilyng, easie in amblyng, and verie swift in running.'[93] Thomas Blunderville, writing in 1565, made no such distinctions:

> The Irish hobby is a pretty fine horse, having a good head and a body indifferently well proportioned, saving that many of them be slender and pin-buttocked. They are tender mouthed, nimble, pleasant and apt to be taught, and for the most part they be amblers and thus they are very meet for the saddle and to travel by the way. Yea, and the Irishmen, both with darts and light spears, do use to skirmish with them in the field and many of them prove to that use very well, by means they are so light and swift.[94]

In 1534, Polydore Virgil said the Irish fed their horses grass in the open air. Probably, the saddle horses were pastured outdoors year round, as used to be the case with the Connemara pony. The lord's stud grazed the waste land of his country, the keepers being entitled to meat and drink from the nearest inhabitants, a custom called *gille-cree*. The references to horses in paddocks are likely the more pampered 'chief horse', and we read of Caher Mac Art Kavanagh having 'four score chief horsses in his stable' in 1549.[95] Paolo Giovio in 1548 noted, 'After a quantity of barley and fodder, the Irish place in the mangers crispy branches of holly that have been burnt up in flames. They have learned from experience that with this nutrition they can cure cramps and invigorate digestion.'[96] In 1397, Ramón de Perilhos had noted similarly that Irish horses 'eat only grass instead of oats, and the leaves of the holly, which they roast a little on account of the prickles which are on the leaves.'[97] The Irish horseman would only ride a stallion. Stanihurst recorded that: 'they pasture mares only for the purpose of breeding: nothing in the estimation of a horseman is more disgraceful, more likely to provoke the mockery of the onlookers, than to be seated on a mare.'[98] This is confirmed by other writers, such as Moryson. The Irish horseman required a string of three horses minimum, including a saddle-horse for himself and at least one of his horseboys, while his 'chief horse' was always a led spare. Horseboys are considered in a separate chapter.

---

93 Holinshed, *Holinshed's Irish Chronicle*, p.38.
94 Goodall, *Foals of Epona*, p.156.
95 Hore, *Social State*, p.282.
96 Harris, 'Paolo Giovio', p.287.
97 Mahaffy, 'Two Early Tours', p.8.
98 Stanihurst, *Great Deeds*, p.123.

6

The Galloglass

Galloglass figures from Roscommon Abbey, County Galway. Late fifteenth century. (Journal of the Royal Historical and Archaeological Association of Ireland, 4th series, vol. 1, no. 1 (1870), p.252)

Third in the hierarchy of Irish fighting men, the galloglass was the heavily armed foot soldier, armed with an axe. They were families of hereditary mercenary warriors, originally from the Western Isles of Scotland, who had settled in the North of Ireland during the thirteenth century. The name *gallóglaigh* (galloglass) means 'foreign young champion' in Irish, and refers to their origin in the Hebrides, which the Irish called *Inse Gall*, or 'Isles of the Foreigners.' That name harks back to the centuries of Norse rule in the Islands. The galloglass were thus foreign in the sense of having a Norse element in their background, but would have found the Gaelic language and social and geographical conditions in Ireland very similar to those at home. They eventually spread south, and by the Tudor era could also be found in Connacht, Leinster and Munster, as can be seen with a glance at the tables of the 'Power of Irishmen'. Every chief who could afford it sought to hire a company of them, while the great magnates might have three or four companies.

Next to the MacDonnell's of Leinster, who are discussed in the chapter on the Pale, the MacSweeney galloglass of the O'Donnell lordship of Tyrconnell are the best documented of the septs of galloglass. Their organisation and armament are recorded in surviving documents which provide the foundation of this discussion. The O'Donnell lordship had hired Scots Highland chieftains and their retinues on a temporary basis during the thirteenth century, and the annals already refer to them as *gallóglaigh* during the succession conflict of 1290–1303. In the wake of the Scottish War of Independence of 1296–1314, many of these Highland gentry, having fought on the losing side, sought a permanent home in Ireland. The MacSweeneys were the most successful in this endeavour, three septs of the family acquiring major sub-chieftaincies in the Lordship of Tyrconnell. They held their estates in return for professional military service, on the same basis as the kin-groups of the *aosdána*, or learned class of poets, brehons, harpers, et cetera.[1] Although the galloglass lineages retained their identity, the bulk of their recruits were drawn from the general Irish population. Yet, to the end of their existence, galloglass captains were generally of the original stock, and as a whole the galloglass continued to be referred to in Latin by the term *Scotici*. A typical instance of this comes from 1553, when the MacDonnells of Leinster were described as 'the King's *Scotici*, otherwise galloglass.'[2]

Recruitment and Organisation

The MacSweeneys of Donegal served the O'Donnells as the most venerable and established of galloglass lineages in Ireland, and they were comprised of three septs. In the late sixteenth century under Magnus Ó Domhnaill and his son Aodh Ruadh (Red Hugh), the leaders of the septs were: Eóghan Og Mac Suibhne na dThuath (MacSweeney Doe, foster father to Red Hugh and principal leader of his galloglass), Domhnall Mac Siubhne Fánad (MacSweeney Fánad), and Donnchadh Mac Suibhne na Tír Boghaine (MacSweeney Banagh). The muster of the three septs is recalled by O'Donnell's steward

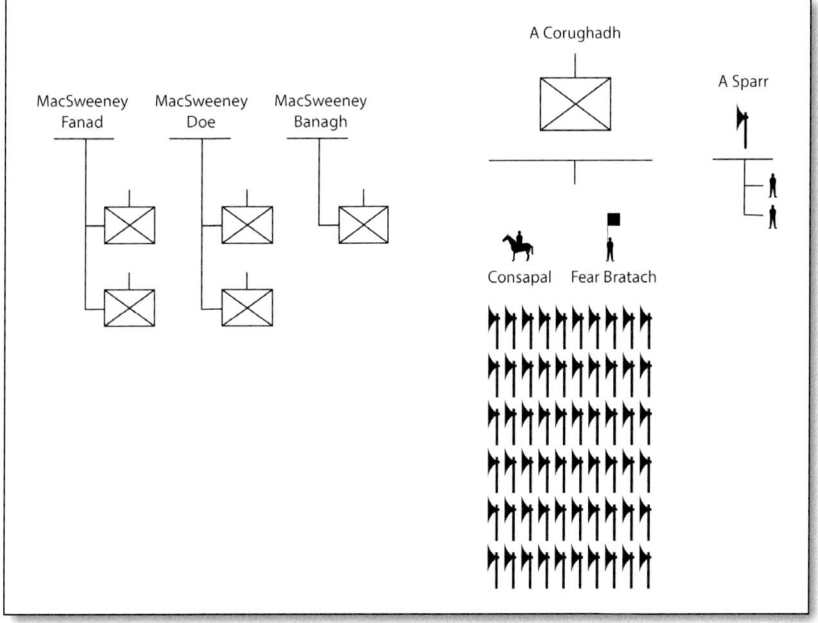

MacSweeney organization

---

1 Katherine Simms, 'Late Medieval Donegal' in William Nolan, Liam Ronayne and Mariead Dunleavy (eds), *Donegal History and Society: Interdisciplinary Essays on the History of an Irish County* (Dublin: Geography Publications, 1995), p.188.
2 Kenneth Nicholls, 'Scots Mercenary Kindreds in Ireland, 1230–1600' in Seán Duffy (ed.), *The World of the Galloglass* (Dublin: Four Courts Press, 2007), p.86.

'OF KERNS AND GALLOWGLASSES'

MacSweeney grave slab at Killybegs, County Donegal. Late fifteenth century. (Author's drawing)

in an anonymous eighteenth century manuscript in the Cambridge Manuscript Library:

> This is the evidence of Donnell O'Gallagher, who is eight-one years, concerning every old custom that O'Donnell had in the land of Conall anno Domini 1626.
>
> - Due from McSweeney Fánad, 18 marks for beefing from him and 10 marks for permanent hired soldiers and one hundred and twenty galloglasses with mail shirts, and a bullock as price for a lacking mail shirt, except for a galloglass man who had been promised.
> - Due from McSweeney Doe, the same amount.
> - Due from McSweeney Banagh, sixty galloglasses with mail shirts, a man to carry the mail shirt and stone of Columcille in addition to these.[3]

Thus the MacSweeney galloglass company, or 'battle' (*corughadh*), consisted of 60 men 'on their feet', to use the contemporary expression. The 'Power of Irishmen' says 'A Batayle of Galoglas be 60 or 80 men harneysed on foot wth sparres Everi one wherof hath his knave to beare his harneys wherof sume have speares sume have bowes.'[4] In 1575, it was reported that in Ulster, 'The captain of galloglasse hath for a quarter, one chief horse and a hackney, or for the hackney an habergeon, and in a band of 100 he hath to advance his wages, 13 dead pays out of the 100; so the band of 100 is but 87 men. The captain is also allowed for his own victuals six men's allowances.'[5] Deadpays were a number of galloglass by which the battle was allowed to fall short, and whose pay went into the pocket of the captain, or 'constable' (*consapal* or *constábla*), a concession to corruption possibly adopted from English usage. High Constables and Chief Constables are occasionally mentioned.

---

[3] McGettigan, Darren, *Red Hugh O'Donnell and the Nine Years' War* (Dublin: Four Courts Press, 2005), p.131.
[4] Price, 'Armed Forces', p.206.
[5] *Calendar of the Carew Manuscripts*, vol. 2, 1575–1588, J. S. Brewrer and William Bullen eds. (London: Longman & Co., 1867), p.9, (?) April, A Note of Ulster, Malby.

A. MacGillapatrick Chieftain, c. **1510–40.**
(Illustration by Seán Ó Brógain © Helion & Company 2024)
See Colour Plate Commentaries for further information.

B. A Mounted 'Spear' of the Pale, 1515.
(Illustration by Seán Ó Brógain © Helion & Company 2024)
See Colour Plate Commentaries for further information.

C. Standard Bearer of Irish kern, 1544.
(Illustration by Seán Ó Brógain © Helion & Company 2024)
See Colour Plate Commentaries for further information.

D. Irish Horseman, c. **1550.**
(Illustration by Seán Ó Brógain
© Helion & Company 2024)
See Colour Plate Commentaries for
further information.

E. Redshank, *c.* **1550**
(Illustration by Seán Ó Brógain © Helion & Company 2024)
See Colour Plate Commentaries for further information.

F. Galloglass, *c.* **1570**
(Illustration by Seán Ó Brógain © Helion & Company 2024)
See Colour Plate Commentaries for further information.

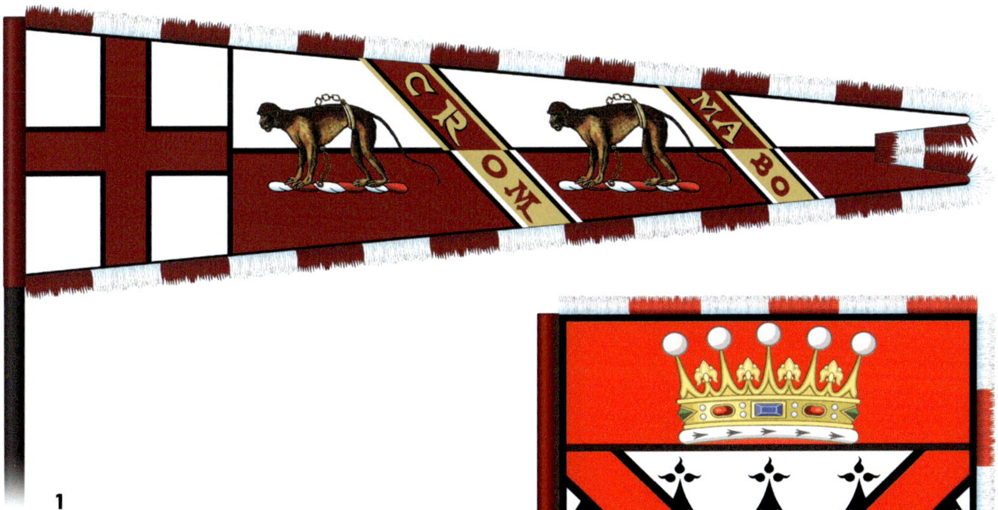

1

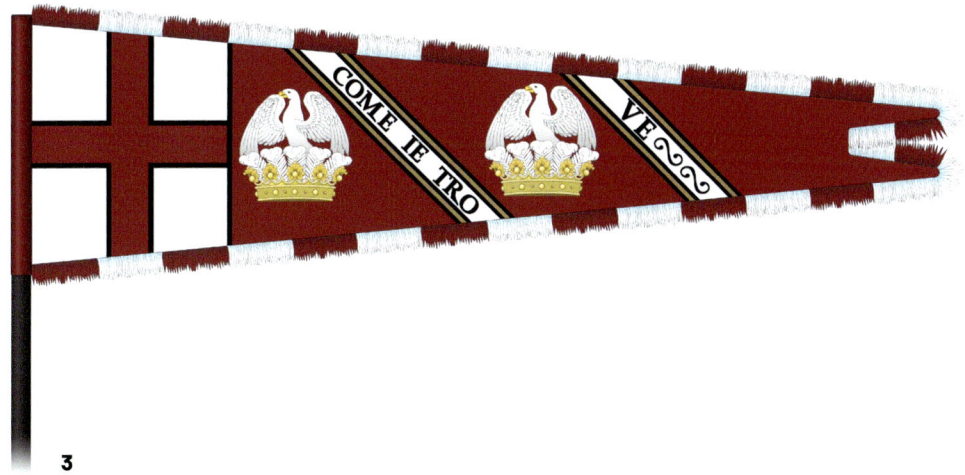

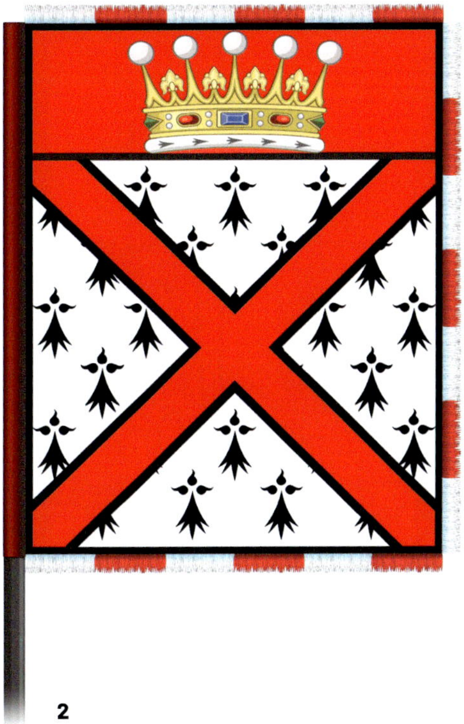

2

3

G. Irish Standards and Banners
(Illustrations by Anderson Subtil © Helion & Company 2024)
See Colour Plate Commentaries for further information.

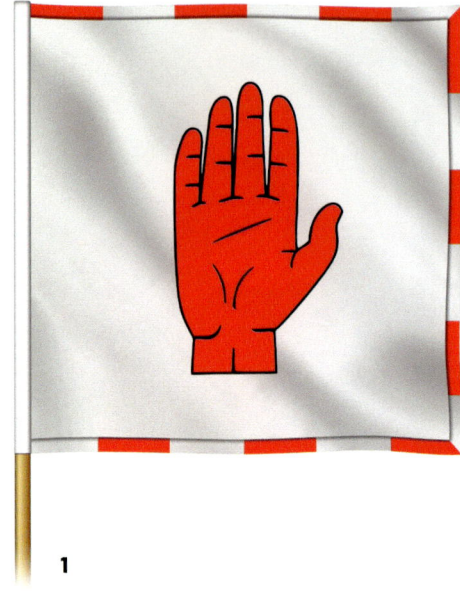

H. Irish Banners
(Illustrations by Anderson Subtil © Helion & Company 2024)
See Colour Plate Commentaries for further information.

Contemporary writers are almost universally complimentary regarding the galloglass as soldiers. Deputy St Leger, in 1543, spoke of the galloglass as being 'harnessed in mail and bassenettes, having every one of them his weapon, called a sparre, much like the axe of the Tower.'[6] He says 'their boys bear for them three darts, which darts they throw, ere they come to the hand strife: these men be those that do not lightly abandon the field, but bide the brunt to the death.' In 1600, John Dymmock famously called them 'picked and selected men of great and mighty bodies, cruel without compassion. The greatest force of the battle consisteth in them, choosing to die rather than to yield, so that when it cometh to handy blows, they are quickly slain or win the field.'[7] Stanihurst said they were a class of cloaked soldiers, 'of great stature, muscled beyond what is normal, brave fighters, utterly bloodthirsty and ruthless soldiers.' He asserted that they harbour an *odium humanitatis* (a hatred of humanity), and that 'before anyone is enrolled into their company, he swears, with religious solemnity [*magna religione iurat*], that whenever he comes to fight in the front line, he will never turn his back – although this practice is becoming increasingly outdated.'[8] Father Good, *c.* 1566, spoke of them as 'Veteran soldiers reserved for the rear whom they terme Galloglasses, and who fight with most keen hatchets.'[9] Paolo Giovio spoke of them in similar terms in 1548 as 'heavily armed foot soldiers, called galloglass in their own language, who are like veterans brought up in the camps and bringing forth wars from wars …. But the galloglass fights with such tenacity that, without fear of death, he thinks to be defeated bravely or to be killed honourably in the moment.'[10] The English Administrator Cowley, writing in 1537, took a different view: 'Galloghaghes are noon other but as a kynde of sowchynners [switzers], that serveth for their wages, and not for love ne affection to their maister, that they serve; and emonges 200 of theme shalbe skaunt 8th, that are gentilmen, or to loke like hable men, and all the residue sklawes and out of the Irishrie.' Cowley, speaking very loosely, and with great antipathy towards the Irish system, seems to think the galloglass should be classed with the unfree labourers, since they are not freeholders in the usual sense. But, as noted above, they held lands as members of the professional class, which included poets, lawyers, et cetera. Cowley is correct in that their ranks were increasingly recruited 'out of the Irishrie', and this was particularly true in the south of the country. He goes on to describe the galloglass captains filling their ranks with recruits drawn from the territory in which they held land, and arming them out of their

---

6   Maxwell, *Irish History*, pp.220–1.
7   Maxwell, *Irish History*, p.221.
8   Stanihurst, *Great Deeds*, p.123.
9   William Camden, *Britain, or a chorographical description of the Most Flourishing Kingdomes, England, Scotland, and Ireland* (London: F. Kingston, R. Young and I. Legatt, for George Latham, 1637), p.147.
10   Harris, 'Paolo Giovio', pp.287–8.

'OF KERNS AND GALLOWGLASSES'

stock of mail shirts: 'And then the capitaynes of the galloglaghes, having a numbre of mayle harneysse, as they are accustumed alway, at tymes when the warres so require, being wadgid by the cyntrey, to trye and take up within the same cuntrey, of the chosen folkes of the same cuntrey birthe, to the number wadgid and reteynid.'[11] In the south, and in more Anglicised districts, the galloglass may have lost some standing as professionals. This is indicated by the harsh discipline mentioned by Lord Deputy Sussex, describing a Desmond galloglass in 1558 being nailed to a post for stealing a mail shirt, while another was hanged for drawing a weapon in camp.[12]

Donat O'Suibne grave slab at Sligo Abbey, County Sligo, 1577 (Author's drawing)

The smaller sub-unit of the galloglass battle was the 'sparr', named for the galloglass axe or 'sparth'. This consisted of the galloglass himself plus a man for his harness bearer and a boy to carry his provision, according to Dymmok. Referring to these camp servants of the galloglass, the Irish annalists record the 'galloglasses and *gíománachs*' of the rebel Butler brothers being defeated by the Earl of Desmond.[13] The term *gíománach* meant a lackey, and was a loan word derived from the English 'yeoman'. The Government's MacDonnell galloglass in Leinster were only allowed one such attendant, and this is also the number indicated by the 'Power of Irishmen' ('Everi one wherof hath his knave'), which likely reflects the practice as it existed in the province of Leinster. While the number of sparrs in a battle of galloglass was usually either 60 or 80, the difference can't be pinned down geographically. As given in Chapter 1 above, battles of 60 served the MacWilliam Burkes in Connacht, while MacCarthy Mor battles could be either 60 or 80. Thus, he cessed '60 axes or sparres' on Irreight, but also '160 axes' (two battles of 80) in MacMorrice's country. Note that the synonyms

---

11 *State Papers: Henry VIII*, p.448, n.d., R. Cowley to Henry VIII.
12 G. A. Hayes-McCoy, *Scots Mercenary Forces in Ireland, 1565–1603* (Dublin: Burns Oates & Washbourne, 1937), p.58.
13 Edmund Hogan, *The Description of Ireland in Anno 1598* (Dublin: H. M. Gill & Son, 1878), p.52.

used for 'galliglasse' in these documents, 'mail', 'sparres', and 'axes', all indicate the expected equipment for each galloglass; a mail shirt and an axe.

The system by which galloglass were maintained was called 'Bonnaght', and was of three sorts. Basic Bonnaght or *Buannacht Bhuna* (Bonaght-Bonny) referred to the quartering of galloglass upon a territory, as negotiated between the lord and his tenants. *Buannacht Bhairr* (Bonney-Bur) meant an imposition above that of Basic Bonnaght, usually for additional galloglass hired in wartime. *Buannacht Bheag* (Bonaghtbeg) was the substitution of a money payment 'towards the finding of galliglasse' in place of providing actual *Buannacht*. *Soren* was an allowance beyond *Buannacht*, extracted from the people as spending money for the galloglass, at the rate of 2s 8d for a day and a night, divided between three sparrs for their meat, drink and lodging.[14] In Munster, each of the three spars received 12d for a day and a night, and *soren* was paid as a 'sroan' (*srubhán*), which was an oatcake a foot and a half broad, or 1.5 gallons of oatmeal, valued at 6d, and a 'quirren', or 4lb of butter, also valued at 6d.[15]

In 1568, the government asked the captains of the Leinster MacDonnells to provide information on the wages of galloglass. They replied that in Leinster, Munster and Ulster, galloglass were engaged by the quarter, and every sparr received 5s 8d Irish. The country also had to provide them with a daily allowance for victuals, consisting of 1d per day in money plus 'bred corne and butter.' In Connacht, the quarterly wages were higher, at 7s per quarter, while the daily victual allowance was half that of the other provinces.[16] In 1575, the pay for a galloglass in Ulster 'for a quarter of a year, when it is best cheap, is one beef for his wages, and two beefs for his feeding and diet.'[17] Stanihurst mentions the galloglass feeding mostly on beef, pork and butter, but we get a more detailed view of the galloglass diet from presentments made before a jury at the Kilkenny Sessions in 1537. There, the Lord of Ossory was accused of charging the inhabitants coign and livery for 160 galloglass, 'being in number 320 persons.' The diet was, 'on fleshe dayes, fleshe, breade, and ale, and on fyshe dayies, fyshe and breade.'[18] The fish was most likely salt hake and salt herring, important exports for Ireland. For Barnaby Rich wrote of 'the Kearne of Ireland, amongst whom there is not so notable a wretch to bee found, that will not obserue his fasting daies, three daies a weeke at the least, and those are Wednesdaies, Fridaies and Saturdaies: then they haue other Vigiles, and such Saint Eeues, as I neuer heard of but in Ireland.'[19]

---

14   Simms, *Kings to Warlords*, pp.139 & 171.
15   W. F. Butler, 'The Lordship of Mac Carthy Mór' in *Journal of the Royal Society of Antiquaries*, pt. 4, vol. 36 (1906), p.354.
16   Butler, 'Rate of the Wages', pp.87–90.
17   *Cal. Carew Mss*, p.9., ? April, A Note of Ulster, Malby.
18   Hore, *Social State*, p.88.
19   Barnaby Rich, *A new Description of Ireland* (London: William Jaggard, 1610), p.11.

'OF KERNS AND GALLOWGLASSES'

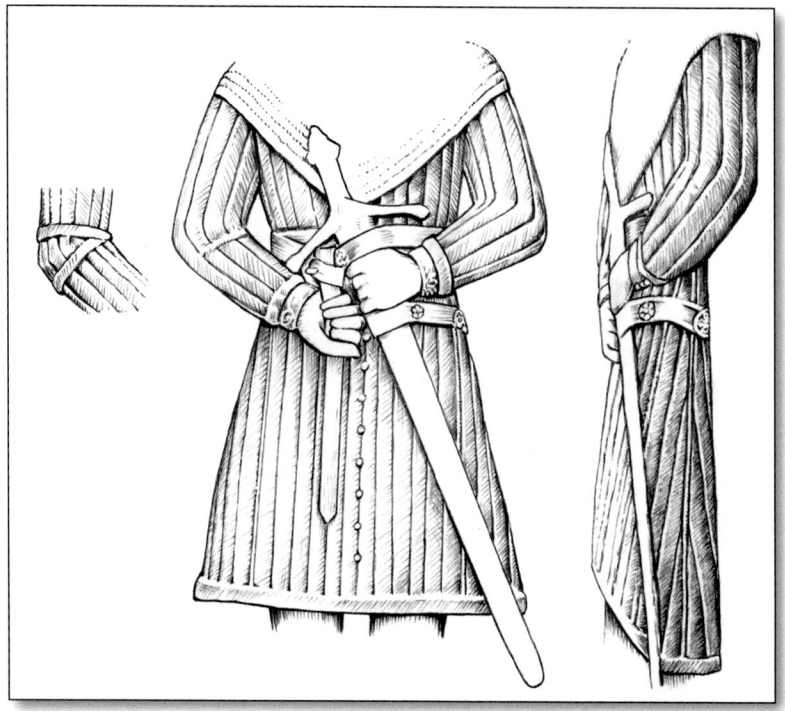

A *cotún*, from an unidentified effigy at Oransay Priory, c. 1350–1500. It fastens down the front with small round buttons, and the skirt has been widened by having two gores shaped like right triangles let into each side seam from waist to hem. This same tailoring technique was used in the long Irish coats, as on that worn by the driver of carriages shown earlier. The insert, from an effigy at Kilmory, shows elbow bands of unknown function. These bands are also present on the galloglass carvings from Roscommon, shown above. (Author's drawing, after Steer and Bannerman)

Edward Tremayne implied that the galloglass had a higher social standing than other Irish soldiers: 'The galloglass for the most part being gentlemen, and in time of peace using to live honestly upon their lands.'[20] It seems that the galloglass, because of his status as a trusted professional, could serve as his lord's personal attendant or emissary. In the indictment of Brian O'Rourke is: 'In April, 1586, the said Sir Brian O'Rourke sent one Ashernan, his gallyglasse, to Surloghe boy his sonn, called Alexander, to come to hym with such force as he could make …. Also Gillispicke, a galliglasse, was likewise sent to Alexander McSurloy.'[21] These may have been the 'lord's galloglass' (*gallóglach tierna*), a personal servant of an Irish chieftain who 'waited on him in his chamber.'[22] He was a bodyguard drawn from the ranks of the lord's galloglass companies, each of which provided one 'dead pay' towards his upkeep. This office was actually adopted by the English Lord Deputy's household, which included a 'galloglass' who carried the Deputy's helmet while running at his stirrup. The man holding an axe in Derricke's depiction of an Irish chief preparing to mount is likely the lord's galloglass. Lord Deputy Fitzwilliam's household accounts lists the clothing provided: 'The Galloglass: 2½ yards of grene Carsey to make him Trowses, 6s. 6d.; 1 pr of brogges, 12d.; a band and towards the buying of a shirt, 2s. 6d.; strings for shirt-bands, 5d.'[23] Writing a century later, in 1704, Martin Martin lists the household of a Hebridean chief, among whom he notes the 'galloglass' as the chief's armour bearer.[24] This is seconded by James Kirkwood, in a less well known manuscript of *c.* 1699, who says: 'The Head of ane Family hath commonly ane Armour Bearer who goes in his full Armour before his Master, intervening betwixt him and all Hazard in tyme of Warr. This is

---

20 Quinn, *Elizabethans and Irish*, p.40.
21 Hayes-McCoy, *Scots Mercenary*, p.360.
22 Nicholls, 'Scottish Mercenary', p.87.
23 Hayes-McCoy, *Scots Mercenary*, p.360.
24 Martin Martin, *Description of the Western Islands of Scotland* (London: Andrew Bell, 1703), p.104.

called *Galloglach*.'[25] This seemingly out-of-place use of the term 'galloglass' may indicate that the function of galloglass as retainer was adopted in the Hebrides after the Irish example.

'Galloglass Well Armed According to the Usage of the Country'

Bagenall, in 1598, recalled that the MacSweeney's were 'all Galloglases, That is men armed with Coates of Mayl Steel Bonetts, Swords and pole axes.'[26] The *Book of the MacSweeneys*, written some time after 1514, gives a more complete description of the equipment required:

> 31. And it was then that a levy of galloglasses was made on Clann Suibhne, and this is how the levy was made: two galloglasses for each quarter of land, and two cows for each galloglass deficient, that is, one cow for the man himself and one for his equipment. And Clann Suibhne say they are responsible for these as follows, that for each man equipped with a mail shirt and a pisane collar, a second man should have a jack and a helmet; that there should be no forfeit for a helmet deficient except the galloglass's brain [dashed out for want of it]; and no fine for a missing axe except a shilling, nor for a spear, except a groat, which shilling and groat the Constable should get, and O'Donnell had no claim to make on either. And previous to this arrangement no lord had a claim on them for a rising-out or a hosting, but they might serve whomsoever they wished. It was the Scottish habit [of military service] they had observed until that time, namely each man according as he was employed.[27]

This passage is sometimes interpreted to mean that one sort of galloglass has a mail shirt and pisane collar, while a second sort has a jack and helmet. The term 'second man', or *dara fher*, is ambiguous and could mean the primary warrior's second, or apprentice, or theoretically, a second line soldier. In fact, I believe this passage may describe how the full armour of a galloglass should be divided between the two attendants that 'bear his harneys'. The words used for mail shirt and pisane collar are *luirech agus sgabal*, and for jack and helmet, *seca agus cinnbert*, while the term for axe is *tuaigh*. All of these elements are listed as early as 1428, when Swayne describes the galloglass accompanying Lord Grey: '8 batazllys of fotmen arrayde of the

---

25   James Kirkwood (J. L. Campbell ed.), *A Collection of Highland Rites and Customs, c. 1699*, (Rochester: D. S. Bewer, Ltd., 1975), p.41.
26   Hogan, *Description Ireland 1598*, p.29.
27   Paul Walsh, *Leabhar Chlainne Suibhe* (Dublin: Dollard, printinghouse, 1920), pp.44–45.

gyse of this contre, that is owry man in acton, habirchon, pischane and basnete.'[28] Clearly, these four items together formed the complete galloglass harness. It defies logic to accept that a man clad in expensive mail would forgo the protection of a helmet, and the MacSweeney regulation goes on to indicate that any galloglass foolish enough to present himself for muster without a helmet need not be fined since he would pay for it by having his brain dashed out. And one cannot wear mail effectively without a padded foundation garment. This was called a *cotún*, from the French haqueton, or else *seca*, from the word jack or side jack (i.e., long jack), found in Anglo-Irish documents. It was a vertically ridged garment reaching just below the knees, seen extending below the hem and elbows of mail shirts in grave slab depictions of fifteenth and sixteenth century Irish armours, and made of many layers of linen stitched together.

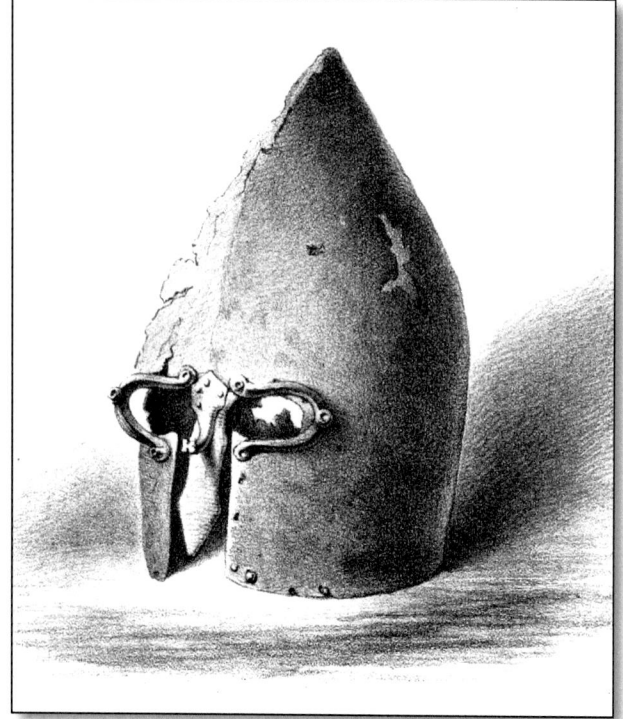

Typically high-pointed Irish helmet, of barbute form, from Lough Henny, County Down. Note upturned nasal of brass. Compare to the De Burgo horseman above. (Ulster Journal of Archaeology (UJA), 1st series, vol. 3, 1855, p.52).

This form of armour is well illustrated in the late fifteenth century galloglass carvings from Roscommon Abbey. These show absolute uniformity, each man being harnessed in a pointed and faceted bascinet, deep pisane collar, mail shirt and padded jack or *cotún*. The uniformity could extend to the colour of the fabric 'syde jack' or *cotún*, for of the Irish contingent sent to the Siege of Rouen in 1418, 18 score were clad in white *cotuin*, and 18 score in red *cotuin*.[29] This full panoply was worn by the MacSweeneys into the late sixteenth century, as seen in the contemporary illustrations above. Note the spreading (horsehair?) crest seen on the scull of galloglass in both images, and the similar styles of axe. The galloglass depicted in John Derricke's woodcuts of 1581 are armed more simply in a longer sleeved shirt of mail and a scull, without a pisane collar. But the MacSweeney grave slabs provide examples of the same armour found on the Roscommon effigy still in use well into the sixteenth century. In fact, Lord Justice Drury wrote in 1579 of meeting a number of mounted O'Reillys, 'most of them wearing glibes, and armed in mail, with pesants [pisane collars] and skulls.'[30] The Irish bascinet was unusually high-pointed, and several surviving examples show them to have been closely fitted, curving gracefully inwards towards the neck at their

---

28 Peter Harbison, 'Native Irish Arms and Armour in Medieval Gaelic Literature, 1170–1600', *Irish Sword*, vol. 12. (1975–76), p.282.
29 Harbison, 'Native Irish Arms', p.183.
30 Maxwell, *Irish History*, p.222.

bottom edge. They are a close match to the Roscommon Abbey galloglass carvings, as is a surviving mail shirt, with slightly flaring elbow length sleeves, that was published in 1877 by Robert Day of the Royal of Society of Antiquaries of Ireland.

This harness survived even later in the Western Isles of Scotland, used into the seventeenth century by the chief's personal retainer, called 'galloglass'. A military census of Athollmen taken on the eve of the Civil War in 1638 shows that of 523 men, 10 retained helmets, mail shirts and a long 'halbert aix'.[31] And the Woodrow Mss, describing the 'Highland host' of 1678, mentions 'steel-bonnets raised like pyramids', obviously the same faceted bacinet seen on the Roscommon Abbey galloglass above.[32] Around 1699, Rev. Kirkwood's *Collection of Highland Rites and Customs* states that 'Of old they used …. Mailcoats, Head-pieces …. and that which they called Scapul, which covered their Shoulders.' In fact, a powder horn carving of around this date shows a 'lord's galloglass' manservant still wearing the vertically ridged *cotún* or jack.

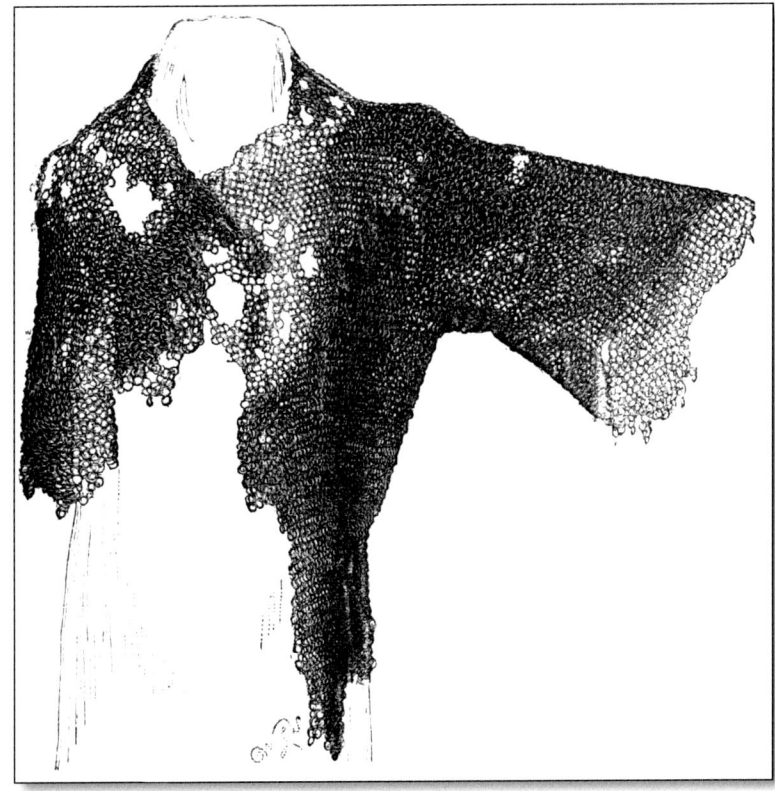

Shirt of mail displayed by Robert Day in 1876. Note the flaring, elbow length sleeves, as often seen in Irish armours. (Journal of the Royal Society of Archaeology of Ireland, volume IV, 4th series, 1877, p.495.)

The Galloglass Axe

The axe used by the Irish galloglass was a direct descendant of the old 'Dane axe' of archaeological classification Petersen Type M. This is a reflection of the Norse ancestry of the galloglass. The Irish galloglass axe was called a sparth or sparr in Anglo-Irish documents, and was called *taugh* in Irish. It represents the latest practical employment of an axe of the Petersen Type M. The Dane Axe emerged in the northern world in the eleventh century,

---

31 John Murray, *Chronicles of the Atholl and Tullibardine Families,* vol. 1 (Edinburgh: Ballantyne Press, 1908), Appendix, pp.x–xx

32 James Drummond, *Ancient Scottish Weapons* (Edinburgh/London: George Waterston & Sons, 1881), p.15.

spreading throughout a broad area of Norse influence. It was exclusively a two-handed axe, with a large head and a handle from four to six feet long. With a head of remarkably thin construction, it was much handier to flourish than its size might suggest. We are told its stroke could take off a horseman's leg and topple his horse.[33] Indeed, it was to counter the mounted Norman knights that the galloglass were first introduced to Ireland.

The Western Isles of Scotland, from whence the original galloglass migrated to Ireland, were a Norse kingdom for hundreds of years. The Dane Axe had already begun to undergo some local modifications in the Isles before its likely appearance in Ireland starting around *c*. 1260. The earliest surviving galloglass axes, from Co. Mayo and Co. Donegal, are in the National Museum of Ireland and have a long straight cutting edge, a convex or 'humped' upper edge, and a concave lower edge. Such axe heads are described in a sixteenth century poem as being broad, narrow-necked, and curve backed (*cul-croma*).[34] They are a uniquely Gaelic development, and seem to be a direct outgrowth of that form of Dane Axe that had a pronounced fore-tip on the blade's upper edge. Recently, dredging operations in the River Blackwater in Co. Tyrone recovered three more galloglass axes of this type, published by Cormac Burke in 2001 as 'Class 21'.[35] These three axe heads, firmly dated to the sixteenth century, are larger than the examples from Co. Mayo and Co. Donegal, and seem to represent a further development of the type. They have an elongated blade with a cutting edge characteristically diverging from the line of the haft by being tilted slightly forward. But the 'hump' of the concave upper edge of the blade has been extended higher, while the concave lower edge is extended down in a 'beard'. This gives a cutting edge about a foot broad, as Stanihurst had described in 1584: 'Their weapons are one foot in length, resembling double-headed hatchets [*bipennis*], almost sharper than razors, fixed on shafts of more than ordinary length.'[36] In 1529, John Major, writing like Stanihurst in erudite Latin, also described the Scottish Leith axe of his day as *bipennis*, strictly a 'double-headed axe', but this seems to have been a conventional way of referring to an axe.[37] Alongside this highly distinct axe, the earlier form of Petersen Type M (Bourke Class 11) may have persisted, though these are hard to date archaeologically. Their continuing presence is suggested by Derricke's woodcuts, and the galloglass on the Dublin Charter of 1583. A written reference to such an axe in the hands of galloglass occurs in a letter of 1583, from Jerome Bowes, Elizabeth's ambassador at the Court

---

33 Ewart Oakeshott, *A Knight and His Weapons* (Wyomoissing: Dufour Editions, 1964), p.45.
34 Harbison, 'Native Irish Arms', p.279.
35 Cormac Bourke, 'Antiquities from the River Blackwater III, Iron Axe Heads', *Ulster Journal of Archaeology*, vol. 60 (2001), pp.63–93.
36 G. A. Hayes-McCoy, 'The Gallóglach Axe', *Journal of the Galway Archaeological and Historical Society*, vol. 17 (1937), pp.105.
37 Claude Blair, *Scottish Weapons and Fortifications, 1100–1800* (Edinburgh: John Donald, 1981), p.20.

of Ivan IV of Russia. He describes the Czar's personal guards, the *Rindis*, 'holding upon their shoulders each of them a broad axe, much like to a galloglass axe of Ireland, thin and very sharp, the 'steal', or handle, not past a half yard long.'[38] As in Ireland, these Russian axes were a cultural artefact of Norse origin. Bowes noted the Russian axes had a short 'steal' or handle, and while not suggesting that the galloglass axe shared this characteristic, his words call to mind Spencer's description of Grantorto, quoted below, who also carried an axe whose 'steel …. was not long', called in Irish *gearrsamtac*, or short handled. The lone axe featured in the Roscommon galloglass carvings appears short handled, but this may be an artistic distortion, possibly introduced to ensure a more robust monument.

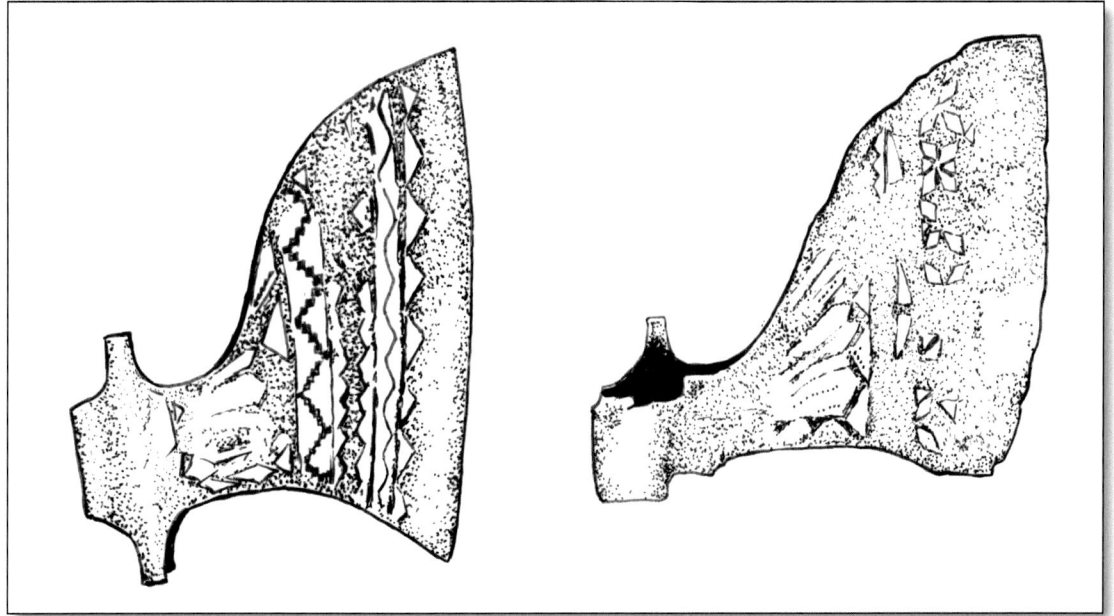

Galloglass axes from Counties Donegal and Mayo, both have silver decoration. Possibly late fifteenth century. (Author's drawing)

Unlike sword blades, galloglass axes were readily produced by sixteenth century Irish smiths, and they were manufactured locally in large numbers. In 1589, a letter preserved in the State Papers notes that the rebel Burkes had employed the MacDonnell galloglass sept of Mayo. These MacDonnells were said to have 'made of late 400 galloglass axes.' Another letter from the same source confirms that 'daily they are making Galloglass axes, and other weapons.'[39] There is also a reference to the specialised manufacture of wooden handles for galloglass axes. In the 1590s, when Feagh Mac Hugh O'Byrne was modernising his forces, substituting the pike for the galloglass axe, it was reported that he 'set all the axemen to make pikes, and the smiths to make heads for them.'[40]

---

38   Quinn, *Elizabethans and Irish*, p.98.
39   Hayes-McCoy, *Scots Mercenary*, p.112.
40   G. A. Hayes-McCoy, 'The Army of Ulster, 1593–1601', *Irish Sword*, vol. 1, no. 2

Domhnall Mac Siubhne Fánad, Chief of MacSweeney Fánad from 1570–1619, is described in bardic poetry as having a specially decorated axe: 'an ogham inscription is on his axe whose bounty is victory.'[41] The Ogham Tract in the *Book of Ballymote*, c. 1400, shows that this alphabet continued to be studied in the bardic schools of the late medieval era. Ogham inscriptions were often notched on lengths of wood, and it is possible the MacSweeney poem described an actual practice. The veteran Captain Nicholas Dawtrey, writing in 1597, made a unique observation regarding the galloglass axe:

> they haue Galloglass, and ar armed with jackes and shirtes of Maile down unto ther knees, and haue sculls on ther heads, and Axes which haue broade bittes or Edges, sett upon very good staues, as longe as the steel of a browne Bill, and the poles of ther Axes sett full of square steel pinnes, to strike with the pole of ther Axe, to pearce Armour.[42]

In 1543, as stated above, St Leger said that the galloglass sparr was 'much like the axe of the Tower.' The axes carried today by the Yeomen Warders of the Tower date to the sixteenth century. Their shafts are five feet four inches in length, the head being a remarkable survival of a Petersen Type M, with spurs top and bottom of the neck, and a very pronounced fore-tip. The shafts are studded with four rows of brass nails. Is something similar indicated by Dawtrey's pole 'set full of square steel pinnes'? This seems to be the meaning of Spencer's description of the giant Grantorto in the *Faerie Queen*, who was modelled after a galloglass:

> All armed in a coat of iron plate,
> of great defence to ward the deadly fear,
> And on his head a steel cap did wear
> of colour rusty brown but sure and strong;
> And in his hand an huge poleax did bear,
> Whose steel [handle] was iron-studded but not long,
> With which he wont to fight, to justify his wrong.[43]

Significantly, the two earliest identified galloglass axes, from Co. Mayo and Co. Donegal, are both decorated with appliqué bands of silver foil, cut in simple patterns of zigzags and stepped pyramid shapes. This style of decoration is matched by the carving on a cross slab at Kilmaha, Argyll. The later galloglass axe from Clonteevy, Co. Tyrone, also has its blade overlaid with silver foil in a series of parallel vertical strips, cut in chevron and lozenge

---

(1949–53), p.115.
41 Simms, 'Images of Galloglass', p.118.
42 Dawtrey, 'A Booke', p.90.
43 Quinn, *Elizabethans and Irish*, p.93.

THE GALLOGLASS

shapes. Mahr suggested 'that ornamented axes were not an everyday rank-and-file weapon, but a better class of axe used on ceremonial occasions.'[44] Perhaps, but if so, it is remarkable that three of the surviving galloglass axes bear such decoration. Of course, silver decoration is occasionally found on the Dane Axe from which the galloglass axe derives. And similar silver appliqué adorns an axe head found at Loch Leven in Scotland and dated to c. 1470.[45] It is certainly noteworthy that when in 1552 the English Court required suitably Irish props for 'An Irisshe playe of the State of Ireland', these included: 'An Irysshe howlbarte the blade foyled with syluer.'[46] Finally, as we will see below, in 1538 we have another reference to a 'galloglasse with a silver spear [sparr] or axe …. the hilt thereof hanging full of silk.' While not resolving the question of how common such silver decoration was, this last quote raises the subject of the use of the galloglass axe as a ceremonial weapon.

The galloglass axe seems to have served as the sign of a chief's authority. In 1538, Lord Deputy Grey was criticised for placing himself in danger, having received a rather slender safe passage from O'Brien while crossing

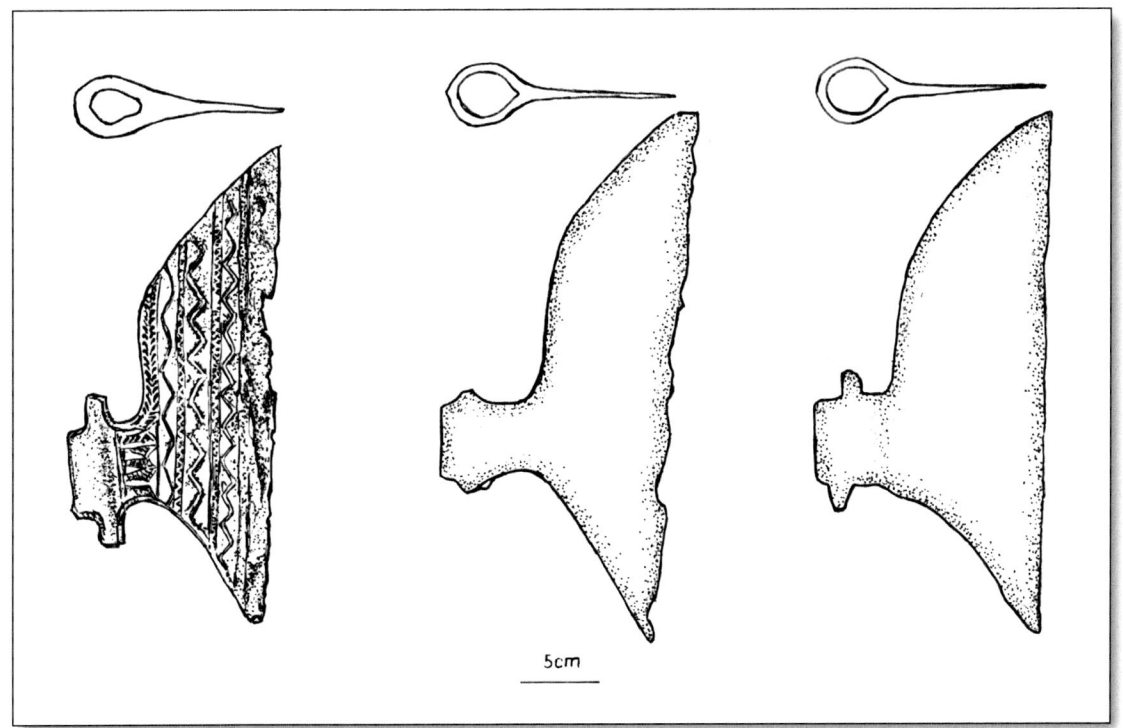

Galloglass axes from County Tyrone. One with silver decoration. Sixteenth century. (Author's drawing)

---

44 Adolph Mahr, 'The Galloglach Axe' in *Journal of the Galway Archaeological Society*, vol. 18 (1938), pp.66–68.
45 Blair, *Scottish Weapons*, p.208–9.
46 Albert Feuillerat, *Documents Relating to the Revels at Court in the time of King Edward VI and Queen Mary, 1550–54* (Louvain: A. Uystpruyst, 1914), pp.66–68.

his territory. O'Brien merely 'sent a galloglasse with him [Grey] for his conduct and salve passage; who, going before him with an axe, conducte him thoroughe Thomonde, wherin they had soche streightes and narrow passages, that if a hundred men had set upon my Lord, they mought have distressed him and all his company.' John Darcy, who accompanied Grey, later complained: 'And the said Lord Deputy having O'Brien's promise to have been conducted by him to Ulicke de Burghe, in the end he [O'Brien] deceived him, sending but one galloglasse with a silver spear [sparr] or axe, and the hilt thereof hanging full of silk, to be his guide, and so went with them to Galway.' When Ulicke de Burghe finally greeted him, he demanded to know why he came so meagerly attended through such a dangerous passage. Grey said 'Lo! Seest thou not yonder standing before me O'Brien's axe for my conduct.'[47] The great student of Irish folkways, E. Estyn Evans, once cautioned that it was never safe to assume that any custom had entirely died out in Ireland. And indeed, it is a remarkable fact that as late as the 1890s, O'Connell of Derrynane – styled the King or *Ri* by the local people – could ensure the safe passage of even an exciseman through his territory by the carrying before him of the 'crooked knife', an old pruning hook which was known as the sign of his authority: 'A tenant would walk out and give up his holding at the bidding of the bearer of the crooked knife.'[48] The galloglass axe could also serve as a sign of victory. In 1569, during the Butler Rebellion, a battle occurred at Kilkenny, and 'When the fighte was ended and the enymyes overthrown, everye man toke a galloweglasse axe of theires who were slain, and caryed it with theyme into the towne in signe of victorie.'[49]

Training

When asked to commence the fight at Knockdoe in 1504, a galloglass captain famously replied: 'I am glad. You can do me no more honour, be Gods blode, and he took his axe in his hand and begane to flouryshe.'[50] Would that we knew exactly how this professional handled his weapon. Certainly there was an art to it. Turlough MacDonnell, who died in 1435, is described in the *Annals of Ulster* as being *sai galloglaig*, 'a galloglass artist.'[51]

In fact it may be possible to glean something from sixteenth century fighting manuals. In *Paradoxes of Defence*, the English soldier George Silver mentions the battle-axe among such polearms as the halberd and

---

47 Mahr, 'The Galloglach Axe', p.68.
48 Caoimhín Ó Danachair, '*An Ri* (the King) An example of Traditional Social Organisation' in *Journal of the Royal Society of Antiquaries of Ireland*, vol. 111 (1981), pp.14–28.
49 T. Phillips, 'The Life of Sir Peter Carew' in *Archaeologia*, no. 27 (1839), p.139.
50 Hayes-McCoy, *Irish Battles*, p.60.
51 Paul Walsh, 'Scots Clann Domhnaill in Ireland', *Irish Ecclesiastical Record*, ser. 5, no. 48 (1936), p.37.

MacSweeney Galloglass depicted on Gough's map of Ulster, 1567. The two standing figures have red *cotuin*, or aketons. Note typically Irish spreading crest and the flared, elbow length sleeves of the mail shirts. (Author's drawing)

bill[52]. He says it should be five or six feet in length and it is just possible that he is describing the galloglass axe, which he might have encountered in Ireland. This has been a starting point for practitioners of HEMA, who have published their work on this subject.[53] More basic training certainly included the grappling we see depicted on the MacSweeney grave slab from Killybegs, Co. Donegal, which shows two figures engaged in what appears to be backhold wrestling, or *barróg*, practised into the early twentieth century in the rural West of Ireland. The galloglass remained primarily an elite individual warrior whose weapon required power and trained skill to use effectively. The galloglass were also described as powerful swordsmen, and were practised in the throwing of darts, which they discharged before taking the axe in hand for close combat.

---

52   George Silver, *Paradoxes of Defense* (London: Edward Blount, 1599).
53   Christopher Scott Thompson, et. al., *Scorners of Death: Fighting Skills of the Medieval Gaelic Warrior* (Glasgow: Fallen Rook Publishing, 2018), pp.138–150.

7

The Kern

The kern was the ordinary light armed Irish foot soldier. 'Kern' (*ceithern*) means war-band and is technically plural, though in English the term was used both for the band and the individual. Occasionally, contemporaries referred to a single kern more properly in English as 'kernagh' (*ceithernach*). In the sixteenth century, the term 'kern' was applied to the infantry portion of a territory's 'rising out' of free men. But it also referred to the permanently retained members of a chief's household kern, called 'kernety' (*ceithern tigh*), who carried out police duties in the lordship, and to out-of-pay professional soldiers turned brigand, known as 'wood kern' (*ceithern coille*). As the century progressed, and the Government's programme of conquest acquired a bitter tone, 'kern' was adopted as a term of abuse applied to all Irish rebels. In Anglo-Irish documents, the kern are described in medieval Latin as *turbarii* or *turbales*, meaning 'troopers.'

Edmund Spencer says it was the kern 'whom only I took to be the proper Irish soldier.'[1] Indeed, in both armament and function, the kern had the oldest lineage amongst Irish soldiers, descending from the *fianna*, or roving heroes of the Fenian Cycle in early Irish literature. At the opening of the sixteenth century, the kern retained essentially the same arms as the pre-Viking *gaisced*, a term for the unarmoured Irish warrior that derived from the spear (*gae*) and shield (*sciath*) presented to him with his coming of age. The tradition of the war-band persisted into the early medieval era in Ireland. Noble youths whose fosterage ended at age 14 would take to the woods in bands while awaiting their inheritance. Before rejoining society at age 20, they hunted, fought amongst themselves, and harboured the last druids in their camps. They were opposed by the church for their pagan associations, and the ritual practice of swearing to take vengeance on a given person, wearing a *signa diabolical* (demonic sign) on a fillet around their heads until the oath was fulfilled. The term *ceithern*, designating these

---

[1] Spencer, *State of Ireland*, unpaginated (text search required), CELT, the Corpus of Electronic Texts. <https://celt.ucc.ie/published/E500000-001/>

THE KERN

war-bands, had appeared by *c.* 900, and was initially associated with a particular territory, e.g., the *ceithernn* of Muntir Thadgain.²

Under the pressure of the Anglo-Norman invasion, mercenary bands of professional kern had emerged by the thirteenth century, called *ceithirne congbhála*, or 'retained bands'.³ By the fourteenth century, Anglo-Irish lineages had themselves adopted the institution of semi-permanent bands of kern. The first Anglo-Irish Parliament in 1297 complained of the exactions of these retained kern and forbade 'degenerate' Englishmen from adopting the *culan*, the hairstyle then popular among Irish kern, which featured long back-hairs with the front of the head shaved. Some of these Anglo-Irish bands were described as 'armoured kern', and were captained by gentlemen, such as Geoffrey Christopher of Waterford, who 'began to make kerns', gathering his gentry relatives for this service.⁴ Retained kern were maintained upon the lord's tenantry by *coinnmheadh*, or 'coign and livery', meaning billeting and provision. These were often called 'holding kern' in the sixteenth century. Among Anglo-Irish magnates, the Earls of Desmond were reputedly the first to adopt this Gaelic Irish practice. In 1467, an abbot complained to the Pope that Desmond maintained his 'kernety', or household kern, upon the local householders while also enforcing the latter's obligation to temporary military service as both horse and foot as part of the 'rising out'. Even the less Gaelicised Ormond lordship had adopted kernety and galloglass in the early fifteenth century, as Anglo-Irish forces became hybridised. Interestingly, Ormond's 120 man kernety was actually drawn from the English-descended Purcells and Codys.⁵ The kernety, or household kern, were sometimes called *fircheithernn* (true kern), and charged with guarding prisoners and assisting the lord's stewards in collecting rent, duties for which they seem to have worn livery badges. They are described in 1589 as overseers and controllers of the serjeants, or rent collectors, 'of which Kernety there should be 12 in number.'⁶ In the more Anglicised marcher lands of the English Pale, it was the Sheriff whom the kernety assisted in 'making distraints

Kern with saffron shirt worn full length. Note the typically Irish spreading crest, and short skean on a lanyard around his neck. The image possibly derives from Henry VIII's expedition to France in 1544. (Biblioteka Cyfrowa, Creative Commons)

---

2 Kim McCone, 'Werewolves, Cyclopes, Díberga and Fíanna: Juvenile Delinquency in Early Ireland' in *Cambridge Medieval Celtic Studies*, no. 12 (1986), pp.1–22.
3 Simms, 'Gaelic Warfare', p.100
4 Robin Frame, 'Military Service in the Lordship of Ireland, 1290–1360' in Robert Bartlett and Angus MacKay (eds.), *Medieval Frontier Societies* (Oxford: Clarendon Press, 1989), pp.119–120.
5 Duffy, *Medieval Ireland*, p.332.
6 *CSP Ireland*, p.203, ? May, Sir Warham St Leger.

and apprehending malefactors.' The Government's extensive use of kern is covered in more detail in the chapter on the Pale.

As discussed in Chapter 5 certain families of household kern formed their lord's hunting establishment and had hereditary duties as dog keepers and horn blowers (*stocaire*), in return for which they held land among the lordship's household, or *lucht tighe*. The Irish for horn is *stoc*, and Dürer's depiction of a kern holding a large horn is significant, whatever the origin of his imagery. While this meaning of *stocaire* is clear, it seems also to have had a derived connotation, referring to the larger boys among the attendants of the kern. For example, in April 1580, Thomas Masterson, Constable of Ferns, wrote that Donyll Spayniaghe Kavanaugh (*Domhnall Spáinneach Caomhánach*) assembled '9 score' kern, and descended upon County Wexford, oppressing the subjects with coign and livery, 'taking for every Kernaghe, every meale beside his meat 6d. st. for every Stokaghe every meale beside his meate 4d. and for every boy 3d. st. for every meale besyde his meate,' also taking free quarters, 'besids money for theire pipers and gunners which they call birts [*beirt*, two people, thus possibly a double portion, but also meaning help or assistance], and in this order they continued in the Country 3 nights.' Later, Donyll was accused of forcing the town of Ballyfarnoge to pay his band, 'to every kernagh 6d., to eche greate stokaghe a groate, and to every smale boy 3d. ster.' Masterson suddenly set upon these 180 kern, and they 'loste 4 of theire Captains' and 'fled to Castles and bounde the famylies of the houses and kepte the Castells as longe as they coulde and wounded some of my men with shot.'[7]

Spencer also enumerates the Irish soldiery as 'Kearne, Gallowglasse, Stocagh, Horsman, and Horseboy,' complaining that as most of the Irish can derive themselves from the head of some sept, they scorn labour and 'becometh a horseboye, or a stocage, or some kerne, inuring hyme selfe to his weapone.'[8] This is the sense in which *O'Reilly's Dictionary* defines *stócach* as an idle fellow, living off the labour of others.[9] Donyll's charges were in keeping with what kern in government pay received throughout this period; 4d per day or, in exceptional circumstances, 6d. A 1575 report on the forces of Ulster chieftains, quoted in the section on 'O'Neill Armies' in Chapter 1, gives gunners the same wages as galloglass, or one beef per quarter for wages and two for feeding, whereas the kern received one heifer per quarter, valued at 8s, with his victuals.

The kernety and retained kern were professional soldiers, as distinct from the kern of the rising out. The required 'rising out' (*coimhéirghe*) of freeholders subject to the hosting summons (*gairm shluaigh*) was

---

7 Herbert Philip Hore, *History of the Town and County of Wexford* (London: Elliot Stock, 1912), pp.68–71.
8 Alexander B. Grossart (ed.), *The Complete Works in Verse and Prose of Edmund Spencer*, vol. 9, (London: Hazell, Watson, and Viney, 1884), p.236.
9 Edward O'Reilly, *O'Reilly's Irish-English Dictionary* (Dublin: James Duffy, 1864).

specified for each territory or sub-lord.[10] Thus, as discussed in Chapter 1, the *Composition Book of Connaught* includes among MacWilliam's claims upon the barony of Tirawley 'eighteen-score of a rising-out there, being three-score horsemen armed and accoutered, six-score kern, nine-score horseboys and horses, bringing their own provision.' Failure to attend the hosting summons resulted in a fine of 15s for a horseman, while a kern's fine for non-attendance was a cow or 5s. The kern represented that portion of the freemen subject to 'rising out' who were unable to afford a horseman's equipment. Holinshed described him thus: 'the kernagh, and he also is a gentleman or freeholder born, but not of abilitie to mainteine a horse with his furniture, and therefore he is a light soldier on foot.'[11] According to Captain Nicholas Dawtrey, a man with decades of experience in Ireland: 'They haue another kinde of men of warr, which they call kernes, that are footemen, yett they serue chiefly with the horsemen, they are furnished with a sworde, and a Target, a skull and each of them 5 or 6 casting spears in his hand.'[12] Dawtrey associates the kern with the horsemen, the noble portion of the 'rising out'. He says the kern and horsemen together 'do always lie where their Creaghts [cattle herds and attendants] feed,' while the hired mercenaries, the 'shot, bowmen and armed men', are thrown forward to man the straights and passes against the incursion of the English army. Like their armed guards, the 'herdsmen among the Irish which keepe their cowes .... are altogether most commonly of the best bloud and discent amongst them.'[13] Doubtless there is some exaggeration in that claim, but it is worth noting that when Hugh O'Neill, Earl of Tyrone, made his escape in the 'Flight of the Earls' in 1607, one of his sons was left behind as he was in the hills with the *creaght*, or cow herd. The kern could display signs of nobility, as in the fourteenth century 'Triumphs of Turlough' (*Cathreim Thoirdhealbhaigh*), which describes a band of kern trapped against the banks of the river Shannon after attempting to flee with their prey of cattle. Left leaderless, their chief having crossed the river, they were slowly picked off by their enemies, as 'One after another perpetually they appointed over themselves a "master of the pack" (*taisech cuanairte*) to head them, until at last is was a commander of but six good men.'[14] Their descendants were the 'kindreds of kerns .... the tail ends of noble families,' eulogised in the seventeenth century by a bardic poet who castigated the upstart peasantry

---

10   *gairm shluaigh*, literally the 'hosting shout', could refer both to the summons and the penalty for non-attendance. In its alternate phrasing, *sluagh-ghairm*, it is the origin of the modern English term 'slogan', just as *sluagh* gives us the English term 'slew'.
11   Raphael Holinshed, *Holinshed's Chronicles of England, Scotland, and Ireland*, vol. 3 (London: J. Johnson, 1807), p.6.
12   Morgan, 'A Booke', pp.90 & 95.
13   Hiram Morgan and Kenneth Nicholls (eds), 'Discourse of the Mere Irish of Ireland', CELT, the Corpus of Electronic Texts. <https://celt.ucc.ie/published/E600001-004.html>
14   Simms, 'Gaelic Warfare', p.106.

under the new English order, who were boors, 'and not the company of kerns; for a company of kerns is so called by reason of its edges of prowess and encounter and of razor-sharp weapons.'[15]

The kern were renowned for physical hardiness, and Stanihurst, who admired their ability to subsist on meagre fare, tells a story indicative of this. Two kern, having kept watch all night, prepared to sleep in the open in a frosty field. One had put a large snowball under his head, causing his comrade to chide him: 'Surely you deserve to be whipped, you cowardly womanish recruit. I ask you, are you so flushed with softness that, after being awake all night, you cannot sleep without a pillow?'[16] Burt, in *Letters from the North*, recalls being told a version of this tale in the Highlands, which he understood to be apocryphal. But he was willing to credit stories of Highlanders sleeping in plaids steeped in water to retain body heat.[17] This same expedient is described among the Irish by Fynes Moryson in 1617, who adds the critical details that the sleeper must be otherwise naked and cover the head.[18] The proverbial 'footmanship' of the Irish, discussed in Chapter 8, was particularly noted among the kern. They also had a somewhat cutthroat reputation. Stanihurst recounts a proverb among the Irish which was used of deliberations in which they had no confidence; 'the considered verdict of the kern.' Meaning, the longer the kern deliberate, over the life of a captive for instance, the nearer they come to a wicked decision, seeking his head. And he says a slain foe is further wounded lest he revive, the kern not believing a man dead until his head be off: 'Are there any men more cautious than these kern?'[19] They were noted for superstitious observations, and wore protective amulets around the neck, such as scraps of paper with prayers written on them or ancient flint arrow heads called 'elf darts' (*saighead shíth*). The martial culture of the kern was particularly associated with the bagpipe, and their sword dance is described in Chapter 13.

Wood Kern (Ceithern Coille)

Despite the status of some kern as gentlemen, by the late sixteenth century they had inspired a pseudo-etymology deriving the name kern (*ceithern*) from *cith Ifrinn*, or a 'shower of hell, because they are taken for no better then for rake hells or the devils blacke garde.'[20] This may hark back to their semi-pagan associations in the early Middle Ages, but, like other soldiers, unemployed kern were simply liable to turn brigand. Apart from the kern

---

15 Williams, *Chloinne Tomáis*, p.167.
16 Stanihurst, *Great Deeds*, p.139.
17 Edmund Burt, *Letters from the North of Scotland*, vol. 2 (Edinburgh: William Patterson, 1876), pp.119–121.
18 Quinn, *Elizabethans and Irish*, pp.70–71.
19 Stanihurst, *Great Deeds*, p.125.
20 Alan Harrison, 'The Shower of Hell' in *Eigse*, 18/2 (1981), p.304.

of the rising out and household kern, there was therefore a third category called *ceithern coille,* or 'wood kern'. An early instance of a band of wood kern robbers (called *ladranna,* i.e. *latrones* in Latin) occurs in 1206, when the *Annals of Mac Carthaigh's Book* recalled a monastery in County Louth being plundered by kern in the service of MacMahon, Lord of Monaghan. Their leader was called *Bratach Buile* (Crazy Banner), which suggests that colourful nicknames were sometimes applied to the headmen of wood kern.[21] Indeed, in 1585 a robber chief emerged in Connemara, a Joyce who went by the name Cloasearlykane (*Cluas a Leiceann,* 'Ear to Cheek'). The nickname was apparently in reference to a scar. He was a follower of Sir Murrough O'Flaherty, and having gathered wood kern, he became the leader of a band of robbers. His gang of 50 were apparently among those hanged at the sessions at Galway the following year.[22]

The Curlew mountains were a noted haunt of wood kern, Thomas Gainsford in 1618 remarking that 'These Curlewes are mountains full of dangerous passages, especially when the kern take a stomach and a pride to enter into action, as they term their rebellion or tumultuary insurrections.'[23] Lord Deputy Sidney recalled marching out of Ulster in 1566 through the 'craggie mountayne of the Curlue, a passage bad inough, where I chased and chastised the ancient outlaws of that quarter called Garron Bane; and so descended into the playnes of Conach.'[24] Garran Bane was not the only fastness in which 'ancient outlaws' lurked. The Walsh Mountains in South-West Kilkenny was a district notorious for harbouring cattle rustlers. Shane Brenagh Fitz Robert, 'a mean gentleman of the surname of the Walshes,' led a band of a dozen other Walshes, raiding as far as Wexford and Waterford. Under pressure, he finally came into Waterford city in 1578 with a withy halter around his neck as a sign of surrender, while his gang were hunted down. These same Walshes were also a mainstay of the Butler Army.[25]

In 1544, Lord Deputy St Leger had written to the King, describing a remote wilderness along the Shannon which he said was the hiding-place 'of theffs and outlawes, called properly the *Olde Evill Children* by reason whereof few or none of your Grace's subjects could travel between Limerick and Waterford.' In 1581, the Exchequer Roll also remarks on 'the county Limerick Thieves called the Old Children.'[26] The band held a castle close to the River Shannon, until the Earl of Desmond finally expelled them and bestowed the castle on one of his followers.[27] This was the duty of an

---

21 Katherine Simms, 'The MacMahon Pedigree: A Medieval Forgery' in David Edwards (ed.), *Regions and Rulers in Ireland, 1100–1650* (Dublin: Four Courts Press, 2004), pp.29–30.
22 Knox, *History Mayo,* p.205.
23 Quinn, *Elizabethans and Irish,* p.165.
24 Hebert Hore (ed.), 'Sir Henry Sidney's Memoir of his Government in Ireland, 1583', *Ulster Journal of Archaeology,* vol. 3 (1855), p.40.
25 Edwards, *Ormond Lordship,* p.265.
26 Hore, 'Sidney's Memoir', p.48.
27 Bagwell, *Ireland Under,* vol. 1, p.265.

'OF KERNS AND GALLOWGLASSES'

Irish chief or lord. Upon his inauguration in 1592, Red Hugh O'Donnell cleared out a nest of bandits in the pass of *An Bearnas Mór*, in the Bluestack Mountains. Since, as the annals says, 'he did not allow robbery or plundering in the country since he was inaugurated.' They celebrated his reign, affirming that 'From Foyle to Howth none raises the cry, none watches his cattle, the woods are void of marauders.'[28]

The Kern's Arms

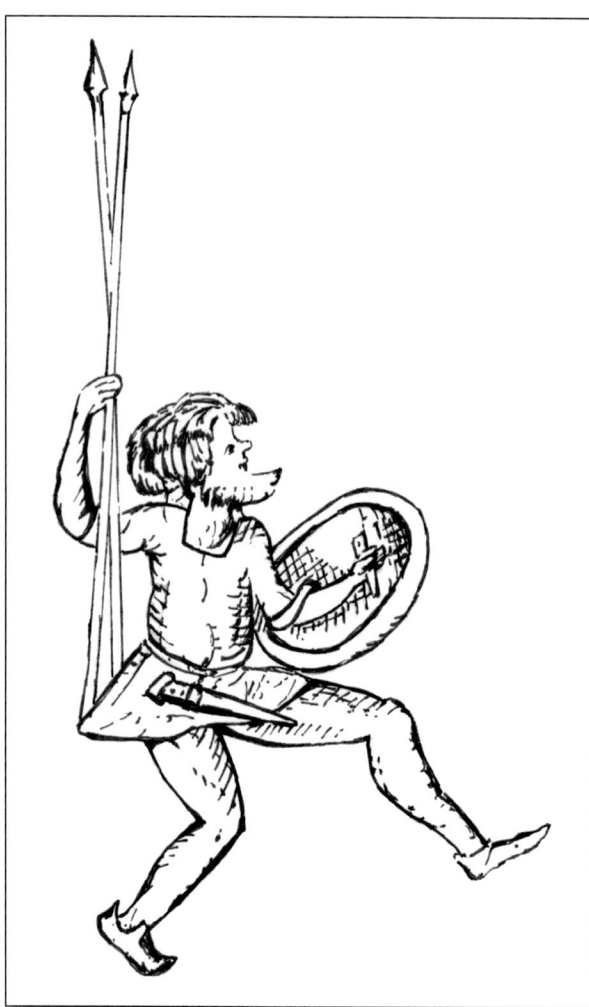

Kern with two darts, shield and short skean at waist. After a map of c. 1600. (Author's drawing)

Kern are generally described as unarmoured, with the exception of Fynes Moryson's strange statement: 'Secondly the Kerne, and some of their Footemen, are armed with waighty Iron males, and Iacks.'[29] Perhaps this echoes back to the 'armoured kern' of the fourteenth century mentioned above, but both must be considered anomalies, as the kern are most noted for their light equipment. Holinshed says: 'The second degree is the kernagh ..... he is a light soldier on foot – his armour is but light and slender, being a scull and left gauntlet, or a target and sword, a skein, and three or foure dartes.'[30] The Dubliner Richard Stanihurst's description of the kern, written in erudite Latin and using classical vocabulary, also mentions the gauntlet: 'The third rank comprises others, also foot soldiers, who are light armed swordsmen [*Machairaphoroi*: i.e. a type of ancient Seleucid light foot, unarmoured, fighting with sword, shield, and spear]. The Irish call them Kerns [*Karni*]. They whirl spears, which are fitted with thongs, so manfully by strength of muscle that the spears seem to be forced into an orbital circuit like a ring. They are armoured with shields [*Caetra*, i.e., the circular leather covered wooden buckler of the ancient Celtiberians] or an iron gauntlet; going into battle they wear no

---

28   O'Clery, *Beatha Aodh Ruadh*, vol. 1, pp.224–227.
29   Graham Kew, 'The Irish Sections of Fynes Moryson's Unpublished Itinerary' in *Analecta Hibernia*, no. 37 (1998), p.70.
30   Raphael Holinshed, *Holinshed's Chronicles of England, Scotland, and Ireland*, vol. 3 (London: J. Johnson, 1807), p.6.

heavy armour.'[31] Dymmock, writing around 1600, also mentions the shield: 'The kerne is a kind of footman, slightly armed with a sword, a target of wood, or a bow and sheaf of arrows with barbed heads, or else three darts.'[32]

There are several surviving illustrations of the elbow length gauntlet for the left hand, worn slung around the neck on a lanyard. These images relate to the participation of Irish kern in Henry VIII's French war of 1544–45. The *Codex de Trajes* illustration, of around the same date, shows a kern with a sleeve of plate on the left arm, apparently of munition grade armour. A contemporary Irish bardic poem to Hugh O'Byrne refers to 'a sheltering gauntlet (*bolard*) on thy forearm down to the fingers.'[33] As noted in the chapter on the Pale, the Ordinances of 1515 specify that the Anglo-Irish horseman of the militia of the Pale was to have a gauntlet for his left hand. John Hunt noted that the long left-hand gauntlet became a feature of the armour of the seventeenth century mounted arquebusier, and as such was issued to the English shot on horseback sent to Ireland in the later stages of the Nine Years' War. Hunt speculated that this may have been inspired by Irish practice.[34] While there is only one surviving image of a kern with a target, from a map of *c.* 1600, there are two surviving examples which show it to have been comparable to the later Highland targe.

Gaelic Irish shields in the sixteenth century appear to have been of two distinct varieties. The general word for shield, *sciath*, was originally applied to the most ancient form, an oval, concave wicker shield. Round, flat targets of wood, covered with leather and studded with brass nails, were known as *starga*, or *targaid*. As with so many cultural traits, this distinction between two types of shield is mirrored in Highland Scotland.

Edmund Spencer writing in 1596 makes clear reference to this wicker shield in *View of the Present State of Ireland*. Pursuing his theory that the Irish are descended from ancient Scythians, he says: 'Moreover, their long, broad shields, made but of wicker rods, which are commonly used amongst the said northern Irish, but specially of the Scots, are brought from the Scythians, as ye may read in Olaus Magnus, Solinus, and others.'[35] A few pages later, he adds, 'also that they used long wicker shields in battle that should cover their whole bodies, and so do the northern Irish. But because I have not seen such fashioned targets used in the southern parts, but only amongst those northern people and Irish Scots.'[36] Then, noting cultural parallels between the Gaelic Irish and contemporary Spain: 'Likewise, round leather targets is the Spanish fashion, who used it for the most part painted, which in Ireland they use also in many places coloured after their

---

31   Stanihurst, *Great Deeds*, p.125.
32   Richard Butler (ed.), *Tracts Relating to Ireland*, vol. 2 (Dublin: M. H. Gill, 1842), p.7.
33   Knott, *Bardic Poetry*, vol. 2, pp.168–9.
34   Hunt, *Irish Sculpture*, p.66.
35   Edmund Spencer, *A View of the State of Ireland* (Dublin: Laurence Flin, 1763), pp.88–9.
36   Spencer, *A View*, p.96.

rude fashion.'[37] We have here the distinction of two types of shield, a long one of wicker, and a round one of leather, probably over wood. In 1596, a Spanish delegation visited the rebellious northern Irish lords to deliver aid, assess their strength and needs, and plan an invasion. Ensigns Jimenez and Montero filed a report afterwards, which is in the *Calendar of State Papers, Spain*. They note that 'they have darts, bows and arrows, shields like ours, and like Hungarian bucklers.'[38] This echoes Spencer's note that there are two types of Irish shield, one of round leather form like those of Spain, and another that the ensigns say resembles a Hungarian buckler. The latter is apparently the wicker shield. Barnaby Rich's long military career from 1540 to 1617 involved a great deal of time in Ireland, and his many books make frequent reference to conditions in that country. In his *Martiall Conference, between Captaine Skill and Captaine Pill*, Captaine Skill compares the trajectory of an arrow unfavourably with that of a musket ball, noting that an arrow can be defended against with a shield:

> as our barbarous Irishmen, that inuented targets made of small wickers, like basket liddes, which weighing not aboue two pownd weight, would couer them from the toppe to the toe, and sometimes with their mantles hanging loose about their armes, which was the cause that our captains of that countrey, long sithence haue conuerted all their bows to caliuers, and from that time haue so continued.[39]

The Scottish Wodrow manuscript of 1678 says the Highlanders had 'targets and shields of the most odd and antique form.'[40] This also appears to affirm two types of shield. In 1699, Rev. James Kirkwood produced *A Collection of Highland Rites and Customs*. Dealing with the old Highlander's 'Warrs and Armour' he says: 'Shield of Oak and Willow Wands, narrow below and broad above. Targets made of Oak covered with bull-hyde of an orbicular Form…'[41] Thus he distinguishes two types of shield, one of oak covered in hide and round, and the other of wicker, narrow below and broad above. This description of the wicker shield is interesting and bears comparison with Eugene O'Curry's description of the old Irish *sciath*:

---

37 Spencer, *A View*, pp.94–5.
38 *Calendar of State Papers, Spain (Simancas)* vol. 4, 1587–1603, Martin A. S. Hume, ed. (London: Eyre and Spottiswoode, 1899), p.627, ? June, Relation of Ensigns Jimenez and Montero.
39 Barnaby Rich, *A Martial Conference between Captaine Skill and Captaine Pill* (London: John Oxenbridge, 1598), unnumbered, last page. (Early English Books Online Text Creation Partnership, 2011) <http://quod.lib.umich.edu/e/eebo2/A10710.0001.001?view=toc>
40 Telfer Dunbar, *History of Highland Dress* (London: B.T. Batsford Ltd, 1979), p.205.
41 Rev. James Kirkwood, *A Collection of Highland Rites and Customs* (Trowbridge: Redwood Burn Ltd., 1975), p.41.

> The common potato-*sciath* is a simple construction of stout wickerwork, of an oblong form, about three feet long and nearly two feet wide; having a depth of about six inches; the oblong not squared or of equal width at both ends, but tapering gradually to its termination, to a rounded and somewhat broad end at the top, and more gradually to a much sharper angle at the lower end.[42]

He is describing the lowly farmyard basket of his own day, tellingly called a *sciath*, but O'Curry believed this *sciath* preserved the memory of its more martial ancestor. He points out that old Irish texts, like the *Book of Invasions* (*Leabhar Gabhála* – Ireland's mythical origin legend) describe the pages repairing the wicker rods of the champion's shields before battle. Though such descriptions date to the early medieval period, they may nonetheless serve to elucidate the form of the old Irish shield in the sixteenth century. Indeed, it survived in vestigial form as a workaday basket nearly into our own time. It is indeed possible for old forms to survive for a very long time, and a shoe dated to 7,000 B.C. recently discovered in an Armenian cave in no way differs from the rawhide pampootie still made in the Aran Islands up to the 1980s.

Ring Pommel Swords

The Irish ring pommel sword is a distinctive design that was associated with the kern. The type is very homogenous and forms Group 3 in Andrew Halpin's analysis of medieval Irish swords.[43] All those of known provenance have been found in Gaelic areas. The blades were manufactured in the major blade making centres of Germany, and brought to Ireland as trade items by Basque fishing fleets. The swords were hilted locally by Gaelic Irish smiths. They appear to wilfully eschew the trend towards more complex hilt types occurring elsewhere. The most well preserved surviving example of a ring pommel sword has a 'double-edged blade of stiff, thick construction which appears to be parallel-sided but in fact exhibits an almost imperceptibly slight taper, being 3.2cm wide at the hilt and 3.0cm a little distance from its spatulate tip. The ricasso extends for 8.5cm from the hilt, beyond which the blade is of lenticular section.'[44] This sword type features in imagery dating to Henry VIII's invasion of France in 1544, including the watercolours of Lucas DeHeere and 'Dravne After the Qvicke', a woodcut in the Ashmolean

---

42 Eugene O'Curry, *On the Manners and Customs of the Ancient Irish, vol. 1* (Dublin: John F. Fowler, 1873), p.330–1.
43 Andrew Halpin, 'Irish Medieval Swords, *c.* 1171–1600', *Proceedings of the Royal Irish Academy* (1986), pp.183–230.
44 Tony Willis and Andrew Halpin, 'A Recently Discovered Sixteenth Century Irish Open Ring Pommel Sword', *Spring 2017 Park Lane Arms Fair Catalogue* (2017), p.16.

Museum, Oxford. It is a mystery why this print and the series of related drawings do not also show the famous Irish dart. The ring pommel swords are carried in square-ended, fringed scabbards, either loose in the hand or tucked in the crook of the elbow. The kern thus avoided having a scabbard dangling about the legs by simply discarding it upon drawing the sword – 'Now was the Sword drawn, and the Scabbard flung away, and no room left for an Accommodation.'[45] Regarding the bulbous blade tips depicted in the Oxford cut, Tony Willis noted: 'When holding swords of this form, the blade ends "feel" heavier than they actually look. Hence the Oxford print is not too far off the mark in communicating the "feel" of these swords, even if in so doing the effort has created a visual inaccuracy.'[46]

Reproduction of the Tullylough open ring pommel sword. (Author's collection)

Dating is difficult, but based on surviving iconographic evidence, the Type 3 can be roughly placed in the second quarter of the sixteenth century, although, of course, its use might plausibly extend some decades before or after that. The earliest depiction of the Irish ring pommel is in Albrecht Dürer's famous drawing of the 'War Men of Ireland,' dated 1521, and showing a curiously large example. The equally well-known series of drawings by Lucas DeHeere – and their derivatives in Continental costume books – indicate its use by the levies of kern sent to France in 1544. At least, this still remains the best hypothesis for the origin of this series of closely related images. This idea of their genesis was first posited by H. F. McClintock, who included the 'Dravne After the Qvicke' woodcut, which he suggested was cut after a life drawing probably made while the kern were passing through England on the way to Boulogne.[47] McClintock suggested that 'the Qvicke' and the DeHeere series derive from a set of originals made at that time, and I find this still the most plausible theory. Notably, all the images that we have show the ring pommel sword in the hands of the kern, or light armed Irish foot.

---

45 Richard Cox, *Hibernia Anglicana, or The history of Ireland*, vol. 1 (London: H. Clark, 1689), p.232.

46 Tony Willis, 'A Two Handed Gaelic Irish Sword of the Sixteenth Century', *Fifteenth Park Lane Arms Fair Catalogue* (1998), p.25.

47 McClintock, H. F., *Handbook on the Traditional Old Irish Dress* (Dundalk: Dundalgan Press, 1958), p.7.

THE KERN

This type of sword never appears on lordly funeral monuments, and by the 1570s Derricke's *Image of Ireland* and the Dublin Charter galloglass seem to show the Gaelic Irish using a sword with closed disc pommels and downward-curved quillons, not unlike the more Anglo-Irish type represented by the so-called Kinsale sword.

It should be noted that the dozen surviving open ring pommel swords of Halpin Group 3 may have no greater claim as a characteristic Gaelic weapon than the 13 surviving 'V-guard' swords of Halpin Group 2. These 'proto-claymore' single-handed swords of Group 2 straddle Highland Scotland and Ireland, are dated to the late fifteenth/early sixteenth century, and appear on funerary monuments in both countries in the hands of high status warriors and galloglass. Their appearance on the effigies of Malachy MacOwny O'More in Laois (1502) and a MacGillapatrick knight in Kilkenny (*c.* 1510–40) confirms this, and the type seems to overlap with the Type 3 open pommel swords chronologically. They are thought to give rise to the claymore proper later in the century.

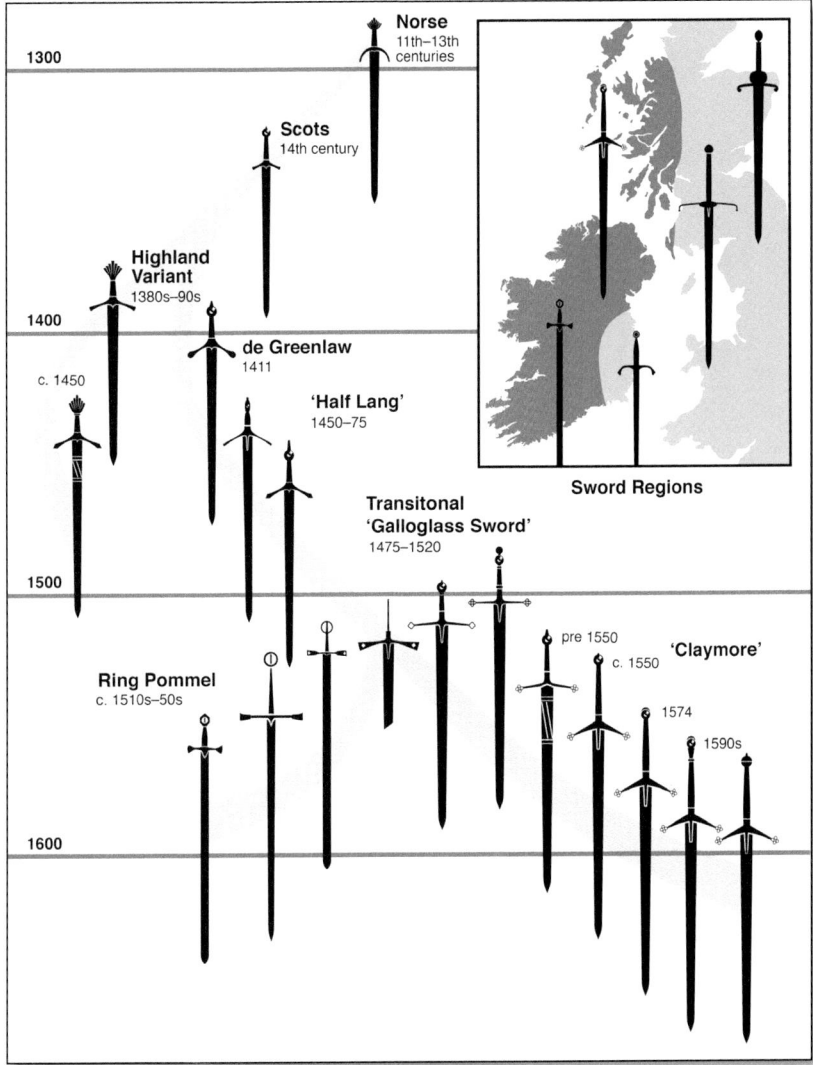

Suggested development of the Irish ring pommel sword and West Highland claymore. The author's interpretation of the work of Willis and Halpin.

Thus the Halpin Type 3 open ring pommel sword is part of a 'weapon set' used by the Gaelic Irish kern in the first half of the sixteenth century. This weapon set also included the Irish dart or throwing spear, the skean (*scian*) or long fighting knife (either alongside the sword or in place of it), and limited defensive equipment (wooden target, steel 'lyft gauntlet' or scull). Writers from later in the century distinguished the sword and target combination, and this may relate to the increasing appearance of dedicated targeteers in the 1570s and 1580s. The best description of the sword's use is from Stanihurst who, in 1584, wrote of the kern:

> They are armoured with shields or an iron gauntlet …. but they have no knowledge of how to use their weapons in a well-trained manner: they have no familiarity with the art of the fencing schools, rarely piercing the foe with a thrust, more often wounding him by slashing. They have an amazing love for their swords, which are kept sharp and not pitted: they care for them diligently so that they may not become rusty or blunt. The story is told that a man of this class, returning from battle having received four or more dangerous wounds, inspected his sword: when he saw that it was nowhere chipped or bent he gave great thanks to God that the wounds were inflicted on his body, not on his sword.[48]

Note the following points from this account: the kern swordsmen were unarmoured, but carried a round target or 'lyft gauntlet'; Stanihurst considers them untrained in the techniques of the fencing schools; the kern do not use the point to thrust, but make slashing cuts instead; they are eager to keep their swords sharp.

We may consider here the impressions of those who have had the opportunity to handle the surviving Irish open pommel swords. Tony Willis and Andrew Halpin note: 'the ring pommel swords are …. blade heavy. The deceptive weight, thickness and almost parallel-sided profiles of both blades, combined with the relatively lightweight hilts, pushes the point of balance much further down the blade than would usually be expected on European single-handed swords.'[49] The light weight of the open ring pommel thus seems calculated to induce a slashing, chopping action, while discouraging the thrust. The blades are sharp down to the blunt point, increasing their cutting capacity. Since parrying would be cumbersome, plate armour for the left hand or arm, or a target, would form the primary defence.

An interesting parallel is found in the nineteenth century Beja swordsmen of the Sudan. Their *kaskara* swords are very similar to the blades of Irish ring pommel swords, but at 35 inches long, they are slightly longer than the Irish ring pommel sword blades, which are about 33.25 inches. Like the Irish sword, the *kaskara* has a blade with several fullers on the ricasso area, inscribed as narrow grooves. Both feature nearly parallel sides, ending in a spatulate tip. *Kaskaras* were hilted locally with a simple cross guard with the wooden grip wrapped in leather and instead of a pommel, they were capped with a disc of leather to prevent the hand slipping off the grip when in use. Without the weight of a pommel, the point of balance is much further out than on European swords, at 12 inches out from the guard. As a result the blade is not balanced in the hand or nimble at the tip, and could not be used to parry a blow. Rather, it was a dedicated striking instrument for making big slashing cuts from far off. The spatulate tip would cut right

---

48 Stanihurst, *Great Deeds*, p.125.
49 Willis, 'A Recently Discovered', p.17.

out to its end, unlike a more tapered pointed blade, thus maximising the swordsman's reach. Its use required the protection of a shield, so it was part of a 'weapon set' that also included round shields of rhinocerous hide and spears.

In words that echo Stanihurst's comments on the swordsmanship of the Irish kern, Sir Samuel White Baker questioned the fencing skill of the Beja swordsmen, 'the Arabs have not the slightest knowledge of swordsmanship; they never parry with the blade, but trust entirely to the shield, and content themselves with slashing …. they cannot recover the sword sufficiently quick to parry, therefore they are contented with the shield as their only guard.'[50] Like the Irish kern, the Sudanese obsessively kept their swords sharp, and as Baker noted, 'after trying both edges with his thumb, he carefully strops the blade to and fro on his shield until a satisfactory proof of the edge is made by shaving the hair off his arm.' Baker held that 'such a weapon possesses immense power, as the edge is nearly as sharp as a razor …. one good cut delivered by a powerful arm would sever a man at the waist like a carrot …. Notwithstanding their deficiency in the art of the sword …. when the sharp edge of the heavy weapon touches an enemy, the effect is terrible.'[51] Bearing in mind the above list of points drawn from Richard Stanihurst's account of the kern's swordsmanship, we can make a closely parallel list regarding the Sudanese *kaskara*: the Beja were unarmoured, but carried a round shield; Baker said they have not the slightest knowledge of swordsmanship; the Beja content themselves with slashing; the greatest care is taken in sharpening the swords.

Practitioners of HEMA have experimented with the *kaskara*, and their impressions confirm the above observations. Some of these practitioners have turned their attention to the weapons of the medieval Irish and Scots, for which there are no surviving sixteenth century manuals. Christopher Scott Thompson in particular has considered the woodcut 'Dravne After the Qvicke', and feels the kern with drawn ring pommel sword depicts the basic guard stance for this weapon: left foot forward with the sword held back behind the head, blade angled forward, its striking edge held away from the opponent.[52] 'Thompson points out that his left hand is held up besides his cheek, as in the advice of eighteenth-century practitioners like McBane and Lonnergan, who advise this stance when cutting or defending on the inside. This seems to indicate the *equilibrio* style of swordplay advocated, for instance, by Page in his brief treatise on the eighteenth century Highland broadsword.

The kern were superstitious regarding their weapons, and in 1600 Haynes recorded: 'Soe doe the Irishe Connjure and charme theire Swordes by makinge a cross on the Grounde with them, and thrustinge the pointe

---

50   Sir Samuel White Baker, *The Nile Tributaries of Abyssinia: and the Sword Hunters of the Hamran Arabs* (London: MacMillan and Co., 1867). pp.169–70.
51   Baker, *The Nile*, p.170.
52   Thompson, *Scorners of Death*, p.37.

into the Grounde before they goe to Battaile holdinge yt a mean of better Successe; likewise they sweare by their Swordes.'[53] He was paraphrasing Father Good, an English Jesuit living in Limerick in the 1560s, who said he could not tell whether the Irish yield divine honour to the moon, for upon seeing the new moon, they bow and say the Lord's Prayer, asking the moon to leave them as it found them.[54] This is echoed in the Caucasus Mountains, where nineteenth century Circassian tribesmen had an extensive lore of weapons, and 'for good luck, the kindjal was used to slash a cross, skywards, when the new moon appeared.'[55]

The Irish Dart

There are more names for spear in Irish than for any other weapon, indicating the centrality of the Irish dart. Peter Harbison's study of the Irish terminology for medieval arms and armour provides some general observations, but the various terms were not used with precision. The *gae* or its diminutive, the *foga,* are usually translated as a kind of dart. The *sleag* was a slender spear, thrust or thrown. And the *craisech* is a heavier spear, used for pushing and thrusting, and sometimes mentioned as being carried by horsemen, retained after they have flung their *gae*. The throwing cords of flax or silk were called *suaineamh* (soonev). The finger loop is an ancient device, appearing in Homer's Iliad and known to the Romans as the *ammentum,* and in the 'Cattle Raid of Cooley' is reference to Cúchulainn's smooth handled throwing spears with cords of full-hard flax upon them. They were fastened on mid-shaft for a *sleag* and towards the butt for *gae*. The cord was wound around the shaft several times, securing a loop about three or four inches long. The forefinger of the right hand was inserted into the loop, and added to the force of the cast. Experiments with darts thrown with the finger loop have achieved distances of 70 yards, though it was typically used at much closer range. The Irish annals often mention a protagonist putting his finger in the loop of his spear before making a cast. The portraits of Sir Thomas Lee and Sir Neil O'Neill, both in the Tate Galleries Collection, illustrate this well, as does the *Codex de Trajes* drawing (see illustration opposite). It seems that, in general, three of the smaller *gae* would be carried, or two of the tall *sleag*, the '*Da Sleag*' of heroic tales.[56] But, as already mentioned, Nicholas Dawtrey said the kern carried five or six throwing spears. Stanihurst indicated that the finger loop was used for

---

53 Edmund Hogan (ed.), 'Haynes' Observations of the State of Ireland in 1600', *Irish Ecclesiastical Record*, vol. 8 (1887), p.1121.
54 Cox, Richard, *Hibernia Anglicana, or The History of Ireland*, vol. 1 (London: H. Clark, 1689), 145–6.
55 Lesly Blanch, *Sabres of Paradise* (New York: Carrol and Graf, 1984), p.52.
56 Harbison, Peter, 'Native Irish Arms and Armour in Medieval Gaelic Literature, 1170–1600', *The Irish Sword*, vol. 12 (1976), pp.270–284.

adroit handling of the dart in a display that seems akin to baton twirling: 'They whirl spears, which are fitted with thongs (*ammentum*), so powerfully by the force of their muscles that the spears seem to be forced into an orbital circuit like a ring.'[57] There may be indications of this in Irish literature, such as the fourteenth century *Book of Maguaran*, in which a chieftain is praised with the lines: 'The hand of this Youth of Eine can make his spear-shaft spin; he can make its steel head spin like the shaft when he shoots it', while another poem reads 'Strong is the captain's hand; he can brandish his spear by its end.'[58]

Kern, using finger loop on dart. Image possibly relates to Henry VIII's French war of 1544. Codice De Trajes. (Biblioteca Nacional de España. Creative Commons)

Overall, the kern are most often described as carrying three darts, and sets of three darts repeatedly appear in arraignments at the assizes in Kilkenny, as in 1547, when an offender 'stole three spears (lancea) and a faling (mantle)', and 1551, when another 'stole three spears and a lock.'[59] They were manufactured locally, as noted by Sir Thomas Phillips in 1611, when he reported on iron being smelted in Ulster by the local population,

---

57 Stanihurst, *Great Deeds*, p.125.
58 Lambert McKenna, (ed.), *The Book of Maguaran* (Dublin: Dublin Institute for Advanced Studies, 1947), pp.342 & 391.
59 *Calendar of Ormond Deeds*, vol. 5, 1547–1584, Edmund Curtis, ed. (Dublin: The Stationery Office, 1935), pp.2 & 69.

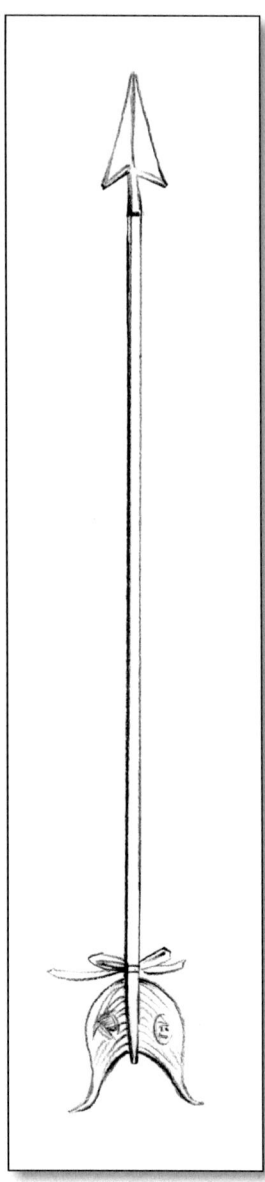

Dart of the City of Cork. Used during the inauguration of the Mayor, and possibly reflecting a sixteenth century original. It is about five feet long, and fletched with stylised peacock feathers. (Author's drawing)

who used it to make 'skeynes and darts.'[60] English armouries may also have manufactured them, and an inventory taken in 1547 shows 'Dartes for Irishemen, croked' [barbed] were stored for the use of the remaining Irish kern in the Calais garrison.[61] The barbed head of the darts in Wright's portrait of Sir Neil O'Neill appear to be plated in copper alloy, which was a Gaelic Irish smithing technique, the remnants of which have been detected on the hilts of some sixteenth century swords and arrow heads, including a forked one resembling the forked arrowhead under the warrior's arm in the famous Dürer drawing of 1521. The tale of 'O'Donnell's Kern,' from internal evidence written about 1537, has the main character, a very down at the heel kern, carrying 'three limber javelins (*trí gaethe boga bunloiscthe*) of the holly wood charred [i.e. fire-hardened rather than iron-headed].'[62] The ancient saga of the 'Cattle Raid of Cooley' also refers to sharpened holly sticks, fire-hardened and without a metal head, called *bir*, which were thrown as darts. These were used by the boys of the camp, but whether such weapons remained in use to any degree during the sixteenth century is uncertain.

Fynes Moryson praised the Irish 'dexterity of using their skeans and Darts.'[63] Casting darts with accuracy required practice from childhood, and in an enactment of 1498, the Dublin Parliament complained that the Palesmen had abandoned the bow and taken up the Irish dart, though 'they had not the profound way and feat of it.'[64] There is a reference to practise with the dart during the Baltinglass revolt of 1569, when Sir Edmund Butler caused 'English dead men's bodies to be stripped out of their English garments, and their hose and dubletts (being stuffed and trussed) he would set up as marks for his kernes to throw their darts at.'[65]

The dart and skean were the most characteristic weapons of the Irish kern, and perhaps because of this, the dart acquired a symbolic status. For Edward VI's Christmas Revels of 1553 an *Irish Play of the State of Ireland* was to be performed, and the six sets of clothing for 'Irish keyrens' included 'vj darts garnished with colours and lease gowlde.'[66] The dart could symbolise the country, as it did during a pageant held for Queen Elizabeth at Rycote in 1592. There she was presented with a 'Dart of gold' embossed with diamonds, with the motto 'fly onely for my soueraigne' written upon it 'in Irish,' and presented by a mute Irish 'lackey' – probably a local man

---

60 Paul Rondelez, 'Ironwork in late Medieval Ireland: AD 1200 to 1600'. Unpublished University College Cork PhD thesis, 2001, p.35.
61 Gervase Phillips, 'Irish Ceatharnaigh in English Service, 1544–1550, and the Development of Gaelic Warfare', *Journal of the Society for Army Historical Research*, vol. 78, no. 315 (Autumn 2000), p.172.
62 Standish Hayes O'Grady, *Silva Gadelica*, vol. 2 (Edinburgh: Williams and Norgate, 1892), p.312.
63 Kew, 'Fynes Moryson's Itinerary', p.110.
64 Hayes-McCoy, *Irish Battles*, pp.59–60.
65 Hore, 'Sidney's Memoir', p.97.
66 Feuillerat, *Revels at Court*, p.58.

in costume.[67] And Perrot in his *Irish Chronicle* recalls a strange occurrence during an English foray into O'More's country in 1597. After Owney O'More had failed to appear before him:

> the Lord Deputy was departinge Northward, he sent unto hym two bundells of dartes as a token; which, when the Lord Deputy did see, he asked what Onys meaning might be to send hym such things. To whom some of experience (that knew the fashion and condition of that countrie people), sayd: 'Your lordship may perceive he means maddely, and sends you this you may know he wantes not this countrie weopens; and you shall see he will shortly shew hymself in rebellion.'[68]

Kern, with fletched dart. (Author's drawing after Andrew Boorde, *First Book of the Introduction of Knowledge*, Early English Texts Society, extra series 10 (London: N. Trübner, 1870), p.131.)

A late example of this symbolic use of the dart can be seen in the civic darts thrown by the Mayors of Cork and Limerick during inauguration ceremonies. In both cities, the new mayor casts the dart from shipboard into the coastal waters of his town to symbolise his sovereignty. The dart of Cork City (opposite) is preserved in the city museum and appears to retain the shape and proportions of the sixteenth century version; the dart is about five feet in length, and is fletched like an arrow. A sketch from Andrew Boorde's 1548 *The Fyrst Boke of the Introduction of Knowledge*, shows an Irishman with a dart similarly fletched, as does Hieronymous Tielch's drawing of an Irish horseboy, *c.* 1600. This particular type of dart is associated in European imagery with 'exotic' easterners, but was used extensively in the Iberian peninsula, where it was known as *dardo*. Its use in Gaelic Ireland may indicate cultural connections with Spain, which were strong in this period. Like the

---

67   Rory Loughnane and Willy Maley (eds), *Celtic Shakespeare: The Bard and the Borderers* (London: Routledge, 2013), p.368.
68   Sir James Perrot (Herbert Wood ed.), *The Chronicle of Ireland, 1584–1608*, (Dublin: Stationery Office, 1933), p.132.

throwing loop, fletching imparted stability to the dart. The heavy darts found on board the Mary Rose were fletched with wood, which would correct any deviation caused by striking rigging when they were thrown from the tops. Fletching would have worked similarly for the much lighter Irish dart when thrown in secondary growth woodlands.

Englishmen who served in Ireland repeatedly emphasise the light nature of the Irish dart, and its particular use against horses. John Dymmock said the kern carried '3 darts, which they cast with a wonderfull facillity and nearnes, a weapon more noysom to the enemy, especially horsemen, then yt is deadly.'[69] Sir John Perrot commented: 'For theyr light throwinge weapons they were but dartes, much lesse and lighter then our javellinges, which they could nimbly handle and throw steadily; but they could not pearce farre or had any greate power agaynst armed men. Chiefly they could annoy horsemen, and sometimes kill or wounde such as were unarmed.'[70] This is echoed by Fynes Moryson, who says, 'the *Kerne* .... assayle horsemen aloof with casting darts and at hand with the sword,' aloof meaning at a distance.[71] Stanihurst says 'With spearpoint they inflict wounds from a distance on men and horses; then at close quarters they enter the fray with drawn swords.'[72] There are two instances worth noting in which this tendency to use the dart against horses is well illustrated. In September, 1580, Sir Walter Raleigh was riding with a party six horsemen near Cloyne, when they were set upon by a group of kern who immediately killed five of the horses, including Raleigh's. Whereupon: 'One Nicholas Wright, a Yorkshireman, observing his master's horse to plunge (being wounded with a dart), cried out to an Irishman, one Partrick Fagan, to assist his captain,' and they made a narrow escape.[73] Similarly, in March of 1579 Lieutenant Nicholas Parker, riding with 5 horsemen and 3 shot, was set upon at Rathkeale by '100 of the traitors, who discharged 16 or 18 shot at him, and many darts .... Mr Parker was hit with two casting spears, but defended with his armour, and had his horse hurt.'[74]

The Bow

While greatly favouring the dart, the Irish kern made occasional use of a short, recurved bow. The best depiction of it is Dürer's galloglass, who carries one in his left hand, with arrows tucked under his arm. The Dürer bow has a slight recurve, and is clearly yew, although the artist has reversed the usual

---

[69] Maxwell, *Irish History*, p.222.
[70] Perrot, *Chronicle of Ireland*, p.16.
[71] Kew, 'Fynes Moryson's Itinerary', p.70.
[72] Stanihurst, *Great Deeds*, p.125.
[73] Harles Smith, *Ancient and Present State of the County and City of Cork*, vol. 2 (Dublin: 1749), pp.31–32.
[74] David Edwards (ed.), *Campaign Journals of the Elizabethan Irish Wars* (Dublin: Irish Manuscripts Commission, 2014), p.74.

THE KERN

positions of the red belly and yellow sapwood. The red belly should be on the inside and the yellow sap wood on the outside face of the bow. Another depiction, with a more dramatic recurve, is in the *Recuiel Herbier* book, which shows one in the hands of an Irish kern (probably from the 1544 levy to France), with again no quiver. In 1397, Perelhos had said, 'some make use of bows, which are as short as half a bow of England, but they shoot as far as the English ones.'[75] Spencer compared them to Scythian bows, while in 1518 Laurent Vital called them 'little Turkish bows.'[76] They are variously said to be less than three-quarters of a yard long, or a yard long. The string is of 'wreathed [twisted] hemp slackly bent' according to Spencer, while Vital says 'the string was a big sinew and the arrows were steel tipped reeds

An Irish archer, c. 1544. He wears a skull with a typically Irish spreading crest. The hand and a half ring pommel sword at his waist has a skean attached to the scabbard, as in the related *Códice De Trajes* image. The quiver resembles a canvas medieval arrow bag, with the addition of typically Irish fringe. He carries a short recurved bow, apparently of yew (or it may be a composite bow?) (Author's drawing, after an image in the Stibbert Museum, Florence)

---

75 Harbison, 'Irish Arms', p.176.
76 Laurent Vital (Dorothy Convery trans., Hiram Morgan ed.), 'Ireland, an extract from Le Premier Voyage de Charles-Quint en Espagne, de 1517 à 1518', at CELT, Corpus of Electronic Texts Edition: T500000-001, p.288.

'OF KERNS AND GALLOWGLASSES'

Kern with short recurve bow. Long boots of rawhide, discussed below under early Highland dress. The image possibly relates to Henry VIII's French War of 1544. (Biblioteka Cyfrowa, Creative Commons)

and feathered to shoot.' Spencer says the 'shorte Bearded arrowes' are 'not above half an elline longe, tipped with steel heades, made like common broad arrows, but many more sharp and slender.'[77] An English ell was 45 inches, so this indicates an arrow about 22 inches long. The 'Power of Irishmen' of *c.* 1490 says that some kern carry 'a bow and a sheaf.' In 1600 Dymmock also speaks of a 'sheaf of arrows with barbed heads.'[78] Spencer, however, does mention little quivers. In an Irish tale of about 1537, *O'Donnell's Kern* discussed above, the title character uses a bow and 24 arrows. A sheaf of arrows is the amount sufficient to fill a quiver for one archer, or a quantity of arrows, usually 24.

Stanihurst mentions that the kern 'are notable stone-throwers,' without specifically mentioning the sling. The *Triumphs of Turlough* (Caithréim Thoirdhealbhaigh), written in 1459 about events *c.* 1317, mentions gathering a good store of round pebbles in preparation for battle.[79] The men of the Claddagh fishing village at Galway were said to be accomplished slingers in the mid-nineteenth century, and held slinging matches among themselves.[80]

The Skean

The skean was a fighting knife particularly associated with the kern, although galloglass and horsemen are also described carrying the skean on occasion. It was a single-edged knife with a thick back, dropping to an acute point. The long version, called *scian fada*, could have a blade up to 22 inches in length. A smaller version, called a *miodóg*, was about the size of a modern Scottish dirk, and could have a blade as short as 10 inches. The wooden handles were elegantly waisted, and carved either in a spiral groove, or with crossed bands of three-strand plait Gaelic revival interlace. There is a thin ferrule around the top and bottom edge of the handles, often plated with copper alloy. The pommel is perfectly flat, with a large countersunk nut securing the peened-over tang, with iron wedges hammered in around it, sometimes in a zigzag pattern. They were worn on lanyards slung around the neck, in leather sheathes heavily carved with four-strand plait knot work and geometric designs. Sometimes, as in Derricke's woodcuts,

---

77 Spencer, *A View*, p.88.
78 Maxwell, *Irish History*, p.222.
79 Standish Hayes O'Grady (ed.), *Caithréim Thoirdhealbhaigh, The Triumphs of Turlough*, 2 vols (London: Irish Texts Society, 26, 27, 1929), p.92.
80 McE, J., 'Ethnological Sketches, No. 1, The Fishermen of the Claddagh, at Galway in *Ulster Journal of Archaeology*, vol. 2 (1854), pp.163–164.

THE KERN

the sheath has a three-inch chape of wound bronze wire, an example of which has been excavated. The *scian fada* could function as a short sword, while the *miodóg* was sometimes thrown 'adroitly at 15 paces distance' as a projectile. The origin of the skean is unknown, though it may descend from the seax. Certain seax sheaths, in particular, bear a strong resemblance to the sheaths of the latter skean. However, the skean blade is more like that of late medieval bollock knives having single-edged blades. Bollock knives sometimes had handles carved in a spiral twist, like a number of Irish skeans. The known surviving examples have been described in detail in a recent publication by the present author.[81]

Like the famed Irish mantle, the skean had long been one of the manufactured exports of Ireland, though in smaller quantities. A fourteenth-century inventory of the Duke of Gloucester includes a lavishly decorated Irish skean; 'A short knife of Ireland garnished with silver finish'. And a roughly contemporary inventory of Mortimer includes two 'falding de hib[er]n' (Irish *fallainn*), i.e., Irish mantles.[82] In 1473, Cornelius O'Duhy, a Gaelic Irish merchant of Drogheda, sailed to Wales and travelled overland to Pembroke to sell his wares, which were 'fallings' or Irish mantles, and knives (*cutellos*). The later were presumably skeans.[83] The Bristol Port Books show two further instances of Irish knives being exported to England in 1526. From the rather high prices, which were 3s 4d and 6s 8d, these were likely skeans with elaborately carved handles and tooled sheaths.[84]

The long skean, with a blade up to 22 inches in length, could be used much like a sword. In 1566, the Irish merchant ship *Sunday of Wexford* was seized by the English pirate Tim Pickery off Land's End. She was making the return voyage from La Rochell, having delivered coal, hides and Irish mantles. The largest part of Pickery's crew were '20 wild kernes very desperat'. His men were armed with 'divers …. abiliments of warres. The kernes with long skeyns and targetts'. This pairing of long skeans with targets suggests they were considered the equivalent of a sword.[85]

The Kern's Dress

The sources for sixteenth century Irish dress were comprehensively catalogued by H. F. McClintock in 1943.[86] Since then, important new

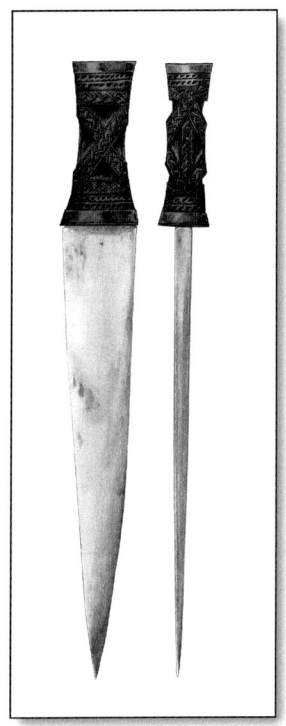

Short skean from Athlone. Restored with a blade about nine inches long. Larger versions had blades up to 22 inches in length. (Author's drawing)

81　Robert Gresh, *The Skean: The Distinctive Fighting Knife of Gaelic Ireland, 1500–1700* (Atglen: Schiffer, 2023).
82　Moffat, Ralph, 'A Sign of Victory? 'Scottish Sword' and other weapons in the possession of the Auld Innimie', Arms & Armour, vol. 15, no. 2, pp.122–43.
83　Timothy O'Neill, *Merchants and Mariners in Medieval Ireland* (Dublin: Irish Academic Press, 1987) p.122.
84　Rondelez, 'Ironwork', p.35
85　Hore, *History Wexford*, vol. 5, pp.173–4.
86　H. F. McClintock, *Old Irish and Highland Dress* (Dundalk: Dundalgan Press, 1943).

'OF KERNS AND GALLOWGLASSES'

Long skean and sheath. The sheath at left is from Kilcumber, and is 23 inches long. It would have fitted the long skean from Corbally, at right, which had a blade 22 inches long. This is the type of skean depicted in Derricke's woodcuts. (Author's drawing)

sources from early in the century have come to light, which are reviewed below.

The dress of the Irish held an importance for the colonial administration in Dublin which is difficult for modern people to understand. During the course of the sixteenth century the Government moved from seeking to prevent the English colonists from adopting Irish fashions, to banning traditional Irish dress altogether. It is important to initially understand the cultural and ideological motivations that shaped Irish dress.

During the 'Gaelic Revival' c. 1350 to 1450, much of the English conquest was recovered by the native Irish. This political revival was accompanied by a cultural revival, one focus of which was the 'Warriors of the Red Branch' and their legendary hero, Cú Chulainn. New manuscript editions of these sagas were commissioned, which have helped preserve them for our own time. In 1387, Niall Og O'Neill built a feasting hall on the mound of Emain Macha, where the Warriors of the Red Branch had feasted in ancient times. This desire to re-enact the heroic past was reflected in clothing as well. In 1397 Niall Og hosted Ramón de Perelhos, a Catalan knight, for Christmas feasting. Perelhos found that in the depths of winter, the lords, ladies, clerics and bishops all wore neither hose nor shoes, and their tunics were cut very low in the neck. This was a conscious emulation of an imagined heroic past, and a display of militant vigour amid the winter frost. Perelhos mentions spurs being worn on bare feet, and this is actually illustrated in the famous miniature painting of Art Mór Mac Murchadha Caomhánach riding to meet the Earl of Gloucester in 1399.[87] This was conscious antiquarianism, and had nothing to do with poverty. The horse MacMurrough was riding had cost him 400 cows. The court ladies were fully affected by this fashion, and Perelhos indicated that many of the women at the Christmas feast were topless, 'with their shameful parts showing,' although wearing skirts, as later illustrated by Lucas DeHeere.[88] While clothing trends shifted, as with the adoption of the saffron dyed smock in the mid-fifteenth century, elements of this heroic fashion remained a century after Perelhos' visit. In 1518, Laurent Vital made an unplanned visit to Kinsale. He describes the Irish 'savages' going barefoot and bare legged, and in what may have seemed a traveller's 'tall tale,' seeing women's breasts fully exposed. Without the context of the Gaelic Revival of the previous century, we might doubt his veracity, but some of his most unlikely details seem to have truth behind them.

He asked his host in Kinsale why some of the bellicose 'savages' had faces smeared with blood. He was told that it was to keep away freckles, 'of which several of them had full faces', the men going bareheaded in summer

---

87 This in an illustration in Jean Creton's *Histoire du roy d'Angleterre Richard II*. British Library Harley Ms 1319.
88 Katherine Simms, 'The Barefoot Kings: Literary Image and Realty in Later Medieval Ireland' in *Proceedings of the Harvard Celtic Colloquium*, vol. 30 (2010), pp.1–21.

THE KERN

Albrecht Dürer's watercolour drawing of Irish 'war men', 1521. While it may be a costume piece, many elements are corroborated from other sources, including the hairstyles, the mantle, the ring pommel sword and the projecting peaks or nasals of the helmets. (Berlin State Museums)

with the hair shorn above the ear. In the late nineteenth century, Lady Wilde made a collection of 'ancient cures, charms, and usages' of Ireland, including: 'For freckles: Anoint a freckled face with the blood of a bull, or of a hare, and it will put away the freckles and make the skin fair and clear.'[89]

During Laurent Vital's visit in 1518, he recorded impressions of Irish dress that correspond to Albrecht Dürer's wash drawing of 'the war men of Ireland' of 1521. It has been suggested that this is because Dürer had read Vital's account, but this is not proven, and perhaps his drawing can be regarded rather as independent verification. Vital said the men were shaved one palm above the ears, only the tops of their heads being covered with hair, which was allowed to fall to their eyebrows,

> like a tuft of hair which one leaves hanging on horses between the two eyes. They are strangely bearded, some shave their beards to just above the mouth and others to below the mouth. Others shave some places and let their beards grow in tufts. These men have their shirts

---

[89] Lady Wilde, *Irish Cures, Mystic Charms and Superstitions* (New York: Sterling Publishing Co., 1991), p.19.

open down to the belt, without sleeves so that they have bare arms. They wrap themselves in a big linen cloth which goes around them one and a half times and stretches nearly from neck to foot, and they have bare feet and bare legs .... These men wear and cover themselves in big hairy coats, over their heads in the same way as the women in Brabant wear their cloaks. This coat only goes a half quarter beyond the belt and over this is a long linen apron. Thus shorn, bearded, armed and barefoot – as I said – imagine how strange this costume is to look at. I must say, I have never seen anything like this before even in a painting.[90]

Polydore Virgil, in 1534, made similar observations,

They wear a linen tunic, and do not change it until it becomes threadbare and, lest it show dirt, they dye it with saffron. When they venture out in public, or for the sake of keeping warm, over this they wear a woolen cloak (and a shaggy one at that, with fringes at the top), and this is the common dress of men and women alike. But their nobles dress in clothes reaching down to the ankles, a hooded cape that extends to the heel. They also wear shoes, whereas the rest of the people go about hatless and barefoot. The skin of their feet is so calloused that even boys whose feet are not yet hardened by long practice and labour run about with surprising speed, even in rough places. They crop their hair a little above the ears, although some of them maintain the ancient manner by cutting off their hair in back but wearing long locks in front. They often shave off their beards, leaving only their upper lips unshaven (as is reasonable to believe) as a terror for their enemies.[91]

Paolo Giovio, in his *Descriptio* of 1548, says the Irish go bareheaded unless wearing a helmet, and:

It is their custom to march with their hair shaggy, cut around at the ears, beard often trimmed, and upper lip covered with twisted bristles, so that they may appear more ferocious in war. Meanwhile, almost all their clothes are of the one kind: a soldier's woollen cloak, with a fringed and variegated edge for elegance, which is hung around the shoulder with the left hand protruding through. A prince prefers his to be purple, leaving the dark blue or red cloak to the soldier, which we therefore call Irish, since it comes from there. We often see it on ship's captains and their sailors, and they are covered down to the

---

90   Vital, 'Ireland', p.288.
91   Virgil, *Anglica Historia,* unpaginated.

knees with saffron dyed tunics, the silken edges of which they decorate most skillfully with colours embroidered by the needle.[92]

In 1537, English administrator Robert Cowley recommended that:

> that no silk or saffron be set upon shirts; for especially against High Feasts at Christmas and Easter there is no Irishman of war – horseman, kernagh, nor galloglass – for the most part but will steal, rob out of churches or elsewhere to go gay at a feast; yea, and bestoweth for saffron and silk to one shirt many times five marks, so that more robbery and felony is against such feasts committed as all the year following.[93]

Also in 1537 'The Act for the English Order and Habit' prohibited English subjects from shaving above the ears or wearing long locks on their head called glibbes, or to have hair growing on the upper lip called crommeal, or to wear a shirt or smock dyed with saffron, or to use more than seven yards of linen in a shirt, or to wear any mantle, coat or hood made in the Irish fashion. Likewise, that same year, a verdict of the heads and commoners of Clonmel advised that the 'bigge Irish sherts be dampned and put back and brought to lasse making and facyon,' and that all the nations wear English apparel and use English customs.[94] An Act of Parliament at Dublin in 1541 limited the amount of linen that could be used in the Irish shirts by the various social ranks:[95]

English mariner wearing an Irish mantle, as described by Paolo Giovio in the text. The shaggy mantle was spongy and soft, and shed water readily. If wet, it could be wrung dry. Engraving by De Bruyn, from *Omnium pene Europae, Asiae, Aphricae, Atque Americae Gentium Habitus*, 1540–87. (Los Angeles County Museum of Art)

Table 26. Limits of Linen in Irish Shirts

Noblemen	20 cubits (12 yards)
Vassal or horseman	18 cubits (11 yards)
Kern (*turbarius*) or Scot	16 cubits (9 yards)
Groom, messenger or other servant of lords	12 cubits (7 yards)
Husbandman or labourer	10 cubits (6 yards)

---

92 Harris, 'Paolo Giovio', p.286.
93 *State Papers: Henry VIII*, p.450, n.d., R. Cowley to Henry VIII.
94 *Letters and Papers, Henry VIII*, Vol. 12, Pt. 2 (London: Eyre and Spottiswoode, 1891), p.314, 17 August, Verdict of Clonmel jurors.
95 McClintock, *Old Irish Dress*, p.85.

'OF KERNS AND GALLOWGLASSES'

In spite of this agitation, the records of the government levy of kern made in 1544–45 for service in France and Scotland show that it was the custom to advance a payment of 40 shillings to newly recruited kern to buy silk and saffron for them: 'Wise was charged with Lord Power's kerne, and had delivered to each of them 40s to buy them silk and saffron.'[96] This is discussed below in the account of Kern in English Overseas Service. As noted elsewhere, the context of our most numerous surviving set of images, the 'Dravne After the Qvicke' print and the DeHeere watercolours, is this war of Henry VIII in France, 1544–1545. Shortly thereafter, there is mention of white woollen cloth being issued to kern in government pay in August 1548, when Thomas Barnewall petitioned the Lord Deputy: 'For payment of the money which he and Sir Thomas Cusake had advanced for buying white cloth for the kern. The Lord of Dunsany owe 7l. 11s. 4d., prays Lord Deputy to compel him to pay it.'[97] There is no indication of how this cloth was made up, or whether it resulted in any kind of uniform clothing. There are, however, suggestions of insignia being worn. Katherine Simms has noted a mid-fifteenth Irish manuscript with a religious text in which heavenly *ceithearn tighe*, or household kern, are distinguished by golden

Dravne After the Qvicke, an English woodcut made from a life drawing. Possibly showing Irish kern on their way to France in 1544. The cap with ear flaps worn by the second figure from the right shows signs of being quilted longitudinally. (North Wind Picture Archive/Alamy Stock Photo)

---

96 Dean Gunther White, 'Henry VIII's Irish Kerne in France and Scotland, 1544–1545' in *The Irish Sword*, vol. 3, no. 13 (1958), p.213.
97 *Calendar of State Papers Ireland: Henry VIII, Edward VI, Mary and Elizabeth*, vol. 1, 1509–73, Hans Claude Hamilton ed. (London: Longman, Green, Longman & Roberts, 1860), ? August, Barnewall to Bellingham.

crosses on their foreheads, and silver crosses on their backs. She suggests this may indicate that mortal kern wore their earthly master's badges as well.[98]

A Venetian report of 1554 describes the Irish still going barefoot both winter and summer, and wearing a long linen shirt, dyed in saffron, which reached the ground and is worn until it is in tatters. Over this was thrown a mantle of coarse woollen cloth, and when they take the field, 'the infantry raise their linen garment up to the waist, fastening their sleeves at the shoulder, and carry two or three darts which the hurl wonderfully.'[99] This is a good description of the blousing of the ankle length linen shirt over the belt to shorten it to knee length. The mention of the long sleeves being fastened at the shoulder may be depicted in the drawings of Irish kern at the Siege of Boulogne, 1544, based on the lost murals at Cowdray House. These seem to show the kern bare armed, and their long sleeves may be fastened out of the way in some manner, perhaps tied together behind the shoulders. The last description we have of this form of Irish dress is from William Good, writing in 1566. He says the Irish wear saffron dyed linen shirts, 'exceedingly large', with wide sleeves flowing to the knees, over these, 'Little jackets they have of wollen, and those very short,' and plain breeches close to their thighs, with a fringed mantle or shag rug with a fringed border thrown over all.[100]

From the beginning of the century, all descriptions of the great linen shirt mention it being dyed with saffron, and there can be no doubt this was regularly done. Research on Irish trade in the sixteenth century has shown imports of very large amounts of crocus for the saffron shirts and orchell for the 'prince's purple cloak', as mentioned by Paolo Giovio above. These dye stuffs fall off sharply around 1570 in the trade records, when other significant changes also appear. The modifications may have been brought on partly by fashion, but starting in the 1570s there was a more dramatic cooling of the climate, which would have played a role as well. Campion, who was in Ireland from 1569 to 1571, says the linen shirts were worn for show, with wide hanging sleeves, and were pleated, needing at least 30 yards of linen. But he adds, 'They have now left their saffron.'[101] The well known woodcuts in John Derricke's *Image of Ireland* illustrate Sidney's second Deputyship of 1575–1578, and show Irishmen almost always wearing brogues and trews, with the linen shirt greatly shortened in length, 'not reaching past the thigh.' Like Campion, he also states clearly that the skirts of these shirts are now tailored, 'with pleats on pleats they pleated are, as thick as pleats may lie, whose sleeves hang trailing down, almost unto the shoe.'[102] Apart from the sleeves, this is quite different from the flowing,

---

98 Simms, *Kings to Warlords*, p.93.
99 McClintock, *Old Irish Dress*, p.68.
100 Cox, *Hibernia Anglicana*, 148.
101 McClintock, *Old Irish Dress*, p.57.
102 Derricke, *Image of Irelande*, p.50.

'OF KERNS AND GALLOWGLASSES'

Irishman in 1581, reflecting changes in dress that seem to have occurred in the 1570s. This is probably the 'lord's galloglass', handing the chieftain his spear. From Derricke's first plate. (Creative Commons)

ankle length linen tunic dyed with saffron of the first half of the century. Derricke makes no mention of saffron. His 'kernogh's coat' or 'parti-pleated jack', a doublet with a sort of pleated peplum, is similar to the very short version worn by Irishmen earlier in the century, but has lengthened, and now sits on the natural waist. A surviving sixteenth century kern's jacket from Kilcommon in the National Museum of Ireland, is the version illustrated by Derricke. Falling as it does to the natural waist, experience has shown that this close fitting jacket was not likely to have been worn with the long linen smocks used earlier in the century, because of the bulk created around the waist when the long skirt is hiked up to knee level. It had to have been worn with Derricke's newly tailored shirt with a short pleated skirt, a shirt that was probably no longer being dyed with saffron, although as late as 1578, the old combination of silk and saffron still constituted a medium of exchange in Gaelic Ulster when it was offered for the return of stolen cattle or for military assistance.[103] Nonetheless, by the arrival of the Spanish Armada in 1588, this shirt has entirely disappeared, possibly reflecting the progressive destruction of Irish linen manufacture wrought by the wars.

Kern in English Service Overseas

Our best picture of the organisation of sixteenth century Irish kern is found in the detailed records of levies for overseas service in 1544/1545 and 1550, during the reigns of Henry VIII and Edward VI. With the suppression of the 'Silken' Thomas Rebellion (1534–1535), a conciliatory period in Anglo-Irish relations began, with many chieftains submitting to 'surrender and regrant': i.e., surrendering their clan's land to the Crown in order to receive it back in the form of a personal hereditary title. This newly affirmed loyalty made the chieftain's armed followers a potential source of military power for the Crown.

Before looking in more detail at the levies, we may briefly summarise the organisation of the kern as follows. In 1544, a 'Captain General' was appointed over the whole force, while in 1550, there was a 'General' with a 'Lieutenant' as his second in command. For the 1544 levy, each company was headed by a 'Capytayne' with one or two 'Peticapitaynes' in the larger companies, whereas in 1550 a 'Petty Capten' alone headed each company. Pay records show that there were also one or two 'wyffelers' and a standard bearer in each company in 1544, and we are told that in addition to the kern, there were 'marshals, pipers, surgeons, and suchlike.' Out of 20

---

103 *Cal. Carew Mss*, pp.147–8, undated, Mayor and Townsmen of Knockfergus.

companies appearing in the full muster of 1544, 11 have pipers listed by name, such as 'Gilpatric Piper'. For the 1550 levy, there are three pipers for 340 men. Thus, in both levies, there was a ratio of roughly one piper to every 100 men. The three 'Soergeons' for the 1550 levy are listed separately. Interestingly, the first man listed among the 'Byrnes Kerne' was 'Sir John O Kerwyn Chapleyn.' While 'Gonners' are listed separately in 1544, there is no indication that they received more pay than an ordinary kern at the time. In both the 1544 and 1550 levies, the size of companies varied from 80 to 30 or even 10 men. It is not clear that they were subsequently reorganised into more consistently sized units. The Irish Council cautioned that captains of smaller units would expect to be entertained as captains, and would not have agreed to go otherwise, and thus, 'we say nothing to the contrary, seeing they entered not into wages here to be joined into numbers there; and yet it might please your Majesty that those gentlemen, though they have not full numbers, may be entertained, as both they and their masters shall not judge themselves disparaged.'[104]

Gervase Phillips has argued that these episodes of service abroad exposed the Gaelic Irish to contact with the very best European soldiers and the most advanced tactics and technology at a much earlier date than is generally realised.[105] Phillips' main concern was to counter John Michael Hill's thesis of the 'Distinctiveness of Gaelic Warfare', an anachronistic notion blurring the Highlanders and Irish together as practitioners of unchanging 'blade dominated offensive tactics.'[106] Phillips' main contention is undoubtedly correct, and the Government clearly did aspire to modernise the arms and training of these Irish contingents. But it must be noted that there still remained the distinctively gruelling Irish way of war, characterised by flight and pursuit. This is quite different from Hill's 'attack and die' proposal, which we must limit to the case of galloglass fighting the relatively rare set-piece battle. The kern sent to France and Scotland would be dispersed in the performance of their specialist raiding role, and it is hard to say what proportion of them were eventually armed with firearms as intended. Certainly, in places along the Scottish border, that percentage rose to half of their number. The presence of standard bearers and whiffers may be a further indication of modernising English influence. The whiffler acted as the NCO of an infantry company, armed with the two-handed 'slaugh sword' which he used 'to keep the people in array.' Whiffers marched at the head of the company with the musicians and ensign. Without overstating the impact of these deployments, it is likely they accelerated the existing

---

104 White, 'Henry's Irish Kern', p.217.
105 Gervase Phillips, 'Irish Ceatharnaigh in English Service, 1544–1550, and the Development of "Gaelic Warfare", *Journal of the Society for Army Historical Research*, no. 78 (2000), pp.163–172.
106 John Michael Hill, 'The Distinctiveness of Gaelic Warfare, 1400–1750', *European History Quarterly*, no. 22 (1992), pp.323–345.

'OF KERNS AND GALLOWGLASSES'

trend towards the adoption of firearms in Ireland. It is less obvious that training and tactics were much affected.

In 1543, Henry VIII and the Emperor Charles V had agreed to jointly attack France within two years. In both of Henry's previous French expeditions (1512–13 and 1522–23), the Scots had seized the opportunity of his absence to attack the northern borders. This time the King was determined to guard against that likelihood, and was persuaded to use Irish troops to that end.

The Levy of 1544

With 'a bruit of war with the Scots and Frenchmen', Sir Anthony St Leger, Lord Deputy of Ireland, promptly wrote to Henry in April of 1543, recommending the services of Irish troops. After describing the horsemen and galloglass, he concludes:

> The other sort, called kerne, are naked men, but only their shirts and small coats; and many times when they come to the bicker, but bare naked, saving their shirts to hide their privities; and those have darts and short bows; which sort of people be both hardy and deliver to search woods or morasses.

He suggests that if Henry

> convert them to morris pikes and handguns, I think they would in that feat, with small instructions, do your highness great service; for, as for gunners, there be no better in no land than they be, for the number they have, which be more than I would wish they had, unless it were to serve your Majesty.[107]

Perhaps with this offer in mind, the Privy Council in December of 1543 had conveyed a warning to Argyle that if his loyalty failed, they would send men from Ireland (as well as Scottish mercenaries) to burn his lands. In

Irish men and women in the service of Henry VIII. Painted by Lucas DeHeere c. 1574, from earlier depictions likely drawn from the Irish levy of 1544. (Ghent University Library, Creative Commons)

---

107 White, 'Henry's Irish Kern', p.213.

March 1544 war preparations accelerated, and 3,000 kern were suddenly demanded from the Irish Council: 1,000 for the Scottish border, and 2,000 for France. On 11 March the Earl of Hertford, Lieutenant of the North, was advised he would soon have 1,000 kern and should send to London for demihakes for them. He was assured that money would be sent to Chester to entertain them after their landing. Two days later, Hertford duly signed a letter requesting '1,000 demihakes by sea with the Lord Admiral for the 1,000 kern, hackbuttiers, coming from Ireland.'[108]

Meanwhile, the Lord Justice and Council of Ireland had responded to this sudden summons, complaining that though the Irish nobility were willing to go, 'idle men' to fill the ranks were not so readily available without some prominent noblemen to lead them. The Irish Council initially claimed it would be Michaelmas (29 September) before the force could be raised, and they promptly split up to visit the various lords and discuss executing the levy. They reported that a reduced levy of 1,000 kern would be ready to send over at the following Easter (13 April), but would require an escort for fear of pirates, 'for if these Kerne, which shall pass but in "pickardes", should be taken, many inconveniences might ensue.'[109] They were advised by the Privy Council that the King now required only the available 1,000 kern. Five hundred were to be sent to Fowdrey, or as near there and Chester as was possible. The other five hundred were to be put in readiness to join the expedition to France on one hour's notice.

The said kern were to be picked and chosen men, all gunners, 'or as many as can be gotten.'[110] In the event, besides able and sufficient men, the Commissioners were authorised to enlist those 'retained for any felony within said counties or liberties.'[111] In early May, with the kern camped near Waterford awaiting favourable winds, 10 men were killed in fighting over provisions that broke out between Brereton's and Ormond's contingents, possibly an outcome of having extended the recruitment effort to the jails. Lord Power's 25 kern each reportedly received an imprest of 40s to pay for silk and saffron. St Leger said that most of the lords supplying kern 'reared upon the country 40s for every kern,' except his brother Robert, who made the payment at his own cost.[112] This traditional payment was still in place when another government levy was made in 1586 for Stanley's expedition to the Low Countries. Stanley's levy included 500 kern, so it is interesting to read: 'Stanley was paid 40s. as "impress" per man to carry out the levy.'[113] A woodcut of an Irish soldier by Caspar Rutz, printed at Amsterdam in 1588 and thought to represent one of Stanley's kern, shows him wearing a *léine*.

---

108 White, 'Henry's Irish Kern', p.214.
109 Viscount Dillon, 'Irish Troops at Boulogne in 1544', *Journal of the Society for Army Historical Research*, vol. 1, no. 3 (1922), p.81.
110 Dillon, 'Irish Troops', p.82.
111 White, 'Henry's Irish Kern', p.215.
112 White, 'Henry's Irish Kern', p.215.
113 Grainne Henry, *The Irish Military Community in Spanish Flanders, 1586–1621* (Dublin: Irish Academic Press, 1992), pp.40–1.

'OF KERNS AND GALLOWGLASSES'

Detail from one of a series of contemporary wall paintings at Cowdray House, Sussex, depicting scenes of Henry VIII's campaign in France. Fortunately, a series of engraving was made of the paintings before the house was destroyed by fire in 1793. Shown here is a column of Irish kern returning to the English camp, driving a prey of sheep and cattle before them and led by a piper. Their hair was depicted in the original painting as red, and they are barefoot and bare legged, wearing their 'Irish shirts' belted at various lengths. Their arms are bare; the sleeves of the shirt pulled up and fastened in a manner not visible here. As discussed in the text, the Venetian ambassador describing the Irish in 1554 said 'the infantry raise their linen garment up to the waist, fastening their sleeves at the shoulder.' Three are shown wearing helmets and with mantles wrapped around their bodies, and all are armed with a pair of six-foot darts with diamond shaped heads. At their left side they wear long skeans with small cross-guards (unusual, but not unknown for skeans), with asymmetrically patterned sheaths. (Author's drawing)

It is possible that even at that late date, the 40s was intended to buy silk and saffron, as it had been during the reign of Henry VIII.

The reduced levy totalled 1,154 – 920 kern and 234 boys. The Council had advised the King that 'within this realm every two kern used to have a page or boy, which commonly is nevertheless a man, to bear their mantles, weapons, and victuals for 2, 3, or 4 days, when they go on a volant journey,' as well as marshals, pipers, and surgeons, who were each to receive 'like entertainment as for themselves.'[114] The Council had reduced this

---
114 White, 'Henry's Irish Kern', p.217.

proportion to one boy to every four kern, as they expected the kern to be otherwise provided for in the Army Royal, and thus able to spare the usual complement of boys. Ormond's nephew Lord Power was appointed Captain General of the whole force, while another nephew, Piers Butler, was to be captain of the first 100 men Ormond had raised, with James Robynet as petty captain. The second company raised by Ormond would have Edmond Purcell as captain, and Patrick Archdeacon as petty captain, men from these two families being the hereditary captains of Ormond's kern. In the end, the actual number of men in each of Ormond's two companies was 80, with 20 boys, and there were 18 gunners in the first company, 23 in the second. These were initially the only firearms in the entire force (see Appendix I).[115] The Council assured the King: 'No doubt they will be easily trained to be good gunners, whereunto they will do you grace high service: many of them be gunners, though they have no guns, whereof there is no provision here.'[116] The rates of pay for the initial levy are given below, along with the rates for the company of Captain Patrick Sherlock, who remained as part of the Calais garrison after the rest of the kern were repatriated to Ireland in September 1544. Only the wages of the footmen differ.

Table 27. Pay of Irish Kern, 1544

Initial Per Diem Rates, May 1544		Captain Sherlock's Company, October 1544	
Captain	3s 4d	Two captains, each	3s 4d
Petty captain	1s 8d	Two petty captains, each	1s 8d
Wyffelers	1s	Two whiffers, each	1s
Standard bearer	1s	Standard bearer	1s
Foot soldier	6d	140 footmen, each	4d

The Contingent for Scotland

The kern had shipped for West Chester by 7 May. At West Chester they were met by John Lyne, the Earl of Hertford's representative from the borders, and Walter Pipard, who was to select the best 600 kern for France. The 400 kern and boys sent to the Scottish borders arrived there by 25 May. They were intended to relieve the Northern horse that had gone to France. Hertford said they were 'very unruly …. their weapons are swords and darts; not past 40 can shoot in hackbuts, but it is intended to teach 100 of them shortly.'[117] Although Callough O'Byrne had been appointed their

---

115 Dillon, 'Irish Troops', p.82.
116 White, 'Henry's Irish Kern', p.217.
117 W. G. Strickland, 'Irish Soldiers in the Service of Henry VIII', *Journal of the Royal Society of Antiquaries of Ireland*, vol. 13 (1922), p.94.

overall leader, upon arrival at Newcastle they were split up, with 100 sent to the West Marches, and the rest divided between the Middle and Eastern Marches. Lord Warden Wharton recommended dividing up the 100 kern for the West Marches by placing 30 at Docliffe, 20 at Burgeons (1½ miles distant), 10 at Drumbeughe (2½ miles further on), 20 at Bownes (1½ miles on), and 20 at Hollme (5 miles further). In the Middle March, Lord Warden Evers made a favourable report of the captain of kern there, and his efforts to discipline the kern, 'who are by nature wild.'[118] Evers suggested the kern be paid monthly rather than fortnightly, to spare their captain some travel to collect their pay, as his presence was required with the men. The kern continued to serve in these small groups on the border for some time. Ten of them formed part of the garrison of Coldingham in December 1544, half of these being armed with half-hakes.

This conflict in Scotland is known colloquially as the 'Rough Wooing', and Hertford held a commission of fire and sword, burning and killing man, woman and child wherever there was resistance. On 12 June he returned from a raid on Jedburgh, having lost only one Irishman and one Englishman, and reported: 'The Irish did good service, are dreaded by the Scots as they take no prisoners after the Border custom but say that the King gives them money to live on.'[119] The raid on Jedburgh did bring in 200 prisoners, so clearly not everyone was killed. Phillips has argued that the lead role taken by the kern at the sacking of Jedburgh was a significant exposure to 'a tactically sophisticated three-pronged assault supported by artillery bombardment, in which the *ceatharnaigh* successfully cooperated with both the gunners and the accompanying English infantry.'[120] In September 1545, the Irish took part in a second raid on Jedburgh, then on 27 September 1545, the King commanded the Irish kern on the borders be paid off and repatriated, their captain, Callough O'Bryne, receiving £13 6s 8d.

The Contingent for France

The 600 kern and 150 boys for the 'Enterprise of Paris' moved south, and in May 'passed through the citie of London in warlike manner, to the number of seaven hundred Irishmen having for their weapons darts and handguns, with bagpipes before them; and in St Iames Park besides Westminster they mustered before the King.'[121] These 600 kern were divided among the three 'battills' into which army was formed. Henry commanded 42,000 men, the

---
118 White, 'Henry's Irish Kern', p.222.
119 Blake Butler, 'King Henry VIII's Irish Army List', *The Irish Geneologist*, vol. 1, no. 1 (1937), p.3.
120 Phillips, 'Irish Ceatharnaigh', p.170.
121 David Potter, *Henry VIII and Francis I: the Final Conflict* (Leiden: Brill, 2011), p.232.

greatest part of which were the 28,000 English foot and 4,000 English horse, supplemented by 10,000 mercenaries, mostly German and Burgundian. Only 7 percent of Henry's English foot had firearms, so the Irish were not exceptional in this regard.[122] Along with the pike, firearms were a key element in the blend of old and new weapons that characterised the 'Army Royal' of 1544. The pike remained largely a specialist weapon handled by German and Swiss mercenaries. The English army's arquebuses were mostly from Italy, chiefly Brescia, with limited home production being carried out by foreigners in Henry's workshops. We may doubt that Hertford received all of the 1,000 hackbutts he requested for the kern, but he certainly stated his intention to train 100 men in their use, and some groups of kern on the borders had half their number armed with them. A like provision must have been made for the contingent for France, though we have no record of it.

Lord Power, overall commander of the Irish kern, was posted in the vanguard with Ormond's two companies. Patrick Sherlock commanded three companies in the main guard, and Gerald de Courci commanded the remainder in the rearguard. The existing muster lists have the Irish placed with specialist troops, as it was evident they were intended for special purposes. In the vanguard, there were 'Irish kerne, 200. Northern horsemen, 100. Pioneers, 400.' The main battle includes 'Irish kerne, 200. Miners, 200. Brewers and bakers, 235.' The rearguard has 'Irishmen, 200. From the sea, 400. Northern horsemen, 100.'

The van landed at Calais on 6 June, 1544, and within three days the Irish were involved in a skirmish up to the gates of Arde, where they operated in close support of English horsemen. Norfolk, commanding the van, reported 'divers of the Irishmen did very well,' saying they 'skirmish very galyardly; and [are] reckoned by the Frenchmen, as the prisoners say, to be *gens mervelous sauvaige* and also *gens experimentés à la guerre.*'[123] The van and rear guards had laid siege to Montreuil by 14 July, and the contingents of Power and de Courci serving there were charged with providing victuals to the besiegers by raiding the local countryside. The peasants had been hiding their crops and valuables in caves since the war of 1513, as Norfolk discovered on his march to Montreuil. He thought the 'paysones, which keep the forest' should be well searched, 'which woulde be best done with the Yrishe men.' During the siege of Montreuil, the kern are said to have burnt 200 houses and some boats in the village of Berck, and another 270 houses at Verton.[124] These long-suffering villages had been attacked by French troops in 1542 and 1543, and after the Irish raids of 1544, they would be visited by landsknechts in 1545.

---

122 James Raymond, *Henry VIII's Military Revolution: The Armies of Sixteenth Century Britain and Europe* (London & New York: I. B. Tauris, 2007), p.3.
123 White, 'Henry's Irish Kern', p.222.
124 David Potter, *Henry VIII and Francis I: the Final Conflict* (Leiden: Brill, 2011), p.230.

'OF KERNS AND GALLOWGLASSES'

Meanwhile, Patrick Sherlock's three companies served with the main guard before Boulogne under the Duke of Suffolk. Richard Stanihurst, writing in 1571, recalled that these kern served the army well in rounding up cattle from neighbouring villages to feed the camp, saying, 'they would range 20 or 30 miles into the mainland, and having taken a bull, they used to tie him to a stake, and scorching him with faggots, they would force him to roar, so as all the cattle of the country would make towards the bull, all which they would lightly lead away and furnish the camp with store of beef.'[125] He goes on to say 'If they took any French man prisoner …. his only ransom should be no more but his head.' A French ambassador visited the camp to complain to Henry VIII in person, demanding to know whether he had brought beasts or men, but the King made a jest of it, so that 'the French men ever after, if they could take any of the Irishe scattering from the company, used first to cut off their genitors, and after to torment them with as great and as lingering pain as they could devise.'[126]

The Siege of Boulogne continued through the summer, until the city capitulated on 13 September. There is no record of the Irish taking part in work in the trenches or in assaults. Having taken the city, the King was anxious to return home, so the Siege of Montreuil was to be raised. But before that could happen, Norfolk commanding at Montreuil, reported: 'This evening came hither certain Irishmen, with whom, at their arrival, the Almaynes had a skirmish, and have thrust one of the Irishmen in under the pap with a boar spear, without occasion given on the Irishman's part that we can find by any inquiry.'[127] This was a daily occurrence between the English forces and their German mercenaries. The bulk of the Irish were repatriated at the end of September when the King returned to England, although at least one company of Irish kern, probably that of Patrick Sherlock, remained in the Boulogne garrison after the withdrawal. Stanihurst recalls the response made by a man of this company to a Frenchman who approached the edge of the haven, challenging any of the English garrison to fight with him hand-to-hand. 'An Irishman named Nicholl Welsh, who was after retained to the Earl of Kildare, loathing and disdaining his proud brags, flung into the water, and swam over the river, fought with the challenger, strake him for dead, and returned back to Boulogne with the Frenchman's head in his mouth,' for which he was bountifully rewarded.[128] The list in the table below is from Butler, and the numbers in brackets represent variations in the two sources he drew from.

---

125 Holinshed, *Holinshed's Irish Chronicle*, p.302.
126 Butler, 'Irish Army List', p.4.
127 White, 'Henry's Irish Kern', p.220.
128 Holinshed, *Holinshed's Irish Chronicle*, p.302-3.

THE KERN

Table 28. List of the Irish Army sent into England, 1544.

#	Company ruled by	Captain	Petty Captain	Kern	Boys	Gunners
1	Earl of Ormond	Pierce Butler	James Robyneet	80	20	18
2	Earl of Ormond	Edmond Purcell	Patrick Archdeacon	80	20	18
3	Earl of Desmond	Gerald de Courci	George Grenelef	115	29	
4	Earl of Tyrone	Arthur O'Quin	Walter Ecyle, Walter Bathe	76	18 (19)	
5	Baron Delvin	Pierce Nugent	William Nugent	28	7	
6	Baron Power	Edmond Power		29	5	
7	Baron Cahir	Tyrrelagh O'Doyll		24	9	
8	Baron Dunboyne			16		
9	Baron of Slane	Thomas Halfpenny		26	7	
10	Sir Gerald FitzJohn Fitzgerald of Dromany	Patrick Sherlock		24 (34)		
11	O'Raylye	John Barron	Edmond Bahan	68	7 (17)	
12	O'Conor	Cormocke O'Conor	Tiege O'Conor	30	8	
13	Magunessa (Macguiness)	Eyer McTnnose		21	5	
14	Kavanagh (Cahir McArte)	Edmond McKayes		15	4	
15	Baron of Carberry	William Bermingham		24	7 (6)	
16	Lord of Louth (Uryell)	Thomas Bathe		32	8	
17	Sir Thomas Cusack the Borderers of Meath and Westmeath, including Magoghegan	Nicholas Field	James Oge	74	30 (19)	
18	Robert Sentleger	Richard Keating	Edmond Keating	72	18	
19	The Brynes	Roger Finglass	Callow O'Brien Bowlyn, McKayer Roe	41	9 (11)	
20	Arte Uge O'Thole, Tiege O'Farrell	Roger Finglass	Cahir O'Farrell	26	7	
			Total	901 (911)	218 (220)	36
			Total	1,155 (1,167)		

The Levy of 1545

In August 1545, a second levy of Irish troops was called for to support 'the gentlemen of the Isles', the King's allies in Scotland. Matthew Stewart, 4th Earl of Lennox, with Donald Dubh MacDonald, who claimed the title Lord of the Isles, had together visited Carrickfergus that month with 180 *birlinnean* or galleys, carrying a force of 4,000 Islesmen in mail with bows and long swords. They requested 100 gunners from Dublin, which was declined as it would have required all the gunners in the Irish retinue. The King did take 3,000 of the Islesmen in wages, and the Irish Council was to find a further 2,000 Irishmen to be sent to join them in Scotland. Ormond was again given the lead in carrying this out, but this levy is not as well documented as that of 1544. Lord Deputy St Leger was instructed by the King to draw the levy 'out of the most wild and savage sort of them,' whose absence would do more good than harm.[129]

The force that sailed on 17 November consisted of 2,000 men. The Irish retinue provided 50 archers and 50 'half-hakes', and there were 400 galloglass, and 1,500 kern and archers of the country, of whom 250 were gunners. The shipping was provided by 10 or 12 ships chiefly registered in Irish ports. There had been delays in obtaining casks for the expedition's beer supply, but eventually victuals of 45,000lbs of biscuit, 17,000lbs of butter, 44 barrels of herrings, and 116 tuns of beer were provided, along with quantites of beeves, sack and gascony wine. The Irish Council provided the firearms, ordnance and powder for the expedition. Ormond was requested to accompany the Irish troops as commander, the Earl of Lennox 'being neither acquainted with the people of that country, nor their language.'[130]

Richard Stanihurst gives a different account of the force's composition, based on traditions of the Power family of Waterford, among whom he was raised: 'The Lorde of Ormonde .... levied of his tenants and retainers 600 galloglasses, 400 kerns, three score horsemen, and 440 shot: so in the whole he mustered on Osmantowne green near Dublin 1,500 soldiers.'[131] After anchoring at Olderfleet, the ships were driven by gales to Dumbarton. Threatened there by a French fleet, and facing political uncertainty in Scotland, Lennox decided to turn back. Lennox and his 500 men returned through the Ards Peninsula, while Ormond landed at Belfast and discharged his 1,500 men at Dundalk. Thus the expedition ended without ever disembarking in Scotland. It is unfortunate that musters do not appear to exist, as they would have added to our knowledge of galloglass organisation, as well as that of the Irish retinue.

---

[129] White, 'Henry's Irish Kern', p.222.
[130] White, 'Henry's Irish Kern', p.222-3.
[131] Holinshed, *Holinshed's Irish Chronicle*, p.303.

The Levy of 1550

In 1550, a third levy of Irish kern was recruited for service either in Scotland or France. They never moved beyond the port of Chester, their services suddenly rendered moot by the collapse of Somerset's Protectorate. They were left in the charge of the Mayor of Chester until money could be found for their voyage home. This episode was examined by Gervase Phillips, who argued that these kern were the first category of Irish soldier exposed to modern warfare and technology. However, there is no evidence that the organisation and composition of the bands of kern in this and the earlier levies was changed in any way from that which already prevailed in Ireland. St Leger, in advocating the use of Irish troops for overseas service in 1544, had described a system that already existed, and was now to be utilised on the Crown's behalf.

The hierarchy seen in the levies of Irish kern was that used at home, where it had doubtless been influenced over time by English practice, but it was not a new imposition called into being by service overseas. And the kern sent to France were used in Continental warfare as 'scourers', engaged in raiding and skirmishing. This differed in no way from their usual employment. Even standards, or 'little guidons', had been made use of by companies of kern in the Pale marches from at least the beginning of the century. More firearms were certainly made available for these levies, along with training in their use. But this was a trend already underway, and while increasing lethality, does not seem to have noticeably altered Irish tactics. An inventory of 1547 still shows 'Dartes for Irishemen croked [barbed]' in store at Calais for the use of the Irish kern in the garrison. The real impact of firearms came after *c.* 1550, with their mass adoption by the new English garrison troops, ultimately in conjunction with the pike. The Irish employed their shot in specialised bands that were not numerous enough to counterbalance the Crown's forces until the 1590s.[132]

The levy of 1550 was commanded by Patrick Sherlock, general, with Piers Sherlock as lieutenant. Two ensigns, three surgeons, and three pipers are listed separately, possibly indicating higher pay. They were organised into 11 companies, each led by a 'petty capten'. As in the earlier levies, the companies were not standardised, varying in size from between 20 to 45 men, the average being 30. There was a ratio of one officer to every 23 men, which was comparable to that in contemporary English foot bands. Part of the muster roll is transcribed below, in which some companies appear to have been family affairs.[133]

---

132 Phillips, 'Irish Ceatharnaigh', pp.163–172.
133 Chester City Records Office: Mayor's Military Papers, 1/1–2, Muster Roll of Kern, 1550.

Table 29. List of the Irish Army sent into England, 1550.

Patrick Sherlok genrall, Peirs Sherlok lotetennt	
Stndert Berrers	Redmond Brymmyngham & Nicholas Dobbyns
Soergeons	Malarthe Ploddye, James Ley, Sodbyngh Trohe
Pipers	Tege O Donoghow, Gylpatrik O Shilleday, Shane O Doersse
Thomas McGoghgan, petty capten, 27 men	**Gerrald O Boyle, petty capten, 21 men**
Pheylime McGoghgan	Bryen McJrmonde
Nyall McGoghgan	Rychard McRys
Bryen Berys	Lydeghe McBryen
Thomas O Malaghlan	Doolan O Morthoer
Tybbott Dyllon	Rys More
Doerchayry McPheaghin	James Bramaghe
Moryertegh McDual	Donyll Duff
Doerchogry McMoylie	Donyl O Brenan
Tege Boeye	Poerrys O Chamy
Llyame McMorghe	Pheylime O Boyle
Shane Duff	Gilpatrik O Duffe
Toerhell O Synge	Oerene Bane
Pheylime Shnnogh	Gilpatrik McDavye
Thomas O Bromane	Llyame Gall
Morryertegh Beoy	Piers Leynegh
Tegge McDollyofe	Donogh O Doerhell
Brien OMagheard	Mogtho O Derraine
Llyame O Fobane	Rys O Loerbett
Bryen McMorcho	Pieres Praneres
Thomas O Dollane	James Grant
Pheyllime McShane	Martyne Thomas
Shane O Charny	
Morryshe McMaleghlen	
Pieres Roche	
Rye McTgylt	
Rychard Laerons	
Bryant Bergn	

8

The Horseboys: Dalonyes and Daltins

Horseboys, 'for so they call their horse-keepers be they never so old knaves', were the lowest strata of the Gaelic Irish military, outdoor servants who also fought as demanded.[1] It is often assumed the term 'horseboy' encompassed the servants of the kern and galloglass, but period documents in English tend to limit its use to those who did the 'meating and dressing of horses.' There is an instance of the servants of kern being referred to as 'grooms', when in 1542 Rory Caoch O'More of Laois is permitted to 'have 72 kerne (*turbari*) – grooms (*garcii*) being computed in that number – for the rule of the said country.'[2] Usually, the servants of foot soldiers are simply called 'boys' in English. The Irish terms were *giolla* (boy) and *giolla na n-eich* (horseboy). Derricke, who tended to use the term 'karne' for Irishmen in general, is very clear about the lowly standing of the horseboys. In 1581 he writes: 'Behold here the difference twixt Karne and their men – The Karne haue the best meate, the horsboyes eate then, of Inmeats and pudding,' devouring unwashed puddings of entrails laid upon the embers for want of gridirons.[3] Derricke's description of the horseboy's meagre fare is remarkably paralleled by a contemporary Irish expression, *Cuid ghiolla an eich don gheirrfhiadh*, that is, 'The horseboy's portion of the hare' meaning a very small portion of it.[4]

Horseboys were usually in a three-to-one ratio to horsemen, as shown in the *Composition Book of Connaught* describing the rising out of Tirawley 'being three-score horsemen armed and accoutered, nine-score horse-boys

---

1 Baldwin, *Beware the Cat*, p.12.
2 *Calendar of the Carew Manuscripts*, vol. 1, 1515–1574, J. S. Brewrer and William Bullen eds, (London: Longman & Co., 1867), 13 May, Indenture of Rory O'More.
3 Derricke, *Image of Irelande*, p.53.
4 Roland M. Smith, 'The Irish Background of Spencer's "View"', *The Journal of English and Germanic Philology*, vol. 42, no. 4 (1943), pp.499–515.

and horses bringing their own provision.'[5] This is because 'Every horsman hath two horses, sume three …. Every Horss hath a knave & their chefe horss is ever ledd, and one of his knaves ride alway & bear his harneys & spears if he have harneys.'[6] In 1600, John Dymmok adds: 'If there be four or five boys to a horse (as sometimes there be), the poor tenants must be contented therewith and yet reward the boys with money.'[7] The authorities in the Pale strove constantly to limit this proliferation of horseboys. Johan Bale, who was briefly bishop of Ossory in 1553, wrote disapprovingly of the 'brechelesse souldiers' of the Irish and their horseboys: 'with their horses and horsegrooms, sometime. iii. waiting upon one jade, they enter into the villages with much cruelty and fierceness …. leaving nothing behind them for payment but lice.'[8]

The 1515 State of Ireland report, discussed in Chapter 3, had complained of this 'infynyt nombre of horsseladdes', while an indenture with the Anglo-Irish Earl of Kildare in 1524 says he is 'to take but for every horsseman 2d. a meale, and for every horsekeeper 1d. …. and but 1 boye for a horsse.'[9] Likewise, Cahir MacArt Kavanaugh was advised upon his submission in 1543, 'and every horseman to have but one horse and a nag.'[10] The excess of horseboys was also limited by an indenture of 26 September 1543, forced upon the Gaelic Irish Munster lords (MacCarthy, O'Sullivan, MacDonough, O'Callaghan, et cetera). This enacted 'that no horseman shall keep more garsons or boys, than horses, on pain of twenty shillings.'[11] This term 'garson' (*garsun* in Irish) is used in Munster and sometimes Leinster, meaning a youth or a serving boy, and derives from the French *garçon*.

Dalonyes and Daltins

English writers often give the contemporary Irish terms for these servants as dalonyes and daltins. Dymmok, enumerating the Irish soldiery, says: 'Dalonyes or horseboys to be a fourth sort, for that they take them into the fight: they are the very skumme, and outcaste of the cuntrye, and not lesse serviceable in the campe for meatinge and dressing of horses, then hurtfull to the enemy with their dartes.'[12] A letter of 1537 in the State Papers distinguishes the daltin, and gives his duties: 'Item, the horsemen of this countre to the charge of the poore fermors have usid to have hymself 3

---

5   Freeman, *Booke of Conought*, p.52.
6   Price, 'Armed Forces', p.206.
7   Butler, *Tracts Relating to Ireland*, p.9.
8   Johan Bale (Peter Happé and John King eds), *The Vocacyon of Johan Bale, 1553*, (Binghamton: Renaissance English Text Society, 1990), p.85.
9   *State Papers: Henry VIII*, p.115, 4 August, Indenture of Earl of Kildare.
10   Herbert Hore, 'Clan Kavanagh Temp. Henry VIII' in *Journal of the Royal Society of Antiquaries of Ireland*, Seventh Series, vol. 2, no. 1 (1858), p.81.
11   Cox, *Hibernia Anglicana*, p.271.
12   Butler, *Tracts Relating to Ireland*, p.8.

THE HORSEBOYS: DALONYES AND DALTINS

horseis, 3 horseboyes; and many of them one other boye, to keep his spores and hose, and to make them clene, namid a Dalten.'[13] Stanihurst (in Holinshed's 1577 *Irish Chronicle*) adds, 'The basest sort among them are little young wags called Daltins: these are lackies and are serviceable to the grooms and horsboies, who are a degree above the Daltinnes.'[14]

The term 'dalonye' is *doílmhaineach* (pl. *doílmhainigh*) in Irish, meaning one free from liability; a hired soldier; a privileged person or noble. The term 'daltin' is *dailtín* (pl. *dailtinedha*), the modern Irish term for a student, but meaning also an orphan, brat or fosterling. Doubtless, these terms were also used to describe the camp servants of galloglass and kern. Although there are some exceptions in the preceding chapters, with the larger boys among the servants of the kern being called *stocaire* in Leinster, while the servants of galloglass were sometimes called *gíománach*.

In 1584, Stanihurst went into more detail concerning this 'fourth rank of soldiers who are called daltinnes.' He says they are a number of runners that in Latin are called *scurras velites*, or light armed servants, and describes their duties, grouping them together with the horseboys:

> They advance without armour and they act as grooms for the horsemen – although they also wield thonged spears – and they clean harness, which has become stained with filth. In the paddocks, they rub down the horses with currycombs until they have them shining, with their manes combed. These horseboys strain every sinew of their bodies at this careful grooming, and as they fail in this diligence, so their reputation drops: for they gain a reputation for especial diligence through the elegance and cleanliness of their horses. Beyond all others, they are careless of restraint in speech, being for the most part addicted to scurrilous wit and filthy conversation.[15]

Edmund Spencer, writing in 1596, looks forward to seeing the horseboys 'cut off', for 'out of the frye of these rakehelly horseboyes, growinge up in knavery and villany, are theire kerne contynewally supplied and mayntayned. For hauinge benn once brought up an idle horseboye, he will never after falle to labour, but is only made fitt for the halter.'[16] He says that having been bred up among Englishmen and learning to shoot a piece, after becoming kern they are more fit to cut the Englishmen's throats. This seems to have been understood as a natural progression, an anonymous observer in 1607 noting: 'In Ireland there are certain kind of swordsmen called kern, descended from horseboys, idle persons, and unlawful propagation.'[17]

---

13 *State Papers: Henry VIII*, p.505, n.d., Luttrell to St Leger.
14 Holinshed, *Holinshed's Irish Chronicle*, p.114.
15 Stanihurst, *Great Deeds*, p.125.
16 Spencer, *A View*, p.116–7.
17 Quinn, *Elizabethans and Irish*, p.120.

The horseboys fought to some degree. As noted, Dymmok says 'they take them into the fight,' while Stanihurst says 'they also wield thonged spears.' We saw that Paolo Giovio assigned the horseboy a more limited role in combat, saying the Irish horsemen carry a couple of darts while 'other are supplied by attendants on foot.' These attendants are the horseboys, and as Giovio describes it, their role was akin to that of the pages in the contemporary Spanish equestrian exercise of *juego de cañas*, who ran behind their masters carrying bundles of spare darts. Certainly, the proud aristocratic Irish horsemen would not ride into battle alongside lowly horseboys. There is, however, an indication that at least in the following century, horseboys may have occasionally fought on horseback. At the Battle of Castlelyons in 1643, 'Squadrons of boys on horseback' in the Confederate army, numbering 120, broke in among the rear of the horse of the Munster Protestants.[18] A rain shower may have assisted their attack, and the Munster horse were routed. The horseboys on that occasion were described as 'coming on as the Moorish and Getulian Horse, mention'd by Salust in Jugarth's War, not in Order and Warlike manner, but by Troops and scattering Companies at adventure, that the Fight rather resembled an Incursion than a Battel.'[19] The comparison to the Numidian horsemen of ancient times suggests they were armed with javelins.

Did They Ride or Run?

Around the year 909, the annals record the death of Cearbhall, son of Muirigen, King of Leinster. As he rode past a combmaker's shop the craftsman happened to throw out a piece of antler which caused the King's horse to rear up. The horse started back 'so that the King struck his own javelin, which was in the hand of his own horseboy.'[20] So, at this early date, the horseboy rode a hackney behind his master carrying his spear, as described in Tudor times by Dymmok and Nowell above. No doubt in both cases, the spare 'chief horse' was led and not ridden. But many of the horseboys ran, since they often outnumbered the horses. And Fynes Moryson certainly felt it was better that way, saying 'let them wittnes who haue kepte Irish footemen, if euer they could bring any of them on foote agayne, whome once they had sett on horsbacke, and if they haue not had better seruice from them whom they kepte most bare in apparrell or mony.'[21]

---

18   Edmund Borlase, *The History of the execrable Irish Rebellion, trac'd from many preceding acts to the grand eruption, the 23 of October, 1641, and thence pursued to the Act of Settlement, 1662* (London: Robert Clavel, 1680), p.118.
19   James Tuchet, *The memoirs of James, Lord Audley, Earl of Castlehaven, his engagement and carriage in the wars of Ireland from the year 1642 to the year 1651 written by himself* (London: Henry Brome, 1680), p.33.
20   John O'Donovan (ed.), *Annals of Ireland: Three Fragments by Dubhaltach Mac Firbisigh* (Dublin: University Press, 1860), p.225.
21   Kew, 'Fynes Moryson's Itinerary', p.104.

THE HORSEBOYS: DALONYES AND DALTINS

Contemporaries saw running at the stirrup as inferior to riding upon one of the master's ambling horses. Stafford, in 1600, recalled that Redmund Burke 'once took the White Knight prisoner, and led him out of the Province in hand-locks, and trotting like a horseboy besides Redmund as he rode'.[22] Likewise, around the same time, Fynes Moryson was surprised to see 'the chief of a sept ride, with a gentleman of his own name (and so learned that he spake good Latin) running bare footed by his stirrup'.[23] Polydore Virgil's *Anglica Historia* says of the Irish: 'The skin of their feet is so calloused that even boys whose feet are not yet hardened by long practice and labour run about with surprising speed, even in rough places.'[24] The German noble, Ludolf von Münchhausen, wrote a brief account of Ireland in 1590, and speaking of Irish horsemen says: 'Their servant runs some 10 or 20 paces behind. The servants wear helmets and carry a broad sword; they are otherwise naked [i.e., unarmoured]'.[25]

In general, sixteenth century Irish were noted for their footmanship, their fleetness of foot. Laurent Vital visited Ireland in 1518: 'I have seen some of these savages, as quick in the fields – one might say – as horses; that is how it was.'[26] On his way to Kinsale in December 1601, O'Donnell avoided an intercepting English force by stealing a night march across a mountain which 'without any rest, was above 2 and 30 Irish miles, the greatest march with carriage (whereof he left much upon the way) that hath beene heard of.'[27]

Irish horse boy, painted in London c. 1603-06, for the album of Hieronymus Tielch. Such servants served as tangible signs of conquest, as turbaned Indian footmen did in nineteenth-century London. The saffron shirt has disappeared and he wears a blue military style cassock and red trews. Note the barbed and fletched dart. (Huntington Museum, San Marino, California)

---

22 Stafford, *Pacata Hibernia*, vol. 1, p.47
23 Kew, 'Fynes Moryson's Itinerary', p.67.
24 Virgil, *Anglica Historia,* unpaginated.
25 Melosina Lenox-Conyngham, *Diaries of Ireland: An Anthology, 1590-1987* (Dublin: Lilliput Press, 1998), p.6.
26 Vital, 'Ireland', p.289.
27 Stafford, *Pacata Hibernia*, vol. 2, p.12.

J. O. Bartley noted that the playwrights of Shakespeare's England were especially struck by this:

> swiftness of foot and endurance which particularly fitted the Irish for running footmen. In Shirley's *Hyde Park* (1632) a race between an English and an Irish footman crosses the stage amid cries of "A Teague! A Teague! Well run, Irish!" Termock in *Hey for Honesty* "runs for te credit of his heels." The footmen in Johnson's *Irish Masque* "vil runne t'rough fire, and vater for tee, over te bog, and te Bannoke ..." and in *Every Man His Humour* (1598) "our nimble-spirited Catso's ... will run over a bog like your wild Irish; no sooner started, but they'le leap from one thing to another,"[28]

This 'footmanship' of the Irish would remain proverbial into the seventeenth century. The Irish Brigade of Alasdair MacColla serving under Montrose in Scotland in the winter of 1644–45 made a famous march over the supposedly impassable Grampian Mountains, ravaging the Campbell's lands. A German broadside of 1632 describes the 'Ihrlander' serving in the Swedish army: 'They hurry over land and ice, where they go 30 miles in a day, the Irishmen running over a morass without caving in.' However, by 1682 Henry Piers reported 'that the footmanship for which the Irish forty years ago were very famous is now quite lost among them.'[29]

---

28   J. O. Bartley, *Teague, Shenkin and Sawney* (Cork: Cork University Press, 1954), p.30.
29   Henry Piers (Charles Vallency, ed.), *A Chorographical Description on the County of Westmeath, 1682*, Collecteana Rebus Hibernicus, vol. 1, no. 1 (Dublin: L. White, 1786), p.108.

9

Scots Redshanks

As the pressure of the government's programme of conquest picked up after *c.* 1550, the Irish chiefs began hiring large numbers of Scots mercenaries. Ancient ties of blood and culture connected the peoples of the West Highlands and the Gaels of Ireland, and in the sixteenth century, dynastic marriages remained common across both sides of the North Channel. The West Highlands and Isles long stood as *terra incognita* to the Edinburgh Government, in much the same sense as Ulster did to Dublin. Indeed, the Islesmen were commonly referred to in Edinburgh as 'Erishe' and their territory as 'Ireland'. However, the advancing power of the Scottish monarchy had brought about the forfeiture of the well-ordered Lordship of the Isles in 1493. The struggle to re-establish that lordship lasted until 1545, with subsequent unrest continuing until *c.* 1609, an era remembered as the *Linn nan Creach* (Age of Forays). This played a role in the increasing mercenary activity in Ireland during this period, with a large number of 'broken men' without clan ties becoming available for service. The impact of worsening climatic conditions on crop yields may have furthered the trend, as temperatures dropped in the third quarter of the century, falling sharply after 1570. However, Highland involvement in Ireland had never entirely ceased since the permanent settlement of Scottish galloglass families following the Bruce Wars. From the outset of the sixteenth century, the Ulster lords, particularly O'Donnell, sought Scottish alliances against local rivals and the Government's prolonged offensive. These alliances and agreements produced a wave of Highland mercenaries, called 'New Scots' by historians to distinguish them from the earlier wave of galloglass settlers, and called 'redshanks' by the Lowlanders and English because of their bare legs. These sixteenth century Highland mercenaries remained primarily seasonal warriors who returned home at the summer's end. While the O'Donnells of Tyrconnell pioneered the use of New Scots, as early as 1433 the *Annals of Ulster* records a war breaking out between O'Neill and O'Donnell, in which 'Mac Domnaill of Scotland came with a numerous fleet to Ireland into the muster of Ua Neill to aid him.' As a notable exception to the typical seasonal service of New Scots, the Clan Donald South (MacDonnells) established a permanent settlement in Antrim during the early sixteenth century, at the expense of the resident MacQuillans. In 1539, Treasurer Brabazon wrote to Henry VIII's Chief Minister, Thomas Cromwell, stating, with some exaggeration:

> all the power of that O'Donnell and O'Neill trust in is in the Scots of the Out Isles, which be scant obedient to their King there; and also they trust in the Scots in Ireland. I do certify your lordship, that there is of Scots now dwelling in Ireland [i.e. Antrim], above 2,000 men of war, as I am credibly informed, which Scots have as well driven away the freeholders, being Englishmen of that country as others, Irishmen, and have builded certain castles there. The head captain of them is one Alexander Karrogh, otherwise called MacDonnell.

Available Numbers and Organisation

The romantic notion that 'all Highlanders were warriors' should be tempered by the knowledge that the musters were limited to 'those who do not till.' Fighting was the province of the chieftain and his *daoine uaisle*, or clan gentry, which formed a core of professional fighting men who were maintained by the tenantry under a custom called 'sorning', equivalent to the coign and livery in Ireland. A second level of minor householders provided the non-professional bulk of the force, and both they and the gentry would have regarded the lowest social stratum, the *bodaich* or earth tillers, with contempt. It has been suggested that a larger proportion of the Highland population bore arms than was the case in Gaelic Ireland, possibly reflecting the influence of feudalism in Scottish Gaeldom, which can also be seen in the charters of the Lords of the Isles.[1] However, Hayes-McCoy's estimate of one in every six or seven males serving in the musters of the Isles should be compared with the roughly comparable figure of one in every five recently estimated for Gaelic Ireland (see discussion in Chapter 1).[2] Highland troops serving in Ireland were not seen primarily as shock troops committed to headlong assaults, but were rather hired as specialists in the longbow, which was their favoured weapon. They were considered light infantry, or *cearnach*, rendered 'caterans' in lowland Scots. This is the same term as the Irish 'kern or kernogh,' and among the Highlanders: 'The name of cearnach was reckoned honourable, and was applicable to those chiefs who distinguished themselves.'[3] The weapon set used in the Highlands – the two-handed sword and bow – was not common among the Gaelic Irish. It might seem reasonable to assume that this preference for the bow was due

---

1 Steven Ellis, 'The Collapse of the Gaelic World, 1450–1650', *Irish Historical Studies*, vol. 31, no. 124 (1999), p.461.
2 Hayes-McCoy, *Scots Mercenary*, p.357.
3 Logan, James, *The Scottish Gael* (London: Smith, Elder, and Co., 1831), p.108.

to the Norse influence in the West Highlands and Isles, the Gaelic word for bow, *bogha*, being a Norse loan word. But the Highland Gaels were equally influenced by the particular requirements of Anglo-Scottish warfare. Since 1424, the Scottish Crown had emphasised the use of the bow to counter the missile superiority of England. In this context, the Highlanders' role was to provide missile support for the pikemen of the Scottish schiltrons. To that end, each Highlander liable for the musters was required to shoot six arrows a week at the butts, at least.[4]

In the best recent work on the subject, that by Ross MacKenzie Crawford, he has convincingly refuted claims that as many as 35,000 men would have been available for mercenary service in Ireland.[5] This grossly exaggerated sum perhaps fits with the prevailing *Linn na Creach* narrative of the West Highlands and Isles as a lawless region, constantly at war. A late sixteenth century muster of Islesmen, probably prepared for King James VI, totals about 7,000 fighting men, though the summary claims only 6,000 (see table below). The table reflects only the muster of the Isles, and excludes mainland holdings of the Campbells, MacLeods and MacDonalds. These estimates are consistent with the muster of the Lord of the Isles for the Battle of Harlaw in 1411, when 10,000 men were mustered, but only 6,600 of the best men were chosen.

In 1545 'McConnell' (Donald Dubh MacDonald, claimant to the title of Lord of the Isles) sailed to Carrickfergus in Ulster with 4,000 men, 'three thousand of them very tall men, clothed for the most part in habergeons of mail, armed with long swords and long bows, but with few guns; the other thousand, tall mariners that rowed in galleys.'[6] MacDonald was supporting Henry VIII's cause in Scotland. Another 4,000 Islesmen had been left at home facing his rivals – Argyle and Huntly. MacDonald's total strength was therefore 8,000 men, and he requested that 3,000 of this number, who were 'gentlemen [who] must be sustained', be taken into wages by the King. This number of 3,000 mailed 'gentlemen' (*daoine uaisle*) represented roughly one-third of the total, a recurring percentage of armoured men found in forces from the West Highlands and Isles. The muster of the clans summarised in the table states this clearly: 'The common accustomat of raising of thair men is 6,000 men, quhairof the 3d pairt extending to 2,000 men aucht and sould be cled with attounes and haberchounis, and knapshal bannetts, as thair laws beir …. na labourers of the ground are permittit to steir furth of the cuntrie …. except only gentlemen quhilk laboris not.'[7] The 2,000 armed in aketons, habergeons and bascinets were the *daoine uaisle*. The remaining 4,000 were said to use bows, and increasingly as the century

---

4 Phillips, 'Irish Ceatharnaigh', p.165.
5 Crawford, Ross MacKenzie, 'Warfare in the West Highlands and Isles of Scotland, c. 1544–1615'. PhD Thesis, University of Glasgow 2016
6 Denis Rixson, *The West Highland Galley* (Edinburgh: Birlinn, 1998) p.88.
7 William F. Skene, *Celtic Scotland: A History of Ancient Alban*, vol. 3. (Edinburg: David Douglas, 1886), p.439.

progressed, firearms. Thus, at the Battle of Glenlivet, in 1592, Argyll's van was commanded by MacLean, 'to the number of 3,000, wherof 2,000 were hagbutters, the third made vp of bowmen and swordmen, with dartes and targets, wherof the last were for the most part armed with coates of mail reaching to their knee.'[8]

Table 30. Muster of the Hebrides by Clan, *c.* 1577–95[9]

Lord	Muster	By Island
Clan Donald/MacDonald of Sleat	1,520–1,524	700 – Sleat, Skye; 500 – Trotternish, Skye; 300 – Uist; 20–24 – 'Helsker'
MacLean of Duart	1,386–1,390	600 – Mull; 400 – Islay; 300 – Tiree; 50 – Jura; 20 – Scapla; 16–20 – Gometra
MacLeod of Lewis	1,040	700 – Lewis with Rona; 200 – Waternish, Skye; 80 – Raasa; 60 – Bernera
MacDonald of Dunnyveg	650	400 – Islay; 100 – Gigha; 100 – Rathlin; 50 – Jura
MacLeod of Harris (Siol Torquil)	560	240 – Duirinish, Skye; 140 – Harris; 140 – Barcadale, Skye; 40 – Pabay
Lord Hamilton	400	300 – Bute; 100 – Arran
MacDonald of Clanranald	386–7	300 – Uist; 60 – Eigg; 20 – Canna; 6–7 – Rhum
MacNeill of Barra	200	200 – Barra
MacLean of Lochbuie	217	200 – Mull; 17 – Scarba
MacLean of Coll	190	140 – Coll; 50 – Mull
MacKinnon of Strath	160	160 – Strathardle, Skye
MacDougal of Lorn	160	100 – Lismore; 60 – 'Hwnayis'
Earl of Argyll (Campbell)	120	120 – Seill
MacDuffie	100	100 – Colonsay
John Stewart Appin	60	60 – 'Hwnayis'
MacQuarrie	60	60 – Ulva ('Ulloway')
MacKynvin	50	50 – Mull
Laird of Ardinmwrthe (Maken)'	16	16 – Eilean nam Muc
Total	**7,275–7,284**	

---

8   James Maidment (ed.), *The Spottiswoode Miscellany: A Collection of Original Papers and Tracts*, vol. 1 (Edinburgh: Alex. Laurie & Co., 1844), p.264.
9   Skene, *Celtic Scotland*, pp.428–440.

Donald Dubh's force in 1545 was unusually large, representing the united strength of the Hebrides in an attempt to restore the Lordship of the Isles. Donald Dubh's total of 8,000 men is in keeping with the muster of roughly 7,000 men seen in the table, as well as the 6,600 men taken to Harlaw. The most powerful West Highland magnate, Campbell of Argyll, might routinely field a private force of 1,000–1,500 men, and could potentially raise as many as 6,000 under the pressure of a Royal summons. Yet it must be emphasised the numbers listed in the table probably represent the maximum each clan could muster, and this could not be maintained for more than a few months. The most typical employment of armed men, the cattle raid, usually involved tens rather than hundreds.[10] Parties of 30 or 40 seem to have been typical on such occasions, and even larger forces on mercenary service were divided into companies of 30 or 40 men. These numbers reflect the size of the crew of a Highland galley (*birlinn*). There may also have been dedicated seamen, such as the 1,000 'tall mariners' of Donald Dubh's army, who were not taken into pay by England.

Armies raised for mercenary service in Ireland were noticeably larger than those employed in clan warfare at home, possibly attracted by the profit to be made. The hiring of redshanks was often based on marriage alliances. MacDonald of Dunnyveg had supported the O'Neills with redshanks during the 1550s. In 1560, Calvagh O'Donnell signed bonds of manrent with the 5th Earl of Argyll, and married the 4th Earl of Argyll's widow, Catherine MacLean, gaining thereby the service of her father, MacLean of Duart, with 1,000 to 1,500 redshanks. Shane O'Neill, his main opponent, had that same year the services of a like number of Scots, of uncertain origin. In 1563, Shane O'Neill captured Calvagh and married his wife, Catherine MacLean, and was thereafter served by 800 MacLeans and Campbells.[11] Lady Agnes Campbell of Kintyre brought a dowry of 1,000 Campbell and MacDonald mercenaries to her marriage with Turlough Luineach O'Neill in 1569, and his bodyguard were 'Scots of the Earl of Argyle's surname.'[12] In 1581, at the height of the second Desmond Rebellion, Turlough retained 2,500 redshanks. The Burkes of Mayo had been hiring large numbers of Scots from the 1550s. By 1572 the State Papers record their appearance in Munster, when 1,200 Scots, brought in by the Burkes were reported crossing the Shannon with James Fitzmaurice.[13]

---

10   Crawford, 'Warfare in West Highlands', p.84.
11   Muríosa Prendergast, 'Scots Mercenary Forces in Sixteenth Century Ireland' in John France (ed.), *Mercenaries and Paid Men: The Mercenary Identity in the Middle Ages* (Boston: Leiden 2008), pp.363–381.
12   *Calendar of State Papers Ireland: Elizabeth*, vol. 2, 1574–1585, ed. Hans Claude Hamilton (London: Longmans, Green, Reader and Dyer, 1867), p.73, 7 July, Earl of Essex.
13   *Calendar of State Papers Ireland: Henry VIII, Edward VI, Mary and Elizabeth*, vol. 1, 1509–73, Hans Claude Hamilton ed. (London: Longman, Green, Longman & Roberts, 1860), p.482, 1 September, Thomas Arthure to Sir John Perrot.

'OF KERNS AND GALLOWGLASSES'

Scots depicted theatrically in the Elephant Tapestry, c. 1575, from cartoons by Lucas DeHeere. Tartan is already thought characteristic of the Highlanders, who are represented here with exotic darts rather than their more typical long bows. (Tapestry workshop of Brussels, Attack on an elephant turret. Pitti Palace, Le Cacce depot, Inv. Tapestries n. 474. By permission of the Ministry of Culture. All further reproduction by any means is prohibited.)

In 1575, the pay of a Scot serving in Ulster was the same as that of a galloglass; one beef per quarter for his wages, and two beefs for his feeding and diet. The captain of 100 Scots received the same as a galloglass captain, that is one chief horse and a hackney, or an habergeon in place of the hackney, per quarter. Out of a band of 100, he would be allowed 13 dead pays, so that the band was only 87 men. And for his own victuals, he received six men's allowances.[14]

Around the year 1580, a party of Highland redshanks from Kintyre under Colla Dubh MacDonald joined MacQuillan in a foray against his enemies. MacQuillan then quartered the MacDonald redshanks among his tenantry up and down 'the Root,' two by two; one of his own galloglass and a Highlander in each house. It happened that the galloglass of MacQuillan were entitled to a mether of milk by custom.[15] According to the tale, in one cabin a Highlander called M'Il-Hargy, a brawny man of quick temper, questioned why he should not also receive a mether of milk. The galloglass sharing his billet responded: 'Would you, a Highland beggar as your are, compare yourself to me or any of MacQuillan's gallogloughs?' Naturally a fight broke out and the poor tenant threw open the two doors of the cottage,

---

14 *Calendar of the Carew Manuscripts*, vol. 2, 1575–1588, J. S. Brewrer and William Bullen (eds) (London: Longman & Co., 1867), p.9, April, A Note of Ulster, Malby.
15 Hayes-McCoy, *Scots Mercenary*, p.60.

giving them liberty to fight it out in the open field.[16] Such were the disputes that could arise among mercenaries at bonnaght.

The mether was a communal drinking vessel cut from solid wood, with a square mouth that tapered to a round bottom, and was usually fitted with four handles. The mether could vary from 15cm to 30cm in height, and was considered a unit of measure variously reckoned as equal to one or two gallons. Like all Irish measures, it seems to have varied locally and over time.

Redshanks in the 1580s

By the 1580s, changes are seen in the Scots mercenaries in Ireland, as dedicated targeteers, trained shot, and horsemen all begin to appear. The latter may have been Gaelic Irish horsemen, some of whom had joined the Scots at Ardnaree in 1586, but some *may* have been Scots border horse. Horsemen were almost unknown in Highland warfare, and attempts were certainly made to recruit Scots border horse for Tyrone's army in the 1590s. In autumn 1580, Captain Malby, the President of Connacht, is reported tangling with a large force of Scots at the Moy, who had sent their baggage over the river. The Scots drove him back 'by their shot and arrows' and then crossed the ford themselves, where 'they abandoned many sculls and bows, which my men picked up in following them.' Malby added: 'They were about 600 men – 180 horsemen, 180 targets, 100 long swords, the rest were darts, shot, and gallowglass axes, as well appointed men as ever I saw for their faculty.'[17] The fight of the Scots against Malby seems mainly to have been by bow and shot, and the implication is that as well as targets and long swords they also carried bows. Later that year he reported that the Burkes had hired 600 Scots, perhaps the same force. In July of 1582, Malby was again pursuing a 'great company of Scots' who were supporting the rebellious sons of Clanricarde Burke. Interestingly, he reported '200 of the Scots were furnished with a case of pistols or snaphaunces.'[18] They retreated across the Erne, where some drowned and again, 'most of them left their baggage.' These references to baggage are curious, as Highland forces preferred to live off the land, particularly when in enemy territory. However, a glimpse of the proportion of 'carriage' that accompanied one Highland host is found in the report of an English spy just prior to the Battle of Solway Moss in 1542. He reported, with some

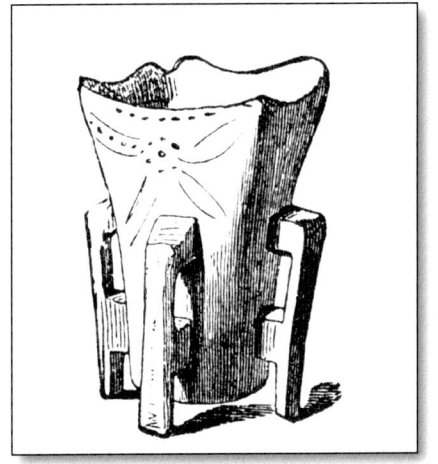

A mether was a communal drinking vessel also used for food storage. This example is about 20cm tall, which is about average. (from W. R. Wilde, *A Descriptive Catalogue of the Antiquities in the Museum of the Royal Irish Academy* (Dublin: M. H. Gill, 1857) p.214.)

---

16 William Hamilton, *Letters Concerning the North Coast of the Country of Antrim* (Dublin: George Bonham, 1790), pp.122–124.
17 Knox, *History Mayo*, p.193.
18 *Calendar of State Papers Ireland: Elizabeth*, vol. 2, 1574–1585, ed. Hans Claude Hamilton (London: Longmans, Green, Reader and Dyer, 1867), p.385, 12 July, Malby to Walsingham.

'OF KERNS AND GALLOWGLASSES'

'Le Capitaine Sauvage', a Highland chief. Woodcut by François Desprez, from *Recueil de la Diversitié des Habits*, 1562. (The Metropolitan Museum of Art, New York)

exaggeration as to numbers: 'therle of Argile had with him in the Scottisshe ost xii ml [12,000] Yerishe men and ij ml [2,200] cariage horses.' [19]

In 1584, Lord Deputy Perrot reported the arrival in Ulster of 'Mac Ilanes' sons and …. 1,100 bows, 500 shot, "and of them 200 inland trained men in the service of the Low Countries," and 800 swords.'[20] This is the classic proportions of ⅔ bow or shot (1,600), and ⅓ swordsmen in mail (800). The presence of the 200 Low Countries veterans, who were said to be 'inland', or Lowlanders, is clear evidence of the connivance of the Scottish Government. In early September of 1586, Richard Bingham, the Governor of Connacht, learned there were 1,400 or 1,500 Scots on the river Erne, who had taken a prey of 500 cows, money and shirts of mail from Sir Owen M'Tool. They had fortified a ford on the river. Bingham marshalled 120 horsemen and 400 foot, with 80–100 kern and 40 Irish shot, to keep these Scots out of Connacht. But Donnell Gorme M'Donnell and Alexander Carragh M'Donnell, sons of James M'Donnell, had now led them across the Erne, drawn in by the rebellious Clanwilliam Burkes and their Clandonnell galloglass of Connacht, 'who are their cousins.' Bingham sent to know their intentions, and they replied that, having no other shift, they took on this enterprise as offering them the best opportunity, 'as all other soldiers in the world do use.' A full muster was compiled afterwards by Bingham. The force had been divided equally between the MacDonnell brothers, 1,300 under Donnell Gorm, and 1,000 under Alexander Carragh, besides an equal number of women and children, which may imply that this was in fact an intended migration.[21]

---

19 Ellis, 'Collapse of the Gaelic World', p.452.
20 *CSP Ireland*, p.524, 21 August, Perrot to Privy Council.
21 *Calendar of State Papers Ireland: Elizabeth*, vol. 3, 1586-88, July, Hans Claude Hamilton ed. (London: Longman & Co., 1877), p.154, 23 September, Sir Richard Bingham.

Table 31. Scots Captains and their Companies Killed at Ardnaree, 23 September 1586.

Of the sept of the Clandonnells	
Donnell Gorm, son of James M'Donnell	300
Alexander Carragh, his brother	400
Of the House of Argyle (Campbell): Gillaspick MacDowell	400
The Clanallestrans	300
The Clanvees	300
Alexander M'Hugh Galt	100
M'Mick Hugh Duff	100
Neil Oge M'Evee	100
Alexander M'Ranolle Boy	50
Murrough Ne Marte, a Munster man	100
The Gwirkins of Gallen, Mayo	30
Shane M'Garrot, Lord Kildare's base brother	30
Of horsemen, some O'Cahan's men, some O'Donnell's, et cetera	80

After a lengthy pursuit, Bingham came upon this force encamped with their backs to the Moy at Ardnaree. The Scots 'ranged themselves in order,' throwing out a 'vorward', which loosed a first volley of arrows. Bingham changed them with his horse, driving them back on the Scots 'battaill', and pursuing both into a bog. While mounted English shot played upon them, Bingham's own Battle came up, and joined the horse in a second charge, upon which the Scots broke for the river. Bingham claimed 1,400 were slain or drowned in the Moy and 'There is about 300 or 400 of their long swords, with many of their bows and sculls found and taken out of the water the day.'[22] Two years later, in 1588, Bingham again reported news 'brought hither that there should be a 600 Scots with bows, 600 shirts of mail, and 300 English Scots landed in the north under the leading of Angus M'Donnell's youngest brother, viz., Callough M'James M'Donnell.'[23] Having slain Captain Merriman and 30 of his company, they intended to 'come into Connacht for a revenge' against those who had massacred their kin at Ardnaree. Their '300 English Scots' may be the trained lowland shot noted above as being in Ulster in 1584.

---

22 *CSP Ireland*, p.164, 23 September, Bingham to Loftus.
23 *Calendar of State Papers Ireland: Elizabeth*, vol. 4, 1588, August–1592, September, Hans Claude Hamilton ed. (London: Longman, 1885), p.30, 10 September, Bingham to Fenton.

'OF KERNS AND GALLOWGLASSES'

Scottish Highlander shown by Lucas DeHeere, c. 1574. The saffron shirt is not in use, but the jacket with pleated skirt is akin to those shown by Derricke, and this Highlander wears short trews. (Ghent University Library, Creative Commons)

With regard to the tactics employed in the small scale actions typical of Ireland, a late example of the use of Scots in harassing an English column on the march comes from September 1595, when Tyrone engaged Sir John Norris' force on its return southward through fairly open country after supplying the garrison of Armagh. Approaching a river crossing with a wood and a bog on its left, Norris hurried his column forward to seize the pass while he held the rearguard against the Irish pursuing him. Tyrone had a force of redshanks sent by James MacSorley, and these were hurried forward with Irish shot to occupy the wood and bog. From the bog, 100 Scots archers and Irish shot kept a harassing fire at long range, retiring when Norris used his vanguard to charge across the ford.[24]

An incident from clan warfare demonstrates the interaction between the bowmen and the mailed swordsmen. In 1491, Alexander of Lochalsh led a raiding party of 1,800 MacDonalds against 600 MacKenzies at the Battle of Park (*Blair na Pairc*), fought over a stretch of bog and rough ground. Outnumbered, Mackenzie hid his unarmoured bowmen in ambush, and led his armed men in an attack on Alexander's camp to draw him out into range of the bowmen. MacLean of Loch Buie led Alexander's van straight into the MacKenzies, driving them back over the bog until he found himself caught in a withering cross-fire from the Mackenzie bowmen. MacKenzie quickly wheeled his swordsmen in order to take the discomfited MacDonalds in their right flank, routing them into the River Conan, where many drowned. MacLean of Loch Buie, clad in mail, was beheaded by a Mackenzie called *Donnchadh Mor na Tuaighe* (Big Donald of the Axe).[25]

Pitched battles might occasionally be fought among the Irish and Scots, as at Glentasie in 1565, when a force of 1,000 MacDonalds was nearly annihilated in a stand-up fight by a larger force under Shane O'Neill. But skirmishing actions were more typical when opposing the government, as in May 1563, when Shane and his Scots skirmished with Sussex's column in the woods between Dungannon and Lough Foyle from eight in the morning until seven at night: 'All that while the woods so rang with the shot that it

---

24 G. A. Hayes-McCoy, 'Strategy and Tactics in Irish Warfare, 1593–1601', *Irish Historical Studies*, vol. 2, no. 7 (1941), p.275–6.

25 Ronald Williams, *The Lords of the Isles* (London: The Hogarth Press, 1984), p.237.

was strange to hear, and also the noise of the Scots that O'Neill had, crying all that day till a little after night.'[26]

The West Highland Panoply

Redshank mercenaries in Ireland specialised in the use of bow and sword. Highland forces therefore had an elite of noble professional warriors with iron helmets, 'haberjouns and tua handit suordis, quhilk was the airmor of the hielandis men,' numbering about a third of the total.[27] The remainder were 'naked' bowmen, sometimes with iron helmets, targes and one or two-handed swords. The bow could be used by both types. It was the preferred weapon for hunting, and held mythic significance, so naturally the elite armoured warriors could choose to use it. However they are generally not depicted as doing so, except on small raids where 'bowis, dorlochis (quiver) and haberschonis (habergeons)' could all be used. And these roles were not fixed. In 1596, MacLean offered to raise 2,000 men for English service in Ireland: '1,500 bowmen and 500 fyremen. In this number we will not want our two-handed swords and armour of mail, to be used if battle be offered us, at which time we will change some of our bowmen to use their two-handed swords the time of battle.'[28] Generally however, archers are described as being unarmoured by custom, to facilitate their usual role as skirmishers. But even mail armoured professionals were considered light troops. In his return to Scotland in 1544, Holinshed records Lennox was supported by 'seven score men of the head of Lennox, that spoke both Irishe and the English Scottish tongues very well, light footmen very well armed in the shirtes of mayle, with bows and two-handed swords; and being joined with the Scottish archers and shotte, did much available service in streyghts, marishes, and mountayne countries.'[29]

Also writing in the 1590s, Dioness Campbell, a Highlander serving as Dean of Limerick, made this same distinction when promoting the use of his countrymen for English service in Ireland: 'theire bowmen are verie fitt and skillful; for feats, assaults and handy blowes, theire swordsmen shall serve verie good use, for that generallie they be men of stronge bodyes.'[30] These two categories also characterised the standing household guards maintained by some chiefs, such as the 'Three hundred Scots of James M'Donnell's household men' reported as arriving in Ulster in 1563.[31]

---

26 *Calendar of the Carew Manuscripts*, Miscellaneous, *The Book of Howth*, J. S. Brewrer and William Bullen eds, (London: Longman & Co., 1871), p.197.
27 Robert Lindesay of Pistcottie (J. G. MacKay ed.), *History and Chronicles of Scotland*, vol. 12. (London & Edinburgh: William Blackwood & Sons, 1899), p.400.
28 Crawford, 'Warfare in West Highlands', p.98.
29 William F. Skene, *The Highlanders of Scotland, Their Origin, History, and Antiquities*, vol. 2 (London: John Murrat, 1837), p.158.
30 Crawford, 'Warfare in West Highlands', p.99.
31 George Hill, *An Historical Account of the MacDonnells of Antrim* (Belfast: Archer

'OF KERNS AND GALLOWGLASSES'

Alexander MacLeod tomb, Rodel, Harris, 1528. A Highland chieftain in the usual array, with an axe of the same type as that found among the galloglass in Ireland. (Author's drawing)

MacLean of Duart also had a guard of 300 picked men; 100 in mail and iron helmets with two-handed swords, 100 'fyirmen' or gunners, and 100 bowmen. Likewise, Grant of Freuchie had a similar force of 80 men, 40 of whom were in mail with iron helmets with two-handed swords, and 40 that had only iron helmets, bows, one-handed swords and targes, 'according to hiland custowme.'[32]

In 1574, an Act of the Scottish Parliament for general 'wapinshcawings', reiterating earlier legislation, specified distinct equipment for the Highlanders which was quite different to that of the Lowlanders, namely 'habirschonis, steilbonettis, hektonis, swordis, bowis and dorlochis, or culvernings.' The word *dorloch* is Gaelic for a quiver or, as it is often termed in Scottish documents, 'a bag of arrows'.[33] These arms are listed in the poetic 'runs' describing the arming process in 'The Army and Arming of the Last Lord of the Isles', which included over his shirt (*leine*) a 'gusseted silk *cotún*' (*cotún síoda*), embroidered with foreign birds and branches of gold. Then a meshed steel coat of mail (*luithrech*), gold ornamented. A clasped belt over this, set with stones and flying birds. And over this an angled cape (*sgaball*),

---

& Sons, 1873), p.131.
32   Crawford, 'Warfare in West Highlands', p.99.
33   Drummond, *Ancient Scottish Weapons*, p.12.

gold bordered, buckled, and pointed. And he received a helmet (*cenbheirt*) a sword (*cloidhemh*) and an axe (*taugh*).³⁴

This is the same harness and nomenclature used in Ireland by Irish horsemen and galloglass, and is described in the section on the galloglass above. Depictions of it on monumental sculpture in the Western Isles do include coats of mail by the early sixteenth century, although earlier carvings had often shown the *cotún* worn alone. This carving tradition had ended by 1550. In Irish literature the quilted *cotún* is described as being of multi-layered linen. But two authors, John Major in 1521 and John Lesly in 1578 describe the Highland *cotún* as being made either of leather or quilted linen, daubed with wax or pitch and covered with deerskin, 'stout and of handsome appearance, which we call an acton.'³⁵ The late use of the aketon in the Highlands may have reflected its usefulness to a maritime people, as a warm, all weather garment that could also have doubled as a flotation device.³⁶ Axes seem to have been carried only by exceptional individuals, and one is depicted being carried on the tomb of Alasdair Crotach MacLeod in Rodel, dated to 1528. The chieftain Lachlan More MacLean carried an axe at Glenlivet in 1594, 'Having a jack upon him and two habergeons, with a morion and a Danish axe', while Gordon of Gight also wore a jack, and was struck by bullets that drove two of its plates into his wounds.³⁷ The targe is little mentioned until specialist targeteers appear in the 1580s, possibly because the use of the two-handed sword made it superfluous. Highlanders at the siege of Haddington in 1549 were described carrying targes like those of the Lowlanders, but the targe is usually limited to individuals. The old harness survived even into the seventeenth century, used by the Highland chieftain's personal retainer called the 'galloglass'. This is covered in detail in the discussion of Galloglass armour in Chapter 6.

The two-handed 'claymore' (*claidheamh mòr*) was the iconic weapon of the Highland warrior, fully developed by *c.* 1550. It is shown being carried in the crook of the elbow, and could be carried 'at the slope' on the shoulder, with or without a scabbard. Scabbards sometimes resemble those of the Irish, with squared ends, flaring like the seriph of a capital 'I,' as in the *Black Book of Taymouth*, and Hieronymus Tielsch's drawing of a Highland archer, *c.* 1603. There is certainly no indication of it being carried slung on the back, although experimentation has shown it could be worn on a waist belt or baldric without greatly impeding archery. It was a fearsome cutting weapon, requiring skill and strength to wield, and it held aristocratic associations. For the Highland gentry nurtured a heroic self-

---

34 Alexander MacBain and John Kennedy, eds., *Relique Celticae*, vol. 1, (Inverness: Northern Counties Publishing Company, 1894), pp.261–63.
35 Drummond, *Ancient Scottish Weapons*, p.8.
36 David Caldwell, 'Having the Right Kit: West Highlanders fighting in Ireland' in Seán Duffy (ed.), *The World of the Galloglass* (Dublin: Four Courts Press, 2007), pp.159.
37 Ross Cowan, 'Lairds of Battle', *Military History Monthly*, No. 32 (2013), pp.45, 48.

image, and if their form of warfare was not entirely 'blade-centric', as some have claimed, they were certainly daunting opponents in single combat. While the popularly entrenched term for this weapon, the term claymore has recently been revealed as an anachronism, applying in fact to the basket hilted sword of the following centuries, however it seems pedantic not to use it.

There is some disagreement over terminology for Highland swords. The 'halflang' mentioned in accounts from earlier in this period seems to have been a hand-and-a-half hilt, of 'proto-claymore' or Halpin 2 type. This was primarily a fifteenth century sword, but it may have lasted into the early sixteenth century. In 1488 1,000 men of Strathearn armed with 'halflang swordis and haberjeons' joined the Scots army before the Battle of Sauchieburn. And at Flodden, in 1513, the MacLean contingent also carried 'halflen' swords. But Huntly's men are described as fighting with 'bows and two-handed swords' at Flodden in the same source.[38] These would be full sized two-handed swords of a transitional type dubbed 'galloglass swords' by Willis. They flourished c. 1475–1530, with the classic sixteenth century 'claymore' developing out of them by c. 1550.[39] The heyday of the two-handed claymore was 1550–1600, as the swords became more readily available due to improved production methods in Germany and better trade routes. The number of swords recovered from the river at Ardnaree in 1586 indicates it was certainly common by then. This sword had an exceptionally long handle, with a high-collared quillon block, long langets, and downward-sloping quillons ending in a quatrefoil of open rings. It is often referred to as an 'Islay hilt'. The terror this weapon inspired is suggested by the fact that the Statutes of Iona outlawed it in 1609, declaring that is should be replaced by the basket hilted broadsword and targe. Bollock knives worn as side arms are called 'dirks' in contemporary Scottish documents, but the distinctive Highland dirk did not evolve from them until c. 1650, or 1600 at the earliest.

All primary documentation indicates the redshanks used a longbow of yew, and not the short recurve bow sometimes used by the Irish. While Scottish monarchs engaged in fitful attempts to promote the bow, suitable yew was not readily available, so as in Ireland, legislation required merchants returning from abroad to bring bows with them. Indeed, English bows were acquired and distributed to the King's Gaelic subjects. In 1532, payment was made to 'the English bowar for a dozen of bows and six dozens of arrows, delivered at the King's command to Alexander Canochson,' i.e. Alexander MacDonald of Dunnyveg. Note that six arrows per bow were provided. About six years later, a dozen hand bows were delivered to Alexander's son and successor, 'by the King's Grace's command, to James Canochson, of the which one half were Scotish bows, and the other half English. The price

---

38   Lindesay of Pistcottie, *History of Scotland*, pp.205, 270.
39   Tony Willis, 'The Scottish Two-Handed Sword', *Barrels & Blades*, series 3, no. 60 (2022), pp.32–70.

of each English bow 16sh. of each Scotish bow 9sh.'[40] Wet local conditions promoted early growth of yew, preventing it from seasoning properly, and Mediterranean yew was preferred. However, the cold and windy Scottish Isles were also suited to growing properly seasoned yew, and Gaelic poetry records that bows continued to be manufactured locally in the Highlands well into the seventeenth century, long after they went out of use in the Lowlands.[41] Gaelic literary sources indicate the 'yellow-backed bow' was comparable to that of England, about six feet long, 'studded with knobs', and made 'of the yew of Easragan.'[42] Nonetheless, professionally made bows seem to have been preferred, and in 1638, the royalist MacDonnell of Antrim, agitating for war against Campbell of Lorne, requested the Dublin government to supply him with 500 longbows, each with four bowstrings and 24 arrows.[43] Bowstrings were of waxed hemp, though the poetry mentions silk being used by some gentry. Horn nocks and bracers are not mentioned. The arrows are conventionally described as being made of birch or yew, the 'shafts sealed with beeswax' and fletched with grey goose feathers bound with silk. George Buchanan in 1582 said the arrows were 'hooked, the iron barbs standing out on both sides.'[44] They almost invariably had broad barbed iron heads, though Jon Taylor in 1633 said 'their weapons are long bowes and forked arrows.'[45]

The Highland quiver was called a *dorlach*, and Gaelic poetry repeatedly describes it as being made of badger skin. By tradition, the *Baobh an Dorlaich*, or Fury of the Quiver, was the last of the 18 arrows a quiver was supposed to contain.[46] A valuable description of the *dorlach* was given by an English spy who observed the Highland archers on the eve of the Battle of Newburn, 1640, 'the greater part bow and arrowes, with a quiver to hould about 6 shafts, made of the maine of a goat or colt, with the haire hanging on, and fastened by some belt or such like, soe as it appeares allmost a taile to them. These were about 1,000, and had bagg-pipes …. for their warlick instruments.'[47] The earliest portrait depicting Highland dress is John Michael Wright's painting of Sir Mungo Murray c. 1683. In the background, Sir Mungo's *cearnach* is clearly depicted carrying a six-foot

---

40 Donald Gregory, 'Notices Regarding Scottish Archery', *Archaeologia Scotica, Proceedings of the Society of Antiquaries of Scotland*, vol. 3 (1831), pp.248–254.
41 David Adams, 'Archery in the Highlands: Muskets and Bows', *Military Illustrated*, no. 111 (August 1997), pp.44–46.
42 Sobieski Stuart, *Costume of the Clans*, p.li.
43 David Stevenson, *Alisdair MacColla and the Highland Problem in the 17th Century* (Edinburgh: John Donald Publishers, Ltd, 1980), p.68.
44 George Buchanan, *History of Scotland, Rerum Scoticarum Historia, 1582* (London: Edw. Jones, 1690), p.23.
45 *Collectanea de Rebus Albanicis,* Iona Club eds (Edinburgh: Thomas G. Stevenson, 1847) Appendix, p.40.
46 I. F. Grant, *The MacLeods: The History of a Clan* (Edinburgh: Holmes McDougal Ltd, 1959), p.189.
47 John Crawford Hodgson ed., *Six North Country Diaries* (Edinburgh: Blackwood & Sons, 1910), p.28.

longbow without any recurve towards the tips, with a hairy quiver sticking out behind, greatly resembling a bushy animal's tail.

Highland archers would make a name for themselves in Ireland. As noted earlier, in 1584, 2,400 Scots landed in Ulster, 1,100 of them being archers. Lord Deputy Perrot noted afterwards: 'The Scots bowmen have done more hurt in the skirmishes then our shott have done.' Several key persons were wounded by them that year in Ulster, including Captain Nicholas Dawtrey at Carrickfergus, one of 102 hurt there. And Captain George Stanley received three Scots arrows in the body during a nightime attack on Donanynie Fort. These experiences seem to have prompted Perrot's temporary effort to reverse the abandonment the bow.[48]

West Highland Banners

In the sixteenth century, the raven wing form of banner, with four points in the fly, appears on several West Highland carvings of galleys. It is mounted on deck, often at an angle, and intended to be carried ashore. A peculiarly West Highland form of heraldry had emerged by the sixteenth century, totemic and making frequent use of quartering, and has been described by Alastair Campbell of Airds.[49] Campbell links its emergence to the forfeiture of the Lordship of the Isles, proposing its use as a vehicle for making claims to the lost lordship. The ready adoption of heraldry may be another indication of the greater influence of feudalism in the Highlands, compared to Gaelic Ireland. West Highland heraldry had a degree of consistency, if not so regular as the highly developed heraldry of Scotland at large. It shared many aspects with the heraldry later adopted by the Gaelic Irish, but did not carry the negative association that English sponsored heraldry held in Ireland, where it was seen as a sign of submission to the authority of the English Crown. After *c.*1540, the adoption of heraldry by Gaelic Irish chiefs was part of the process of 'surrender and regrant', whereby the chief handed his clan lands over to the Crown to receive them back as a noble title, inheritable through primogeniture.

There is abundant evidence of the Highlanders and Irish alike carrying banners. At Glentasie, in 1565, Shane O'Neill gave James MacDonnell 'the overthrow, and took of their baners and ancients xiii', i.e., 13 banners among a force of 1,000 men.[50] As with the Irish, we have instances of the smaller guidon being used by Scots, and these are discussed in Chapter 12. The position of the Chief's Standard Bearer was hereditary, as in Ireland.

---

48   Halpin, 'Archery in Medieval Ireland', p.120.
49   Alastair Campbell of Airds, 'A Closer Look at West Highland Heraldry', St Andrew's Day Lecture (1996), <http://www.heraldry-scotland.co.uk/ Westhighland.htm>
50   George Hill, 'Shane O'Neill's Expedition against the Antrim Scots, 1565' in *Ulster Journal of Archaeology*, 1st. series, vol. 9 (1861/62), p.132.

For instance, the Vic Mhurichie branch of MacLeods held this office under MacLeod of Dunvegan.[51]

It was in the sixteenth century that the Highlanders adopted the bagpipe as their military instrument. This development also occurred among the Irish at about the same time, and there is a larger amount of extant material on early Irish piping, which is discussed in Chapter 13. It seems to have been a shared tradition in the sixteenth century, preserved into modern times through the agency of the British Army's Highland regiments. An early instance of pipers is Jean de Beaugue's account of the Earl of Argyll's contingent at the siege of Haddington in 1549, where 'the wild Scots encouraged themselves to arms by the sound of their bagpipes.'[52] The Highland pipers would develop a highly sophisticated form of pipe music, *piobaireachd*, in the late sixteenth and early seventeenth centuries. There are four compositions in this genre that relate to Rory Mor MacLeod's expedition to Ireland to assist O'Donnell in 1594. But this occurs outside the time period of this study. As in Ireland, the horn was used as well as the pipes, and this too was a hereditary position in the Lordship of the Isles, where MacInstocker (*Mac-an-Stocair*) held the office.[53]

Early Highland Dress

The Highlander's dress was largely identical to that of the Gaelic Irish until the last quarter of the sixteenth century. They are repeatedly described as being long haired, bareheaded, and barelegged to the knee, to which John Elder, in 1543, explicitly attributed the nickname, 'redshanks'.[54] Bishop Lesley, writing in Latin in 1578, says retrospectively: 'Their clothing was made for use (being chiefly suited for war) and not for ornament' and included mantles of several colours, as well as 'shaggy rugs, such as the Irish use at the present day.' Lesley adds that they also wore 'a short wollen jacket, with the sleeves open below for the convenience of throwing darts …. They also made of linen very large shirts, with numerous folds and wide sleeves which flowed abroad loosely to their knees. These the rich coloured with saffron and others smeared with some grease to preserve them longer clean.'[55] This compares very closely with DeHeere's drawings of Irish kern from the 1540s, pictured while in the service of Henry VIII. The exception is the mantle of several colours, clearly a proto-tartan plaid.

The shaggy rugs Lesley mentioned were possibly imported from Ireland, where they were a popular export from Waterford, being sought after

---

51 Grant, *The MacLeods*, p.70.
52 I.F. Grant and Hugh Cheape, *Periods in Highland History* (London: Shepheard-Walwyn, 1987), p.130.
53 Grant, *Periods in Highland*, p.83.
54 Grant, *Periods in Highland*, p.126.
55 McClintock, *Old Irish Dress*, p.114.

abroad particularly by mariners. Lesley adds that the Highlanders also had 'plain breeches close to the thighs' (*foemoralia simplicissima*), which offered little protection. Fr Good had used the same phrase to indicate trews when describing Irish dress in 1566. As they offered little protection, these may actually be 'Irish Dimmie-Trouses', or half trews, as described by Gabriel Archer in 1602.[56] These are depicted on ancient Irish high crosses, and like the full length trews with foot straps depicted in the *Book of Kells*, had survived into the sixteenth century. The only depiction of the 'demi-trews' is DeHeere's drawing of a Highlander of the 1570s, who wears a shaggy rug mantle, and whose clothing reflects later changes also seen in Gaelic Irish dress at that time. As climate became noticeably colder, Derricke's woodcuts overwhelmingly depict the Irish wearing trews on their legs, brogues on their feet, and a new form of jacket, longer in the waist with a pleated peplum, also seen on DeHeere's Highlander. The proto-tartan plaid remained evident, and in 1596, Angus MacDonald of Islay offered gifts of 'plaids and sculls' to O'Neill during negotiations.[57] As the saffron shirt (*léine croich*) went out of use in Ireland sometime in the early 1580s, it was replaced there by the coat and trews. The Highlanders (who may have imported linen from Ireland) invented the belted plaid instead, and are described in the service of O'Donnell in 1594, wearing 'mottled cloaks, belted and hanging to their calves.'[58] Trews were worn quite often too, and not just by gentry. A contingent of Highland bowmen sent to France in 1627 wore 'Trewis & blew cappis' as well as 'Marlit Plaidis'.[59] The earliest reference to caps being worn by Highlanders is among the Scots contingent of the Laird of Wemyss, at the Battle of Arques in 1589. They were described by the Count of Angoulême: 'We laughed to see them armed and clothed like figures of antiquity represented in the old tapestries, with coats of mail and iron helmets covered with black cloth like a priest's cap (*bonnet de prebstre*), using bagpipes and oboes as they went into battle.'[60] Rawhide shoes, like the 'pampootie' of the Aran Islands, are frequently mentioned, but a longer version existed. Nicolas de Nicolay, describing James V's voyage around Scotland *c.* 1540, says the Islemen wore 'ankle boots made in an antique style, which go up to the knees.'[61] That is, high fur buskins, reaching above the calf, and laced in front with a leather point, which are seen in John Speed's depiction of a Wilde Irishman in 1610, as well as the related print of the 'Le capitaine sauvage,' a Highland chief published in Paris in 1562.

---

56   Quinn, *Elizabethans and Irish*, p.23.
57   Grant, *Periods in Highland*, p.126.
58   J. Telfer Dunbar, *History of Highland Dress* (London: B. T. Batsford, Ltd., 1979), p.32.
59   Gregory, 'Scottish Archery,' p.253.
60   Michel Francisque, *Les Écossais en France, Les Français en Écosse*, vol. 2 (London: Trübner & Co., 1862), p.123.
61   Sobieski Stuart, *Costume of the Clans*, p.67.

West Highland Naval Power

The seafaring tradition of the West Highlands and Isles was part of a Norse cultural legacy. The sixteenth century was to be the twilight of Hebridean naval activity, and compared to previous centuries, fleets were already greatly reduced in both number and the size of ships. The mercenary trade in Ireland had become key to financing the galleys, and Ireland was the source of much of the timber used to build them. With the conquest of Ireland in 1603, both disappeared, heralding the end of the tradition.

West Highland galleys were fast and hard to catch, making good troop transports that were highly manoeuvrable inshore. Galleys might be sent back to Rathlin Island for safekeeping drawn up on shore. This left them vulnerable to destruction, and in 1575 11 galleys of Sorley Boy MacDonnell's people were burnt there as he watched helplessly from the Ulster shore.

Hebridean galleys were of three types: the *long-fhada*, or longship, commonly called 'lymphad' in English; the *birlinn* (from Norse 'byrdingr' – a cargo ship); and the *naibheag*, or little ship. A government report of 1615 explained that a galley was a vessel of 18 to 24 oars, while a 'birling' was a vessel of 12 to 18 oars, and the number of men they could carry was estimated as three per oar.[62] Thus, the full complement of a *long-fhada* was 54 to 72 men, while the smaller *birlinn* carried 36 to 54 men. The *naibheag* may have been the 8 oared boat, or 'open sculls of boats', noted as having been used when large numbers were transported, as in 1545 and 1595. (The naevog is a now type of currach in Ireland, which may give some idea of size.)[63]

The clinker-built West Highland galleys of the early sixteenth century resembled their Norse predecessors, but with extremely high stem and stern posts, sometimes topped with bronze wind-vanes. They had a single mast with a square-rigged sail, and are chiefly distinguished from their Scandinavian ancestors by a 'stepped' stern-rudder mounted with pintles and gudgeons. David Caldwell has criticised the reconstruction of a West Highland *birlinn*, the *Aileach*, for conforming too literally to monumental sculpture. With a complement of 16 oars, the crew should have been 48 men. But with a length of just 40 feet, the *Aileach* could only accommodate a crew of 10 or 11, and was too cramped to allow the use of all oars. Citing a long ship depicted on a fourteenth or fifteenth century carved slab in the Abbey Museum, Iona, and a ship graffito on the wall at Dunluce Castle, Caldwell suggests that the *birlinn* was in fact longer than depicted on most

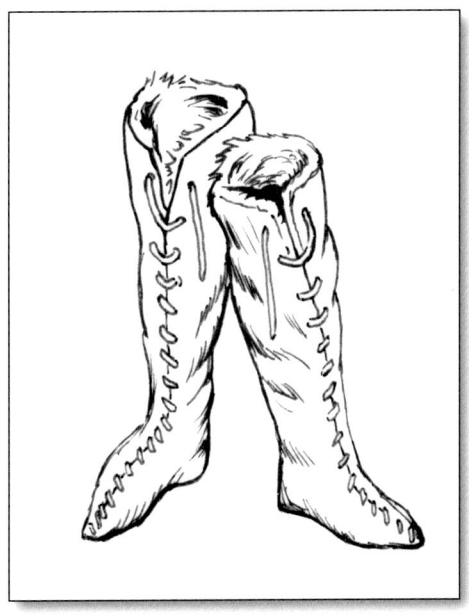

'Boots made in an old fashioned way, which come as high as their knees.' Such boots appear on Irish kern occasionally as well, and examples were excavated in Ireland during the eighteenth century. (Author's drawing)

---

62 Crawford, 'Warfare in West Highlands', p.88
63 Denis Rixon, *The West Highland Galley* (Edinburgh: Birlinn, 1998), pp.74–78.

'OF KERNS AND GALLOWGLASSES'

West Highland galley represented on a grave slab from Iona (Author's drawing)

monuments. He argues that in order to fit them on the narrow grave slabs, the sculptor condensed the length and exaggerated the height of the prow and stern. This suggests that they were much closer in appearance to their Norse forbearers such as the Gokstad ship, which is nearly twice the length of the *Aileach*.[64]

The main body of evidence for galley design is the series of monumental slabs dating from 1350 to 1550. It is clear there was a fundamental change in galley design after 1550, with the appearance of a long prow, as on a Mediterranean galley, and a stern that projected aft, fitted with a cabin on the poop. There is still a single mast, the sail being set with a sloping yardarm and resembling a lug or even lateen sail. Caldwell doubts any such change took place, but it is indicated by a much larger data set than he acknowledged, appearing on no less than four maps as well as late sixteenth century monumental and armorial art in both Scotland and Ireland.[65]

Table 32. Hebridean Naval Expeditions to Ireland[66]

Date	No. of galleys	No. of men	Average crew	Comment
1545	180	4,000	22	Donald Dubh to Ireland
1569	32 + 'many boats'	4,000	<125	
1579	16	700	43	in the Bann
1584	30	2,400	80	MacLean landings
1585	24 'long ships'	2,000	83	Sorley Boy and 2,000 men from Islay to Antrim
1589	26	2,000	77	under a MacLean commander
1589	7	600	86	probably MacNeills in Erris, Mayo
1591	13	700	54	MacLeans/MacNeills/MacLeods in Erris, Mayo

---

64 Caldwell, 'Having the Right Kit', p.150.
65 Lord Archibald Campbell, *Argyllshire Galleys* (London: Charles J. Clark, 1906)
66 Rixon, *The West Highland Galley*, p.43.

Part III

Ships, Castles, Banners and Pipes

10

Irish Naval Power

There was significant shipbuilding in the ports of Tudor Ireland, so that a ship bearing the name of a particular port, such as the *Gabriel of Waterford*, can be assumed to have been built there.[1] In fact, the percentage of Irish trade conducted on Irish-built ships actually rose from 50 percent in 1503–4 to 75 percent by the 1540s.[2] Besides merchant carracks and fishing boats, military galleys were being built down to the end of Elizabeth's reign. Irish ports had long been under Royal command to provide themselves with galleys to collect revenues and guard against pirates. In 1234, two galleys of 60 oars and four galleys of 40 oars had been ordered to be built. A decade later, Drogheda and Waterford were required to maintain two galleys, while Cork and Limerick were each to maintain one.[3]

Medieval tracts on the rights of an Irish King include among his household such officers as Standard Bearer, Keeper of Hostages, and not infrequently Commander of the Fleet (*cennus cabhlaigh*).[4] As early as 1154, a MacLaughlin King in Ulster hired a West Highland fleet under Mac

---

1 Timothy O'Neill, *Merchants and Mariners in Medieval Ireland* (Dublin: Irish Academic Press, 1987), p.112.
2 Evan Jones and Susan Flavin, 'Ireland-Bristol Trade in the sixteenth century', University of Bristol research project, <www.bris.ac.uk/Depts/History/Ireland/research.htm>
3 O'Neill, *Merchants and Mariners*, p.114.
4 Simms, *Kings to Warlords*, p.412.

Scelling, to defend against the galleys of Torlough O'Connor.[5] In the Tudor era, several Gaelic Irish maritime lordships still maintained fleets of galleys and smaller boats. Principally used to patrol commercial fisheries and collect revenues from visiting French and Spanish fishing fleets, they could also be used for piracy and as troop transports on raids. Galleys operated in conjunction with strategically sited tower houses on shore, which allowed a chieftain to oversee his fishing grounds. It is often assumed that they were of the clinker-built Hebridean type, but the carving on the O'Malley tomb suggesting this probably dates to the seventeenth century and may be more a heraldic device than an accurate representation.

A late instance of domestic galley construction comes from 1598, when Tibbot ne Longe, son of the famous Grania O'Malley, offered his services to the Government if they would build him two galleys in either Carrickfergus or Wexford, one to be of 30 oars and the other of 24 oars.[6] These two ports were particularly noted for building and providing timber for galleys. For example, in 1568 the Lord Justices reported from Dublin that they 'have restrained the export of boards from Carrickfergus and Wexford, to impede the Earl of Argyle in making galleys.'[7] By 1599 Tibbot ne Longe was indeed operating 'three very good galleys' carrying 300 men each, 'built by an Englishman of Richard Bingham's' (Bingham was Governor of Connacht). It was further noted that: 'There are no galleys in Ireland but these.'[8] From this last statement, and the number of men carried, these would seem to have been galleys of Mediterranean type, which begin to appear in iconography during the sixteenth century. A mid-sixteenth century map of Bantry and Beara shows, besides conventional shipping, two O'Sullivan galleys of this type in line ahead and under oars with masts lowered. The first galley has a trumpeter in the bow, while the second has a horn blower in the stern, and what appears to be a drummer in the bow. Such trumpeters are often seen on the stern of galleys and galleons in contemporary naval paintings. The type is also represented on Jobson's map of Munster of 1589, and on Bartlett's map of East Ulster of 1602, the seal of Waterford, and a number of West Highland heraldic arms of the second half of the century. This form of galley would not have been clinker-built, though smaller boats of the older form may have remained in use alongside it. Its fore-and-aft rig gave greater manoeuvrability close in to shore, where the masts could be lowered to create a lower profile. The sails in many of the depictions resemble lug sails, an intermediate form between the square sail and the lateen sail. Lug sails were popular with pirates and smugglers during the next two centuries, and this series of images may depict an early use of it. The long prow would have facilitated boarding, as with the Algerian xebec. There is no indication of any Irish galley carrying cannon, although in 1601 Captain Plessington

---

5 Simms, *Gaelic Ulster*, p.82.
6 Rixon, *The West Highland Galley*, p.44.
7 Rixon, *The West Highland Galley*, p.110.
8 Rixon, *The West Highland Galley*, p.44–5.

IRISH NAVAL POWER

reported a fight with one of two galleys belonging to Grace O'Malley and manned by O'Flahertys, that was 'rowed with thirty oars and had on board ready to defend her 100 good shot'.[9] Following is a brief summary of the known Irish naval forces of the era.

'Developed' Irish and Highland galleys represented on maps by Francis Jobson and an anonymous map of Lough Neagh, c. 1600. Such depictions also occur in heraldic art, and strongly suggest that a change had occurred in construction design. (Author's drawing)

O'Driscoll

Presiding over a portion of the south-west coast running from the harbour of Baltimore to Cape Clear, the O'Driscolls controlled one of the finest fishing grounds in Europe and were subject to the overlordship of MacCarthy Mor. They were a prominent maritime clan who drew income from intensive local fishing and the fees charged to foreign fishing fleets. They frequently clashed with the merchants of Waterford and famously lost three galleys in 1447 in a war with the men of that city. These galleys were commemorated thereafter in the Waterford town arms, whose changing iconography over time may indicate development in the design of galleys in Irish waters.[10] The naval power of the O'Driscolls was finally broken in 1538, when they seized three Portuguese vessels loaded with wine. The Mayor of Waterford launched a punitive expedition with 400 men in three vessels, including the recovered Portuguese ship *La Santa Maria de Soci*, the great galley of Waterford, and possibly a pickard under Piers Dobin with 24 men well armed with artillery. The Waterford men attacked Fineen O'Driscoll at his chief seat of Baltimore, destroying his castles, the abbey, and 'Fynyn's chief galley of 30 oars, and three or four small pinnaces', which were taken.[11] From

---

9   Anne Chambers, *Granuaile: The Life and Times of Grace O'Malley, c. 1530–1603* (Dublin: Wolfhound Press, 1983), pp.25–26.

10 Connie Kelleher, 'The Gaelic O'Driscoll Lords of Baltimore, Co. Cork: Settlement, Economy and Conflict in a Maritime Landscape' in Linda Doran and James Lyttleton (eds), *Lordship in Medieval Ireland* (Dublin: Four Courts Press, 2007), pp.130–159.

11 Edward O'Mahony, 'Waterford and the Sack of Baltimore, 1538' in *The Mizen*

'OF KERNS AND GALLOWGLASSES'

An O'Driscoll galley represented on a cast iron plaque bearing the date 1593. It commemorates capture of galleys in 1447, but probably reflects later sixteenth century galley design. (Author's drawing)

O'Sullivan galleys depicted on a map of Bantry and Beara. Thought to be mid-sixteenth century. Trumpeters and drummers are seen in bow and stern. (Author's drawing after a map in The National Arhives, Kew MPF/1/94)

one of the most powerful clans in Munster, and the premier maritime power in the south-west, the O'Driscolls power diminished after 1538. After losing their fishery rights after 1601, the clan largely disappears from the historical record.

O'Sullivan

The O'Sullivan Beare Lordship of County Cork were a maritime clan controlling Bantry Bay and the Beara Peninsula. As with the O'Driscolls, they were subject to MacCarthy Mor's overlordship. Domhnall O'Sullivan wrote to Phillip III in 1605, recalling that at least 500 fishing boats had visited his ports and that each paid a substantial sum of money for fishing rights. The O'Sullivans used galleys to control these fishing grounds. The imposition of levies could be collected at sea or when fishermen came ashore for processing and to get fresh water and supplies. The fishing fleets often spent the summer working the grounds. Earlier in the sixteenth century, an English ship had seized a Spanish fishing vessel off Dursey Island. The captain of the English vessel was subsequently captured by the galleys of Dermot an Phudair O'Sullivan, and executed. Dermot himself was killed when gunpowder exploded in his castle in 1549, giving rise to his post-mortem nickname of *an Phudair* (of the powder) and by which he is known to history.[12] As mentioned above, two O'Sullivan galleys appear in a mid-century map of Bantry and Beara in the National Archives.

Journal, no. 7 (1999), pp.29–45.

12 Colin Breen, *The Gaelic Lordship of the O'Sullivan Beare: A Landscape Cultural History* (Dublin: Four Courts Press, 2005), pp.116–117.

Earl of Desmond

The Earls of Desmond held the liberty of Kerry, encompassing a series of ports in the south-west over which they held admiralty, the right to wrecks and 13s 4d out of every stranger's ship arriving there.[13] Like Ormond, rather than owning ships Desmond would hire a ship from one of the port merchants as needed. In 1462, the future 8th Earl of Desmond lost four such hired ships in a sea battle with Thomas, brother of the Earl of Ormond. It is not clear that any Desmond vessels were involved in 1497 when the Earl joined Perkin Warbeck at the siege of Waterford, the documented shipping having been provided by the Emperor Maximilian. James, 12th Earl, used English ships to recover Youghal from John Fitzgerald of Dromana in 1528. The following year, James requested four great vessels of 200 tons, and six smaller ones, when negotiating with the envoy of Charles V, but these do not seem to have been delivered.

In 1551, a Biscay ship of 70 tons, loaded with Gascon wine, was led into Youghal as a prize by two vessels. One of the captors was the *Mary Winter of Waterford*, of 30 tons, reportedly either owned by the Earl of Desmond, or his in partnership with a Davey Poore. The wine was quickly dispatched on a picard for sale in England. Such occasional piracy was one source of income for all maritime lordships, and this instance netted the Earl at least £25. With Gerald, 14th Earl, (1558–1583), clear evidence exists for ownership of a vessel, the *James of Desmond* of 120 tons. In 1566, the *James* was hired by three Kinsale merchants to carry hides, herrings and mantles to La Rochelle, going thence to Bordeaux to take on wine for the return voyage. This voyage brought the Earl £160. It is clear, however, that by the two Desmond rebellions any such naval capability on the Earl's part was a thing of the past.

O'Malley and O'Flaherty

The O'Malleys took tolls from ships passing through their waters to the neighbouring port of Galway, which was visited by 600 merchantmen a year. They also carried on a lively overseas trade, principally with Spain, as well as engaging in opportunistic piracy. Based on the numbers of ships operated by individual members of the clan, the O'Malleys seem to have maintained a large number of ships. In 1413, Tuathal O'Malley was lost at sea with seven ships, and in 1513, Eóghan O'Malley raided Killybegs with three ships. Grace O'Malley offered the Lord Deputy her services 'with three galleys and 200 fighting men, either in Scotland or Ireland.' In 1591, after being raided by Hebridean pirates, Grace prepared 20 boats to pursue them in revenge.[14]

---

13   Niall O'Brien, 'The Earl of Desmond's Navy', *Journal of the Kerry Archaeological and Historical Society*, ser. 2, vol. 8 (2008), pp.87–96.
14   Chambers, *Granuaile*, pp.24–5.

The living conditions along the west coast of Connacht greatly resembled those in the Western Isles, and the O'Malleys, and the closely related O'Flahertys, had engaged in mercenary service on a similar basis to the redshanks since the early fifteenth century. Using the mobility of their galleys, they appear in service from Desmond to Tyrconnell. They also provided transport for bodies of Scottish redshanks. In 1568, the *Annals of the Four Masters* records the defeat of James Fitzgerald and his MacSheehy galloglass by Thomas MacMaurice of Kerry. Thomas had 50 MacSheehy galloglass himself, and the aid of 'John-na-Seoltadh, son of Donnell O'Malley, with the crew of a long ship, who being friends to the fleet of MacMaurice, had come to visit him.'[15] The O'Flahertys of Connaught provided naval support for the rebel James Fitzmaurice during the second Desmond Rebellion. Upon Fitzmaurice's landing in the country in July 1579, they sent two galleys for his use. These transported a potion of Fitzmaurice's force back into Connacht to foment rebellion there. Fitzmaurice himself was killed at Barrington Bridge while going overland to join these forces.[16] In 1599, the State Papers report 'the Malleys and Flaherties, with five or six galleys, and many boats, are now arrived within this river of Limerick.'[17] Besides galleys, their fleet included pinnaces and 'baggage boats'.

O'Donnell

The lords of Tyrconnell were not dependent upon the Pale or England for links to mainland Europe, but had their own direct relationships. They maintained a fleet of 12 or 13 ships, of uncertain type, used to conduct maritime trade and diplomatic missions, to patrol their extensive territorial waters, and to convey pilgrims. The *Annals of the Four Masters* records a sea battle in 1369, won by the sons of Niall O'Donnell against Philip Maguire and 'a large fleet,' fought on Lough Erne. O'Donnell ships are noted in the *Annals of Ulster* in 1508, patrolling the Erne and venturing as far inland as Cavan. In 1514, 'a flotilla of long ships and boats was drawn by O'Domnaill on Loch-Erne,' to enforce his supremacy. The wealth of the O'Donnell fisheries and trade attracted pirates to the coasts of Donegal, mainly O'Malleys and O'Flahertys, as well as Hebrideans. While there are no later sea battles recorded in the annals, throughout the first half of the sixteenth century the O'Donnells are frequently found ambushing pirate gangs who had come ashore.[18]

---

15 O'Donovan, *Annals of Ireland*, p.1627.
16 O'Brien, 'Desmond's Navy', p.92.
17 *Calendar of State Papers Ireland: Elizabeth*, vol. 8, 1599, April–1600, February, Ernest George Atkinson ed. (London: HMSO, 1899), p.153, 14 September, Thomond to Cecil.
18 Mac Eiteagáin, 'Renaissance Tír Chonaill', pp.207, 212 & 225.

11

The Tower House

Perhaps the most iconic archaeological features of the Irish countryside are the tower houses that dot the rural landscape, dating from 1400–1650. They form a particular category of small castle, said to have originated in a £10 subsidy granted by statute of Henry VI in 1429 to any Palesman who would build a castle within 10 years. The purpose was to defend the English Pale around Dublin, and the money was to be raised by levy within the counties of Louth, Meath, Dublin and Kildare, 'the four loyal shires'. The measurements were to be a modest 20 feet by 16 feet, and 40 feet high (6.1m x 4.9m x 12.2m). In fact, tower house building had been well underway in the Pale already during the early fifteenth century. This simple form would spread from the Pale to the Anglo-Irish lordships of the south and west, with tower houses eventually becoming common among the Gaelic chieftains as well. As their usage spread westward over the sixteenth century, tower houses became larger and more sophisticated. Over 3,000 were built in all but with some estimates ranging as high as 7,000, with Ireland becoming the most encastellated part of Europe in the late Middle Ages.[1] The distribution map below shows they were never as common above the lake and drumlin borders of Ulster, reflecting both an environment that favoured the continued use of crannogs, and which was less open to English cultural influence. Interestingly, there are a handful of Ulster tower houses evidently built by lowland Scots masons for Irish chiefs prior to 1603. These feature conical-roofed corner turrets, corbelled out in the Scottish style, as found at Enniskillen, Burt and Dunluce Castles.[2]

---

1   Terry Barry, 'The Study of Medieval Irish castles: a bibliographic survey', *Proceedings of the Royal Irish Academy*, vol. 108C (2008), p.129.
2   E. M. Jope, 'Scottish Influences in the North of Ireland: Castles with Scottish Features, 1580–1640' in *Ulster Journal of Archaeology*, 3rd. ser., vol. 14 (1951), pp.31–47.

'OF KERNS AND GALLOWGLASSES'

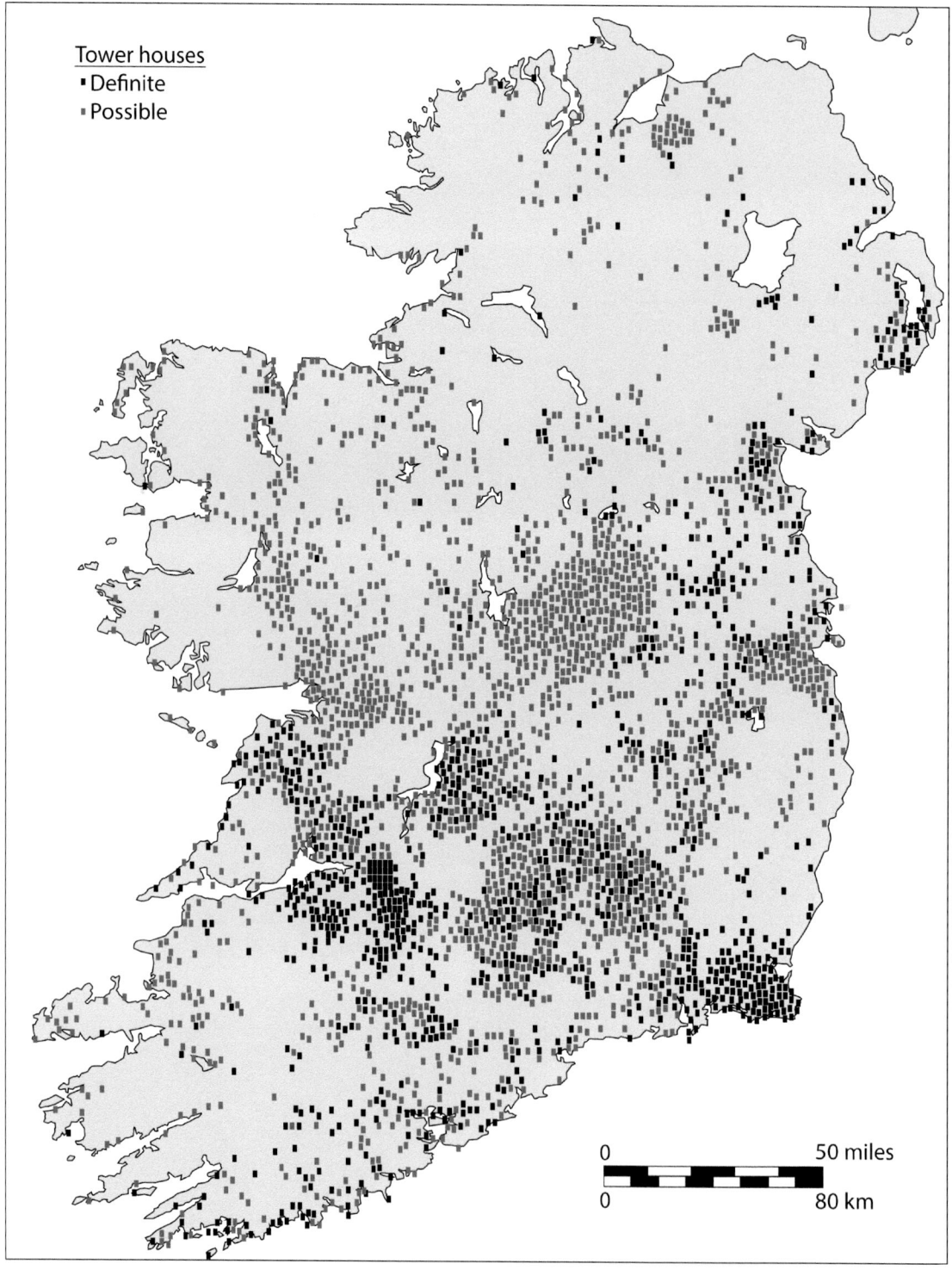

Tower House Distribution. (Author's drawing, after *Atlas of the Irish Rural Landscape*)

THE TOWER HOUSE

Tower houses were at least four stories high. The ground level was a storage room, often with a vaulted ceiling in fifteenth century examples in the eastern part of the country, the vault serving to guard the upper stories against fire. Typically, the first floor could serve as sleeping quarters for the ward and servants, with a kitchen on the second floor, and the chief's living space, the solar, on the third, with the hall usually being uppermost in the sixteenth century, located directly over the vaulted ceiling. The location of the hall on the top floor became a feature of the newer Gaelic tower houses of the midlands and west. The hall's high wooden ceiling and flagstone floor, originally with a central hearth, gave a sense of occasion that was central to its function.

The castle proper could be surrounded by a bawn (from the Irish *bó dún*, a cow enclosure) – either a masonry wall, or a ditch and hedge. Cattle could be driven into the bawn at night for safekeeping. About 20 percent of surviving tower houses show evidence of a masonry bawn.[3] Some castles, such as Aughnanure, had a separate hall built alongside the tower house for receptions and banqueting, sometimes of stone, sometimes of wattle and daub or sods with thatched roofs. It is not clear what relationship these external halls had to the hall proper within the castle. Possibly the external hall was a communal hall while the castle hall was the lord's hall. But the owners would choose to sleep in the tower for security.

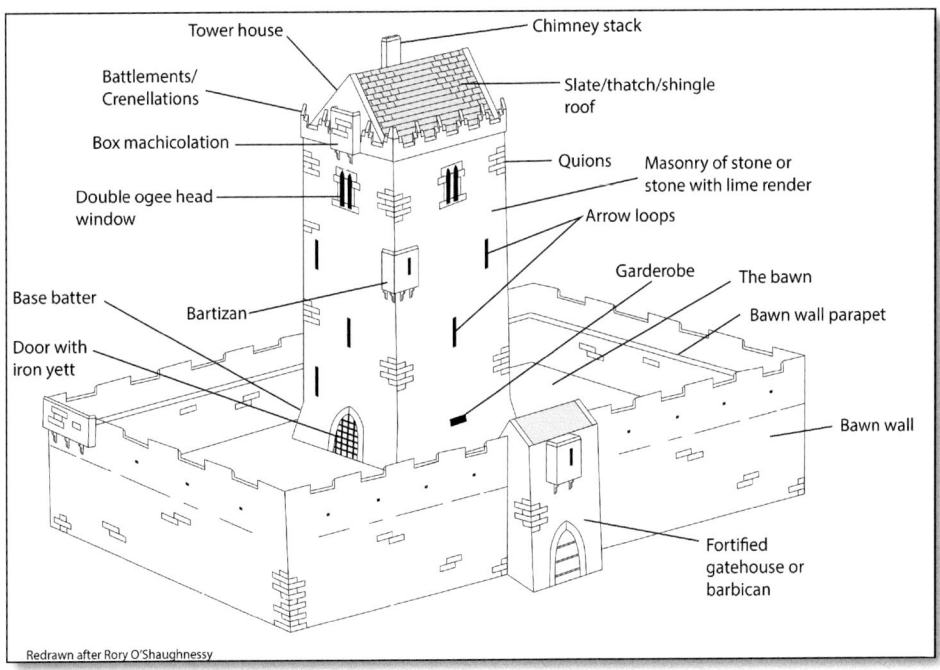

Features of the tower house (Author's drawing, after Rory O'Shaughnessy)

---

3   Victoria McAlister, *The Irish Tower House: Society, Economy and Environment, 1300–1650* (Manchester: Manchester University Press, 2019), p.22.

'OF KERNS AND GALLOWGLASSES'

Tower House Features: punch-dressed door jambs and ogee-headed windows. (Author's drawing, after Leask)

Leask identified the key features of tower houses: a vault constructed on wickerwork centring; punch-dressed stone for window surrounds and door jambs; ogee-headed windows and angle loops; box machicolations atop the walls over the doorways; battlements with 'Irish' crenellations with stepped merlons. Stepped merlons are a distinctively Irish form of crenellation, and are also found on sixteenth century churches and bridges, as at Tintern Abbey in Wexford. Their only occurrence outside Ireland is in depictions of castles on contemporary West Highland tomb sculpture, although they do not appear in surviving structural examples. The peculiarly Irish stepped merlons are not an isolated case, northern Italy having a distinctive regional style of crenellation as well.[4]

The Gaelic tower houses of the west and midlands generally date to the sixteenth century, and are distinguished by the more frequent use of bartizans, machicolation and gun loops, with any vaulted ceilings being on an upper storey when they are present. The vaulted ceiling was constructed on a framework of temporary timber supports holding up a wicker matting over which the lime mortar bed was laid. When the supports were removed, the wicker matting was often left in place. Today, the impression of the wicker matting can be seen in the vault ceiling – sometimes the embedded matting itself remains. This may be the explanation of the curious observation of the French visitor, Boullyae le Gouz (1644), who said: 'and many of them ornament the ceilings with branches.'[5]

Strategic Siting

Castles were constructed for chieftains and other leading members of the local ruling family or clan. Regional overlords would often maintain castles within the territory of a sub-king or *ur-rí* (*urraight*). Tower houses were also built for galloglass captains, poets, and other members of the professional classes, as well as churchmen, such as the infamous apostate Bishop Miler Magrath, who built Termon Castle in Donegal. Interestingly, Coole Castle in Co. Offaly was built in 1575 by John MacCoghlan specifically for his wife, according to the date stone.[6] And incoming planters in the early

---

4   H. G. Leask, *Irish Castles and Castellated Houses* (Dundalk: Dundalgan Press, 1995), pp.7–88 & 97–98.
5   Leask, *Irish Castles*, p.91.
6   Rolf Loeber, 'An Architectural History of Gaelic Castles and Settlements, 1370–1600' in Patrick J. Duffy, David Edwards and Elizabeth Fitzpatrick (eds), *Gaelic*

THE TOWER HOUSE

seventeenth century would continue building in the tower house tradition, employing Irish masons, when establishing their new settlements.

In urban settings the tower house saw use by merchants as a kind of city row-house, serving as living quarters in its upper stories, with the commercial space at street level having a separate entrance. Examples of urban tower houses include in Lynch's Castle in Galway, and Taffe's Castle and the Mint in Carlingford. Merchants also acquired tower houses in the hinterlands of the coastal corporate towns, which facilitated their commercial access to the products of the countryside.

The castle was likely the single largest outlay an Irish lord or freeholder would incur in his lifetime. Around 1600, the German planter Mathew De Renzy estimated the 'meanest' tower house would cost £600 or £700. Twenty-five years earlier, the costs of building a tower were estimated at a more reasonable £300 or £400 in County Down.[7] In this regard, the economic importance of the migration of great shoals of herring into the warmer waters off the western and southern coasts of Ireland during the fifteenth century cannot be overestimated. The resultant income from the fishing accrued to regions under Gaelic control throughout the sixteenth century, which denied the Crown any revenue from the windfall. The increased wealth was reflected in a building boom of tower houses and ecclesiastical structures. Tower houses, apart from their defensive function, were statements of wealth which formed centres of nucleated settlement and economic activity.

An interesting agreement exists for the building of a sixteenth century tower house. In 1547, a castle was built for Richard Butler in return for lands he had given to the Earl of Ormond. The agreement states that the castle shall have:

- three floors, with a vault over the ground floor.
- walls were to be six feet thick below the vault, and four feet thick above.
- the height of each floor is prescribed.
- a slate roof and two chimneys.
- the door to be protected by an iron grate [yett].
- a berbikan and doors, windows and all things necessary to a castle.

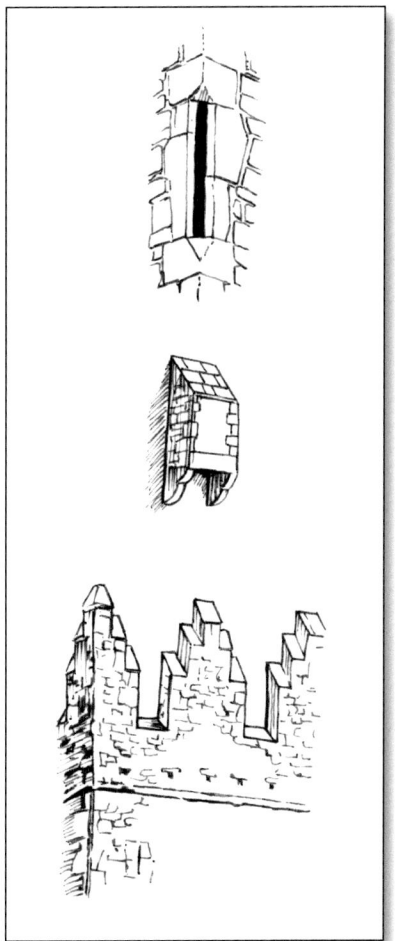

Tower House Features: angle loops, machicolations, and Irish crenellations. (Author's drawing, after Leask)

Ireland: Land, Lordship & Settlement c. 1250–1600 (Dublin: Four Courts Press, 2001), p.308.

7 McAlister, *The Irish Tower House*, p.7.

'OF KERNS AND GALLOWGLASSES'

A tower house of the type common in the west during the sixteenth century, based on that of Kilcrea, and situated in a landscape. The next tower house is just visible on the right horizon, as found in parts of east and north Cork. (copyright JG O'Donoghue)

Tower House interior. The ground floor, with porter's lodging to the right of the entrance door, and the stairway to the left, while a storage cellar lies straight ahead. The first floor has sleeping quarters for the ward, servants and guests. The second floor has a kitchen and further sleeping quarters. The third floor is the lord's living quarters, with two fireplaces and painted walls. The fourth floor is the dining hall, but during the course of the sixteenth century, most entertaining shifted to external dining halls, often built of perishable materials that have not survived. (copyright JG O'Donoghue)

Derby Ryan was to supervise the work along with the treasurer of Lismore, who would employ a master mason and a master carpenter.[8] Labour for castle building, a service called 'musteroon', was among the chiefly exactions required of tenants, and food and lodging would also be exacted for itinerant professional masons. Ireland had good and highly mobile masons, the State Papers showing 'Forty masons of the west' were 'taken up for the service of Berwick' in 1561, and sent from Dublin in February by way of Chester.[9] Again, in December of 1561, a further '200 good and fit masons and hewers of rough stone' from Ireland were to be employed in the fortification of Berwick. We are told that for their return home, they purchased honest English clothing, including civil caps.[10] Skilled workmen occasionally came from abroad – in May of 1561 James M'Donnell was reported in the State Papers to have 'many carpenters come out of Scotland to build him a house in the Red Bay.'[11]

Use and Construction

Tower houses were commonly built on bedrock foundations, and often strategically sited to guard river crossings, bridges, and passes. The original tower houses of the English Pale were constructed along the borders with Offaly to stem the incursions of O'Connor Faly, and they were incorporated into the larger network of ditches and palisades guarding the Pale. While strategic considerations may be evident, many tower house locations are not particularly strong in terms of their immediate landscape setting. A clan often held a network of castles, as with the O'Malleys in Mayo, and the O'Flahertys in Galway. In more densely occupied areas like Clare or Limerick, tower houses could constitute individual nodes on a defensive network, and were built within sight of one another. A chief would often build additional castles on his demesne lands, which served to assert his control locally, as well as providing residences for members of the senior line of the clan.

Tower houses are strongly associated with rivers and waterways in particular and frequently occur in proximity to salmon weirs and fish ponds. Waterways were an important means of communication, as well as a source of income through fishing and trade, and tower houses could help dominate both. O'Donnell was known abroad as the 'King of Fish' and the salmon so prominent in the arms of the O'Neill lordship are said to reflect

---

8   Tom McNeill, *Castles in Ireland: Feudal Power in a Gaelic World* (London: Routledge, 997), p.211.
9   *Calendar of State Papers Ireland: Henry VIII, Edward VI, Mary and Elizabeth*, vol. 1, 1509–73, Hans Claude Hamilton ed. (London: Longman, Green, Longman & Roberts, 1860), p.166, 23 February, Jaques Wingfield to Sussex.
10   *CSP Ireland*, p.184, (?) December, Warrant from Queen.
11   *CSP Ireland*, pp.170–1, 28 April, Capt. Pers to Fitzwilliams.

the O'Neills' exploitation of the Bann fisheries. In the tower houses of the Gaelic O'Connor Sligo Lordship, which were the normal residences of the landholding families, two or three members of the family sometimes owned the tower house together. The O'Connor tower houses were strategically located, some around the Sligo Coast and Ballysadare Bay, others guarding bridges or river crossings leading into their territory. The wall walk around the roof of the house served both as a look out post as and a functioning rain gutter.[12]

Wall walk view, Dysert O'Dea Castle, Co. Clare (Author's photograph)

A network of Geraldine castles ran along the south bank of the Shannon Estuary in the north of Cos Limerick and Kerry. These served to secure the region, from the old O'Connor stronghold of Carrigafoyle in the west, to the walled and castellated city of Limerick further east, with its many urban tower houses. From their main seat at the great Norman keep of Askeaton, the semi-Gaelicised Geraldine Earls of Desmond oversaw a realm that included strongholds held by their sub-lords, the 'three knights': The White Knight (Kilmallock), the Knight of Glin (Glin, Ballyguiltenane), and the Knight of Kerry (Lixnaw, Listowel and Beale). Carrigafoyle, having been occupied by the Geraldines, acted as a customs house where duties were levied on merchandise being shipped upriver. Goods could then be landed at Tarbert, or further upriver at Limerick itself. The coastal tower houses of Doon and Beal acted as beacons, alerting the Earl of his right to

---

12 Margaret Mac Curtain, 'A Lost Landscape: the Geraldine Castles and Tower Houses of the Shannon Estuary' in John Bradley (ed.), Settlement and Society in Medieval Ireland (Kilkenny: Boethius Press, 1988), p.437.

THE TOWER HOUSE

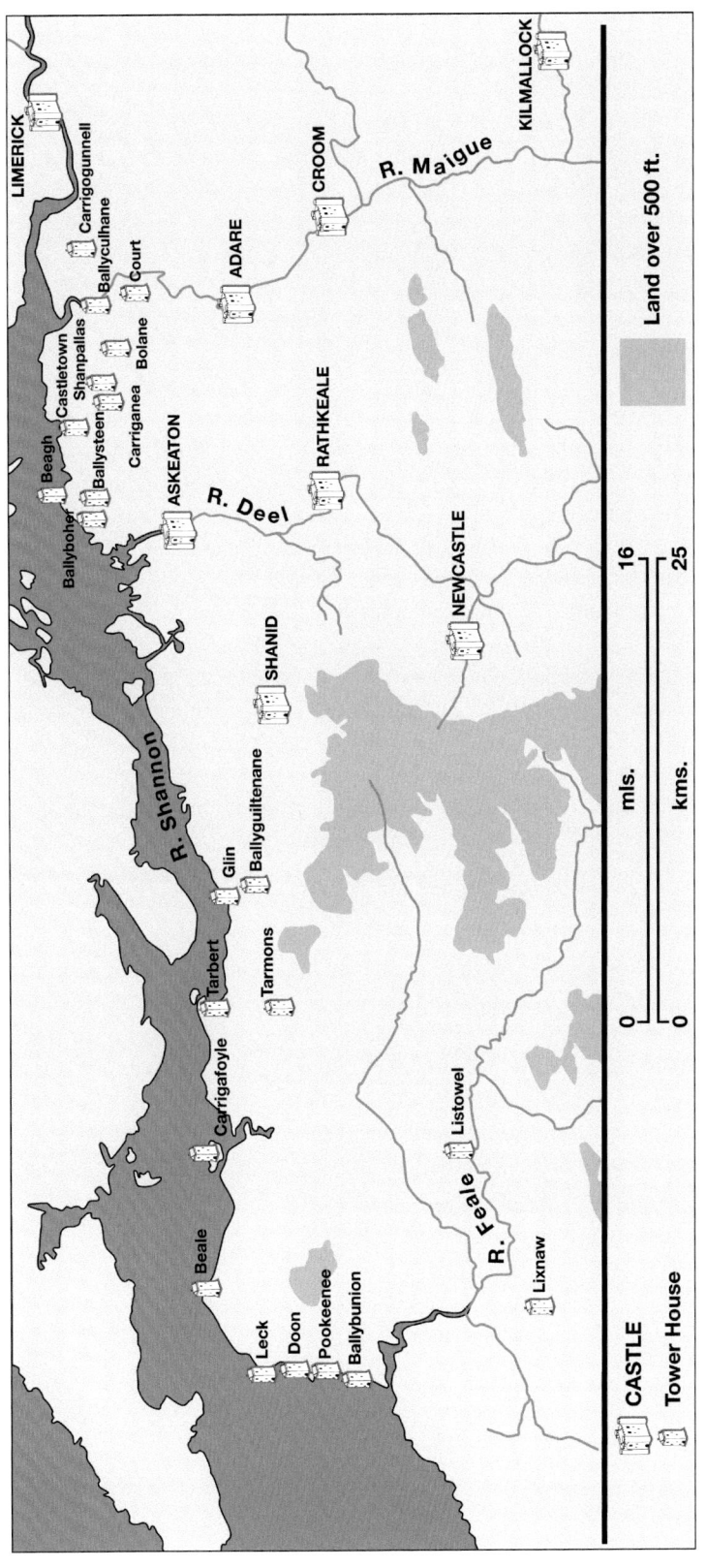

Geraldine castles and tower houses along the Shannon Estuary (Author's drawing, after Mac Curtain)

salvage in case of shipwreck. Running east–west along the Shannon estuary, the Geraldine castles form three successive lines of defence, in support of one another.[13]

Tower houses were primarily living spaces, the lower storey having a porter's lodge by the entrance, with the rest of this level being devoted to storage. The hall, for communal activities such as audiences and feasting, was usually located above the vaulted ceiling – which after 1500 is often found on an upper floor. As noted above, this is a feature of western tower houses, often of Gaelic origin. The stone floor above the vault was more suitable since the hall frequently contained a central floor hearth, mural fireplaces only being added later.

The principal living quarters (the 'solar') are often found immediately below the hall in post 1500 tower houses. In the pre-1500 examples of the east, the vault often has several floors above it, in which cases the living quarters may be located on the floors above the hall, which is immediately over the vault. Based on these considerations, Rory Sherlock has devised five categories of tower house, his dating aided by radiocarbon samples from hazel twigs from the wicker found in some castle vaults.

The lime rendered walls of the living chambers could be enlivened with wall paintings, which was probably fairly common though only four examples survive. Higher status tower houses might also have panelling and stucco plasterwork to accentuate the hall, which sadly do not survive. The hall frequently had a timber partition supporting a loft in which musicians or singers could perform.

Rory Sherlock has explored some of the nuances to be discerned in how differently space might be used in outwardly similar tower houses. Evidence for suites within a single tower house being owned by different individuals occurs only in Gaelic areas and is a late sixteenth century feature. This practice is associated with the discontinuance of the hall as a communal social space within the castle, with the hall itself being partitioned into separate living accommodations and even subdivided vertically with the addition of a new floor in place of the once spacious but smoke-filled ceiling area. This was made possible by the replacement of the central hearth with mural fireplaces. The abandonment of the hall signals the end of the old communal social life of the Gaelic castle and the transition to a more hierarchical social structure, with greater privacy for the Lord in what was now essentially a house.[14]

---

13   Mac Curtain, 'A Lost Landscape', pp.438–9.
14   Rory Sherlock, 'The Evolution of the Irish Tower House as a Domestic Space' in *Proceedings of the Royal Irish Academy*, vol. 111C, Special Issue: *Domestic Life in Ireland* (2011), pp.115–140.

THE TOWER HOUSE

Castle Ward

The 'ward' was the term used for a castle's garrison in Tudor Ireland. Galloglass seem to have been the usual ward during most of the sixteenth century, though firearms were present fairly early, becoming ubiquitous by 1600. In the examination of the MacDonnells of Leinster, above, a number of galloglass – either 9 or 12 – were specified for each land holding, quite possibly representing the ward of the associated castle. In 1536, at the breaking of O'Brien's Bridge (a bridge castellated at both ends), 'both the castles were well warded with gunners, galloglass and horsemen.' The gunners manned a 'ship's piece, a portingal [Portuguese] piece, hagbusshes [arquebuses] and hand guns.'[15] Irish horsemen, being armoured similarly to galloglass, often dismounted to take up position alongside them. By the end of the century the ward were entirely arquebusiers and simply termed 'the shot'. The shot are listed among the immediate household of the chief, and like the galloglass of earlier days, probably lived within the tower house.

Stanihurst discusses the castle ward, who keep watch:

> so that no one may make attack while they are asleep …. they maintain watches at the very top of the castle, like in a watchtower, and these call out very frequently. Thus they keep watch, with frequent outcry for the greater part of the night. They keep up this repeated shouting in order to indicate to thieves and nightwalkers that the head of the house is not so deeply asleep that he will not be fully prepared – and watches rouse him whenever they suspect the approach of an enemy – to drive the enemy from his hearth in manly fashion, and if there is a real need, to take the field under arms and to fight hand-to-hand.[16]

Defensive Qualities

Tower houses were built for defence, but while they could rebuff the attentions of raiding parties, they were not ideal for withstanding a siege. Thus, they were occasionally razed by their owners when their defence became strategically untenable. Less drastically, the tower house's defences might instead be 'slighted' for this purpose, i.e. the crenellated parapets thrown down. The door, being the only entrance, was central to the tower house's defence.[17] Doors were generally protected on the outside by box machicolation overhead, with a 'murder hole' in the interior ceiling just

---

15 Maxwell, *Irish History*, p.99.
16 Stanihurst, *Great Deeds*, p.113.
17 Duncan Berryman, 'The Defensibility of Irish Tower Houses – a Study' in *The Castle Studies Group Journal*, no 24 (2010–11), pp.260–268.

above the lobby, providing a means to defend against intruders who had breached the door. Murder holes are often small enough that their main function may actually have been communication between the lord upstairs and the 'porter' at the door below, concerning admittance to the tower house.

The porter, or doorkeeper, was stationed in the porter's lodge, a small chamber immediately adjacent to the doorway – usually to the right as you enter. In the evening the porter secured the door with a wooden drawbar that recessed into the surrounding masonry. A bolted door just opposite the porter's lodge gave access to the spiral staircase leading to the living quarters upstairs. At Cratloekeel Castle in Co. Clare, masonry evidence shows that this front door drawbar was locked in place by a secondary drawbar pushed against the end of the primary drawbar to secure it, and which was operated from within the bolted stairwell door. Thus the secondary drawbar was only accessible to persons living upstairs, behind the bolted stairwell door. This provided a fail-safe against any treachery by the porter.

The most effective door defence was probably the yett, a hinged iron grill or grate that closed over the tower house door. The yett was secured with a chain drawn through a slot in the masonry door jamb, and it protected the door from attack with battering rams, much like the portcullis of a larger castle. Even if the door was burnt, the yett could still deny entry. However, only about 20 percent of tower houses were fitted for a yett, a fact which has been taken to indicate that defence was a secondary concern to living space. Experimental archaeology by a team from Queen's University Belfast reconstructed two tower house doorways. Fire destroyed one door within 40 minutes, while a battering ram broke the second door, drawbar and all, in a matter of minutes, thus underscoring the importance of a yett for serious defence.[18]

---

18   Berryman, *Defensibility of Tower Houses*, pp.266–7.

12

Banners and Flags

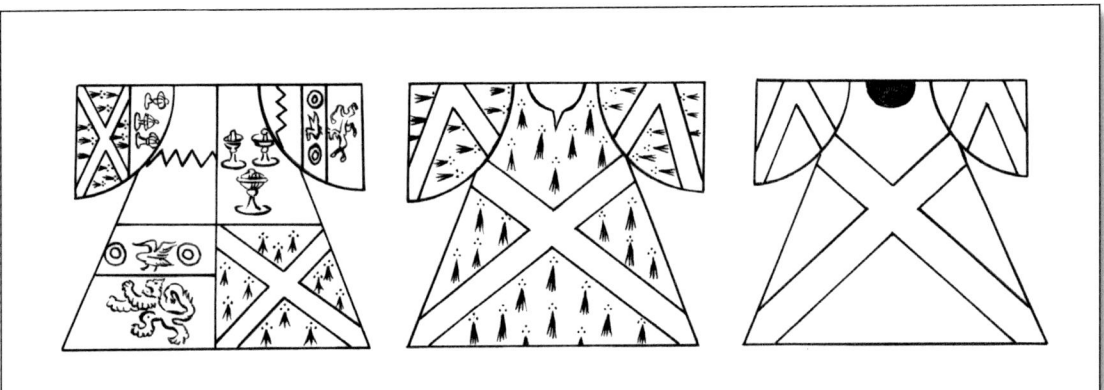

Anglo-Irish heraldic tabards: The arms of Fitzgerald of Kildare are argent, a saltire gules. The Desmond arms are the same, but as a junior branch of the Fitzgeralds, they display an ermine field as a difference. The Ormond arms are, quarterly: 1, or, a chief indented azure; 2, gules, three covered cups or; 3, argent a lion rampant gules, on a chief of the last a swan close of the first between two annulets; 4, ermine, a saltire gules. After the Funeral Entries of Ulster's Office, in the National Library of Ireland.

Anglo-Irish Banners

The Anglo-Irish magnates displayed conventional English heraldry.[1] Their often striking banners and standards came into special prominence in the late sixteenth and early seventeenth centuries when they were used in sumptuous heraldic-themed funerals. These are recorded in the Funeral Entries of the Genealogical Office, and displayed the standards under which such a lord would have marshalled his 'rising out' earlier in the century. These are the flags referred to after the great Battle of Knockdoe in 1504, when the *Four Masters* record the victorious Earl of Kildare being urged to gather his scattered forces, and 'to pitch a camp, for our soldiers and attendants will join us on recognising our standards and banners.'[2] They were borne by hereditary standard bearers, such as Robert Halfepennie, 'who wyth his auncestours was Standert bearer to the house of Slane.'

---

1 G. A. Hayes-McCoy, G. A., *A History of Irish Flags from the Earliest Times* (Boston: G. K. Hall & Co., 1979), pp.24–27.
2 O'Donovan, *Annals of Ireland*, p.1279.

Holinshed tells us that at the defeat of Conn Bacach O'Neill at the Ford of Belahoe in 1539, this Halfepennie declined to lead the charge against the 'quicke Iron walles' of 'armed Galloglasses' lining the far shore. Instead, the Baron of Slane entrusted his standard to a substitute, who led the victorious charge.[3] The Family of Walshe served as hereditary standard bearers to the Earls of Kildare until the collapse following the rebellion of 'Silken' Thomas. A private battle 'with banner displayed & trumpet sounding' was fought at Affane in February 1565 between the Anglo-Norman Houses of Desmond and Ormond. In response, the State Papers record that in September of that year, a Commission was to certify 'what be the laws of Ireland, for wilful murder, arson, banners displayed, assembly with force, &c.' For a nobleman to take the field 'with banners displayed' was technically high treason if he was not on Crown Service.[4] This complaint had been brought against the 9th Earl of Kildare in 1531, when he 'displayed his banner openly' while leading his men in an raid on the camp of the allied Butlers while they were both on campaign together with Lord Deputy Skeffington in the North.[5] A document of 1599 on various aspects of fosterage mentions the use of livery as a badge of identity, referring to the individual client as a 'mean castle of that coat', where the aim was to assimilate the foster family into the lord's affinity.[6] It is interesting to note that the heraldic tabards illustrated in the Funeral Entries were actually used, as when complaint was made in 1566 of Gerald, 11th Earl of Kildare's 'liverers', the officers collecting his 'unreasonable duties' and who wore his livery.[7] We also have a late instance when a footman of the 'Queen's' Earl of Desmond in 1600 was sent through the country to encourage support prior to the young Earl's arrival, 'having his master's arms upon his coat before and behind, to show himself in most places of the country.'[8]

Town militias would have served under civic banners, such as the 'new banner charged with the arms or shield of the town' bought for Kilkenny in 1517. The civic flag of Dublin was the 'black standard' dating to the thirteenth century. In 1577, Hollinshed recalled that 'euen to this day the Irishe feare a ragged and iagged blacke standard that the Citizens haue almost, through tract of tyme, worne to the harde stumpes. This standarde they carie with them in hostings, being neuer displayed but when they are readie to enter in battaile and to come to the shocke.'[9]

The 1515 regulations for the musters of the Pale specified that the Warden of a Shire should have a standard of St George, conventionally

---

3   Holinshed, *Holinshed's Irish Chronicle*, p.296.
4   *CSP Ireland*, p.273, 22 September, Memorandum for the Commissioners.
5   Bagwell, *Ireland Under*, vol. 1, p.155.
6   Fiona Fitzsimmons, 'Fosterage and Gossiprid in Late Medieval Ireland' in Patrick J. Duffy, David Edwards and Elizabeth Fitzpatrick (eds), *Gaelic Ireland: Land, Lordship & Settlement c. 1250–1600* (Dublin: Four Courts Press, 2001), p.142.
7   Hore, *Social State*, p.169.
8   Stafford, *Pacata Hibernia*, vol. 1, p.107.
9   Holinshed, *Holinshed's Irish Chronicle*, p.42.

for every 100 men, while the constable of a barony should have a guidon, conventionally for every 50 men. The guidon bore the arms of St David of Wales, a red dragon on a white over green field. The regulations for the musters of the Pale in 1557 ordered that, in place of the former standard of St George, each of the County Dublin baronies was to acquire 'a convenient and warlike ensign with a red cross of St George therein against the day of musters.'[10] All banners of the Pale's rising out were to be 'boughte on the deputies costes,' and the 1519 Ordinances say every shire with their standards should lodge together in one quarter of the field, and that the standards of Dublin, the county of Dublin and the county of Kildare go together, and the standards of Drogheda, Meath and Louth go together. Provision was made that no banner or guidon be reared in the field apart from those appointed by the Deputy, and he was to suffer but few of each to be displayed. Approaching the enemy's country, the Marshal organised the host into a forward, middleward and rearward, and no man was to depart from his ward's banner, on pain of forfeiture of horse and harness. Likewise, only designated foragers were permitted, and these to be accompanied by 'certain guidons of horsemen and banners of footmen', appointed nightly for their protection.[11]

The medieval institution of Scutage, or 'Royal Service', was a surtax laid upon the chief tenants of the Pale, used to pay hired troops. In anticipation of a great hosting, Scutage could be proclaimed by the Lord Deputy by publicly displaying the Royal Banner. There were several such instances in the Tudor era, the last occurring in 1531 for Skeffington's hosting against the O'Tooles of Leinster. The Royal Banner does not appear to have been taken on service.[12] However, Deputies would display their own cognizance in the field. In 1566, Lord Deputy Sidney campaigned against Shane O'Neill under 'my pensel [pennoncelle, or streamer] with the ragged staff.' Shane was alerted to Sidney's presence by a scout, who reported: 'I saw the red bracklok [*bratach*, Ir. flag] with the knotty club, and that is carried before none but himself.'[13]

Gaelic Irish Banners

The idea that the sixteenth century Gaelic Irish made little use of banners and flags may derive from two statements of Fynes Moryson, dating to the Nine Years' War at the end of the century. In July 1601, when the rebels showed themselves along the Blackwater with drums and colours, Moryson dismissed it as mere bravado, since the Irish, 'fighting like thieeues vpon dangerous passages, used not to appear in such warlike manner.' And

---

10 Hayes-McCoy, *History of Irish Flags*, p.25.
11 Maginn and Ellis, *Tudor Discovery*, pp.103–4.
12 Ellis, *England's Irish Pale*, p.97.
13 Hayes-McCoy, *History of Irish Flags*, p.27.

after the defeat of the Irish at Kinsale half a year later, Moryson says the victors waived 'the Colours we had taken in the battell, and among the rest, especially the Spanish Colours, (for such most of them were) the Rebels in woods not using that martial brauery.'[14]

In fact, the record shows that the Gaelic Irish made regular use of banners, standards and guidons throughout the Tudor era, just as they had in the high Middle Ages and earlier. By 1316, the O'Connor had a designated 'standard bearer', reported in the annals as being slain at the Battle of Athenry. This remained a hereditary office in the household of a Tudor era Irish chieftain. Over half of the more than 200 coats of arms in MacLysaght's collection of Irish arms have a silver (argent, white) field, the highest proportion of any European nation.[15] This is thought to reflect the origins of these coats as tribal totems depicted on white banners. The O'Doherty banner, for instance, is described as 'A lion and bloody eagle …. on a white sheet of silken satin.' What may well be examples of this Gaelic proto-heraldry have been identified in the zoomorphic roundels of the Queen Mary harp and Trinity College harp, which display symbols of the MacKinnon and Mac Giolla Phádraig families, respectively.[16] Other such totems include the red hand of the O'Neills, the cat of the O'Cahans, the robin redbreast of the O'Sullivans, and the 'enfield' or *onchú* of the O'Kellys. Some had apparent regional significance, such as the blue lion that was adopted in the arms of a cluster of Gaelic families in the North Roscommon and Sligo area.

A very limited number of Gaelic lords may have begun using heraldry under the quasi 'home rule' of the Kildare Ascendancy, from 1470–1534. The Fitzgerald Earls of Kildare themselves had adopted many aspects of Gaelic culture, and were heavily intermarried with the Gaelic nobility. Kildare's use of English heraldry may, in turn, have inspired allied chieftains to adopt coats of arms. Certainly, the form of early blazons in Irish language sources, as well as other evidence, seem to suggest an independent if fledgling use of heraldry among the Gaelic Irish in the early sixteenth century.[17] After the downfall of the house of Kildare, the policy of Surrender and Regrant adopted in 1540 put a new colour on this use of heraldry. Conn Bacach O'Neill had been addressed by the Pope in 1538 as 'King of our Realm of Ireland' but his bid to effect that title was extinguished at the Battle of Belahoe a year later. In his subsequent submission, Conn was made Earl of Tyrone, receiving a new coat of arms and a Crown Charter to the lands of the O'Neill Lordship, while agreeing to 'utterly forsake the name of

---

14   Fynes Moryson (Litton Falkiner ed.), *Itinerary*, vol. 2, *The Rebellion in Ireland, AD 1600*, (London: J. Beale, 1907), pp.113, 179.

15   Edward MacLysaght, *Irish Families, Their Names, Arms and Origins* (Dublin: Irish Academic Press, 1985)

16   Eóghan Mac Giolla Phádraig, 'A Fitzpatrick Crest on the National Harp', *The Journal of the Fitzpatrick – Mac Giolla Phádraig Clan Society* (2021), pp.1–21.

17   N. J. A. Williams, 'Dermot O'Connor's Blazons and Irish Heraldic Terminology', *Eighteenth Century Ireland / Iris an dá chultúr*, vol. 5 (1990), pp.61–88.

O'Neill.'[18] The office of the Ulster King of Arms was established at Dublin Castle in 1552 to regulate the granting of arms to such newly indentured Gaelic nobility. Naturally, acquisition of arms under English authority was seen as being inimical to the clan system. Some of the early accepters of arms would subsequently rebel, while the vast majority of Gaelic lords remained aloof altogether, and 10 years after the establishment of the new office of heraldry, Lord Deputy Fitzwilliam was still referring to the ongoing 'discountenance of heraldry' among the Gaelic chieftains.[19] Only after the final overthrow of the Gaelic system in the early seventeenth century would the bulk of remaining Gaelic nobility seek arms from Ulster's Office, as they scrambled to secure a place in the new order.

Banners in Use

Sir John Harrington recorded the Tourney Ordinances of 1562, which attempted to regulate the size of flags. A banner for an earl, viscount or baron was to be three feet square, and 'Place under a banner a C. men.' A standard was to be 'slitte at the end' and should be four yards long for a banneret, five for a baron and six for an earl, and 'place under a standard an hundred men.' A pennon is to be two yards and a half long, 'made ronde at the end' and 'serveth for the conduct of 50 men.' Likewise, a guydhomme (guidon) was also to be two yards and a half long, but was to bear no arms, 'onelye a man's crest' and 'Place under a guidhomme 50 men.' 'Pencels or flags for horsemen muste be a yarde and a haulfe longe, wyth the crosse of St George, the creste or worde.'[20]

Contemporary government documents and Irish annalists often refer to 'banners of footmen' and 'standards of horse', and there are clear indications this was more than a figure of speech. On 25 September 1520, the State Papers record the victory of MacCarthy Reagh and Sir Thomas of Desmond over the 10th Earl of Desmond's forces at the Battle of Mourne, with Desmond reputedly losing '18 banners of galoglas, which bee comonly in every banner 80 men, and the substance of 24 banners of horsemen, which be 20 under every baner, at the leest; and under some, 30, 40, and 50.' This gives us an idea of which Irish troops carried banners, and in what quantity.[21]

The 1519 Ordinance for the General Hosting of the Pale states that captains of horse were to have a banner, provided at least 40 horsemen attended each banner. In the State Papers, during Brian O'Connor's rebellion of 1537, the 'galowglassez of the traytors' made a pre-dawn attack on the

---
18 Peter Beresford-Ellis, *Erin's Blood Royal* (New York: Palgrave, 2002), pp.24, 37.
19 *CSP Ireland*, p.191, 14 April, Fitzwilliams to Cecil.
20 Sir John Harrington, *Nugae Antiquae, Vol. I*, ed. Thomas Park (London: J. Wright, 1804), pp.8–11
21 *State Papers: Henry VIII*, p.46, 25 September, Lord Lieutenant to Henry VIII.

government hosting, which included 'too batell of galowglasse .... and there the galowglasse lost their standert.'[22] We know at least some galloglass captains had their own personal banners. In 1576, a MacSweeny captain of galloglass was hung, drawn and quartered by Drury, the President of Munster, for taking a 'prey of cattle, with his banner displayed, from Cork, which banner he had carried before him unto the place of execution.'[23] Indeed, even the kern sometimes carried flags, as the 1519 Ordinance referred to above states also that the captain of 60 kern for Meath was to have a 'lytle bann[er] and all the kerne to follow.' The companies of 60 kern for Carlow and Kildare were each likewise to have a captain, 'and everie captayne their lytle gytton' [guidon, or small ensign].[24] And as stated in the above examination of contingents of kern for overseas service, these also had a standard bearer for each company, who received non-commissioned officer's pay, although this may not have been typical outside government service. In 1626, Randal MacDonnell, the Earl of Antrim, complains that he could not find sufficient 'yellow and crimson taffeta' in Dublin to make a standard for his men, who thus appeared like 'a parcel of Irish kern'.[25]

Irish lords are described displaying multiple banners, even when conducting cattle raids. On 29 October 1564, Calvagh O'Donnell sent six standards, which he had taken from Shane O'Neill, to the Lord Lieutenant, Sussex.[26] An Act of Attainder was subsequently drawn against Shane accusing him of entering the Pale 'with banners displayed as an open enemy.' And in 1537, 'Walter [Roche] came with a banner displayed of Irishmen, and tooke with them ye prey,' while 'David Ketteing .... brought Caire Carrathe [Caher Carragh Kavanagh] with banner displayed, and tooke the prey of Rahaspok.'[27] In October 1568, Lord Roche complains of a devastating raid against him by the Earl of Clancarthy and his followers, 'with six or seven banners displayed.'[28]

The *Annals of the Four Masters* records that in 1561 Calvagh O'Donnell 'sent his own standard to the town [Sligo] and displayed it on the battlements of the tower.' Other forms of standards were sometimes carried. The O'Donnells had a battle talisman called the *Cathach*, a decorated book shrine containing a gospel associated with their patron, St Columcille. In 1567, Hugh O'Donnell made his submission to the government and received a knighthood from Lord Deputy Sidney. He was granted new arms, possibly inspired by those of his wife, a MacDonald of the Isles. Yet at the Battle of Farsetmore the same year, Hugh's hereditary Standard Bearer, McGroarty, is recorded in the *Four Masters* as being slain at the first clash

---

22 *State Papers: Henry VIII*, p.525, 30 December, Brabazon to Cromwell.
23 Bagwell, *Ireland Under*, vol. 2, p.323.
24 Ellis, *England's Irish Pale*, p.97.
25 Hayes-McCoy, *Irish Flags*, pp.32–3.
26 *CSP Ireland*, p.xxvii, 29 October, Calough O'Donnell to Sussex.
27 Hore, *Social State*, p.49–50.
28 Richard Butler (ed.), *Tracts Relating to Ireland*, vol. 2 (Dublin: M. H. Gill, 1842), p.69.

BANNERS AND FLAGS

of opposing horsemen, while carrying the *Cathach*. And one of the three septs of O'Donnell galloglass, MacSweeny Doe, provided 'a man to carry the mail shirt and stone of Columcille', which must have been lesser talismans.²⁹

The guidons being carried by the kern of the Pale marches early in the century are not isolated instances. In 1568, the Dean of Armagh complained of being chased into the woods by Con O'Donnell's 'gydone and force'.³⁰ And in 1572, the same source reports a 'Scottish guidon bearer slain by Capt. Pers's own hands.'³¹ And in 1584 after a fight with the English near Dunluce, Sorley Boy MacDonnell is said to have lost 40 men, 'among the rest Donnell Cassyleye, Sorley's guidon bearer.' Sorley Boy had at least one other 'giddon' also said to have been killed, Donogh Rua MacNaughten.³² Patrick Condon, a rebel who was very active in Cork during the second Desmond Rebellion, would later, 'hoist the Pope's banner with his own guidon, crying Condon above!'³³ The cry is more often rendered *Condon abu*, and the 'Pope's banner' that Condon was flying in 1593, when this report is entered in the *State Papers*, may have been a Counter-Reformation banner left over from the second Desmond Rebellion.

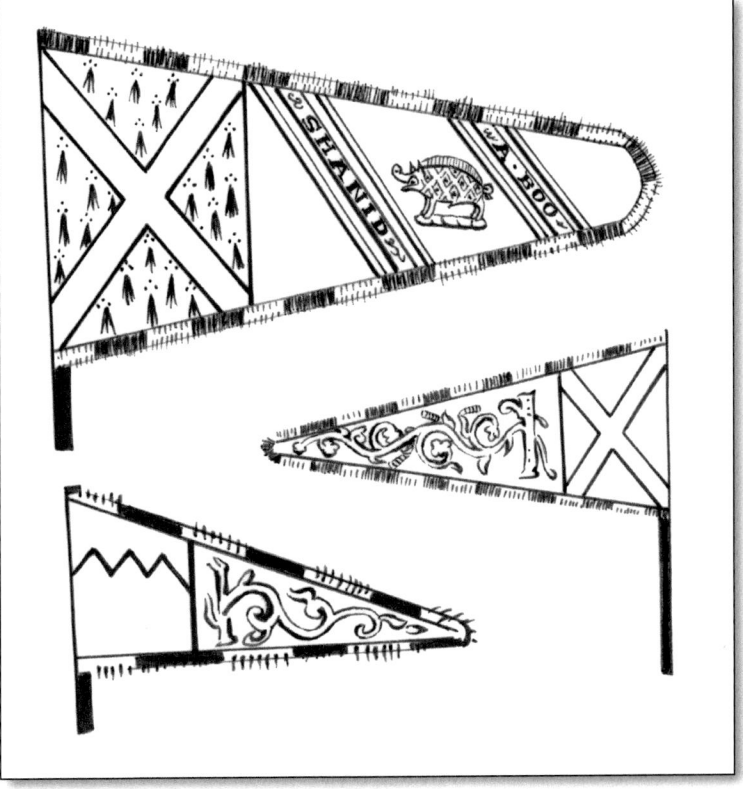

A standard of Desmond, bearing the motto SHANID A BOO on white scrolls across a red field, with the boar of Desmond. Below it are the guidons of Butler and Kildare. The guidons are red, charged with a yellow stump and tendril. That of Butler bears in the hoist the arms; or, a chief indented azure. That of Kildare bears in the hoist the arms; argent a saltire gules. The standard and guidons all have red and white fringe. (After the Funeral Entries of Ulster's Office, in the National Library of Ireland)

Counter-Reformation Banners

In the course of the protracted campaign against the Midlands clans in the middle of the century, government attitudes hardened. The Protestant

---

29 McGettigan, *Red Hugh O'Donnell*, p.27.
30 *CSP Ireland*, p.xxvii, 16 July, Lord Justices to Queen.
31 *CSP Ireland*, p.466, 27 February, Fitzwilliams to Privy Council.
32 George Hill, *An Historical Account of the MacDonnells of Antrim* (Belfast: Archer & Sons, 1873), pp.166 & 168.
33 *Calendar of State Papers Ireland: Elizabeth*, vol. 5, 1592, October–1596, June, Hans Claude Hamilton, ed. (London: Eyre and Spottiswoode, 1890), p.145, 10 September, Mayor of Youghal to Privy Council.

Reformation policies introduced after 1537 injected a religious element to the Crown's campaign against the southern magnates, and in the second Desmond Rebellion of 1579–1583, Counter-Reformation banners make their appearance among the rebels in Munster. James Fitzmaurice brought a Papal Banner with him when he landed in Kerry in 1579. When Fitzmaurice was killed shortly thereafter, Desmond's two brothers continued to carry it, and it was nearly captured when they were defeated at the Battle of Monasternenagh in October 1579. The English commander, Sir Nicholas Malby, described Fitzmaurice's Papal Banner as 'a red ensign about an ell square, and the picture of Christ crucified very gloriously upon it which a horseman did run away withal.' It bore the Latin motto, *In Omni Tribulatione Et Angustia Spes Nostra Jesu Et Maria* (In all Tribulation and Difficulty our Hope is Jesus and Mary).

A more distinctly Papal banner is illustrated in a picture map of the siege of *Dún An Óir*, or the Golden Fort. It flew over the Italian and Spanish troops who were besieged there in 1580, and bore the arms of Pope Gregory XIII beneath the tiara and the crossed keys. In March 1582, 1,000 rebel horse and foot, mostly MacSweeney galloglass, under David Berry and Sir Owen MacCarthy of Carbery, entered West Cork flying an ensign bearing Papal insignia. They managed to draw out the company in garrison at Bantry Abbey and destroy it.[34] The rebels reportedly 'advanced seven Irish pencines displayed besides an ensign of the Pope's arms, the bearer thereof being killed by the soldiers.'[35] The 'pencines' are evidently heraldic pennoncelles, or guidons, noted above as having been carried by the Irish.

---

34 Sasso, 'Desmond Rebellions', p.331.
35 *Calendar of State Papers Ireland: Elizabeth*, vol. 2, 1574–1585, Hans Claude Hamilton ed. (London: Longmans, Green, Reader and Dyer, 1867), p.lxxxvii., 12 March, Sir Warham St Leger to Queen.

13

The Pipers

A distinctive aspect of Gaelic Irish military culture in the sixteenth century was the use of the bagpipe as a martial instrument. William Camden, for example, noted, 'In warre they use the bagpipe in steed of a trumpet.'[1] The instrument had been adopted relatively late in Ireland and Gaelic Scotland. The first definite mention of its use as a military instrument is in an Irish version of the romance of Fierabras, dated 1484–1487: 'Let horns and pipes (*píba*) be sounded by you to gather your host.' A more mundane list of church donors from 1495 in the DeBurgo lordship of Connacht includes 'captainio M'Donnell' (DeBurgo's galloglass captain) and a man described as 'pibyre' (*píobaire*), or piper.[2] The instrument seems to have been avoided in the Pale because of its increasing identification with the Gaelic Irish. It would remain a salient feature of the Gaelic Irish military tradition until the end of the Williamite War. Irish language literary sources of the late seventeenth century refer to it as the *píb mhór*, or great pipe, and include two references to the *dos mór*, or bass drone, as well the *feadán*, or chanter.[3] This is the same terminology used for the Highland bagpipe in Scottish Gaelic. *Píb mhór* is pronounced 'peeb wor', and combined with the instrument's military use, may have given rise to the term by which it is sometimes known today, 'warpipes'.

In 1584 the Dubliner, Richard Stanihurst, gave a complete description of the great pipe: 'This type of pipe is held among the Irish to be the whetstone of martial courage, for as other soldiers are ardently fired up for battle by the sound of trumpets, so are the Irish by the sound of this.' He describes an instrument of the most skilful craftsmanship, generally similar to the Highland bagpipe of today, having a tightly stitched bag of folded hide, into which are glued 'two hollowed out wooden pipes, one longer, one shorter,'

---

1   Camden, *Britain*, p.147.
2   Seán O'Donnelly, *The Early History of Piping in Ireland*, Na Píobairí Uilleann Teoranta and the Royal Scottish Pipe Band Association, N.I. Branch (Newtownabbey: Oakdene Services, 2001), p.9.
3   Seán O'Donnelly, 'The Warpipes in Ireland', *Ceol*, vol. 5, no. 1 (1981), p.56.

i.e., the bass and tenor drones. There is a blowpipe and a chanter with apertures which 'the piper regulates by a rolling action of his fingers.' He says the blow pipe emerges from the side of the bag, and that the piper, with swelling cheeks and neck, blows the bag up while maintaining pressure on it with one arm. The instrument emits a 'sound both loud and shrill.'[4]

In much of Europe, the bagpipe was a mellow pastoral instrument. The Gaelic preference for a louder, shriller pipe was driven by its martial use. Thus, Spencer in his *Faerie Queene* evokes his Irish experience with these lines: 'Now when amid the thickest woods they were / They heard a noyse of many bag-pipes shrill.'[5] Along with its military function, contemporaries noted the great pipe's employment at burial services. These remain two of the most prominent uses of the Highland bagpipe to this day. Vincenzo Galilei, father of the famous astronomer, wrote in 1581: 'It is much used by the Irish; to its sound this unconquered, fierce and warlike people march their armies and encourage each other to deeds of valour. With it also they accompany their dead to the grave, making such sorrowful sounds as to invite, nay, compel the bystanders to weep.'[6]

A description of kern returning from a cattle raid in 1561 says, 'then muste they have a bagpipe bloinge afore them.'[7] By this time, bands of kern were often accompanied by a piper, as with the 12 kern and their piper, Rory Gortaghe, found guilty of murder at Clonmel in 1552.[8] As noted above the 1544 and 1550 musters of Irish kern for overseas service were accompanied by pipers at a ratio of one per 100 men. The pipers were listed separately after the company officers in the muster of 1550, which may indicate a higher rate of pay than the ordinary kern. There are indications as well of the galloglass being accompanied by pipers. Apart from the piper associated with DeBurgo's galloglass captain above, two pipers are listed in pardons granted to the Government galloglass, the MacDonnells of Tinnakill, in the 1570s: 'Alexander piper' and 'Tyrlagh piper.'[9] And Derricke's 1581 woodcut of a battle features a prominently labelled 'pyper' lying slain at the head of a company of galloglass.

Signals and Marches

Derricke, describing the overthrow of the Irish in battle, clearly states that their pipers played recognisable signals: 'And baggepype then instead of Trompe / do lull the back retreat.'[10] At the Battle of Kinsale in 1601, Camden

---

4 Stanihurst, *Great Deeds*, p.121.
5 Herbert Hoare, 'War-cries of Irish Septs', *Ulster Journal of Archaeology*, no. 11 (1855), p.204.
6 O'Donnelly, *Early History*, p.23.
7 Hore, 'Irish Bardism', p.166.
8 *Cal. Ormond Deeds*, vol. 5, pp.72–3.
9 O'Donnelly, *Early History*, p.13.
10 Derricke, *Image of Ireland*, p.63.

says the Earl of Tyrone realised that he had failed to take the English by surprise, 'and soone after by his bagpipers sounded the retraite.' Seán Donnelly suggests that this Irish 'retreat' and other signals were recognised by the English, and he adds, 'More than likely they would have consisted of certain fairly simple note-figures repeated over and over.'[11] There is an unusual tune that survives in the Irish tradition called 'O'Neill's March' (Marcshlua Uí Neill, or O'Neill's Cavalcade) which meets these criteria, and was collected in 1809.[12] Tellingly, the tune fits the limited compass of the great pipe, and consists of three distinct figures, each repeated four times. It sounds like nothing so much as three trumpet calls played end-on-end, and may well preserve some signals of sixteenth century pipers.

The publication of Derricke's *Image of Ireland* in 1581 seems to have occasioned the first known programme of descriptive music. Inspired by the woodcuts of marching English horse and foot, Irish 'karne' following a bagpipe, and battle scenes, William Byrd composed a suite of keyboard music titled *The Battell*. It is found in the musical manuscript, *My Ladye Nevells Booke* (1591), and includes *The Marche of Horsmen*, *The Marche of Footemen*, *The Irishe Marche* and *The Bagpipe and the Drone*. These last two marches fit comfortably on the nine-note great pipe, and may reflect the actual music of sixteenth century Irish pipers. Certainly, music historians consider the other pieces in the suite to be based on the contemporary drum beats and trumpet calls, which could readily have been supplied by Byrd's patron, the Earl of Oxford. And the date of composition likely predates the manuscript itself by 10 years.[13] Byrd would also have had ample opportunity to hear Irish pipers in England.

In the reign of young Edward VI, Royal entertainments at Court in 1551 included a *Masque of Irishmen*, for which three shillings was paid 'For the hier of an yrishe bagpipe plaier'. Over Christmas 1553, expenses for the Lord of Misrule festivities included a 'garment of russet damask' for the 'Lord of Misrule's minstrel – the Irysshe bagpiper.' This piper may have been part of the intended cast of William Baldwin's lost *Irish Play of the State of Ireland*, slated for performance in 1553, but possibly never performed before the King's premature death in July. The play itself does not survive but the properties made for it are inventoried in the 'Revels Accounts'. The provision of six sets of clothing for 'Irish keyrens' with a wooden sword and dart for each, is suggestive that a sword dance was to have been performed, quite likely to the music of the 'Iryishe bagpiper.'[14]

Fynes Moryson noted that the Irish kern performed a sword dance, and he called it 'the Matachine daunse with naked swords which they

---

11 O'Donnelly, *Early History*, p.14.
12 Edward Bunting, *A General Collection of Ancient Irish Music* (London: Clementi & Co., 1809), p.32.
13 Sally Mosher, 'William Byrd's "Battell" and the Earl of Oxford' in *The Oxfordian*, vol. 1 (1998), pp.43–52.
14 Feuillerat, *Revels at Court*, pp.48, 79 & 183.

make to meete in diuers comely postures.' When performed at the end of the century before Lord Mountjoy, Moryson found it dangerous sport 'to see so many naked swords so neere the Lord Deputy and the cheefe Commanders of the Army in the handes of the Irish kerne.'[15] Writing a few years later, palesman Hugh Collier shared Moryson's concerns when listing 'Customes of the Irishry …. which may prove dangerous in suddaine attemptes.' He says 'some are proper to their kierne, as dauncing with naked swordes, some to their Musitianes and mintrelles as their Bagg pipes.'[16] The mattachins, or sword dance, is well described by Arbeau in his contemporary dancing manual, *Orchésographie*[17]. It was known as *rinnce an chlaidhimh* in seventeenth century Ireland. 'At my Lord Barries in Ireland' at Christmas 1632 a dramatic sword dance was performed by six servants dressed as kern 'with swords drawn.'[18] It probably resembled the folk dance called Droghedy's March, noted in the early nineteenth century. Like the kern's dance performed at Lord Barrymore's, the Drogedy involved teams of six facing one another, rhythmically clashing swords or sticks, followed by 'involutions, evolutions, interlacings and unwinding.' It was danced to a tune resembling 'Brian Boru's March'[19] and the dance of today's Wexford Mummers may be a modern echo of it.

Good, an English Jesuit stationed at Limerick in 1566, repeats: 'In war they use the bagpipe instead of a trumpet …. and in joining battle, they cry as loudly as possible they then can 'pharroh.'[20] This is the word *faire* in Irish, meaning 'look out'. Edward Bunting, whose collection of 1809 is cited above, also printed a tune called 'The Pharroh, or war march' (*Faire! Faire! Ar Aghaidh, Ar Aghaidh* or 'Watch, watch, advance, advance!'). Like the others mentioned here, this multi-part march can be fitted on the bagpipe, but its origins are uncertain. Spencer, in 1596, also speaks of this cry of 'Ferragh! Ferragh! that their kern use at their first encounter.' Good says this cry was used by all Irish soldiers, cavalry as well as infantry. He also says the Irish held that those who failed to shout it loud enough would be swept through the air to 'a certain vaile in Kerry …. where he eateth grass, lappeth water …. hath some use of reason, but not of speech', which Donnelly has equated with the legendary *Gleann na nGealt* (the Glen of the Mad).[21]

Bunting's 1809 collection, noted above as preserving *O'Neill's March*, includes on the same page 'Rory O Moor, King of Leix's March.' Rory

---

15   Falkiner, *Illustrations of Irish*, p.322.
16   Morgan, 'Discourse of Mere Irish', unpaginated.
17   Thoinoit Arbeau, *Orchésographie* (Langres, 1589). Reprinted in London in 1925 by C. W. Beumont.
18   Alan J. Fletcher, *Drama, Performance, and Polity in Pre-Cromwellian Ireland* (Toronto and Buffalo: University of Toronto Press, 2000), pp.310–313.
19   Patrick Kennedy, *The Banks of the Boro* (Dublin: McGlashan & Gill, 1875), pp.231–232.
20   Camden, *Britannia*, p.144.
21   O'Donnelly, 'Warpipes in Ireland', p.23.

Óg O'More is the principal antagonist of Derricke's *Image of Ireland*, and production of that book was stopped to include notice of his death in June 1578. The tune has something of the feel of Byrd's *Irishe Marche*, and it has also survived in the oldest stratum of the Highland piping repertoire as the *piobaireachd*, 'Duncan Mac Rae of Kintail's Lament.' Based on this concordance, piper Alan MacDonald has reinterpreted this *piobaireachd* as a martial tune rather than a lament. *Piobaireachd* is a theme and variation form of art music, possibly inspired by the complex music of the Gaelic harpers. It may have had its beginning in the late sixteenth century, or it may only have emerged in the seventeenth century. Several so-called 'Irish pibrach' survive in the Scottish tradition, and perhaps the basic theme of these may have an Irish origin. But the lengthy, florid *piobaireachd* variations seem likely to have developed only in the seventeenth century Scottish context. In any case, the bagpipe in Ireland never attained the high status it would achieve in the Scottish Highlands, where it replaced the harp as the elite instrument during the course of the seventeenth century.

Amongst the English foot, Shakespeare's 'ear-piercing fife', i.e., the Almain whistle, had been adopted alongside the drum during the 1530s. It supplanted the bagpipe, which had to some degree accompanied the march of French and German troops as well as English, and which now remained in service only among the Irish and Scots.[22] Turner, writing around 1670 in *Pallas Armata*, lists the company officers, adding that 'In some places a Piper is allowed to each Company …. the Bag-pipe is good enough Musick for them who love it; but sure it is not so good as the Almain Whistle. With us any Captain may keep a Piper in his Company, and maintain him too, for no pay is allowed him.'[23] This may reflect a tradition of piping common to the North of England and the Lowlands of Scotland, as well as the Gaelic regions. In fact, the tune *Rory O Moor, King of Leix's March*, discussed above, appears in a supplement to the 1657 edition Playford's *Dancing Master*. It is quite evidently a bagpipe tune, and is associated there with a prominent northern family, the Washingtons. It was obviously common to the three kingdoms, but Playford is missing the ending flourishes found in the Irish and Highland versions, which argues for a Gaelic origin.

In the droll seventeenth century poem *Irish Hudibras* – a very anti-Irish piece of doggerel verse – the Irish piper Macshane challenges the trumpeter 'O'Triton' to a contest; 'When with O Triton he'd compare / To Sound as good a Point-of-War.' Macshane is killed 'Because his Pipes were shrill and sharper', so that he goes 'To sound a Charge in Purgatory.'[24] This phrase, a 'point of war', has been identified as early as 1578. It is defined by the *Oxford*

---

22 James Tanner, *Instruments of Battle: The Fighting Drummers and Buglers of the British Army* (Philadelphia: Casemate, 2017), p.37.
23 James Turner, *Pallas Armata, Military Essayes of the Ancient Grecian, Roman…* (London: M.W. for Richard Chiswell, 1683), p.219.
24 James Farewell, *The Irish Hudibras, or Fingallian Prince* (London: Richard Baldwin, 1689), pp.24–26.

English Dictionary as a short strain sounded as a signal, citing Gervase Markham[25], who spoke of the 'soundings which we generally call Poynts of Warre,' meaning six particular trumpet calls. *The Point of War* played by British army pipers today is a version of the fife signal known as 'Three Camps', current in eighteenth and nineteenth century military music, and no doubt dating back much earlier.

Rising Status?

Bardic poets were intensely conservative and their works habitually omitted mention of firearms, bagpipes and other relatively recent innovations, which were not in keeping with their heroic ethos. For them, the aristocratic wire-strung harp which accompanied the recitation of their poetry was the only instrument worthy of notice. O'Donnelly nonetheless cites increasing instances of Irish pipers appearing in English documents over the course of the sixteenth century, possibly reflecting a rise in their status. Initially, notices in the *State Papers* read like this: 'Slew Art O'Connor and his piper.' He cites a subtle change evident in a plea of loyalty submitted by Piers Butler in 1589, when he was under suspicion. Butler, an illegitimate brother of the Earl of Ormond, provided a long list of rebels that he had killed, naming the most notable. Numerous pipers are cited. Thus, he killed 'Bryen Reoghe, piper to Thomas of the Myll' and 'slew Shane O'Forgurtie alias Shane E Cogge, piper to the said Neal Mc Moriertaghe.' Butler never names the many ordinary kern that he killed. Apart from the pipers, he only mentions chief rebels and captains by name.[26] O'Donnelly points out that these are the first historical references we have to a piper being described as 'piper to' some notable person, a possible marker of enhanced status.

Later in the century, special notice is made in the State Papers regarding the taking of the head of Feagh MacHugh O'Byrne's piper, and the slaying of the rebel Richard Tyrrell's piper. These references to pipers become more numerous after the middle of the sixteenth century, a time of intensifying military activity. With the expansion of military strength under Shane O'Neill, and later Hugh O'Neill, Earl of Tyrone, many persons of humble origin were armed for the first time. It has been suggested that they brought with them their instrument, and that it gained status as it became associated with the military profession. But pipers were well established by the time Henry VIII's musters for France were levied in 1544.[27]

---

25 Gervase Markham, *Souldiers Accidence, or an Introduction to Military Discipline*, second edition (London: printed by I. Dawson for John Bellamie, 1625) p.60. 'Poynts of Warre'.
26 O'Donnelly, 'Warpipes in Ireland', p.55.
27 O'Donnelly, *Early History*, p.19.

THE PIPERS

Illustrations of the Pipes

In the absence of any surviving examples, we are reliant upon written descriptions and surviving artwork for our image of the old Irish *píb mhór*. The illustrations of Irish pipers by DeHeere and Derricke seem to owe something to Netherlandish depictions of bagpipes, as they show an instrument with a very large bag pressed against the chest with both forearms, its closely parallel drones issuing from a single stock. This is the arrangement seen in Brueghel's many depictions of pipers. We saw earlier that the eye-witness Stanihurst is quite clear that the bag of the Irish bagpipe was held under one arm, as with the modern great pipe. He is seconded by the more reliable Irish visual depictions (see below), which also clearly show splayed bass and tenor drones set into separate stocks. The drones show indications of tuning slides, and their ends are only moderately flared. These four images are consistent. The figure labeled 'piper' in English script is from a Cistercian ordinal written in 1501, but may have been added decades later. The stone carving from Woodstock castle, thought to be sixteenth century, is somewhat distorted to fit the available space, and the chanter is absurdly large. But the relationship of the drones seems accurate. The definitely sixteenth century carved piper from Galway city maintains natural proportions. The manuscript illustration of a piping pig is similarly dated, and along with the Galway carving, provides the best indication of the proportions of the Irish great pipe. And see Derricke's much more carefully rendered slain 'pyper' from his battle image, which mirrors all the features of these Irish depictions.

Sixteenth century depictions of pipers by native Irish artists (as discussed in the text) (Author's drawing)

In his description of the Irish manner of fighting, written in the early 1540s, Paolo Giovio places the piper among the galloglass, 'where the battle stands,' 'Out from among these [galloglass], while the battle stands disposed in the middle of the field and the bagpiper plays, the light infantry rushes from the wings and fights with darts and arrows which they fire from short wooden bows.'[28] Rather unexpectedly, he adds, 'when the battle-signal calls to arms. They spark battle not with the sound of a trumpet, but with the bellowing of a huge twisted wooden horn [*ligneae buccinae*].' This is intended to mean a separate instrument to the bagpipe, for which he uses the standard Latin terminology, *utriculario tibicine*. Very large wooden horns were common enough among pastoral mountain communities from the Carpathians to the Alps. And early depictions of the Swiss alphorn show a large, crooked wooden horn, spirally wrapped with split willow bindings, which give it a twisted appearance. Giovio's 'huge' or 'great' wooden horn is reminiscent of these early depictions of the alphorn. Considering the importance of cattle herding in Ireland, it is perhaps not surprising to find something similar in an Irish context, although this is our only reference to it. Those of the kern who served as *stocaire*, or horn blowers, are assumed to have carried animal horns, as depicted in Dürer's well-known watercolour sketch of Irish men of war.

---

28   Harris, 'Paolo Giovio', p.287–8.

THE PIPERS

Illustrations of the Pipes

In the absence of any surviving examples, we are reliant upon written descriptions and surviving artwork for our image of the old Irish *píb mhór*. The illustrations of Irish pipers by DeHeere and Derricke seem to owe something to Netherlandish depictions of bagpipes, as they show an instrument with a very large bag pressed against the chest with both forearms, its closely parallel drones issuing from a single stock. This is the arrangement seen in Brueghel's many depictions of pipers. We saw earlier that the eye-witness Stanihurst is quite clear that the bag of the Irish bagpipe was held under one arm, as with the modern great pipe. He is seconded by the more reliable Irish visual depictions (see below), which also clearly show splayed bass and tenor drones set into separate stocks. The drones show indications of tuning slides, and their ends are only moderately flared. These four images are consistent. The figure labeled 'piper' in English script is from a Cistercian ordinal written in 1501, but may have been added decades later. The stone carving from Woodstock castle, thought to be sixteenth century, is somewhat distorted to fit the available space, and the chanter is absurdly large. But the relationship of the drones seems accurate. The definitely sixteenth century carved piper from Galway city maintains natural proportions. The manuscript illustration of a piping pig is similarly dated, and along with the Galway carving, provides the best indication of the proportions of the Irish great pipe. And see Derricke's much more carefully rendered slain 'pyper' from his battle image, which mirrors all the features of these Irish depictions.

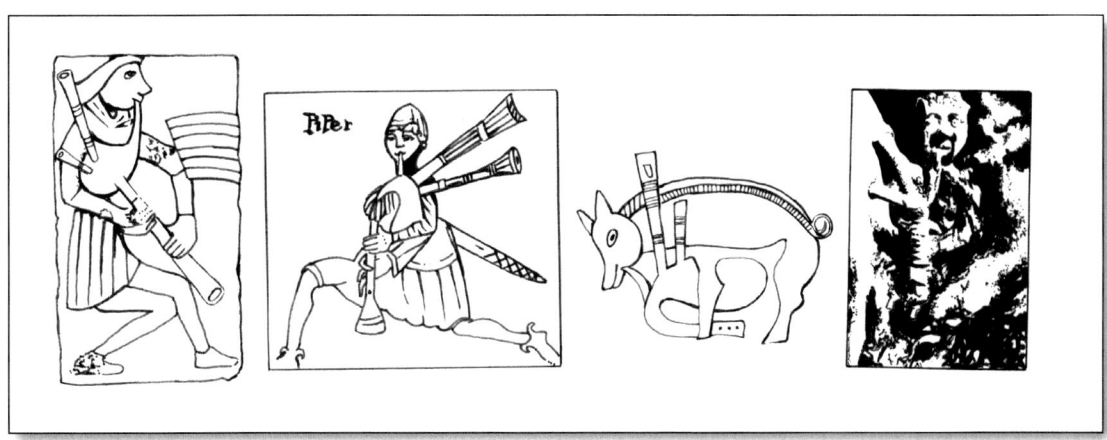

Sixteenth century depictions of pipers by native Irish artists (as discussed in the text) (Author's drawing)

In his description of the Irish manner of fighting, written in the early 1540s, Paolo Giovio places the piper among the galloglass, 'where the battle stands,' 'Out from among these [galloglass], while the battle stands disposed in the middle of the field and the bagpiper plays, the light infantry rushes from the wings and fights with darts and arrows which they fire from short wooden bows.'[28] Rather unexpectedly, he adds, 'when the battle-signal calls to arms. They spark battle not with the sound of a trumpet, but with the bellowing of a huge twisted wooden horn [*ligneae buccinae*].' This is intended to mean a separate instrument to the bagpipe, for which he uses the standard Latin terminology, *utriculario tibicine*. Very large wooden horns were common enough among pastoral mountain communities from the Carpathians to the Alps. And early depictions of the Swiss alphorn show a large, crooked wooden horn, spirally wrapped with split willow bindings, which give it a twisted appearance. Giovio's 'huge' or 'great' wooden horn is reminiscent of these early depictions of the alphorn. Considering the importance of cattle herding in Ireland, it is perhaps not surprising to find something similar in an Irish context, although this is our only reference to it. Those of the kern who served as *stocaire*, or horn blowers, are assumed to have carried animal horns, as depicted in Dürer's well-known watercolour sketch of Irish men of war.

---

28   Harris, 'Paolo Giovio', p.287–8.

Wilde Irishe Living History Group

Wilde Irishe Living History Group photograph

Wilde Irishe is a living history group centred in the Mid-Atlantic States of the USA. It portrays Irish military and civilian life of the sixteenth century, working with its English counterparts. Wilde Irishe welcomes those interested in various interpretations, such as musical and clergy.

Appendix I

Muster of the Earl of Ormond's Kern, 1544

(Source: T. Blake Butler, 'King Henry VIII's Irish Army List', *The Irish Genealogist*, vol. 1, no. 1 (1937), pp.6–7.)

KERNE TO BE TRANSPORTED INTO INGLANDE TO SERVE THE KYNG	
Therle of Ormondes Kerne	
Pyers Butler, Capytayne	James Robynnet, Peticapitayne
Partric Pursel	Shane McMaghies
Gerald Claragh	Shane Odowlan
Teg Omurgho	Waler Ohelan
Edmund Meaghir	William Brennagh
Donogh Omorgho	Piers McJames
Donogh Ohiky	Robert McOliver
William McMoritagh	Edmund Comerford
Hugh McLissey	Thomas Sortall
Piers Fiz Walter	James Cantwell
Oliver Fiz Willm	Robert Pursell
Shane Logh	Robert Roo Pursell
Teg Oboy	Thomas Pursell
Tirrelagh Gukky	Shane Obergyn
William Grennagh	Gilpatric Piper
Philip McPurcel	Shane McThomas
Piers Cantwel	Shane McRobert
Ric Fiz Piers	Donel Obrowe
Dermot Duf McShane	Dermot Olahiff
William Duf McDonogh	Ulic Nyshure
Edmund Cantwel	Donel Oshee
Ric McManus	William O Kerel
Ric Fiz John Butler	Mauric O Shee
William McReymud	William Oge Omaghir
William Fannyng	Malaghlyn Omaghir

MUSTER OF THE EARL OF ORMOND'S KERN, 1544

Piers Fiz John Butler	Neile McGuire
Walter Fiz Richard	William Boy
Piers Power	William Ketting
Jordon Comyn	Donogh Odure
Patric Gangagh Laffan	James Ohedian
William Laffin	Edmund Oge
Gonns	
Edward Sortall	Gerald Tallon
William Reynalde	William McShane
Molaghlen O Kelly	Teg Ohiky
Ric Downey	Teg Obelan
Shane McDonel	Shane Roo Mars
Walter Archer	William O Shee
Conor Omalackney	Mylis Croke
Nicholas Flemyng	Mahon Ohaly
Ric Fiz Piers	Wm McTeg Gdure
Item XX Boies.	Sm^n LXXX Kerne

Annother C Kerne of the Erle of Ormondes.	
Edmud Purcell, Capitayn	Patric Archdeacon, Peticapitayne
Gerald Brennan	Patricke Nolan
Edmonde Kavenagh	Donogh Ocurren
Geffery Lount	Wyllyam Fyn
Nicholas Dobbyn	Callowe Piper
Nele McCostigen	John Odoran
Patricke Fitz Donell	Gylly Duff Odowde
Nele Boy Taylor	Ullicke Stonden
Sir Pyers Byrgen	Bayer Rothe
Donogh McEdmond	Thomas Purcell
John Lonyaghyr	Donogh Lonyaghan
Teg Oflyan	Edmond Leyagh
Olyver Grace	Teg Leygh
Oliver Fitz James	Edmond Oloolge
Robert Fitz James	Walter Synnot
Donell More	Donell McShyre
Donogh Sherif	Pyers Marnell
Morgh Kynshelagh	John Fitz Davyd
Derby Rothe	Donogh Oge

'OF KERNS AND GALLOWGLASSES'

Malaghlyn Owre	Hue Roo
Art Omorgho	Morierlagh O Flyn
Walter Stondon	John Rothe
John Leygh	James Grace
Donogh Leygh	Richard Grace
James Commerford	Geffrey Cantwell
Teg Obryn	Morish Duff
Richard McCode	John Fitz Edmonde
Teg Odoran	Walter Fitz James
Richard Bane Grace	Robert Lont
Theobald Purcell	
Gonners	
Patricke Fitz Gerald, Peticapitayne	
Pyers Walshe	Wyllyam Fertere
Moriertagh Kavenagh	Nicholas Fitz Geron
Davyd Marres	Olyver Drilyn
James Annell	Davyd Fitz Morrishe
Patricke Purcell	Edmond Brothyr
Pyers McCode	Geralde Waton
Wyllyam Brenagh	Symon Marres
Redmond Roche	Arland Graunte
John Ohely	Connor McEgan
Donell Pitcagh	Wyllyam Marres
John Lye	Edward Tobyn
Sm^n LXXX Kerne Item Boyes XX Sm^n C	

Appendix II

The Rate of the Wages of the Galloglas as They be Paid in Money and Victualls, Rated After Their Own Confession Before Sir Thomas Cusack And Mr Secretary

At Dublin, 17º Novembris, 1568

Apon conference had with the captens of the three septes of the Queens Majesties Galloglasses by Sir Thomas Cusacke, Knighte, and John Chaloner, her Majesties Secretarie in this realme, by the apoyntement of the Lorde Deputie, to witt and certifie what the wages and entreteynement of every sparre of her Majesties Galloglasses oughte to be of dutie ordinarilye in every place where the same is leviable: they have related as foloweth, videlicet,

    That in every place where ther is to be levied an wholle quarters bonaghte vnto them, videlicet, for the wholle quarter of the yere they muste have of all places within Leymistre, Mounster or Vlster, for every sparre (which maketh two men), by the name of the quarters wages v^s viij^d Irishe, and the dayly dietts halfe in money, videlicit, a penny sterling the meale for eche man, which for the wholle quarter amounteth vnto xl^s vi^d ob. Irish, and also the other halfe diettes in victuels, videlicet, for every sparre xv. peckes and a hoope of bredd corne for six score and two cakes of bred after the rate of half an hoope of corne for every cake, and also xviij. score and six quartes of butter vnto those cakes, after the rate of three quartes of butter to every cake, and v. quartes to a gallon.

    And that in the Annaley and in Connaught where the wholle quarters bonaght is to be levied vnto them, they muste have for dietts halfe money and halfe dietts as aforeseid, but for the wages of every sparre more videlicet vij^s Irish.

    But where their bonaght is for lesse then the quarter of a yere; there they muste have but the wages and dietts of money onlye, and no victuells, that is to witt, wages as aforesaid, after the rate of the tyme; and dietts for the rate of the tyme only, after iiij^d sterling, per diem for every sparre and no more.

    According to the which rates the Bonaghtes due and leviable upon the Irishe Captenries and countreys by their enformacion conferred with the olde councell booke, so ferre furth as is there registred, and further by sighte of former warrants of their bonaghtes, the countrepaynes of captens indentures not yet perused amount as on the other syde may appere.

'OF KERNS AND GALLOWGLASSES'

Bonaghtes Due To The Queens Majestie For Her Galloglasses.

		Wages in Money	Dietts in Money	Dietts in Victuells
IN CONNAGHTE				
Sparres : iiij^{xx}	Apon Birmingeams contrey, for 14 dayes yerlye	iiij^l vi^s ij^d Irishe	xviij^l xiij^s iiij^d Sterling	Nothing
Sparres : iiij^{xx}	Apon Oconor Roo, for iiij^{or}. weekes	viij^l xij^s iiij^d Irishe	xxxvij^l vi^s viij^d Sterling	Nothing
Sparres : viij^{xx}	Apon Oreiglyes contrey, for the wholle quarter of a yere, yerely	lvj^l Irishe	ccxlij^l vi^s viij^d Sterling and	Bred corne, 2440 pecks. Butter, 58,560 quartes
Sparres : vi^{xx}	Apon the Annaley, for the wholle quarter of a yere, yerely	xlij^l Irishe	ciiij^{xx}ij^l x^s Sterling and	Bred corne, 1830 pecks. Butter, 43,920 quartes
IN MOUNSTRE				
Sparres : xl^{ti}	Apon Odwyers countrey for iiij^{or}. weekes yerlye	lxix^s ix^d Irishe	xviij^l xiij^s iiij^d Sterling	Nothing
Sparres : lx^{ti}	Apon Mac ybrien arra, for iiij^{or}. weeks yerly	v^l iiij^s vij^d ob. Irishe	xxviij^l Sterling	Nothing
Sparres : lx^{ti}	Apon Woney Omulryan, for iiij^{or}. weekes yerelye	v^l iiij^s vij^d ob. Irishe	xxviij^l Sterling	Nothing
Sparres : lx^{ti}	Apon Mac ybrien Ogownaghe, for iiij^{or}. weekes, yerlye	v^l iiij^s vij^d ob. Irishe	xxviij^l Sterling	Nothing
Sparres : iiij^{xx}	Apon William Burke quondam Hugh Burk, of Creigh Clenwilliam, for vi. weekes yerlye	x^l ix^s iij^d Irishe	lvi^l Sterling	Nothing
Sparres : vi^{xx}	Apon Burke, besides Lymerike, for vi. weekes yerlye	xv^l xiij^s x^d ob. Irishe	iiij^{xx}iiij^l Sterling	Nothing
Sparres : vj^{xx}	Apon O Kennedye, for a moneth yerly	v^l ix^s iij^d Irishe	lvi^l Sterling	Nothing
IN VLSTER				
Sparres : iiij^{xx} for his contrey, xl^{ti} for Ferney	Apon Mac Mahon, for a quarter of a yere, yerlye,	xxxiiij^l Irishe	ciiij^{xx}ij^l x^s Sterling	Bred corne 1830 peckes. Butter 43,920 quartes
Sparres : vi^{xx}	Apon Macgynisses contrey, for a quarter of a yere, yerly	xxxiiij^l Irishe	ciiij^{xx}ij^l x^s Sterling	Bred corne 1830 peckes. Butter 43,920 quartes
Sparres : xl^{ti}	Apon Ohanlons contrey, for lyke tyme yerlye	xi^l vi^s viij^d Irishe	lx^l xvi^s viij^d. Sterling	Bred corne 610 peckes. Butter 14,640 quartes
IN LEMISTER				
Sparres : vi^{xx}	Apon the Byrnes, for a quarter of a yere, yerly	xxxiv^l Irishe	ciiij^{xx}ij^l x^s Sterling	Bred corne 1830 peckes. Butter 43,920 quartes
Now the enrollment of the contracte sayth for iiij^{or}, vi, or viii weekes, or for a quarter of a yere, when and as need requireth, not specifieng yerlye				

THE RATE OF THE WAGES OF THE GALLOGLAS

Sparres : vi^{xx}	Apon McEdmond Duffs, Mc Vadak and Mcdavy Mores contreyes, for lyke tyme, yerely	xxxiv^l Irishe	ciiij^{xx}ij^l x^s Sterling	Bred corne 1830 pecks. Butter 43,920 quartes
Sparres : lx^{ti}	Apon the iij. septes of the Cavenaghes, for lyke tyme, yerely	xvij^l Irishe	xci^l v^s Sterling	Bred corne, 915 pecks. Butter, 21,960 quartes
Sparres : xl^{ti}	Apon the Morroughes contrey, for lyke tyme, yerlye	xi^l vi^s viij^d Irishe	lx^l xvi^s viij^d Sterling	Bred corne, 610 pecks. Butter, 14,640 quartes
Sparres : iiij^{xx}	Apon Vpperossirie for lyke tyme, yerlye	xxij^l xiij^s iiij^d Irish	cxxi^l xiij^s iiij^d Sterling	Bred corne, 1220 pecks. Butter, 29,280 quartes
Sparres : iiij^{xx}	Apon Ocaroll, for his owne contrey, for lyke tyme, yerlye	xxij^l xiij^s iiij^d Irish.	cxxi^l xiij^s iiij^d Sterling.	Bred corne, 1220 peckes. Butter, 29,280 quartes.
Sparres : xl^{ti}	Apon Mc Cowghlan's contrey, for lyke tyme, yerlye,	xi^l vi^s viij^d Irishe	lx^l xvj^s viij^d Sterling	Bred corne, 610 pecks. Butter, 14,640 quartes
Sparres : vi^{xx}	Apon O Kelleys contrey, for lyke tyme, yerlye	xxxiv^l Irishe	ciiij^{xx}ij^l x^s Sterling	Bred corne, 1830 pecks. Butter, 43,920 quartes
Sparres : iiij^{xx}	Apon Omoloyes contrey, for half a quater of a yere yerlye	xi^l vi^s viij^d Irishe	lx^l xvi^s viij^d. Sterling	Nothing
Sparres : iiij^{xx}	Apon Omaddens contrey, for a moneth yerlye	vi^l xix^s vi^d Irishe	xxxvij^l vi^s viij^d Sterling	Nothing
	Summa totalis of eche sorte of the seid bonaghts, according their titles and . . . . aforseyd	iiij^{c}li^l vij^s x^d Irishe for iij^{c}xxxviij^l x^s ix^d Sterling	ii^{m}iiij^{c}viij^l xv^s Sterling	Bred corne, 18,600 pecks for after ij^c sterling the peck, i^{m}viij^{c}lx^l sterling Butter after v quartes to the gallon, 89,304 gallons, for after xviij^d sterling the gallon, vi^{m}vi^{c}iiij^{xx} xvii^l sterling

FINIS[1]

---

[1] From: Richard Butler (ed.), 'The Rate of the Wages of the Galloglas' in Richard Butler, Acquilla Smith and James Hardiman (eds), *Tracts Relating to Ireland*, vol. 2 (Dublin: M. H. Gill, 1843), pp.87–90

Appendix III

Clergy Contributions to the Rising Out of the Pale, and the Militias of Corporate Towns

While the musters of the Pale listed in Chapter 3 occurred too late to include them, clergy had been liable to contribute to the Rising Out of the Pale prior to the dissolution of the monasteries after 1541. Thereafter, the duties of the abbots towards the common defense may have been acquired by those who took over their lands. The 1534 Ordinances of Ireland[1] specified that 'all lords, and other personnes of the spiritualitie, shall sende companyes to ostynges and journayes, in maner and forume folowynge.

>The Archbishop of Armagh, 16 able archers, or gonners, appoynted for the warre.
>The Archbishop of Dublin, 20
>The Bishop of Meath, 16
>The Lord of Saint Johns, 20
>The Bishop of Kildare, 8
>The Abbot of Saint Thomas Courte, 10
>The Abbot of Saint Mary Abbey, besides Dublin, 10
>The Abbot of Mellifont, 10
>The Deane of Dublin, 4

And every other person of that Church of Saint Patrick, that may dispend yearly 40 marks, one able archer.

>The Prior of Christs Church of Dublin, 3
>The Prior of Saint Johns of Dublin without Newgate, 2
>The Prior of All Saintes besides Dublin, 2
>The Prior of Saint Wulstones, 2
>The Prior of Holme Patrick, 2
>The Prior of Atherde, 2
>The Prior of Saint Johns besides Trim, 2
>The Abbot of Trim, 3
>The Abbot of Navan, 2

---

1 *State Papers: Henry VIII*, p.212, n.d., Ordinances of Ireland.

The Abbot of Bective, 2
The Prior of Saint Peters beside Trim, 1
The Proctors of Lanthony, 6
The Abbot of Duleek, 1
The Abbot of Kenlis, 1
The Prior of Saint Johns there, 1

Item, out of every 20 pounds by year, which the Abbot of Furnes may distend there, one archer.
The Archdeacon of Meath, 6. The Archdeacon of Nobber, 2. The Person of Trim, 2. The Person of Rathwier, 2.
Every other spiritual person out of 40 marks to send one able archer to the 'ostynge of rodeo' and those of 20 marks annually to send one archer.

Militias of Corporate Towns

The statues of Winchester, promulgated in England in 1285, had been applied to Ireland in 1308. These required towns to close their gates between sunset and sunrise, and to maintain a watch of six men at each gate. And all men between 16 and 60 were to be armed according to their rank and means.[2] A late medieval ballad in Norman-French, c. 1265, celebrating the walling of the town of Ross, claims the town had 363 crossbowmen, 1,200 archers, and 3,000 spearmen, led by 104 mounted men at arms.[3] The militia of Drogheda in 1468 consisted of 500 archers and 200 'poleaxes & pans'. The pans may mean panches, or breastplates. The poleaxes would presumably include bills, glaives and halberds. While the musters of The Pale listed in chapter 3 seem to consist entirely of mounted archers and horsemen, we know that those who were unable to shoot a bow would have carried bills and glaives.[4]

Thus, the militias of corporate towns could be considerable, but they were generally concerned with the security of their immediate vicinities, and only the city of Dublin and the towns of Drogheda and Dundalk contributed regularly to the Rising Out of the Pale. They were required to send archers to the Pale musters, and in 1519, Drogheda sent a sheriff with 24 bows, with a 'banner of footmen', and all of the bows of the county of Louth were to wait upon that banner, which banner itself was to wait upon that of Meath.[5] For the Muster of 1556, the city of Dublin supplied 60 archers and gonners well appoynted', while the town of Drogheda sent

---

2   M. D. O'Sullivan, *Old Galway* (Cambridge, Heffer & Son, 1942), p.33.
3   Graves and Hore, *Social State*, p.30.
4   Andrew Halpin, 'Archery in Medieval Ireland'. Unpublished University College Dublin PhD Thesis, 1990, p.75.
5   Ellis, *English Pale*, p.56.

40 'tall ffeallowes well appointid'.[6] The Ordinances of Ireland of 1534 cited above, specified that Dublin and Drogheda should 'sende companies of archers and gounners, with the Kynges Deputie, to ostynges and journayes', and adds that the cities of Limerick, Waterford, and Cork, and the towns of Wexford and Kilkenny shall do likewise when required.[7] These latter were often less cooperative.

In 1538 Lord Deputy Grey made a successful 'road' upon MacMurrough Kavanagh, and 800 horse and foot were furnished for the expedition by the city of Wexford.[8] Things were different in 1569, during the Butler Revolt, when Lord Deputy Sidney, en route for Cork with only 600 men, arrived at Clonmel. There he sent to Waterford, asking for a muster of citizens to accompany his passage over the mountains for three days. This was refused, though a few seamen and volunteers did come to the Deputy.[9]

The statues of Winchester were periodically renewed, with the caliver gradually supplanting the bow. As late as 1590, the town of Galway was defended by 500 'serviceable men', 200 of whom had calivers with some halberds, while the rest had only old bills.[10] Cox lists the muster of the city and town militias of Munster in 1584 as:[11]

City/Town	Shot	Billmen
The City of Waterford	100	300
Cork	100	300
Limerick	200	600
Clonmel	40	200
Killmallock	20	100
Fethard	20	100
Cashel	20	140
Kinsale	20	100
Carrick	20	40
Total	**540**	**1,880**

---

6 *Facsimiles,* Gilbert, pt. 4.1, Appendix V.
7 *State Papers: Henry VIII*, p.213, n.d., Ordinances of Ireland.
8 *Calendar of State Papers Ireland: Henry VIII, Edward VI, Mary and Elizabeth*, vol. 1, 1509–73, Hans Claude Hamilton (ed.), (London: Longman, Green, Longman & Roberts, 1860), p.46, 30 September, Wm Sayntloo to Sir Wm Kingston.
9 Cox, *Hibernia Anglicana*, p.334.
10 O'Sullivan, *Old Galway*, p.126.
11 Cox, *Hibernia Anglicana*, p.385.

Colour Plate Commentaries

A. MacGillapatrick Chieftain, *c.* 1510–40.

This figure represents Brian '*na Lúireach*' (of the mail coat) MacGillapatrick, Lord of Upper Ossory, who died in either 1511 or 1537. Hunt therefore dated the monument this figure is based on to *c.* 1510–40. It was carved by the same Rory O'Tunney workshops responsible for many of the Anglo-Irish knightly effigies seen elsewhere in this book. However, the harness is quite distinct, and shows the selective adoption of some features of Anglo-Irish armour by a neighbouring Irish Midland clan. Beneath everything, he wears a long sleeved coat, falling below the knees and split in front, which is not quilted and may be of leather. Over this is a knee-length hauberk of mail, the sleeves coming just below the elbows. This is covered by a pair of plates, in the Anglo-Irish style. He wears greaves, sabatons and gauntlets, while a pisane collar defends the neck. The forearms are unarmoured, and the pisane has no besagews attached, as usually seen on Anglo-Irish monuments. Likewise, the bascinet has no visor, in common with other representations of Gaelic armours. The sword belongs to Halpin Group 2, a type of Scottish origin, but in widespread use among the Gaelic Irish. It does not appear in the hands of Anglo-Norman figures, and the distribution of archaeological finds confirms its Gaelic associations. Group 2 swords have hollow pommels, and are remarkably light and nimble, weighing as little as 1½ pounds.

B. Mounted 'Spear' of the Pale, 1515.

A guidon bearing the arms of St. David of Wales was to identify the constable of a barony, and conventionally flew over 50 men. A larger standard of St George marked a shire warden, and conventionally flew over 100 men. A member of the Pale gentry, this horseman is armed according to the Ordinance of 1515. This called for a 'barbeyd horse', interpreted by Hunt as meaning simply a shaffron and crinet, with a steel saddle. He has a typically Irish 'side jack', meaning a long jack. Such jacks were valued for the protection they afforded the legs, and he therefore wears only greaves. Over the jack is a 'halbryk', a French term also used in contemporary Scotland to describe a back and breast with tasses. There is no armour on the arms, apart from the sleeves of the jack, although the left forearm is protected by a long gauntlet of a type also used by Irish kern. He wears a visored, tapered bascinet of the usual Irish form, with an ample pisane collar. He carries a 'Walshe spere', and his halbryk is fitted with a lance rest. Such men were always in short supply, and throughout this period English Governors in Ireland sought additional mounted spearmen from the Scottish and Welsh marches.

C. Standard Bearer of Irish kern, 1544.

All companies of kern sent to France in 1544 included a standard bearer. The Ordinance of 1519 required captains of kern to have a 'lytle gytton' (little guidon) for the kern to follow. This man carries the guidon of the Earl of Ormond, who contributed two companies of kern in 1544. In 1543, Lord Deputy St Leger described the kern as wearing only 'their shirts and small coats,' adding that in battle they wore only their shirts. A Venetian ambassador in 1554 described the kern as raising their shirts up, and fastening the sleeves at the shoulder when going into action. This is how they are depicted in the engravings of the lost Cowdray House paintings, which shows kern returning to the English camp from a cattle raid outside Boulogne. They are bare legged, their shirts shortened to various lengths by blousing them over the belt, while their arms appear quite bare. This last is interpreted as having the long sleeves of the *léine* fastened behind the shoulders. Laurent Vital had commented on the bare arms of Gaelic Irish soldiers in 1518, and it is evident that this was intended to facilitate mobility and weapon handling. He is armed with a long, good quality skean, and wears a type of early morion, sometimes called a cabasset, dating to the late fifteenth or early sixteenth centuries. The one pictured is based on an example in the Royal Armouries at Leeds, which is of North Italian manufacture and resembles those worn by many figures in the Cowdray House paintings, including some of the kern.

D. Irish Horseman, *c.* 1550.

The 'horseman's apparel' (*culaidh mharcaigh*) worn by this figure is essentially identical to the harness of a galloglass. It is seen on the late fifteenth century Burke effigy at Glinsk, Co. Galway, and is identical to the harness worn in the *Book of the de Burgos* by Seaán Mac Oilverus de Burgo, who was the Lower MacWilliam (*Mac William Íochtar*) from 1571 to 1580. The depiction of Seaán Mac Oilverus is not an anachronism, as a group of O'Reilly horsemen were seen wearing bascinets and mail with pisane collars in 1579. As described by Paolo Giovio in 1548, he is hurling a dart fitted with a finger loop, having switched his 'Spanish lance' (*lancea de jinete*) from his right hand to his left. Further darts were held tucked into the belt, or under the thigh. The lance was 12 feet in length, three feet longer than the usual 'horseman's staff' in use by the English. It was held in the middle and wielded overhead rather than being couched under the arm.

He has let go of the reins in order to handle his weapons, 'for nothing is so manageable as an Irish horse.' The smooth ambling gait of his Irish 'hobby' provides a stable platform from which to cast a dart.

E. Redshank, *c.* 1550

A redshank at the time of the battle of Glenshesk, 1565. The one-third of a Highland force that were armoured were 'cled in attounes and haberchounis, and knapshal bannets, as their laws beir.' This figure is so armed, with the habergeon 'side, almost eucn to their heeles.' He is based on the MacLeod monument at Rodel, dated 1528. Offensive weapons were 'twa-handit-swordis, bowis, dorlochis,' the *dorloch* being a fur quiver. The bow is identical to the English longbow, and English made bows were occasionally distributed by the King of Scots to his Island subjects. He also carries a bollock knife, as seen on a monument at Ardchattan that is dated 1502. The distinctive Highland dirk didn't appear until after 1600. There is no specific record of military servants accompanying Highland forces, possibly because of the limits imposed by the capacity of the galleys that transported them. But the proportions of one armed man to two unarmed men was equivalent to the proportions found in the Irish galloglass sparr.

F. Galloglass, *c.* 1570

This figure is based on plate IX in Derricke's *Image of Ireland* of 1581, illustrating a battle in which galloglass are fleeing from English shot. Some details are from the close parallel depiction of a galloglass on the Charter of the City of Dublin (from 1583), which I have argued elsewhere is likely by Derricke's own hand. He is a 'veteran soldier, reserved for the rear,' a senior man though not necessarily a captain. The silver foil appliqué decoration on his axe appears on the majority of surviving specimens, and was evidently thus not rare. A poem on Domhnaill Mac Suibhne of Fanad (ruled 1570–1619) says, 'an ogham inscription is on his axe whose bounty is victory,' and such an inscription has been represented here, notched along the shaft below the axe socket. His skull reflects Spencer's description of the character Grantorto, modelled on a galloglass, who wears a 'steel cap . . . of colour rusty brown.' The large upturned nasal is evident in Derricke's depictions and several other sources, is seen in Ucello's *Battle of San Romano* in the collection of the National Gallery in London, and is on a number of surviving Italian barbutes of the fifteenth century. It was also popular in the Iberian Peninsula, and its use in Ireland may reflect Spanish influence. The spreading crest is seen in several depictions of galloglass from the second half of the sixteenth century. They are generally assumed to be horsehair, but others seem to resemble feathers, and the antiquary W. R. Wilde suggested they might be cock feathers. The implications of masculine vigour would be in line with the use of otter skin to crest these Irish skulls, which is also documented. Trews of green kersey were provided to the Lord Deputy's personal galloglass in 1590, and this man wears trews of 'goose turd' green, as seen on the Dublin Charter galloglass. The brogues are a Lucas Type 5 variant found in excavations at Salterstown, Co. Londonderry, which closely parallel those shown in the Dublin Carter depiction, 'with a flap at the heel to pull them on.'

Flags Captions:

G.

1. The Earl of Kildare's Standard

The hoist of allegiance, nearest to the flag staff, displays the red cross on a white field indicative of loyalty to the Crown of England. The livery field is divided horizontally, white over red, and bears the earl's badge, blazoned a monkey proper, environed about the middle with a plain collar chained or. This badge and the earl's motto are carved into a mantelpiece from Kilkea Castle, dated 1573. The motto, *Crom aboo*, or *Crom Abú* (spelt barbarously on the standard), appears on transverse bands, countercharged. It translates as 'Croom [castle] to Victory.' Croom castle, in Co. Limerick, was a major seat of the Kildare branch of Geraldines.

2. The Earl of Desmond's Banner

The banner bears in chief the coronet of an Earl. The field bears the arms of the Earl of Desmond, blazoned ermine a saltire gules. The ermine field marks the cadet status of the Desmond branch of Geraldines. Kildare's banner bore a red saltire on a plain white field. The banner has a fringe alternating red and white. This, like the other Anglo-Irish banners and standards illustrated here, is based on the funeral entries in the rolls of Ulster's Office, now in the National Library of Ireland.

3. The Earl of Ormond's Standard

The hoist of allegiance, like that of Kildare, bears the cross of Saint George, indicating loyalty to the Crown. The livery field bears the badge of a falcon sitting on a plume of five ostrich feathers, surmounting a ducal coronet. The motto *Come Je Truove* appears on transverse bands, and means 'As I Find.'

H.

1. O'Neill's Banner

The O'Neills began using the heraldic device of a red hand *c.* 1350. The use of this ancient device was part of a propaganda campaign in support of the O'Neill's assumption of the prerogatives of the old Anglo-Norman Earldom

COLOUR PLATE COMMENTARIES

of Ulster, and their subsequent assertion of kingship over all Ulster. This was part of the Gaelic Revival, whereby lands lost by the Gaelic Irish were recovered and wider power was sought by Gaelic regional overlords. It has been pointed out that the red hand symbol appears in the arms of the DeBurgh Earls of Ulster, but its origin is doubtless much older. An elaborate series of traditions associate it with the descendants of Niall of the Nine Hostages, and it appears in the arms of his descendants in both Ireland and Scotland.

2. O'Donnell's Banner

Hugh MacManus O'Donnell made his submission to Lord Deputy Henry Sidney in 1567, receiving this coat of arms. The sign of the cross was traditionally held to have been inscribed by Saint Patrick on the shield of Connell, a son of Niall of the Nine Hostages and an early ancestor of the O'Donnells. Regardless of the veracity of this story, the O'Donnells had likely used a cross of some design long before the adoption of English heraldry after Hugh's submission in 1567. Hugh was married to Iníon Dubh MacDonald, a daughter of James MacDonald of Dunnyveg, and it is likely the adoption of the particular charge of a hand holding a cross crosslet fitchée was influenced by MacDonald symbolism.

3. MacCarthy Mór's Banner

The banner bears the charge of a red stag on a white field. This is an ancient totem of the Eóghanacht Kings of Munster. It was likely adopted into formal heraldry when Donal MacCarthy was created Earl of Clancare in 1565, under the surrender and regrant scheme. Like many Gaelic arms, it consists of a simple totem on a white sheet, indicative of its ancient use as a battle flag, another example of this kind being the oak tree of the O'Connors.

4. Papal Flag of James Fitzmaurice Fitzgerald

Symbols of the Counter-Reformation first appear on Irish battlefields in 1579, during the second Desmond Rebellion. This figure is based on a reconstruction by G. A. Hayes-McCoy of the banner brought to Ireland by James Fitzmaurice Fitzgerald, a cousin of the Earl of Desmond, when he landed at Dingle to infuse the local power struggle with broader religious meaning. The banner, about an ell square, bears the figure of Christ crucified and a golden dragon on a red field, the latter being the arms of Pope Gregory XIII. The Latin motto is translated as 'In all Tribulation and Difficulty our Hope is Jesus and Mary.'

Bibliography

Archive Sources

Chester City Records Office: Mayor's Military Papers, 1/1-2, Muster Roll of Kern, 1550

National Folklore Collection 279: 162-3. Glengariff School, County Cork, 1937/1938. Teacher: Caoimhín Ó Séaghdha

Official Documents

Calendar of the Carew Manuscripts, vol. 1, 1515-1574, vol. 2 1575-1588, J. S. Brewrer and William Bullen (eds), (London: Longman & Co., 1867)

Calendar of the Carew Manuscripts, Miscellaneous, 'The Book of Howth,' J. S. Brewrer and William Bullen (eds), (London: Longman & Co., 1871)

Calendar of Ormond Deeds, vol. 3 1413-1509, vol. 4 1510-1546, vol. 5 1547-1584, Edmund Curtis (ed.), (Dublin: The Stationery Office, 1935)

Calendar of State Papers Ireland: Henry VIII, Edward VI, Mary and Elizabeth, vol. 1 1509-73, Hans Claude Hamilton (ed.), (London: Longman, Green, Longman & Roberts, 1860)

Calendar of State Papers Ireland: Elizabeth, vol. 2 1574-1585, Hans Claude Hamilton (ed.), (London: Longmans, Green, Reader and Dyer, 1867)

Calendar of State Papers Ireland: Elizabeth, vol. 3 1586-88, July, Hans Claude Hamilton (ed.) (London: Longman & Co., 1877)

Calendar of State Papers Ireland: Elizabeth, vol. 4 1588, August-1592, September, Hans Claude Hamilton (ed.) (London: Longman, 1885)

Calendar of State Papers Ireland: Elizabeth, vol. 5 1592, October-1596, June, Hans Claude Hamilton (ed.), (London: Eyre and Spottiswoode, 1890)

Calendar of State Papers Ireland: Elizabeth, vol. 8, 1599, April-1600, February, Ernest George Atkinson (ed.), (London: HMSO, 1899)

Calendar of State Papers, Spain (Simancas). vol. 4 1587-1603, Martin A. S. Hume (ed.), (London: Eyre and Spottiswoode, 1899)

Facsimiles of National Manuscripts of Ireland, part 4.1, John Gilbert (ed.), (Dublin: Public Records Office, 1884)

Letters and Papers, Henry VIII, Vol. 12 part. 2 (London: Eyre and Spottiswoode, 1891)

Manuscripts of Charles Haliday Esq., of Dublin, Acts of the Privy Council in Ireland, 1556–1572, J. T. Gilbert (ed.), (London: Eyre and Spottiswoode, 1897)

State Papers Published Under the Authority of His Majesty's Commission: King Henry VIII, vol. 2 part 3. *Correspondence of the Governments of England and Ireland, 1515–1538* (London: HMSO, 1834)

Printed Primary Sources

Baldwin, William (William A. Ringler Jr and Michael Flachman, eds) *Beware the Cat*, (San Marino: Huntington Library Press, 1988)

Bale, Johan (Peter Happé and John King eds), *The Vocacyon of Johan Bale, 1553*, (Binghamton: Renaissance English Text Society, 1990)

Borlase, Edmund, *The History of the Execrable Irish Rebellion, trac'd from many preceding acts to the grand eruption, the 23 of October, 1641, and thence pursued to the Act of Settlement, 1662* (London: Robert Clavel, 1680)

Buchanan, George, *History of Scotland, Rerum Scoticarum Historia, 1582* (London: Edw. Jones, 1690)

Burt, Edmund, *Letters from the North of Scotland*, vol. 2 (Edinburgh: William Patterson 1876)

Camden, William, *Britain, or a Chorographical Description of the most flourishing Kingdomes, England, Scotland, and Ireland* (London: F. Kingston, R. Young and I. Legatt, for George Latham, 1637)

Cox, Richard, *Hibernia Anglicana, or The history of Ireland*, vol. 1 (London: H. Clark, 1689)

de Peralta, Juan Suárez, *Tratado de Caballería de la Gineta y de la Brida* (Seville: 1580)

Derricke, John, *The Image of Irelande, With a Discouerie of Woodkarne* (London: John Daie, 1581)

Dymmock, John, 'A Treatice of Ireland' in *Tracts Relating to Ireland*, vol. 2 (Dublin: M H. Gill, 1842)

Froissart, Jean (Thomas Johnes, trans.), *Chronicles of England, France, Spain and adjoining countries*, vol. 2, trans. Thomas Johnes (London: H. G. Bohn, 1857).

Gerald of Wales, (A. B. Scott and F. X. Martin trans.), *Expugnatio Hibernica*, (Dublin: Royal Irish Academy, 1978)

Harrington, Sir John (Thomas Park ed.) *Nugae Antiquae, Vol. I*, (London: J. Wright, 1804)

Holinshed, Raphael, *Holinshed's Chronicles of England, Scotland, and Ireland*, vol. 3 (London: J. Johnson, 1807)

Holinshed, Raphael (Liam Miller and Eileen Power eds), *Holinshed's Irish Chronicle, 1577*, (Dublin: Dolmen Press, 1979)

Holinshed, Raphael, *Holinshed's Chronicle, 1587*, vol. 6 (Abingdon: Routledge, 1965)

Kirkwood, Rev. James, *A Collection of Highland Rites and Customs* (Trowbridge: Redwood Burn Ltd, 1975)

Lindesay of Pistcottie, Robert (J. G. MacKay ed.), *History and Chronicles of Scotland*, vol. 12. (London & Edinburgh: William Blackwood & Sons, 1899)

Longfield, Ada K., (ed.), *Fitzwilliam Accounts 1560–65* (Dublin: Irish Manuscripts Commission, Dublin 1960)

MacCarthy, B. (ed.), *Annala Uladh, Annals of Ulster* (Dublin: Her Majesty's Stationery Office, 1895)

Monstrelet, Enguerrand de (Thoas Johnes trans.), *The Chronicles*, vol. 5, (London: Longman, Hurst, Rees, Orm and Brown, 1810)

Moryson, Fynes, *Itinerary*, 7 vols, (Glasgow: James MacLehose and Sons, 1907–1908)

Moryson, Fynes (Litton Falkiner ed.), *Itinerary,* vol. 2 *The Rebellion in Ireland, AD 1600*, (London: J. Beale, 1907)

O'Clery, Lughaid (Paul Walsh ed.), *Beatha Aodh Ruadh Uí Domhnaill (The Life of Hugh Roe O'Donnell)*, (Dublin: Irish Texts Society, 1948)

O'Donovan, John (ed.), *Annals of the Kingdom of Ireland, by the Four Masters*, 7 vols, (Dublin: Hodges, Smith & Co., 1856)

O'Donovan, John (ed.), *Annals of Ireland: Three Fragments by Dubhaltach Mac Firbisigh* (Dublin: University Press, 1860)

O'Grady, Standish Hayes (ed.), *Caithréim Thoirdhealbhaigh, The Triumphs of Turlough*, 2 vols (London: Irish Texts Society 26 and 27, 1929)

O'Sullivan Bere, Don Philip (Matthew J. Byrne ed.), *Ireland Under Elizabeth*, (Dublin: Sealy, Bryers & Walker, 1903)

Perrot, Sir James Herbert Wood ed.), *The Chronicle of Ireland, 1584–1608*, (Dublin: Stationery Office, 1933)

Piers, Henry (Charles Vallency ed.), *A Chorographical Description on the County of Westmeath, 1682*, Collecteana Rebus Hibernicus, vol. 1, no. 1 (Dublin: L. White, 1786)

Polydore Virgil (Dana Sutton ed.), *Anglica Historia, Book XIII*, 1555, The Philological Museum, University of Birmingham. <https://philological.cal.bham.ac.uk/polverg/>

Rich, Barnaby, *A Martial Conference between Captaine Skill and Captaine Pill* (London: John Oxenbridge, 1598), Early English Books Online Text Creation Partnership, 2011)<http://quod.lib.umich.edu/e/eebo2/A10710.0001.001?view=toc>

Rich, Barnaby, *A New Description of Ireland* (London: William Jaggard, 1610)

Spencer, Edmund, *A View of the State of Ireland* (Dublin: Laurence Flyn, 1763)

Spencer, Edmund, *A View of the Present State of Ireland*, (1596), CELT, the Corpus of Electronic Texts. <https://celt.ucc.ie/published/E500000-001/>

Stafford, Thomas (Standish O'Grady ed.), *Pacata Hibernia*, 2 vols, (London: Downey & Co., 1896)
Stanihurst, Richard (John Barry and Hiram Morgan eds), *De Rebus in Hibernia Gestis*, (Cork: Cork University Press, 2014)
Tapia y Salcedo, Gregorio, *Exercicios de la Gineta al Principe Nuestro Señor d. Baltasar Carlos* (Madrid: D. Diaz, 1643)
Tuchet, James, *The memoirs of James, Lord Audley, Earl of Castlehaven, his engagement and carriage in the wars of Ireland from the year 1642 to the year 1651 written by himself*, (London: Henry Brome, 1680)
Vital, Laurent (Dorothy Convery trans., Hiram Morgan, ed.), 'Ireland, an Extract from Le Premier Voyage de Charles-Quint en Espagne, de 1517 à 1518', at CELT, Corpus of Electronic Texts Edition: T500000-001, p.288. <https://celt.ucc.ie./published/T500000-001.html>
Walsh, Paul, *Leabhar Chlainne Suibhe* (Dublin: Dollard's Printing House, 1920)
Williams, N. J. A. (ed.), *Parlement Chloinne Tomáis* (Dublin: Dublin Institute for Advanced Studies, 1981)

Printed Sources

Bagwell, Richard, *Ireland Under the Tudors*, 3 vols (London: Longmans, Green, and Co., 1885–1890)
Baker, Sir Samuel White, *The Nile tributaries of Abyssinia: and the Sword Hunters of the Hamran Arabs* (London: MacMillan and Co., 1867)
Bartley, J. O., *Teague, Shenkin and Sawney* (Cork: Cork University Press, 1954)
Bergin, Osborn (ed.), *Irish Bardic Poetry* (Dublin: Dublin Institute for Advanced Studies, 1970)
Beresford-Ellis, Peter, *Erin's Blood Royal* (New York: Palgrave, 2002)
Berleth, Richard, *The Twilight Lords* (New York: Alfred A. Knopf, 1978)
Berry, James, *Tales of Mayo and Connemara* (Salem: Salem House, 1984)
Blair, Claude, *Scottish Weapons and Fortifications, 1100–1800* (Edinburgh: John Donald, 1981)
Blanch, Lesly, *Sabres of Paradise* (New York: Carrol and Graf, 1984)
Brady, Ciaran, 'The Captains' Games: Army and Society in Elizabethan Ireland' in Thomas Bartlett and Keith Jeffery (eds), *A Military History of Ireland* (Cambridge: Cambridge University Press, 1997), pp.116–135.
Breen, Colin, *The Gaelic Lordship of the O'Sullivan Beare: A Landscape Cultural History* (Dublin: Four Courts Press, 2005)
Bunting, Edward, *A General Collection of Ancient Irish Music* (London: Clement & Co., 1809)
Burt, Edmund, *Letters from the North of Scotland*, vol. 2 (Edinburgh: William Patterson, 1876)
Butler, Richard (ed.), 'The Rate of the Wages of the Galloglas' in Richard Butler, Acquilla Smith and James Hardiman (eds), *Tracts Relating to Ireland*, vol. 2 (Dublin: M. H. Gill, 1843), pp.87–90

Butler, William, *Gleanings From Irish History* (London: Longmans, Green and Co., 1925)

Caldwell, David, 'Having the Right Kit: West Highlanders fighting in Ireland' in Seán Duffy (ed.), *The World of the Galloglass* (Dublin: Four Courts Press, 2007), pp.145–168

Caldwell, David, *Scottish Weapons and Fortifications, 1100–1800* (Edinburgh: John Donald, 1981)

Campbell, Lord Archibald, *Argyllshire Galleys* (London: Charles J. Clark, 1906)

Cannan, Fergus, *Galloglass, 1250–1600: Gaelic Mercenary Warrior* (London: Opsrey, 2010)

Carey, Vincent P., *Surviving the Tudors: The Wizard Earl of Kildare and English Rule in Ireland, 1537–1586* (Dublin: Four Courts Press, 2002)

Carman, W. Y., *British Military Uniforms from Contemporary Pictures* (London: Leonard Hill, 1957)

Chambers, Anne, *Granuaile: The Life and Times of Grace O'Malley, c. 1530–1603* (Dublin: Wolfhound Press, 1983)

Collectanea de Rebus Albanicis, Iona Club, eds (Edinburgh: Thomas G. Stevenson, 1847)

Collins, Arthur, *Letters and Memorials of State*, vol. 1 (London: T. Osborne, 1746)

Corkery, Danile, *The Fortunes of the Irish Language* (Cork: Mercer Press Ltd, 1956)

Cunningham, Bernadette and Raymond Gillespie, *Stories from Gaelic Ireland* (Dublin: Four Courts Press, 2003)

Donnelly, Colm J., Eileen M. Murphy, 'Violence in Later Medieval Ireland: the Osteoarchaeological Evidence and its Historical Context' in Eve Campbell, Elizabeth Fitzpatrick and Audrey Horning (eds), *Becoming and Belonging in Ireland AD c. 1200–1600* (Cork: Cork University Press, 2018), pp.108–128.

Drummond, James, *Ancient Scottish Weapons* (Edinburgh/London: George Waterston & Sons, 1881)

Duffy, Christopher, *The '45: Bonnie Prince Charlie and the Untold Story of the Jacobite Rising* (London: Cassell, 2003)

Duffy, Seán (ed.), *Medieval Ireland: An Encyclopaedia*, (New York: Routledge, 2005)

Dunbar, J. Telfer, *History of Highland Dress* (London: B. T. Batsford, Ltd., 1979)

Dunleavy, Mariead, *Dress In Ireland* (London: B. T. Batsford, Ltd, 1989)

Edwards, David (ed.), *Campaign Journals of the Elizabethan Irish Wars* (Dublin: Irish Manuscripts Commission, 2014)

Edwards, David, 'The Escalation of Violence in Sixteenth Century Ireland' in David Edwards, Pádraig Leinihan, Clodagh Tait (eds), *Age of Atrocity: Violence and Political Conflict in Early Modern Ireland* (Dublin: Four Courts Press, 2007)

Edwards, David, *The Ormond Lordship in County Kilkenny, 1515–1642* (Dublin: Four Courts Press, 2003)

Ellis, Steven G., *England's Irish Pale, 1470–1550: The Making of a Tudor Region* (Woodbridge: The Boydell Press, 2021)

Ellis, Steven G., 'The Tudors and the Origins of the Modern Irish States: A Standing Army' in Thomas Bartlett and Keith Jeffery (eds), *A Military History of Ireland* (Cambridge: Cambridge University Press, 1997), pp.136–159.

Falkiner, C. Litton, *Illustrations of Irish History* (London: Longmans, Green, and Co., 1904)

Falls, Cyril, *Elizabeth's Irish Wars* (London, Methuen & Co., Ltd, 1950)

Farewell, James, *The Irish Hudibras, or Fingallian Prince* (London: Richard Baldwin, 1689)

Feuillerat, Albert, *Documents Relating to the Revels at Court in the time of King Edward VI and Queen Mary, 1550–54* (Louvain: A. Uystpruyst, 1914)

Fissell, Mark Charles, *English Warfare, 1511–1647*, (New York: Routledge, 2001)

Fitzpatrick, Elizabeth, 'Gaelic Service Kindreds and the Landscape Identity of Lucht Tighe' in Eve Campbell, Elizabeth Fitzpatrick and Audrey Horning (eds), *Becoming and Belonging in Ireland AD c. 1200–1600* (Cork: Cork University Press, 2018), pp.167–188.

Fitzpatrick, Elizabeth, *Royal Inauguration in Gaelic Ireland, c. 1100–1600: A Cultural Landscape Study* (Woodbridge: The Boydell Press, 2004)

Fitzsimmons, Fiona, 'Fosterage and Gossiprid in Late Medieval Ireland' in Patrick J. Duffy, David Edwards and Elizabeth Fitzpatrick (eds), *Gaelic Ireland: Land, Lordship & Settlement c. 1250–1600* (Dublin: Four Courts Press, 2001), pp.138–149.

Frame, Robin, 'Military Service in the Lordship of Ireland, 1290–1360' in Robert Bartlett and Angus MacKay (eds.), *Medieval Frontier Societies* (Oxford: Clarendon Press, 1989)

Freeman, A. Martin (ed.), *The Compossicion Booke of Conought* (Dublin: The Stationery Office, 1936)

Flavin, Susan, *Consumption and Culture in Sixteenth century Ireland: Saffron, Stockings and Silk* (Woodbridge: Boydell & Brewer Ltd, 2014)

Fletcher, Alan J., *Drama, Performance, and Polity in Pre-Cromwellian Ireland* (Toronto and Buffalo: University of Toronto Press, 2000)

Frame, Robin, 'Military Service in the Lordship of Ireland, 1290–1360' in Robert Bartlett and Angus MacKay (eds.), *Medieval Frontier Societies* (Oxford: Clarendon Press, 1989), pp.101–126.

Goodall, Daphne Machin and Dent, A. A., *The Foals of Epona* (London: Galley Press, 1962)

Grant, I. F., *The MacLeods: The History of a Clan* (Edinburgh: Holmes McDougal Ltd, 1959)

Grant, I. F. and Hugh Cheape, *Periods in Highland History* (London: Shepherd-Walwyn, 1987)

Greene, David, *Dunaire Mhéig Uidhir: The Poembook of Cú Connacht Mág Uidhir* (Dublin: Dublin Institute for Advanced Studies, 1972)

Gresh, Robert, *The Skean: The Distinctive Fighting Knife of Gaelic Ireland, 1500–1700* (Atglen, Schiffer, 2023)

Grossart, Alexander B. (ed.), *The Complete Works in Verse and Prose of Edmund Spencer*, vol. IX, (London: Hazell, Watson, and Viney, 1884)

Halpin, Andrew, *Weapons and Warfare in Viking and Medieval Dublin*, Medieval Dublin Excavations 1962–81, ser. B, vol. 9 (Dublin: National Museum of Ireland, 2008)

Hamilton, William, *Letters Concerning the North Coast of the Country of Antrim* (Dublin: George Bonham, 1790)

Hayes-McCoy, G. A., *A History of Irish Flags from the Earliest Times* (Boston: G. K. Hall & Co., 1979)

Hayes-McCoy, G. A., *Irish Battles: A Military History of Ireland* (Dublin: Gill and Macmillan, 1980)

Hayes-McCoy, G. A., *Scots Mercenary Forces in Ireland, 1565–1603* (Dublin: Burns Oates & Washbourne, 1937)

Hayes O'Grady, *Silva Gadelica*, vol. 2 (Edinburgh: Williams and Norgate, 1892)

Henry, Grainne, *The Irish Military Community in Spanish Flanders, 1586–1621* (Dublin: Irish Academic Press, 1992)

Hill, George, *An Historical Account of the MacDonnells of Antrim* (Belfast: Archer & Sons, 1873)

Hodgson, John Crawford, ed., *Six North Country Diaries* (Edinburgh: Blackwood & Sons, 1910)

Hogan, Edmund, *The Description of Ireland in Anno 1598* (Dublin: H. M. Gill & Son, 1878)

Hore, Herbert Philip, *History of the Town and County of Wexford* (London: Elliot Stock, 1912)

Hore, Herbert and James Graves (eds), *The Social State of the Southern and Eastern Counties of Ireland in the Sixteenth Century* (Dublin: University Press, 1870)

Hunt, John, *Irish Medieval Figure Sculpture: 1200–1600*, vol. 1 (Dublin: Irish University Press, 1974)

Joyce, P. W., *A Social History of Ancient Ireland*, vol. 1 (New York: Longmans, Greene & Co., 1904)

Kelleher, Connie, 'The Gaelic O'Driscoll Lords of Baltimore, Co. Cork: Settlement, Economy and Conflict in a Maritime Landscape' in Linda Doran and James Lyttleton (eds), *Lordship in Medieval Ireland*, (Dublin: Four Courts Press, 2007), pp.130–159.

Kennedy, Patrick, *The Banks of the Boro* (Dublin: McGlashan & Gill, 1875)

James Kirkwood (J. L. Campbell ed.), *A Collection of Highland Rites and Customs, c. 1699*, ed. J. L. Campbell (Rochester: D. S. Bewer, Ltd, 1975)

Knott, Eleanor, *The Bardic Poems of Tadhg Dall Ó Huiginn* (London: Irish Texts Society, 1922)

Knox, Hubert, *The History of the County of Mayo* (Dublin: Hodges, Figgis & Co., 1908)

Leask, H. G., *Irish Castles and Castellated Houses* (Dundalk: Dundalgan Press, 1995)

Lennon, Colm, *Elizabethan Ireland: The Incomplete Conquest* (Dublin: Gill & Macmillan, 2005)

Lenox-Conyngham, Melosina, *Diaries of Ireland: An Anthology, 1590–1987*, (Dublin: Lilliput Press, 1998), p.6.

Loeber, Rolf, 'An Architectural History of Gaelic Castles and Settlements, 1370–1600' in Patrick J. Duffy, David Edwards and Elizabeth Fitzpatrick (eds), *Gaelic Ireland: Land, Lordship & Settlement c. 1250–1600* (Dublin: Four Courts Press, 2001), pp.271–314.

Logan, James, *The Scottish Gael* (London: Smith, Elder, and Co., 1831)

Longfield, Ada K., *Anglo-Irish Trade in the Sixteenth Century* (London: George Routledge & Sons Ltd, 1929)

Loughnane, Rory, and Maley, Willy (eds), *Celtic Shakespeare: The Bard and the Borderers* (London: Routledge, 2013)

Lucas, A. T., *Cattle in Ancient Ireland* (Kilkenny: Boethius Press, 1989)

Mac Airt, Seán, *The Book of the O'Byrnes* (Dublin: Dublin Institute for Advanced Studies, 1944)

McAlister, Victoria, *The Irish Tower House: Society, Economy and Environment, 1300–1650* (Manchester: Manchester University Press, 2019)

MacBain, Alexander, and John Kennedy, eds., *Relique Celticae*, vol. 1, (Inverness: Northern Counties Publishing Company, 1894)

MacCarthy, Daniel, *The Life and Letters of Florence MacCarthy Reagh* (London: Harrison and Sons, 1867)

McClintock, H. F., *Handbook on the Traditional Old Irish Dress* (Dundalk: Dundalgan Press, 1958)

McClintock, H. F., *Old Irish and Highland Dress* (Dundalk: Dundalgan Press, 1943)

Mac Curtain, Margaret, 'A Lost Landscape: the Geraldine Castles and Tower Houses of the Shannon Estuary' in John Bradley (ed.), *Settlement and Society in Medieval Ireland* (Kilkenny: Boethius Press, 1988), pp.429–444.

McGettigan, Darren, *Red Hugh O'Donnell and the Nine Years' War* (Dublin: Four Courts Press, 2005)

Mac Eiteagáin, Darren, 'The Renaissance and the Late Medieval Lordship of Tír Chonaill' 1461–1555' in William Nolan, Liam Ronayne and Mariead Dunleavy (eds), *Donegal History and Society: Interdisciplinary Essays on the History of an Irish County* (Dublin: Geography Publications, 1995), pp.203–228.

McKenna, Lambert, *The Book of Maguaran* (Dublin: Dublin Institute for Advanced Studies, 1947)

MacLysaght, Edward, *Irish Families, Their Names, Arms and Origins* (Dublin: Irish Academic Press, 1985)

M'Sparran, Archibald, *The Irish Legend, or M'Donnell and the Norman de Burgos* (Coleraine: J. M'Combie, 1854)

Maginn, Christopher and Stephen G. Ellis, *The Tudor Discovery of Ireland* (Dublin: Four Courts Press, 2015)

Mahaffy, J. P., 'Two Early Tours of Ireland' in Members of Trinity College, Dublin, eds, *Hermathena*, vol. 40 (London: Longmans, Green & Co., 1914), pp.1–16.

Maidment, James (ed.), *The Spottiswoode Miscellany: A Collection of Original Papers and Tracts*, vol. 1 (Edinburgh: Alex. Laurie & Co., 1844)

Marsden, John, *Galloglass: Hebredian and West Highland Mercenary Warrior Kindreds in Medieval Ireland* (East Linton: Tuckwell Press, 2003)

Martin Martin, *Description of the Western Islands of Scotland* (London: Andrew Bell, 1703), p.104.

Maxwell, Constancia, *Irish History From Contemporary Sources* (London: George Allen & Unwin, 1923)

Michel, Francisque, *Les Écossais en France, Les Français en Écosse*, vol. 2 (London: Trübner & Co., 1862)

Moore, Thomas, *History of Ireland*, vol. 2 (London: Longman, Orme, Brown, Green & Longmans, 1837)

Morley, Henry, *Ireland under Elizabeth and James the First*, (London: G. Routledge & Sons, Ltd, 1890)

Mullin, T. H. and J. E. Mullan, *The Ulster Clans* (Belfast: The University Press, 1966)

Murray, John, *Chronicles of the Atholl and Tullibardine Families*, vol. 1 (Edinburgh: Ballantyne Press, 1908)

Nicholls, Kenneth, *Gaelic and Gaelicised Ireland in the Middle Ages* (Dublin: Gill and Macmillan, 1972)

Nicholls, Kenneth, 'Scots Mercenary Kindreds in Ireland, 1230–1600' in Seán Duffy (ed.), *The World of the Galloglass* (Dublin: Four Courts Press, 2007), pp.86–105.

O'Connor, G. B., *Elizabethan Ireland, Native and English* (Dublin: Sealy, Bryers and Walker, 1907)

O'Curry, Eugene, *On the Manners and Customs of the Ancient Irish*, vol. 1 (Dublin: John F. Fowler, 1873)

O'Donnelly, Seán, *The Early History of Piping in Ireland, Na Píobairí Uilleann Teoranta and the Royal Scottish Pipe Band Association, N.I. Branch* (Newtownabbey: Oakdene Services, 2001)

O'Dowd, Anne, *Straw, Hay & Rushes in Irish Folk Tradition* (Dublin: Irish Academic Press, 2015)

O'Flaherty, Roderic, *The Territory of West of H-Iar Connaught*, ed. James Hardiman (Dublin: M. H. Gill, 1876)

O'Keefe, Tadhg, 'Medieval Frontiers and Fortification: The Pale and its Evolution' in F.H.A. Aalen and Kevin Whelan (eds), *Dublin City and County: From Prehistory to Present* (Dublin: Geography Publications, 1992), 1–34.

Oman, Sir C., *A History of the Art of War in the Middle Ages*, vol. 1 (London: Methuen & Co. Ltd, 1924)

O'Neill, Timothy, *Merchants and Mariners in Medieval Ireland* (Dublin: Irish Academic Press, 1987)

O'Reilly, Edward, *O'Reilly's Irish-English Dictionary* (Dublin: James Duffy, 1864)

Paul, James Balfour (ed.), *Accounts of the Lord High Treasurer of Scotland, iv 1507–13* (Edinburgh: Her Majesty's General Register House, 1902)

Potter, David, *Henry VIII and Francis I: The Final Conflict, 1540–1547* (Leiden: Brill, 2011)

Prendergast, Muríosa, 'Scots Mercenary Forces in Sixteenth Century Ireland' in John France (ed.), *Mercenaries and Paid Men: The Mercenary Identity in the Middle Ages* (Boston: Leiden 2008), pp.363–381.

Quinn, David Beers, *The Elizabethans and the Irish* (Ithaca: Cornell University Press, 1966)

Rapple, Rory, *Martial Power and Elizabethan Political Culture: Military Men in England and Ireland, 1558–1594* (Cambridge: Cambridge University Press, 2009)

Raymond, James, *Henry VIII's Military Revolution: The Armies of Sixteenth Century Britain and Europe* (London & New York: I. B. Tauris, 2007)

Reid, Stuart, *Highland Clansman, 1689–1746* (London: Osprey, 1997)

Rixson, Denis, *The West Highland Galley* (Edinburgh: Birlinn, 1998)

Simms, Katherine, *From Kings to Warlords* (Woodbridge: Boydell & Brewer, Ltd, 1987)

Simms, Katherine, *Gaelic Ulster in the Middle Ages* (Dublin: Four Courts Press, 2020)

Simms, Katherine, 'Gaelic Warfare in the Middle Ages' in Thomas Bartlett and Keith Jeffery (eds), *A Military History of Ireland* (Cambridge: Cambridge University Press, 1997), pp.99–115.

Simms, Katherine, 'Images of Galloglass in Poems to the MacSweeneys' in Seán Duffy (ed.), *The World of the Galloglass* (Dublin: Four Courts Press, 2007), pp.106–123.

Simms, Katherine, 'Late Medieval Donegal' in William Nolan, Liam Ronayne and Mariead Dunleavy (eds), in *Donegal History and Society: Interdisciplinary Essays on the History of an Irish County* (Dublin: Geography Publications, 1995), pp.183–201.

Simms, Katherine, 'The MacMahon Pedigree: A Medieval Forgery' in David Edwards (ed.), *Regions and Rulers in Ireland, 1100–1650* (Dublin: Four Courts Press, 2004), pp.27–36.

Skene, William F., *The Highlanders of Scotland, Their Origin, History, and Antiquities,* vol. 2 (London: John Murray, 1837)

Skene, William F., *Celtic Scotland: A History of Ancient Alban*, vol. 3 (Edinburg: David Douglas, 1886)

Smith, Charles, *Ancient and Present State of the County and City of Cork* (Dublin: 1749)

Stevenson, David, *Alisdair MacColla and the Highland Problem in the 17th Century* (Edinburgh: John Donald Publishers, Ltd, 1980)

Strutt, Joseph, *A Complete View of the Dress and Habits of the People of England* (London: Henry G. Bon, 1842)

Stuart, John Sobieski, *The Costume of the Clans* (Edinburgh: John Grant, 1892)

Tanner, James, *Instruments of Battle: The Fighting Drummers and Buglers of the British Army* (Philadelphia: Casemate, 2017)

Thompson, Christopher Scott; Grosse; Phrenger, Ken; Guistitis, Randal, *Scorners of Death: Fighting Skills of the Medieval Gaelic Warrior* (Glasgow: Fallen Rook Publishing 2018)

Turner, James, *Pallas Armata, Military Essayes of the Ancient Grecian, Roman…* (London: M.W. for Richard Chiswell, 1683)

Ware, James, *The Antiquities and History of Ireland* (Dublin: A. Crook, 1705)

Whyte, Henry, *The Martial Music of the Clans* (Glasgow: The Celtic Monthly Office, 1904)

Wilde, Lady, *Irish Cures, Mystic Charms and Superstitions* (New York: Sterling Publishing Co., 1991)

Williams, Ronald, *The Lords of the Isles* (London: The Hogarth Press, 1984)

Articles

Adams, David, 'Archery in the Highlands: Muskets and Bows' in *Military Illustrated*, no.111 (August 1997), pp.44–46

Terry, Barry, 'The Study of Medieval Irish castles: a bibliographic survey' in *Proceedings of the Royal Irish Academy*, vol. 108C (2008), pp.115–136

Berryman, Duncan, 'The Defensibility of Irish Tower Houses – a Study', *The Castle Studies Group Journal*, no 24 (2010–11), pp.260–268

Blumberg, Arnold, 'The Jinete', *Medieval Warfare*, vol. 3, no. 1 (2013), pp.18–21

Booker, Sparky, 'Moustaches, Mantles, and Saffron Shirts: What Motivated Sumptuary Law in Medieval English Ireland?' in *Speculum*, 96/3 (July 2021), pp.726–770.

Borrowes, Erasmus, 'Tennekille Castle, Portarlington and Glimpses of the MacDonnells', *Ulster Journal of Archaeology*, vol. 2 (1854), pp.34–43

Bourke, Cormac, 'Antiquities from the River Blackwater III, Iron Axe Heads', *Ulster Journal of Archaeology*, vol. 60 (2001), pp.63–93.

Butler, T. Blake, 'King Henry VIII's Irish Army List' in *The Irish Genealogist*, vol. 1, no. 1 (1937), pp.3–13

Butler, W. F., 'The Lordship of MacCarthy Mór' in *Journal of the Royal Society of Antiquaries*, pt. 4, vol. 36 (1906), pp.349–367

Campbell of Airds, Alastair, 'A Closer Look at West Highland Heraldry', St Andrew's Day Lecture (1996), <http://www.heraldry-scotland.co.uk/Westhighland.htm>

Cowan, Ross, 'Lairds of Battle', *Military History Monthly*, No. 32 (2013), pp.44–49

de Breffny, Brian, 'An Elizabethan Political Painting', *Irish Arts Review*, vol. 1, no. 1 (1984), pp.39–41

DeBurgh, Thomas J., 'Ancient Naas (Parts I. and II.)', *Journal of the Kildare Archaeological Society*, vol. 1, no. 3 (1891–95) pp.184–201

Dillon, Viscount, 'Irish Troops at Boulogne in 1544', *Journal of the Society for Army Historical Research*, vol. 1, no. 3 (1922), pp.81–84.

Edwards, David, 'The Butler Revolt of 1569', *Irish Historical Studies*, vol. 28, no. 11 (May 1993), pp.228–255

G. M., 'Review of Irish Poetry from the English Invasion to 1798 by Russell K. Alspach', *Studies: An Irish Quarterly Review*, vol. 33, no. 132 (1944), pp.561–563

Ellis, Steven, 'The Collapse of the Gaelic World, 1450–1650', *Irish Historical Studies*, vol. 31, no. 124 (1999), pp.449–469

Fitzgerald, Lord Walter, 'Macdonnells of Tinnakill Castle', *Journal of the Kilkenny Archaeological Society*, vol. 4, no. 3 (1904), pp.205–215

Gregory, Donald, 'Notices Regarding Scottish Archery', *Archaeologia Scotica, Proceedings of the Society of Antiquaries of Scotland*, vol. 3 (1831), pp.248–254

Halpin, Andrew, 'Irish Medieval Swords, c. 1171–1600', *Proceedings of the Royal Irish Academy* (1986), pp.183–230

Harbison, Peter, 'Native Irish Arms and Armour in Medieval Gaelic Literature, 1170–1600', *The Irish Sword*, vol. 12 (1975–76), pp.173–199, 270–84

Harris, Jason, 'Ireland in Europe: Paolo Giovio's Description (1548)', *Irish Historical Studies*, vol. 35, no. 139 (2007), pp.265–288

Harrison, Alan, 'The Shower of Hell', *Eigse*, 18/2 (1981), p.304

Hayes-McCoy, G. A., 'The Army of Ulster, 1593–1601', *Irish Sword*, vol. 1, no. 2 (1949–53), pp.105–117

Hayes-McCoy, G. A., 'The Early History of Guns in Ireland' in *Journal of the Galway Archaeological and Historical Society*, vol. 18 (1938), pp.43–65.

Hayes-McCoy, G. A., 'The Gallóglach Axe' in *Journal of the Galway Archaeological and Historical Society*, vol. 17 (1937), pp.101–121

Hayes-McCoy, G. A., 'Strategy and Tactics in Irish Warfare, 1593–1601' in *Irish Historical Studies*, vol. 2, no. 7 (1941), pp.255–279

Hill, George, 'Shane O'Neill's Expedition against the Antrim Scots, 1565' in *Ulster Journal of Archaeology*, 1st. ser., vol. 9 (1861/62), pp.122–141

Hill, John Michael, 'The Distinctiveness of Gaelic Warfare, 1400–1750' in *European History Quarterly,* no. 22 (1992), pp.323–345

Hogan, Edmund (ed.), 'Haynes' Observations of the State of Ireland in 1600' in *Irish Ecclesiastical Record*, vol. 8 (1887), pp.1112–1122.

Hore, Herbert, 'Clan Kavanagh Temp. Henry VIII' in *Journal of the Royal Society of Antiquaries of Ireland*, Seventh Series, vol. 2, no. 1 (1858), pp.73–92

Hore, Herbert, 'Gaelic Domestics' in *Ulster Journal of Archaeology*, 1st. ver., vol. 3 (1855), pp.117–126

Hore, Herbert, 'Irish Bardism in 1561' in *Ulster Journal of Archaeology*, 1st. ver., vol. 6 (1858), pp.165--167

Hore, Herbert, 'The Hosting Against the Northern Irish in 1566' in *Ulster Journal of Archaeology*, vol. 1 (1853), pp.159–164

Hore, Herbert (ed.), 'Sir Henry Sidney's Memoir of his Government in Ireland, 1583' in *Ulster Journal of Archaeology*, vol. 3 (1855), pp.33–52, 85–109, 336–357

Hore, Herbert, 'War-cries of Irish Septs' in *Ulster Journal of Archaeology*, no. 11 (1855), pp.203–212

Jones, Evan and Susan Flavin, 'Ireland-Bristol Trade in the sixteenth century', University of Bristol, <www.bris.ac.uk/Depts/History/Ireland/research.htm>

Jones, Robert, 'Re-Thinking the Origins of the 'Irish' Hobelar' in *Cardiff Historical Papers*, vol. 1 (2008) pp.1–20

Jope, E. M., 'Scottish Influences in the North of Ireland: Castles with Scottish Features, 1580–1640' in *Ulster Journal of Archaeology*, 3rd ser., vol. 14 (1951), pp.31–47.

Kelly, John, 'The Collection of Cess and Pardons and Fines in Carlow in the 1570s' in *Carloviana, the Journal of the Carlow Historical and Archaeological Society* (2017), pp.110–120

Kelly, John, 'Robert Hartpole, Constable of Carlow' in *Carloviana, the Journal of the Carlow Historical and Archaeological Society* (2016), pp.72–84

Kew, Graham, 'The Irish Sections of Fynes Moryson's Unpublished Itinerary' in *Analecta Hibernia*, no. 37 (1998), pp.1–137

Lincoln, Bruce, 'The Indo-European Cattle-raiding Myth' in *History of Religions*, vol. 16 (August 1976), pp.42–65

Lucas, A. T., 'A Hay-rope Pack-saddle from County Louth' in *Journal of the County Louth Archaeological Society*, vol. 15, no. 1 (1961), pp.13–16

Lydon, James F., 'The Hobelar: An Irish Contribution to Medieval Warfare' in *Irish Sword*, vol. 2 no. 5 (1954), pp.12–16

MacCarthy, Daniel, 'My Lord Clanricarde's Tailor's Bill' in *Journal of the Kilkenny and South-East of Ireland Archaeological Society*, vol. 1, new series (1858), pp.247–250

McCone, Kim, 'Werewolves, Cyclopes, Díberga and Fíanna: Juvenile Delinquency in Early Ireland' in *Cambridge Medieval Celtic Studies*, no. 12 (1986), pp.1–22

MacDonald, Archibald (ed.), 'A Fragment of an Irish MS. History of the MacDonalds of Antrim' in *Transactions of the Gaelic Society of Inverness*, vol. 37 (1934–1936), pp.262–284.

McE, J., 'Ethnological Sketches, No. 1, The Fishermen of the Claddagh, at Galway' in *Ulster Journal of Archaeology*, vol. 2 (1854), pp.163–164

Mac Giolla Phádraig, Eóghan, 'A Fitzpatrick Crest on the National Harp' in *The Journal of the Fitzpatrick-Mac Giolla Phádraig Clan Society* (2021), pp.1–21

McGurk, John (ed.), 'The Discovery and Recovery of Ireland with the Author's Apology', Author Thomas Lee, the Corpus of Electronic Texts. <https://celt.ucc.ie/published/E590001-005.html>

Mahr, Adolph, 'The Galloglach Axe' in *Journal of the Galway Archaeological Society*, vol. 18 (1938), pp.66–68

Morgan, Hiram (ed.), 'A Boke of Questions and Answars' in *Analecta Hibernia*, no. 36 (1995), pp.79–132

Morgan, Hiram and Nicholls, Kenneth (eds), 'Dialogue of Sylvynne and Peregrynne', Author H. C., CELT, the Corpus of Electronic Texts. <http://research.ucc.ie/celt/document/E590001-001>

Morgan, Hiram and Kennith Nicholls (eds), 'Discourse of the Mere Irish of Ireland', anon., CELT, the Corpus of Electronic Texts.
<https://celt.ucc.ie/published/E600001-004.html>

Morgan, Hiram (ed.) Hatfield House, Cecil Papers 88/121-2, 'Thomas Walker's Narrative, written to Sir Robert Cecil, 1601', CELT, the Corpus of Electronic Texts
<https://celt.ucc.ie/published/E600001-003/>

Mosher, Sally, 'William Byrd's "Battell" and the Earl of Oxford', *The Oxfordian*, vol. 1 (1998), pp.43–52

Murphy, Rev. Denis S. J., 'The Pale' in *The Journal of the County Kildare Archaeological Society*, vol. 2., no. 1 (1896), pp.48–58

Nicholls, Kenneth, 'Celtic Contrasts: Ireland and Scotland', *History Ireland*, vol. 7, no. 3 (Autumn 1999), pp.22–26

O'Brien, Niall, 'The Earl of Desmond's Navy' in *Journal of the Kerry Archaeological and Historical Society*, ser. 2, vol. 8 (2008), pp.87–96.

Ó Cuív, Brian, 'Fragments of Irish Medieval Treatises on Horses' in *Celtica*, vol. 17 (1985), pp.113–122

Ó Danachair, Caoimhín, 'An Ri (the King) An example of Traditional Social Organisation' in *Journal of the Royal Society of Antiquaries of Ireland*, vol. 111 (1981), pp.14–28

Ó Doibhlin, Éamon, 'Ceart Uí Néill: A Discussion and Translation of the Document' in *Seanchas Armhacha: Journal of the Armagh Diocesan Historical Society*, vol. 5, no. 2 (1970), pp.324–358

O'Donnelly, Seán, 'The Warpipes in Ireland', *Ceol*, vol. 5, no. 1 (1981), pp.19–58.

O Fionnain, Donall (ed.), 'A German Visitor to Monaincha in 1591' in *Tipperary Historical Journal*, County Tipperary Historical Society (1998), pp.228–233.

O'Mahony, Edward, 'Waterford and the Sack of Baltimore, 1538' in *The Mizen Journal*, no. 7 (1999), pp.29–45

O'Neill, James, 'Three Sieges, two massacres: Enniskillen at the outbreak of the Nine Years' War, 1593–92' in *The Irish Sword: The Journal of the Military History Society of Ireland*, vol. 30, no. 121 (2016), pp.241–250

O'Sullivan, M. D., *Old Galway* (Cambridge, Heffer & Son, 1942)

Panaev, A. A. (Mark Conrad, trans.), 'The Eupatoria Affair' in *Russkaya Starina*, Vol. XIX (1877), pp.300–323

Phillips, Gervase, 'Irish Ceatharnaigh in English Service, 1544–1550, and the Development of Gaelic Warfare' in *Journal of the Society for Army Historical Research*, vol. 78, no. 315, pp.163–172

Phillips, T., 'The Life of Sir Peter Carew' in *Archaeologia*, no. 27 (1839), pp.96–151

Price, Liam, 'Armed Forces of the Irish Chiefs in the Early 16th Century' in *Journal of the Royal Society of Antiquaries of Ireland*, vol. 62 (1932), pp.201–207

Quinn, David B., 'Calendar of Council Book of Dublin, 1581–1586' in *Analecta Hibernia*, no. 24 (1967), pp.91–180.

Schlegel, Donald M., 'The MacDonnells of Tyrone and Armagh: A Genealogical Study' in *Seanchas Armhacha: Journal of the Armagh Diocesan Historical Society*, vol. 10, no. 1 (1980–81), pp.193-219

Scott, Brendan and Nicholls, Kenneth (eds), 'The Landowners of the late Elizabethan Pale' in *Analecta Hibernica*, no. 43 (2012), pp.1–15

Sherlock, Rory, 'The Evolution of the Irish Tower House as a Domestic Space' in *Proceedings of the Royal Irish Academy*, vol. 111C, Special Issue: Domestic Life in Ireland (2011), pp.115–140

Shirley, Evelyn Philips, 'Extracts from the Journal of Thomas Dinely' in *Journal of the Royal Society of Antiquaries of Ireland*, series 2, vol. I (1856), pp.143–188

Simms, Katherine, 'The Barefoot Kings: Literary Image and Realty in Later Medieval Ireland' in *Proceedings of the Harvard Celtic Colloquium*, vol. 30 (2010), pp.1–21

Simms, Katherine, 'Images of Warfare in Bardic Poetry' in *Celtica*, vol. 21 (1990), pp.608–619.

Simms, Katherine, 'Warfare in the Medieval Gaelic Lordships' in *The Irish Sword*, vol. 12 (1975), pp.98–108

Smith, Roland M., 'The Irish Background of Spencer's "View"' in *The Journal of English and Germanic Philology*, vol. 42, no. 4 (1943), pp.499–515

Strickland, W. G., 'Irish Soldiers in the Service of Henry VIII' in *Journal of the Royal Society of Antiquaries of Ireland*, vol. 13 (1922), pp.94–97

Swinney, Richard and Crawford, Scott, 'Medieval Hunting as Training for War Insights for the Modern Swordsman' in *Acta Periodica Duellatorum*, vol. 2, no. 1 (Bern: Universität Bern, 2014), pp.179–193

Walcot, Peter, 'Cattle Raiding, Heroic Tradition, and Ritual: The Greek Evidence' in *History of Religions*, vol. 18, no. 4, (May 1979), pp.326–351

Walsh, Paul, 'Scots Clann Domhnaill in Ireland' in *Irish Ecclesiastical Record*, series 5, no. 48 (1936), pp.23–42

Westropp, Thomas, 'Notes on Askeaton, County Limerick' in *Journal of the Royal Society of Antiquaries of Ireland*, series 5, vol. 34 (1904), pp.111-132

White, Dean Gunther, 'Henry VIII's Irish Kerne in France and Scotland, 1544–1545' in *The Irish Sword*, vol. 3, no. 13 (1958), pp.213–225

Williams, N. J. A., 'Dermot O'Connor's Blazons and Irish Heraldic Terminology' in *Eighteenth Century Ireland / Iris an dá chultúr*, vol. 5 (1990), pp.61–88

Willis, Tony, and Halpin, Andrew, 'A Recently Discovered Sixteenth Century Irish Open Ring Pommel Sword' in *Spring 2017 Park Lane Arms Fair Catalogue* (2017), pp.13–23

Willis, Tony, 'The Scottish Two-Handed Sword' in *Barrels & Blades*, series 3, no. 60 (2022), pp.32-7

Willis, Tony, 'A Two Handed Gaelic Irish Sword of the Sixteenth Century' in *Fifteenth Park Lane Arms Fair Catalogue* (1998), pp.18–27

Theses and Dissertations

Crawford, Ross MacKenzie, 'Warfare in the West Highlands and Isles of Scotland, *c.* 1544–1615'. PhD Thesis, University of Glasgow 2016

Dorney, John, 'Florence MacCarthy and the conquest of Gaelic Munster, 1560–1640'. Dissertation submitted to National University of Ireland in partial fulfilment of requirements for the degree of MA at University college Dublin, 2003

Halpin, Andrew, 'Archery in Medieval Ireland'. Unpublished University College Dublin PhD thesis, 1990

Hewerdine, Anita Rosamund, 'The Yeomen of the King's Guard 1485–1547'. Unpublished PhD thesis, University of London, 1998

Lublin, Robert I., 'Costuming the Shakespearean Stage'. Unpublished PhD Thesis, Ohio State University, 2003

Rondelez, Paul, 'Ironwork in late Medieval Ireland: AD 1200 to 1600'. Unpublished University College Cork PhD thesis, 2001

Sasso, Claude Ronald, 'The Desmond Rebellions, 1569–1573 and 1579–1583'. Unpublished Loyola University of Chicago PhD thesis, 1978

About the author

Robert Gresh is an independent researcher of Irish descent, living in the USA. He is a lifelong student of Irish arms and armour and leads a living history group focussed on sixteenth century Ireland. He has researched and reconstructed much of the clothing and leather goods the group uses. He is the author of *The Skean: the Distinctive Fighting Knife of Gaelic Ireland, 1500 – 1700*, published in 2023. His historical blog on sixteenth century Ireland can be found at https://www.wildeirishe.com/blog.

About the artists

Seán Ó'Brógáin is based in Donegal, Ireland. He studied Scientific and Natural History illustration at Lancaster University and works for a wide range of international clients. His previous artwork for Helion has been included in St Ruth's Fatal Gamble: The Battle of Aughrim 1691 and the fall of Jacobite Ireland, and The King's Irish.

Born in Curitiba, in southern Brazil, Anderson Subtil holds a degree in Drawing from the School of Music and Fine Arts of the Paraná State. Since 2018, he has worked as an illustrator for several Helion & Company Series. His artworks have been published in books and magazines in Brazil, the United States, the United Kingdom, France, Austria and Japan.

Other titles in the From Retinue to Regiment series:

No 1 *Richard III and the Battle of Bosworth*
Mike Ingram

No 2 *Tanaka 1587: Japan's Greatest Unknown Samurai Battle* Stephen Turnbull

No 3 *The Army of the Swabian League 1525*
Doug Miller

No 4 *The Italian Wars Volume 1: The Expedition of Charles VIII into Italy and the Battle of Fornovo* Massimo Predonzani & Alberici Vincenzo, translated by Irene Maccolini

No 5 *The Commotion Time: Tudor Rebellion in the West, 1549* E.T. Fox

No 6 *The Italian Wars Volume 2: Agnadello 1509, Ravenna 1512, Marignano 1515*
Massimo Predonzani & Alberici Vincenzo, translated by Rachele Tiso

No 7 *The Tudor Arte of Warre Volume 1: The Conduct of War from Henry VII to Mary I, 1485-1558* Jonathan Davies

No 8 *The Ethiopian-Adal War 1529-1543: The Conquest of Abyssinia* Jeffrey M. Shaw

No 9 *The Ōnin War: A Turning Point in Samurai History* Stephen Turnbull

No 10 *One Faith, One Law, One King: French Armies of the Wars of Religion 1562–1598*
T J O'Brien de Clare

No 11 *The Italian Wars Volume 3: Francis I and the Battle of Pavia 1525* Massimo Predonzani & Alberici Vincenzo

No 12 *On the Borderlands of Great Empires: Transylvanian Armies 1541-1613*
Florin Nicolae Ardelean

No 14 *The Art of Shooting Great Ordnance: A History of the Development, Manufacture and Use of Artillery, 1494–1628* Jonathan Davies

No 15 *The Italian Wars Volume 4: The Battle of Ceresole 1544 - The Crushing Defeat of the Imperial Army* Massimo Predonzani & Simon Miller

No 16 *The Men of Warre: The Clothes, Weapons and Accoutrements of the Scots at War 1460–1600*
Jenn Scott

No 17 *The German Peasants' War 1524–26*
Douglas Miller

No 18 *The Tudor Arte of Warre Volume 2: The conduct of war in the reign of Elizabeth I, 1558–1603: Diplomacy, Strategy, Campaigns and Battles*
Jonathan Davies

No 19 *The Kalmar War 1611–1613: Gustavus Adolphus's First War*
Michael Fredholm von Essen

No 20 *Hojo: Samurai Warlords 1487–1590*
Stephen Turnbull

No 21 *The Battle of Castillon 1453: The Death Knell for English France* Peter Hoskins

No 22 *The Tudor Arte of Warre Volume 3: The Conduct of War in the Reign of Elizabeth I 1558-1603: The Elizabethan Army* Jonathan Davies

No 23 *Sweden's War in Muscovy 1609-1617: The Relief of Moscow and Conquest of Novgorod*
Michael Fredholm von Essen

No 24 *'Of Kerns and Gallowglasses': Irish Armies of the Sixteenth Century, 1487-1587*
Robert Gresh